P9-CAM-174

Chicago

written and researched by

Rich McHugh

with additional contributions by

J.P. Anderson, Chris Barsanti and Mark Ellwood

ROUGH GUIDES

www.roughguides.com

Introduction to
Chicago

Sitting squarely in the middle of America, surrounded by hundreds of miles of pancake-flat prairies, Chicago is, in many ways, the last great American city. Having come of age during the industrial age – the grain, lumber, meatpacking, steel and railroad trades all took turns dominating the economic landscape – Chicago's blue-collar roots still shine through, with all the can-do attitude of a small town, the ambition and diversity of a dynamic metropolis, and a distinct lack of pretension throughout. While the city may stand in the shadow of more cosmopolitan New York or cutting-edge LA, there's no shortage of top-notch art and architecture, or street-level excitement, with less of the hassle and infrastructure problems of the coastal rivals.

Chicago's reputation as the stomping ground of Prohibition-era gangsters like Al Capone may still loom large in most people's minds, along with images of the backroom dealing perfected by politicians, but the truth is rather less lurid. These days, Chicago is better known for its sports obsessions, as Chicagoans are, for better or worse, loyally supportive of their teams; the ever-inconsistent Chicago Cubs' games remain well attended thanks to marquis players like Sammy Sosa and the atmosphere conjured up at grand old Wrigley Field.

Founded in the early 1800s, the city grew up with the country, serving as the main connection between the established East Coast cities and the wide open Wild West frontier. This position on the sharp edge between

Fact file

• Chicago covers approximately **228 square miles**, of which 5 percent (7300 acres) is devoted to parkland.

• The city's **population** is 2,896,016 – up 5 percent from a decade ago – 36 percent of whom are black, 31 percent white, 26 percent Hispanic and 4 percent Asian. The population of the greater metropolitan area is 8,272,768.

• Annually, Chicago hosts 35,000 **conventions**, trade shows and other meetings attracting more than 4.4 million attendees. The city's convention center, McCormick Place, is the largest of its kind in North America, measuring 2.2 million square feet.

• Chicago has the world's largest public library (Harold Washington Library), largest free public zoo (Lincoln Park Zoo), largest food festival (Taste of Chicago), largest aquarium (Shedd Aquarium), largest collection of Impressionist paintings outside Paris (Art Institute of Chicago), as well as the world's busiest roadway (Dan Ryan Expressway), busiest futures exchange (Board of Trade), busiest airport (O'Hare International Airport) and busiest sit-down restaurant (*Berghoff Restaurant*).

• Chicago is known as the birthplace of the electric iron and cooking range, the cafeteria, *McDonald's* restaurant, the grain reaper, the window envelope, the winding watch, the zipper, the bifocal contact lens, the railroad sleeping car, the bowling tournament and the steel-frame skyscraper.

civilization and wilderness made the city into a crucible of innovation, something only enhanced by the chance the city had to start over, after the Fire of 1871, in which much of central Chicago burned to the ground – one of the

Chicago is, in many ways, the last great American city

worst fires in US history. Indeed, many aspects of modern American life, from skyscrapers to suburbia, had their start, and perhaps their finest expression, here on the shores of Lake Michigan.

In the early years of the twentieth century, the city cemented a reputation as a place of limitless opportunity, with jobs aplenty for

those willing to work – and was the obvious destination for those seeking opportunity in the Midwest. The city swelled with immigrants from Eastern Europe, Sweden, Mexico, Italy, Greece, Germany, China and Ireland, as well as migrants from the Deep South, all of whom have left their mark, some more indelibly than others, making Chicago something of a quirky metropolis in America's heartland. What other city, after all, would dye its river green to celebrate St Patrick's Day?

Meanwhile, some eighteen million visitors come to Chicago each year, making it one of the top tourist destinations in the country. While they invariably tour the city's wide range of excellent museums and other high-brow attractions, Chicago's strongest cultural suit is **live music**, with a phenomenal array of jazz and blues clubs packed into the backrooms of its amiable bars and cafés; it's not a stretch to say that modern blues music was invented here. The rock scene is also one of the healthiest in the country, with a profusion of bands having come out of the city in the 1990s. And almost everything is noticeably less expensive than in other US cities – **eating out**, for example, costs much less than in New York or LA, but is every bit as good.

Chicago-style food

Chicago-style is a term you're bound to encounter over and over during your stay in Chicago, roughly translating to hearty, meaty and more often than not, greasy. Undoubtedly the city's biggest contribution to American cuisine is **deep-dish pizza**, a twist on traditional pizza that's like two slices in one: it's twice as thick as an ordinary slice, with twice as much cheese and usually laden with sausage or pepperoni and a host of optional toppings. Although most pizza parlors offer deep-dish, the following places have perfected it: *Pizzeria Uno*, *Lou Malnati's* (pictured above) and *Giordano's*.

Hot dogs (also known as "Red Hots," or simply "dogs") and Polish sausage are similarly large and come topped with the kitchen sink – onions, peppers, sauerkraut, pickles, tomatoes, ketchup and mustard. The best are served at stand-up joints, many of them near Wrigley Field, including *Wiener's Circle*.

Italian beef sandwiches, long, split rolls crammed with thin cuts of roast beef, are best eaten "dipped" in broth – a soggy nightmare for your clothes, but a wonderful treat for the taste buds. Chicago has two famed Italian beef spots: *Portillo's*, in the River North, and *Al's Number 1 Italian Beef* in Little Italy.

To find these and other dining options, see "Eating," starting on p.141.

What to see

The compact heart of Chicago is the Loop; from here the city spreads to the north, south and west, bounded to the east by Lake Michigan, which provides Chicago with some of its most attractive open space, and serves as a clear point of reference for getting your bearings – the lake is always east of the urban grid. The Chicago River, which cuts through the heart of downtown Chicago to Lake Michigan, separates the business district from the shopping and entertainment areas of the North Side, which merit, at the very least, several days' worth of exploring. Few visitors spend any time on the South Side, and only a slightly greater number venture west.

The best place to start exploring Chicago is **the Loop**, the city's downtown and birthplace, and home to perhaps the finest display of modern architecture in the world, from the prototype skyscrapers of the 1890s and the "Chicago School" period to Mies van der Rohe's modernist masterpieces and their postmodern successors. As well, you'll find here the quarter-mile-high Sears Tower and the Art Institute, the city's premier art museum.

Chicago's most commercial area – **Near North** – is where you're likely to spend much of your time. Just north of the river and divided into the River North, N Michigan Avenue and Streeterville areas, Near North is where most of the city's hotels and restaurants are concentrated, as are its fashionable shops and department stores, on the famed Magnificent Mile.

Eating out costs much less than in New York or LA, but is every bit as good

Chicago parks

Chicago may be built on an urban grid, much like other major US cities, but the city does, in fact, have an abundance of open space where you can take in its natural beauty. The enduring legacy of Daniel Burnham's remarkable plan of 1909 is to have preserved the city's lakefront as a public park, an unbroken expanse of greenery stretching some thirty miles north and south of Chicago. North of downtown, **Lincoln Park**, the largest urban park in the country, is the city's playground, offering miles and miles of bike paths and beaches, a free zoo and an excellent conservatory, plus some remarkable city views (see p.93). East of downtown, **Grant Park**'s 200-acre swath is a convenient break from downtown, and is home to some major museums and cultural venues (see p.77), while on Chicago's West Side, you'll find lush Garfield Conservatory, located in the eponymous park (see p.107).

East of Michigan Avenue, on Streeterville's lakefront, is Chicago's most popular tourist destination, Navy Pier, a promenade of chain restaurants, shops and concert venues marked by the hard-to-miss giant Ferris wheel. On the other side of Michigan Avenue, River North is the city's gallery district, the once run-down warehouses now home to a diverse array of art works, not to mention a number of the city's hottest restaurants.

North lies the **Gold Coast**, where a few streets of upscale boutiques and gorgeous brownstones make a pleasant stroll, while **Old Town** to the west is artsier and more unbuttoned, home to the venerable Second City improvisational comedy club and a host of colorful Victorian homes.

Old Town blends into **Lincoln Park**, a leafy residential area that borders the park of the same name and is home to an enclave of young professionals. The streets, lined with restored flats, also hold some of the city's best restaurants and bars, giving the neighborhood a lively social scene.

Low-key **Lakeview** further north draws a younger crowd than Lincoln Park: good for a wander along its commercial stretches, while sports fans will want to head to Wrigleyville, home to baseball's Cubs and Wrigley Field stadium, as well as a bevy of raucous sports bars.

Beyond here, the distinct city neighborhoods thin out, save for **Andersonville**, where a small but worthwhile selection of restaurants, delicatessens and bakeries still serve the remnants of a Swedish enclave.

Heading south from the Loop, the **Near South** encompasses the lakefront Grant Park, with its panoply of museums, the historic Printers Row district and Chinatown's bustling street life. Further south, the **South Side** proper takes over, much of it a no-go zone for visitors, except **Hyde Park**, an island of middle-class prosperity around the Gothic campus of the **University of Chicago**.

Chicago's **West Side** holds the twin culinary attractions of **Greektown** and **Little Italy**, the latter mainly a tourist hangout, and the former considerably less so. The city's large Mexican community makes its base southwest of here in **Pilsen**, known as well for its home-style eateries and colorful murals.

Northwest of here, Chicago's blue-collar side takes over; among the warehouses and old churches are a few areas worth your attention. The **Ukrainian Village**, with its wonderfully ornate churches and Eastern European roots, is worth a stop on your way to the city's hippest neighborhood, **Wicker Park**, full of carefully restored Victorian homes and a flourishing alternative music and club scene. **Bucktown**, just north, is a more gentrified version of Wicker Park, with plenty of restaurants, bars and nightclubs to choose from, along with corresponding high rents and increasingly homogenous make-up.

Nine miles west of the city, the affluent and attractive suburb of **Oak Park** holds the childhood home of Ernest Hemingway and more than a dozen well-preserved examples of the influential architecture of Frank Lloyd Wright; the most interesting and groundbreaking of these are maintained as monuments and open for viewing.

When to go

hicago's **climate** ranges from the unbearably hot and humid in midsummer to well below freezing from December through February, with spring and fall amounting to little more than a month or two in between. The **best times to visit** are in the early summer (May–July) and early fall (Sept & Oct), when the weather is at its most pleasant; there's usually snow from December to March, while the heat of late summer is best avoided. Whatever time of year you come, be sure to dress in layers: buildings tend to be overheated during winter and air-conditioned to the extreme in summer. Also bring comfortable, sturdy shoes – you're going to be doing a lot of walking.

Average Chicago temperatures (°F) and rainfall (inches)

	Jan	Feb	Mar	Apr	May	June	July	Aug	Sept	Oct	Nov	Dec
Av. high	29	34	45	58	70	80	84	82	75	63	48	35
Av. low	13	18	28	39	48	57	63	62	64	42	31	20
Av. rainfall	1.7	1.4	2.7	3.6	3.2	3.8	3.6	4.1	3.5	2.6	2.9	2.2

25

things not to miss

It's not possible to see everything that Chicago has to offer in one trip – and we don't suggest you try. What follows is a selective and subjective taste of the city's highlights: stunning architecture and engaging museums, wide-ranging cultural events, and memorable restaurants and bars. They're arranged in five color-coded categories to help you find the very best things to see, do and experience. All entries have a page reference to take you straight into the Guide, where you can find out more.

01 City skyline Pages **55 & 61** • Whether you see it from the John Hancock Observatory (center) or the top of the Sears Tower, you're sure to be impressed by the city's spectacular skyline.

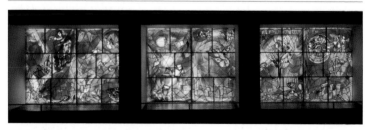

02 Chagall's American Windows Page **47** • There's plenty at the Art Institute of Chicago to hold your attention, though perhaps nothing more enchanting than Chagall's serene stained-glass creations.

03 **Riding the El** Page **28** • There's no better first impression of the Loop – and Chicago – than to ride in on the El, climb down to the street and feel the restless energy compressed within these few city blocks.

04 **Oak Street Beach** Page **71**
• A glamorous summertime playground, right off Michigan Avenue, in a somewhat unexpected location.

05 **Tiffany Dome, Chicago Cultural Center** Page **42** •
Your eyes are likely to be glued to the sparkling roof of Preston Bradley Hall during a concert at the Center.

xi

06 **Chicago Mercantile Exchange** Page **55** • Try to read the frenzied hand signals on the trading floor, as billions of dollars are bought and sold each day.

08 **Billy Goat Tavern** Page **59** • Despite being made famous on TV's *Saturday Night Live*, this smoky, greasy bar has kept much of its no-nonsense charm.

07 **Baseball at Wrigley Field** Page **100** • The ivy-covered walls, the boisterous crowd and free-flowing hot dogs and beer all add up to the quintessential ballpark experience, no matter who wins the game.

09 **Wicker Park mansions** Page **89** • This architectural gem, at 2146 Caton St, is one of numerous homes in the delightful Wicker Park historic district.

11 **A drink at The Drake Hotel** Page **63** • Soak up the Roaring Twenties ambience in the hotel's plush *Palm Court Lounge*, with a sophisticated cocktail or afternoon tea.

10 **Navy Pier** Page **64** • After your head stops swimming from rides soaring through the sky on the giant Ferris wheel or spinning on the merry-go-round, make for the promenade for a relaxing beer and a bite to eat.

12 **Italian beef sandwiches** Page **145** • At *Mr Beef* or countless other Italian beef spots in the city, order "a beef, dipped, spicy".

13 **Museum of Science and Industry** Page **114** • Behind the stately exterior of this popular museum, you'll encounter everything from a submarine to a live-chick hatchery to a replica of a coal mine, among hundreds of others exhibits.

14 **Chicago Symphony Orchestra concerts** Page **189** • When the world-class symphony plays at its stunning venue, you're assured of one of the most rewarding high-culture experiences around.

15 **Frank Lloyd Wright's legacy** Pages **122 & 115** • The great American architect introduced his "Prairie style" in Chicago and left a collection of eye-catching designs in the area, most notably his home in Oak Park (left) and the Robie House in Hyde Park (right).

16 **Boat tours** Page **30** • The Chicago River, which snakes through the city center, is best experienced on a boat tour, with the Chicago Architectural Foundation's cruises being the best.

17 **Shopping on Michigan Avenue** Page **58** • Stop in at the Magnificent Mile, even in the worst weather; the street has plenty of indoor malls packed with major chains and department stores to keep your credit card busy.

19 **Museum Campus** Page **77** • "Sue," the largest T. rex ever unearthed, is the star at the Field Museum of Natural History, just one of three museums (including the Shedd Aquarium and the Adler Planetarium) that merit at least an afternoon's exploration.

18 **Chicago's lakefront** Page **204** • Jog, walk or, even better, rent a bike and explore the spectactular shores of Lake Michigan.

20 **Blues clubs** Page **178** • Like the dozens of blues joints in Chicago, Lincoln Park's cozy B.L.U.E.S. club has been hosting nightly blues acts for decades.

21 **Chicago architecture** Page **241** • Arguably the modern architecture capital, the city's distinctive designs include the corncob–inspired Marina City towers.

22 **Glessner House** Page **83** • Considered a plain-faced addition to Prairie Avenue District when it was built in the late 1800s, the house and its decorative interior are among the well-preserved survivors of Chicago's gilded age.

23
Second City comedy club Page **741** •
Second City rarely disappoints with its raucous brand of improv – chances are good you'll wake in the morning with sore stomach muscles.

24 **Marshall Field's** Page **42** • An afternoon spent sifting through seven stories of merchandise at the city's famed department store is likely to leave you happily exhausted.

25 **Ravinia Festival** Page **190** • This complex of music venues is the place to go for summertime outdoor concerts, a treat whether you're in view of the stage under the Pavilion or sprawled on the adjacent lawn.

Contents

Using the Rough Guide

We've tried to make this Rough Guide a good read and easy to use. The book is divided into six main sections, and you should be able to find whatever you want in one of them.

Front section

The front color section offers a quick tour of Chicago. The **introduction** aims to give you a feel for the city, with suggestions on where to go. We also tell you what the weather is like and include a basic fact file. Next, our author rounds up his favorite aspects of Chicago in the **things not to miss** section – whether it's great food, amazing sights or a special activity. Right after this comes the Rough Guide's full **contents** list.

Basics

The Basics section covers all the **pre-departure** nitty-gritty to help you plan your trip and the practicalities you'll want to know once there. This is where to find out about money and costs, Internet access, transportation, car rental, local media – in fact just about every piece of **general practical information** you might need.

The city

This is the heart of the Rough Guide, divided into user-friendly chapters, each of which covers a specific neighborhood. Every chapter contains an **introduction** that helps you to decide where to go, followed by an extensive tour of the sights, all plotted on a neighborhood map.

Listings

Listings contain all the consumer information needed to make the most of your stay, with chapters on **accommodation**, places to **eat** and **drink**, **live music** and **culture** venues, **shopping**, **sports** and **festivals**.

Contexts

Read Contexts to get a deeper understanding of what makes Chicago tick. We include a brief **history**, plus a look at the city's **architecture** and **blues music**, along with a detailed further reading section that reviews numerous **books** relating to the city.

Index + small print

Apart from a **full index**, which includes maps as well as places, this section covers publishing information, credits and acknowledgements, and also has our contact details in case you want to send in updates and corrections to the book – or suggestions as to how we might improve it.

Color maps

The back color section contains eight detailed maps and plans to help you explore the city up close and locate every place recommended in the guide.

Map and chapter list

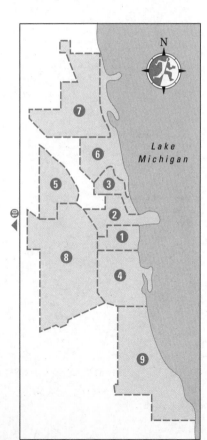

Contents

5

Contexts 227–264

Index and small print 265–274

Color maps at back of book

1. Chicago and around
2. Chicago neighborhoods
3. The Loop, South Loop and Grant Park
4. Near North, the Gold Coast and Old Town
5. Lincoln Park, Lakeview and Wrigleyville
6. West Side
7. South Side
8. CTA train map

Map symbols

maps are listed in the full index using colored text

MAP SYMBOLS

〔80〕	Interstate		⛳	Golf course
〔30〕	U.S. Highway		◆	General point of interest
〔1〕	Highway		ⓘ	Information centre
▬	Railway		⊠	Post office
▬	River		▬	Building
✕	Airport		⊞	Church
⊞	Hospital		⁺₊⁺	Cemetery
Ⓜ	Subway station		▦	Park
METRA	Commuter rail station			

Basics

Basics

Getting there

Chicago is a major hub for domestic and international travel, and is well served by air, rail and road networks. Flying into O'Hare International Airport – the country's busiest – is your quickest and easiest approach, given the sheer volume of domestic and international flights that route through here. One of the country's largest carriers, United Airlines, is based here, and nearly every major airline offers service to Chicago, either through direct flights or in conjunction with other airlines. Midway Airport, on the city's southwest side, sees a much smaller flow of mostly domestic commuter flights, but is nonetheless an option for those already in the US or who have included Chicago on a multi-city itinerary.

Trains can be a scenic alternative to flying, if you have time and don't mind paying the equivalent of airfare. The national train network, **Amtrak**, runs frequent service between Chicago and most major US cities, all of them arriving at Union Station, just west of the Loop.

Buses are far cheaper and more frequent than trains, but can be uncomfortable and time-consuming. The sole long-distance carrier servicing Chicago is **Greyhound**, whose buses arrive at the Greyhound station southwest of the Loop.

Shopping for air tickets

Within the US, prices for **domestic flights** to Chicago depend more on passenger volume than anything else, so it pays to search for flights leaving from an airport with plenty of traffic to the city. Airfares always depend on the **season**, with the highest being around May to September when the weather is best; fares drop during the low season, December to March (excluding around Christmas and New Year's Day when prices are hiked up and seats are at a premium). Note also that flying on weekends ordinarily adds substantially to the cost of a round-trip fare; the price ranges quoted below assume mid-week travel.

If you want to travel during **major American holiday periods** (around Fourth of July, Thanksgiving, and Christmas and New Year's Day), be sure to book well ahead. While prices fluctuate wildly around these times, it's possible to find cheaper fares with some digging, though they'll

require at least the standard three-week (or 28-day) advance purchase.

You can often cut costs by using a **specialist flight agent** – either a consolidator, who buys up blocks of tickets from the airlines and sells them at a discount, or a discount agent, who in addition to dealing with discounted flights may also offer special student and youth fares and a range of other travel-related services such as travel insurance, rail passes, car rentals, tours and the like. Some agents specialize in charter flights, which may be cheaper than anything available on a scheduled flight, but again departure dates are fixed and withdrawal penalties are high. Check the fares advertised in the travel sections of daily and weekly newspapers.

Many airlines and discount travel **websites** offer you the opportunity to book your tickets online – often at a small discount – which may also cut out the costs of agents and middlemen. Good deals can often be found through discount or auction sites, as well as through the airlines' own websites. As Chicago isn't a popular package-tour destination, you're likely to find better deals on your own, especially through one of the online booking sites (see below), who can set you up with air ticket, lodging and car rental.

If you're traveling from Europe or Australasia and the US is only one stop on a longer journey, you might want to consider buying a **Round-the-World (RTW) ticket**. Some travel agents can sell you an "off-the-shelf" RTW ticket that will have you touching down in about half a dozen cities; others will have to assemble one for you, which can be tailored to your needs but is apt to be more expensive. Chicago does figure on some standard itineraries, but cities on the US East and West coasts are more typical stopovers.

Online booking agents and general travel sites

ⓦ**www.cheapflights.com** Bookings from the UK and Ireland only. Flight deals, travel agents, plus links to other travel sites.

ⓦ**www.cheaptickets.com** Discount flight specialists.

ⓦ**www.etn.nl/discount.htm** A hub of consolidator and discount agent Web links, maintained by the nonprofit European Travel Network.

ⓦ**www.expedia.com** Discount airfares, all-airline search engine and daily deals.

ⓦ**www.flyaow.com** Online air travel info and reservations site.

ⓦ**www.gaytravel.com** Gay online travel agent, concentrating mostly on accommodation.

ⓦ**www.geocities.com/thavery2000** Has an extensive list of airline toll-free numbers and websites.

ⓦ**www.hotwire.com** Bookings from the US only. Last-minute savings of up to 40 percent on regular published fares. Travelers must be at least 18 and there are no refunds, transfers or changes allowed. Log-in required.

ⓦ**www.lastminute.com** Offers good last-minute holiday-package and flight-only deals.

ⓦ**www.orbitz.com** Partnership of the top airlines in the US, offering the cheapest fares published, as well as hotel and car booking; best used from within the US.

ⓦ**www.priceline.com** Name-your-own-price website that has deals at around 40 percent off standard fares. You cannot specify flight times (although you do specify dates) and the tickets are nonrefundable, nontransferable and nonchangeable.

ⓦ**www.skyauction.com** Bookings from the US only. Auctions tickets and travel packages using a "second bid" scheme. The best strategy is to bid the maximum you're willing to pay, since if you win you'll pay just enough to beat the runner-up regardless of your maximum bid.

ⓦ**www.smilinjack.com/airlines.htm** Lists an up-to-date compilation of airline website addresses.

ⓦ**www.travelocity.com** Destination guides, hot Web fares and best deals for car rental, accommodation and lodging as well as fares. Provides access to the travel agent system SABRE, the most comprehensive central reservations system in the US.

ⓦ**www.travelshop.com.au** Australian website offering discounted flights, packages, insurance and online bookings.

ⓦ**travel.yahoo.com** Incorporates a lot of Rough Guide material in its coverage of destination countries and cities across the world, with information about places to eat, sleep and so on.

Flights and other approaches from the US and Canada

From most places in North America, **flying** is the fastest and easiest way to reach Chicago. The city is connected with all of the major US cities – New York, Boston, Washington DC, Atlanta and Miami on the East Coast, and Seattle, San Francisco and Los Angeles on the West – with at least several flights a day from each.

As Chicago isn't a popular package-tour destination, you're likely to find better deals on your own, especially through one of the online booking sites (see above), which can set you up with air ticket, lodging and car rental.

Airlines

Aero Mexico ☏1-800/237-6639, ⓦwww.aeromexico.com/ingles/home.html
Air Canada ☏1-888/247-2262, ⓦwww.aircanada.ca

Sample round-trip fares and Flight times to Chicago

From	Flight time	Fare
Boston	2hr 30min	$230
Dallas	2hr 15min	$230
Denver	2hr 30min	$180
Los Angeles	4hr	$240
Minneapolis	1hr 30min	$210
Montreal	2hr	$260
New Orleans	2hr	$300
New York	2hr	$220
Orlando	2hr 30min	$290
San Francisco	4hr 30min	$275
Toronto	1hr 30min	$230
Vancouver	3hr	$350
Washington DC	1hr 30min	$190

Alaska Airlines ☎1-800/252-7522,
⊛www.alaska-air.com
America West Airlines ☎1-800/235-9292,
⊛www.americawest.com
American Airlines ☎1-800/433-7300,
⊛www.aa.com
American Trans Air (to/from Midway Airport)
☎1-800/435-9292, ⊛www.ata.com
Continental Airlines ☎1-800/523-3273,
⊛www.continental.com
Delta Air Lines ☎1-800/221-1212,
⊛www.delta.com
Frontier Airlines (to/from Midway Airport)
☎1-800/432-1359, ⊛www.flyfrontier.com
Mexicana ☎1-800/531-7921,
⊛www.mexicana.com
National ☎1-800/447-4747,
⊛www.nationalairlines.com
Northwest ☎1-800/225-2525, ⊛www.nwa.com
Southwest Airlines (to/from Midway Airport)
☎1-800/435-9792, ⊛www.southwest.com
Spirit ☎1-800/772-7117, ⊛www.spiritair.com
United Airlines ☎1-800/241-6522,
⊛www.ual.com
US Airways ☎1-800/428-4322, ⊛www.usair.com

Discount travel agents

Air Brokers International ☎1-800/883-3273,
⊛www.airbrokers.com. Consolidator and specialist
in Round-the-World and Circle Pacific tickets.
Airtech ☎212/219-7000, ⊛www.airtech.com.
Standby seat broker; also deals in consolidator fares
and courier flights.
Airtreks.com ☎1-877/AIRTREKS or 415/912-
5600, ⊛www.airtreks.com. Round-the-world and
Circle Pacific tickets. The website features an
interactive database that lets you build and price
your own round-the-world itinerary.
Council Travel ☎1-800/2COUNCIL,
⊛www.counciltravel.com. Nationwide organization
that mostly specializes in student/budget travel.
Flights from the US only. Owned by STA Travel.
Educational Travel Center ☎1-800/747-5551
or 608/256-5551, ⊛www.edtrav.com.
Student/youth discount agent.
Skylink US ☎1-800/247-6659 or 212/573-8980,
Canada ☎1-800/759-5465,
⊛www.skylinkus.com. Consolidator.
STA Travel ☎1-800/781-4040, ⊛www.
sta-travel.com. Worldwide specialists in independent
travel; also student IDs, travel insurance, car rental,
rail passes and more.
Student Flights ☎1-800/255-8000 or 480/951-
1177, ⊛www.isecard.com. Student/youth fares,
student IDs.

TFI Tours ☎1-800/745-8000 or 212/736-1140,
⊛www.lowestairprice.com. Consolidator.
Travac ☎1-800/TRAV-800,
⊛www.thetravelsite.com. Consolidator and charter
broker with offices in New York City and Orlando.
Travel Avenue ☎1-800/333-3335,
⊛www.travelavenue.com. Full-service travel agent
that offers discounts in the form of rebates.
Travel Cuts Canada ☎1-800/667-2887,
US ☎1-866/246-9762, ⊛www.travelcuts.com.
Canadian student-travel organization.
Travelers Advantage ☎1-877/259-2691,
⊛www.travelersadvantage.com. Discount travel
club; annual membership fee required (currently $1
for 3 months' trial).
Worldtek Travel ☎1-800/243-1723,
⊛www.worldtek.com. Discount travel agency for
worldwide travel.

Tour operators

AmeriCan Adventures ☎1-800/TREK-USA,
⊛www.americanadventures.com. Camping and
youth-hostel trips that feature Chicago on various
cross-country itineraries. Note: trips do not originate
in Chicago.
Amtrak Vacations ☎1-877/YES-RAIL,
⊛www.amtrak.com/savings/
amtrakvacations.html. Package deals that include
accommodation, car rental and sightseeing tours.
Amtrak Air Rail tickets combine rail travel one way
with a flight on United Airlines or United Express the
other way.
Contiki Holidays ☎1-888/CONTIKI,
⊛www.contiki.com. Planned vacation packages
geared to 18–35-year-olds; the 9-day "Northern
Experience" tour (from $1025, land only) ends in
Chicago and includes a day of sightseeing, plus one
night's accommodation.
Maupintour ☎1-800/255-4266,
⊛www.maupintour.com. Luxury tours, including an
8-day Great Lakes escorted tour, with a night in
Chicago, from $1750 per person (on land only).
Suntrek Tours ☎1-800/SUNTREK or 707/523-
1800, ⊛www.suntrek.com. Small group tours that
mix sightseeing in cities with the outdoors; a few
tours stop in Chicago for a night.
United Vacations ☎1-800/854-3899,
⊛www.unitedvacations.com. Vacation packages
that can combine airfare with hotel accommodation,
car rental and other services.

By rail

Travel by **train** can be a scenic and leisurely
option, though not likely to be much cheaper

than air travel. **Amtrak** (☎1-800/USA-RAIL, ⊛www.amtrak.com) services Chicago and runs trains from most major US cities. It also jointly operates trains between Toronto and Chicago with Canada's national rail company, **VIA Rail** (in Toronto ☎416/366-8411, rest of Canada ☎1-888/842-7245, in US ☎1-800/USA-RAIL, ⊛www.viarail.ca); several trains make the twelve-hour trip daily.

Peak fares are usually in effect from June to September. Round-trip fares from **New York** (18hr) start around $200, from **Boston** (22hr) $220, **San Francisco** or **Los Angeles** (48hr) $415, **Seattle** (48hr) $335, **Detroit** (5hr) $75, **Milwaukee** (1hr) $40, **San Antonio** (31hr) $260, **New Orleans** (32hr) $260 and **Toronto** (12hr) $155.

Amtrak also has a partnership with United Airlines (Air Rail Vacation, ☎1-800/437-3441) that allows you to fly one way to Chicago and take the train the other way.

You'll also find **seasonal special offers** (30 percent discount on select routes during the fall and spring etc), as well as discounts of 15 percent for **seniors** and **students**, for most Amtrak rail journeys; check the company's website or call them for details. If Chicago is part of a longer itinerary, you might consider buying one of Amtrak's rail passes. For US and Canadian residents, the **North America Rail Pass** allows thirty days' unlimited travel throughout Amtrak and VIA Rail's networks ($674 in high season, $475 in low season).

Overseas visitors can buy **USA Rail passes**, which cover six different regions and are valid for fifteen or thirty days with unlimited stopovers. Of these, the most suitable for visits to Chicago are the **West Rail Pass**, allowing travel between Chicago and New Orleans, and westward to the Pacific during a fifteen-day period ($200 in low season, $300 in high season) and thirty-day periods ($270 in low season, $400 in high season); and the **National USA Rail Pass**, good for fifteen-days of unlimited travel anywhere in the network for $440 (high season) or $295 (low), or thirty days for $550 (high season) or $385 (low). Passes must be bought before you travel to North America, and you'll need to present it, along with a passport, at an Amtrak office to be issued tickets before you board your train. Reservations are usually required, and are best made before you arrive in North America.

By bus

The national bus line, **Greyhound** (☎312/408-5800, ⊛www.greyhound.com), runs frequent buses from major Midwestern cities (Cleveland, Indianapolis, Milwaukee, Minneapolis), usually around ten per day from each city. Beyond the Midwest, Greyhound does run a few buses daily from New York, Washington DC and Denver, plus a few that make the two-day journey from the West Coast. Two smaller companies stop at Greyhound's station: **Lakefront Lines** (☎1-800/638-6338, ⊛www.lakefrontlines.com) operates service between Charleston (West Virginia) and Chicago, passing through Ohio, Indiana and Kentucky, while the Michigan-based **Indian Trails** (☎1-800/292-3831) runs buses between Chicago and points in Michigan and Wisconsin.

Fares depend on the season, though on all routes you'll pay slightly more if you travel between Friday and Sunday (see below for standard midweek round-trip fares). The price drops if you buy your ticket seven days in advance or take advantage of student and senior discounts or special offers (eg "two-for-one" companion fares). If Chicago is just one stop on a longer itinerary, check out the **Discovery Pass**, which is open to both US citizens and overseas travelers. It offers unlimited travel in the entire Greyhound network for as little as four days ($140) up to sixty days ($495).

Sample round-trip fares and bus times to Chicago

From	Trip time	Fare
Boston (6 daily)	23hr	$250
Cleveland (9 daily)	6hr	$73
Indianapolis (9 daily)	3hr 20min	$59
Los Angeles (6 daily)	50hr	$210
Milwaukee (14 daily)	1hr 45min	$26
Minneapolis (8 daily)	8hr	$55
New York City (6 daily)	16hr	$143
Washington DC (6 daily)	17hr	$150

By car

Driving to Chicago will give you some flexibility, but once you reach the city you're not likely to need a car unless you're short on time or want to explore outlying areas like Oak Park. You'll pay a lot for parking, so having a car over a long period of time can add up. (For more about driving once in Chicago, see "Arrival," p.23.)

Arranging a car in advance, either online or over the phone, will also save you money. Most rental agreements will include unlimited mileage, though you should confirm this when arranging a car and again when you pick it up. If you want to pick up the car at one location and leave it at another, rates can go up by as much as $200. If you are **under 25**, expect to pay high surcharges on top of the initial rental charge. Be sure to read the agreement carefully before signing out an automobile, especially for details on Collision Damage Waiver (sometimes called Liability Damage Waiver), a form of insurance that often isn't included in the cost of the initial rental charge but is well worth having. At $10–15 per day the waiver can add up, but without it you could end up paying hefty fees for any scratches, dents and other damage to the car – even those that aren't your fault. Credit card holders should inquire with their credit card companies beforehand as some include this type of coverage if you use your card to pay.

Driving to Chicago

From	Driving time	Distance
Miami	23hr	1380 miles
Montreal	14hr	840 miles
New York	15hr	780 miles
San Francisco	35hr	2135 miles
Toronto	9hr	513 miles
Washington DC	12hr	699 miles

Car rental agencies

Alamo US ☏1-800/522-9696, ⊛www.alamo.com
Avis Australia ☏13 63 33, ⊛www.avis.com; Canada ☏1-800/272-5871; New Zealand ☏09/526 2847; Republic of Ireland ☏01/605 7500; UK ☏0870/606 0100; US ☏1-800/331-1084, ⊛www.avis.com
Budget Australia ☏1300/362 848; New Zealand ☏09/976 2222; Republic of Ireland ☏01/9032 771; UK ☏0800/181 181; US ☏1-800/527-0700, ⊛www.budgetrentacar.com
Cosmo Thrifty Northern Ireland ☏028/9445 2565, ⊛www.thrifty.co.uk
Dollar Australia ☏02/9223 1444; US ☏1-800/800-4000, ⊛www.dollar.com
Enterprise Rent-a-Car US ☏1-800/325-8007, ⊛www.enterprise.com
Hertz Australia ☏13 30 39; Canada ☏1-800/263-0600; New Zealand ☏0800/654 321; Republic of Ireland ☏01/660 2255; UK ☏0870/844 8844; US ☏1-800/654-3001, ⊛www.hertz.com
National Australia ☏13 10 45; New Zealand ☏0800/800 115 or 03/366 5574; UK ☏0870/5365 365; US ☏1-800/227-7368, ⊛www.nationalcar.com
Suncars UK ☏0870/500 5566, ⊛www.suncars.com
Thrifty Australia ☏1300/367 227; New Zealand ☏09/309 0111; US ☏1-800/367-2277; UK ☏01494/751 600, ⊛www.thrifty.co.uk

Flights from the UK and Ireland

There are several **direct flights** leaving daily from London Heathrow Airport to Chicago's O'Hare. British Airways offers two flights, one in the morning, the other in the afternoon, while United has three – usually in mid-morning, around noon and in the late afternoon. United Airlines partners with British Midland to service major UK cities, offering direct flights from Manchester to Chicago (one daily, leaving mid-morning). All other British Midland flights first route through London Heathrow before heading to Chicago, which will add extra to the transatlantic fare.

Round-trip fares to Chicago can cost as little as £295 and as much as £500 (June–Aug and at Christmas). If a direct flight to Chicago is not a priority, your flight options increase substantially: several carriers – KLM, Alitalia and Northwest Airlines among them – fly between the London area airports and route either through a European city (Amsterdam, Milan, Paris) or a US city (New York, Washington DC, Detroit, Atlanta) before continuing on to Chicago.

The only carrier flying direct to Chicago from **Ireland** is Aer Lingus, which leaves from Shannon and Dublin once a day (except Tues), with fares starting from around €424. Although other major carriers (ie Continental, Delta and Northwest) do route through Ireland, they don't link directly with Chicago, so you'll be forced to deal with layovers and transfers. Your best bet is to stick with Aer Lingus and make sure to reserve in advance.

Airlines

Aer Lingus UK ☎0845/084 4444, Republic of Ireland ☎0818/365 000, ☺www.aerlingus.ie
Air France UK ☎0845/0845 111, ☺www.airfrance.co.uk, Republic of Ireland ☎01/605 0383, ☺www.airfrance.com/ie
Alitalia UK ☎0870/544 8259, Republic of Ireland ☎01/677 5171, ☺www.alitalia.co.uk
American Airlines UK ☎0845/7789 789 or 020/8572 5555, Republic of Ireland ☎01/602 0550, ☺www.aa.com
British Airways UK ☎0845/77 333 77, Republic of Ireland ☎1800/626 747, ☺www.ba.com
British Midland UK ☎0870/607 0555, Republic of Ireland ☎01/407 3036, ☺www.flybmi.com
Continental UK ☎0800/776 464, Republic of Ireland ☎1890/925 252, ☺www.flycontinental.com
Delta UK ☎0800/414 767, Republic of Ireland ☎01/407 3165, ☺www.delta.com
Iberia Airlines UK ☎0845/601 2854, Republic of Ireland ☎01/407 3017, ☺www.iberiaairlines.co.uk
Japan Airlines UK ☎0845/774 7700, ☺www.jal-europe.com
KLM UK ☎0870/507 4074, ☺www.klmuk.com
Korean Air UK ☎0800/0656 2001, Republic of Ireland ☎01/799 7990, ☺www.koreanair.eu.com
Lufthansa UK ☎0845/7737 747, ☺www.lufthansa.co.uk
Ryanair.com UK ☎0871/246 0000, Republic of Ireland ☎0818/30 30 30, ☺www.ryanair.com
Scandinavian Airlines (SAS) UK ☎0845/607 2772, Republic of Ireland ☎01/844 5440, ☺www.scandinavian.net
Singapore Airlines UK ☎0870/608 8886, Republic of Ireland ☎01/671 0722, ☺www.singaporeair.com
Swiss UK ☎0845/601 0956, ☺www.swiss.com
United Airlines UK ☎0845/8444 777, ☺www.unitedairlines.co.uk
Virgin Atlantic Airways UK ☎01293/747 747, ☺www.virgin-atlantic.com

Flight and travel agents

Apex Travel Dublin ☎01/241 8000, ☺www.apextravel.ie. Specialists in flights to the US.
Bridge the World UK ☎0870/444 7474, ☺www.bridgetheworld.com. Specializing in Round-the-World tickets, with good deals aimed at the backpacker market.
CIE Tours International Dublin ☎01/703 1888, ☺www.cietours.ie. General flight and tour agent.
Flightbookers UK ☎0870/010 7000, ☺www.ebookers.com. Low fares on an extensive selection of scheduled flights, plus Chicago accommodation packages. Recommended.
Flynow UK ☎0870/444 0045, ☺www.flynow.com. Wide range of discounted tickets.
Joe Walsh Tours Dublin ☎01/676 0991, ☺www.joewalshtours.ie. General budget fares agent.
North South Travel UK ☎ & ☎01245/608 291, ☺www.northsouthtravel.co.uk. Discounted fares worldwide – profits are used to support projects in the developing world, especially the promotion of sustainable tourism.
Quest Travel UK ☎0870/442 3542, ☺www.questtravel.com. Specialists in Round-the-World and Australasian discount fares.
STA Travel UK ☎0870/1600 599, ☺www.statravel.co.uk. Worldwide specialists in low-cost flights and tours for students and under-26s, though other customers welcome.
Trailfinders UK ☎020/7628 7628, ☺www.trailfinders.com. One of the best-informed and most efficient agents for independent travelers; Amtrak passes available.
Travel Cuts UK ☎020/7255 2082 or 7255 1944, ☺www.travelcuts.co.uk. Canadian company specializing in budget, student and youth travel, and Round-the-World tickets; Greyhound and Amtrak passes available.
United Vacations UK ☎0870/606 2222, ☺www.unitedvacations.co.uk. Tailor-made package holidays, fly-drive deals, organized sightseeing tours and more.
☺www.travel4less.co.uk Good discount airfares and package deals, including three-night city breaks to Chicago, from £399 in low season (flight and accommodation included).

Tour operators

American Adventures UK ☎01892/512 700, ⓦwww.americanadventures.com. Small group camping trips throughout the US and Canada.
American Holidays Belfast ☎028/9023 8762, Dublin ☎01/433 1009, ⓦwww.american-holidays.com. Specialists in travel to the US.
British Airways Holidays UK ☎0870/442 3820, ⓦwww.baholidays.co.uk. An exhaustive range of package and tailor-made holidays around the world, with Chicago city breaks.
Kuoni Travel UK ☎01306/742 888, ⓦwww.kuoni.co.uk. Build your own holiday package to Chicago; good family offers.
Thomas Cook UK ☎0870/5666 222, ⓦwww.thomascook.co.uk. Long-established one-stop 24-hour travel agency for package holidays or scheduled flights, with bureaux de change issuing Thomas Cook travelers' checks, travel insurance and car rental.
Thomas Cook Holidays UK ☎01733/563 200, ⓦwww.thomascook.com. Range of flight and board deals for Chicago.
Twohigs Dublin ☎01/677 2666. Specialists in US travel, among other regions.
World Travel Centre Dublin ☎01/671 7155, ⓦwww.worldtravel.ie. Discount flights and other travel services.

Flights from Australia and New Zealand

There are no direct scheduled flights to Chicago from either Australia or New Zealand.

Most Chicago-bound flights from **Australia** leave from Sydney or Melbourne and usually route through Tokyo, Los Angeles or Las Vegas. The major carriers – Qantas (in partnership with American Airlines) and United Airlines – offer several flights a day to the US West Coast, from which onward travel to Chicago is easily arranged. Flights take about thirteen hours to the West Coast, and five hours onward to Chicago.

Fares vary depending on the season (between June and September being the most expensive) and flight availability, with fares as low as A$1400 and as high as A$3600, though A$2100–2640 is the more usual range.

Chicago-bound flights from **New Zealand** leave Auckland, Christchurch or Wellington and route through Los Angeles, before making the onward flight to Chicago. The two major carriers, Air New Zealand and Qantas, and their US partners, United Airlines and American Airlines, generally fly from Auckland (add about 15 percent to the fare for Christchurch and Wellington departures). In general, expect to pay NZ$2830–4100.

Airlines

Aer Lingus Australia ☎02/9244 2123, New Zealand ☎09/308 3351, ⓦwww.aerlingus.ie
Air Canada Australia ☎1300/655 747 or 02/9286 8900, New Zealand ☎09/379 3371, ⓦwww.aircanada.ca
Air France Australia ☎02/9244 2100, New Zealand ☎09/308 3352, ⓦwww.airfrance.com
Alitalia Australia ☎02/9244 2445, New Zealand ☎09/308 3357, ⓦwww.alitalia.com
America West Airlines Australia ☎02/9267 2138 or 1300/364 757, New Zealand ☎0800/866 000, ⓦwww.americawest.com
American Airlines Australia ☎1300/650 747, New Zealand ☎09/309 9159, ⓦwww.aa.com
British Airways Australia ☎02/8904 8800, New Zealand ☎0800/274 847 or 09/357 8950, ⓦwww.britishairways.com
Continental Airlines Australia ☎1300/361 400, New Zealand ☎09/308 3350, ⓦwww.flycontinental.com
Delta Air Lines Australia ☎02/9251 3211, New Zealand ☎09/379 3370, ⓦwww.delta-air.com
Japan Airlines Australia ☎02/9272 1111, New Zealand ☎09/379 9906, ⓦwww.japanair.com
KLM/Northwest Airlines Australia ☎1300/303 747, ⓦwww.klm.com/au_en, New Zealand ☎09/309 1782, ⓦwww.klm.com/nz_en
Korean Air Australia ☎02/9262 6000, New Zealand ☎09/914 2000, ⓦwww.koreanair.com.au
Lufthansa Australia ☎1300/655 727, ⓦwww.lufthansa-australia.com, New Zealand ☎09/303 1529, ⓦwww.lufthansa.com/index_en.html
Qantas Australia ☎13 13 13, ⓦwww.qantas.com.au, New Zealand ☎09/357 8900, ⓦwww.qantas.co.nz
Scandinavian Airlines (SAS) Australia ☎1300/727 707, New Zealand agent: Air New Zealand ☎09/357 3000, ⓦwww.scandinavian.net
Singapore Airlines Australia ☎13 10 11, New Zealand ☎09/303 2129, ⓦwww.singaporeair.com

Swiss Australia ☎1300/724 666,
🖲www.swiss.com
United Airlines Australia ☎13 17 77,
🖲www.unitedairlines.com.au, New Zealand
☎09/379 3800 or 0800/508 648,
🖲www.unitedairlines.co.nz
Virgin Atlantic Airways Australia ☎02/9244
2747, New Zealand ☎09/308 3377,
🖲www.virgin-atlantic.com

Travel and flight agents

Budget Travel New Zealand ☎0800/808 480,
🖲www.budgettravel.co.nz. Round-the-World tickets
and tours.
Destinations Unlimited New Zealand ☎09/373
4033. Round-the-World tickets.
Flight Centre Australia ☎13 31 33 or 02/9235
3522, 🖲www.flightcentre.com.au, New Zealand
☎0800/243 544 or 09/358 4310,
🖲www.flightcentre.co.nz. Specialist agent for
budget flights, especially Round-the-World tickets.
STA Travel Australia ☎1300/733 035,
🖲www.statravel.com.au, New Zealand
☎0508/782 872, 🖲www.statravel.co.nz. Discount
flights, travel passes and other services for
youth/student travelers.
Trailfinders Australia ☎02/9247 7666,
🖲www.trailfinders.com.au. One of the best-
informed and most efficient agents for independent
travelers; Amtrak passes also available.

Specialist agents

Adventure World Australia ☎02/8913 0755,
🖲www.adventureworld.com.au, New Zealand
☎09/524 5118, 🖲www.adventureworld.co.nz.
Chicago hotel bookings, car rental and organized
tours.
Canada & America Travel Specialists Australia
☎02/9922 4600, 🖲www.
canada-americatravel.com.au. Flights and
accommodation in North America, plus Amtrak
passes and Greyhound Ameripasses.
Contiki Australia ☎02/9511 2200, New Zealand
☎09/309 8824, 🖲www.contiki.com. Frenetic tours
for 18–35-year-olds, at least one of which passes
through Chicago.
Sydney International Travel Centre ☎02/9299
8000 or 1800/251 911, 🖲www.sydneytravel.
com.au. US flights, accommodation, city stays and
car rental.
travel.com.au Australia ☎1300/130 482 or
02/9249 5444, 🖷02/9262 3525, New Zealand
☎0800/468 332, 🖲www.travel.co.nz.
Comprehensive online travel company.
United Vacations Australia ☎1300/887 870,
🖲www.unitedvacations.com.au. Hotel deals for
Chicago.
Viator Australia ☎02/8219 5400,
🖲www.viator.com. Small selection of Chicago tours
and discounts; also sells City Pass – admission to six
top Chicago attractions for 50 percent off regular
admission (from $39 per person).

Entry requirements

Citizens of the UK, Ireland, Australia, New Zealand or most Western European
countries (check with your nearest embassy or consulate) who plan to visit the
US for less than ninety days need only a round-trip ticket, passport and visa
waiver form. The latter (an I-94W) is available from your travel agency, at the airline check-in desk or on board the plane, and must be presented to immigration
once you arrive.

For a brief excursion, Canadian citizens will
need only proof of citizenship (passport or
birth certificate in conjunction with a photo
ID) to enter the US.

Residents of countries not mentioned
above will need a valid passport, as well as a
non-immigrant visitor's visa, which is valid
for a maximum of ninety days. Visa proce-
dures vary by country and by your status on

application, so contact the nearest US
embassy or consulate for details. Most travelers won't need to be inoculated to enter
the US, unless they're en route from areas
where cholera and typhoid are endemic;
check with your doctor before you leave.

The date stamped in your passport by
immigration upon arrival is the latest you're
legally allowed to stay. Leaving a few days

later may not matter, especially if you're heading home, but more than a week or so can result in a protracted, rather unpleasant interrogation from officials, which may cause you to miss your flight. You may also be denied entry the next time you try to visit the US.

Should you need a **visa extension**, you'll have to apply through the nearest US Immigration and Naturalization Service (INS) office before your time is up. In Chicago, the office is at 10 W Jackson Blvd, (Mon–Thurs, 7.30am–2pm; ☎312/385-1500 or 1-800/870-3676, ✆www.ins.usdoj.gov). Be prepared to discuss why you're hoping to stay on – they're likely to assume you are working in the US illegally, so any evidence of your pre-existing (and abundant) funds might strengthen your case. If you can, bring an upstanding American citizen to vouch for you. You'll also have to explain why you didn't plan for the extra time initially.

US embassies

For details of foreign embassies and consulates in Chicago, see p.224.
Australia Moonah Place, Yarralumla, Canberra, ACT 2600 ☎02/6214 5600 ✆http://us embassy-australia.state.gov/embassy
Britain 24 Grosvenor Square, London W1A 1AE ☎020/7499 9000, ✆www.usembassy.org.uk
Canada 490 Sussex Drive, Ottawa, ON K1P 5T1 ☎613/238-5335, ✆www.usembassycanada.gov
Ireland 42 Elgin Rd, Ballsbridge, Dublin 4 ☎01/668 8777, ✆www.usembassy.ie
New Zealand 29 Fitzherbert Terrace, Thorndon, Wellington ☎04/462 6000, ✆www.usembassy.org.nz

Insurance

You'd do well to take out an insurance policy before traveling to cover against theft, loss and illness or injury. For overseas visitors, travel insurance including medical coverage is *essential*, given the high costs of health care in the US.

Before paying for a new policy, however, it's worth checking whether you are already covered: some all-risks home insurance policies may cover your possessions when overseas, and many private medical schemes include cover when abroad.

In **Canada**, provincial health plans usually provide partial cover for medical mishaps overseas, while holders of official student/teacher/youth cards in Canada and the US are entitled to meagre accident coverage and hospital in-patient benefits. Students will often find that their student health coverage extends during the vacations and for one term beyond the date of last enrollment.

Americans should find that their health insurance covers any unforeseen medical costs they may incur while visiting Chicago.

After exhausting the possibilities above, you might want to contact a specialist travel insurance company, or consider the travel insurance deal we offer (see box below).

Many policies can be chopped and changed to exclude coverage you don't need – for example, sickness and accident benefits can often be excluded or included at will.

A typical travel insurance policy usually provides cover for the loss of baggage, tickets and – up to a certain limit – cash or checks, as well as cancellation or curtailment of your journey. Most of them exclude so-called dangerous sports unless an extra premium is paid, so if you're visiting Chicago as part of a wider trip and are also planning to do some water sports or other similar activity, you'll almost certainly have to pay an extra premium.

If you do take medical coverage, ascertain whether benefits will be paid as treatment proceeds or only after return home, and whether there is a **24-hour medical emergency number**. When securing baggage cover, make sure that the per-article limit – typically under $770/£485 – will cover your most valuable possession.

Rough Guides travel insurance

Rough Guides offers its own travel insurance, customized for our readers by a leading UK broker and backed by a Lloyd's underwriter. It's available to anyone, of any nationality and any age, traveling anywhere in the world.

There are two main Rough Guide insurance plans: **Essential**, for basic, no-frills cover; and **Premier**, with more generous and extensive benefits. Alternatively, you can take out **annual multi-trip insurance**, which covers you for any number of trips throughout the year (with a maximum of 60 days for any one trip). Unlike many policies, the Rough Guides schemes are calculated by the day, so if you're travelling for 27 days rather than a month, that's all you pay for. If you intend to be away for the whole year, the Adventurer policy will cover you for 365 days. Each plan can be supplemented with a "Hazardous Activities Premium" if you plan to indulge in sports considered dangerous, such as skiing, scuba-diving or trekking. For a policy quote, call the Rough Guide Insurance Line: US toll-free ☎1-866/220-5588; UK freefone ☎0800/015 0906; or, if you're calling from elsewhere ☎+44 1243/621 046. Alternatively, get an online quote or buy online at ⓦwww.roughguidesinsurance.com

In case you'll need to make a **claim**, be sure to keep receipts for medicines and medical treatment, and should you have anything stolen, you will need to obtain an official statement from the police.

Information, websites and maps

The main source of city information for tourists is the Chicago Office of Tourism (see below for details). You can contact them before your trip for glossy brochures, maps, visitor guides and event calendars. Once in Chicago, you can visit its walk-in branches. There are also several excellent Chicago-related websites with current information on tours, museums, and the newest restaurants and clubs.

Information

Before setting off for Chicago, you may want to contact one of the tourist organizations listed below under "Tourist offices" for help in planning your itinerary.

Once in the city, you'll want to head for the **Chicago Office of Tourism**, which has three locations, the best and most accessible of which is on the first floor of the **Chicago Cultural Center**, 77 E Randolph St (Mon–Fri 10am–6pm, Sat 10am–5pm, Sun 11am–5pm; ☎1-877/CHICAGO, ⓦwww.ci.chi.il.us/Tourism/CulturalCenter/index.html), which can help you with maps, tours and citywide information. The Office of Tourism has a second location inside the **Chicago**

Water Works building, 163 E Pearson St, at Michigan Ave (daily 7.30am–7pm), and an **Explore Chicago kiosk** at 2 N State St, at Madison Ave (Mon–Sat 10am–6pm).

Tourist offices

Chicago Convention and Tourism Bureau Mailing address: 2301 S Lake Shore Drive, Chicago, IL 60616 ☎1-877/244-2246, outside the US, Mexico and Canada ☎312/201-8847, ☎567-8533, ⓦwww.chicago.il.org
Illinois Bureau of Tourism 100 W Randolph St, Suite 3-4000 Chicago, IL 60601 ☎312/814-732 or 1-800/226-6632, ⓦwww.enjoyillinois.com

Websites

The following is a selective list of Chicago-related **websites** to help get you started.

Chicago Public Library ⊚ www.chipublib.org. A handy resource whose encyclopedic "Learn Chicago" section covers just about everything you want to know, from vital city statistics and symbols to major and minor disasters.

Chicago Tribune ⊚ www.chicagotribune.com. Homepage of the city's morning newspaper, covering local news, sports and weather updates, plus arts and entertainment listings in its extensive Metromix search engine (⊚ www.metromix.com).

City of Chicago ⊚ www.ci.chi.il.us. The city's official homepage, with links to major attractions, accommodation, tours, an events calendar and more in its "About Town" section.

Illinois Hotel and Lodging Association ⊚ www.stayillinois.com. The Association's comprehensive website has detailed summaries of and links to most hotels in Chicago and throughout Illinois.

League of Chicago Theaters ⊚ www.chicagoplays.com. Provides details on venues, showtimes and ticket prices for plays being performed in Chicago. Includes a link to a list of half-price theater shows (under "Hot Tix").

Mayor's Office of Special Events ⊚ www.ci.chi.il.us/SpecialEvents. The best source for information on festivals, parades, holiday and sporting events, as well as what films are currently being shot in Chicago. Updated regularly.

National Weather Service ⊚ weather.noaa.gov/weather/IL_cc_us.html. The organization's Illinois page provides up-to-the-minute weather conditions at O'Hare, Midway and regional airports.

Sports Illinois ⊚ www.sportsillinois.com. Part of the Illinois Bureau of Tourism's extensive site, covering every conceivable sport, and where to participate, throughout the state.

Maps

Our maps should be sufficient for most purposes; commercial maps and the free city plans available from tourist offices can help fill in the gaps. For a pocket-sized map, try the laminated *Streetwise Chicago* ($5.95; ⊚ www.streetwisemaps.com), which is available from most book, travel and map stores.

The **American Automobile Association** (☎ 1-800/222-4357, ⊚ www.aaa.com) provides free maps and assistance to its members, and to British members of the AA and RAC.

Map outlets

In the US and Canada

AdventurousTraveler.com US ☎ 1-800/282-3963, ⊚ adventuroustraveler.com

Book Passage 51 Tamal Vista Blvd, Corte Madera, CA 94925 ☎ 1-800/999-7909, ⊚ www.bookpassage.com

Distant Lands 56 S Raymond Ave, Pasadena, CA 91105 ☎ 1-800/310-3220, ⊚ www.distantlands.com

Elliot Bay Book Company 101 S Main St, Seattle, WA 98104 ☎ 1-800/962-5311, ⊚ www.elliotbaybook.com

Globe Corner Bookstore 28 Church St, Cambridge, MA 02138 ☎ 1-800/358-6013, ⊚ www.globecorner.com

Map Link 30 S La Patera Lane, Unit 5, Santa Barbara, CA 93117 ☎ 1-800/962-1394, ⊚ www.maplink.com

Rand McNally nationwide ☎ 1-800/333-0136, ⊚ www.randmcnally.com. Around thirty stores across the US; dial ext 2111 or check the website for the nearest location. In Chicago: 150 S Wacker Drive, IL 60606 ☎ 312/332-2009; 444 N Michigan Ave, IL 60611 ☎ 312/321-1751.

The Travel Bug Bookstore 2667 W Broadway, Vancouver, British Columbia V6K 2G2 ☎ 604/737-1122, ⊚ www.swifty.com/tbug

World of Maps 1235 Wellington St, Ottawa, ON K1Y 3A3 ☎ 1-800/214-8524, ⊚ www.worldofmaps.com

In the UK and Ireland

Blackwell's Map and Travel Shop 50 Broad St, Oxford OX1 3BQ ☎ 01865/793 550, ⊚ maps.blackwell.co.uk

Eason 40 O'Connell St, Dublin 1 ☎ 01/858 3881, ⊚ www.eason.ie

Heffers Map and Travel 20 Trinity St, Cambridge CB2 1TJ ☎ 01223/333 536, ⊚ www.heffers.co.uk

Hodges Figgis Bookshop 56–58 Dawson St, Dublin 2 ☎ 01/677 4754, ⊚ www.hodgesfiggis.com

The Map Shop 30a Belvoir St, Leicester LE1 6QH ☎ 0116/247 1400, ⊚ www.mapshopleicester.co.uk

National Map Centre 22–24 Caxton St, London SW1H 0QU ☎ 020/7222 2466, ⊚ www.mapsnmc.co.uk

Newcastle Map Centre 55 Grey St, Newcastle-upon-Tyne NE1 6EF ☎ 0191/261 5622.

Ordnance Survey Ireland Phoenix Park, Dublin 8 ☎ 01/802 5300, ⊚ www.osi.ie

Ordnance Survey of Northern Ireland Colby House, Stranmillis Court, Belfast BT9 5BJ ☎028/9025 5755, ⊛www.osni.gov.uk
Stanfords 12–14 Long Acre, London WC2E 9LP ☎020/7836 1321, ⊛www.stanfords.co.uk
The Travel Bookshop 13–15 Blenheim Crescent, London W11 2EE ☎020/7229 5260, ⊛www.thetravelbookshop.co.uk

In Australia and New Zealand

The Map Shop 6–10 Peel St, Adelaide, South Australia 5000 ☎08/8231 2033, ⊛www.mapshop.net.au

Mapland 372 Little Bourke St, Melbourne, Victoria 3000 ☎03/9670 4383, ⊛www.mapland.com.au
MapWorld 173 Gloucester St, Christchurch ☎0800/627 967 or 03/374 5399, ⊛www.mapworld.co.nz
Perth Map Centre 1/884 Hay St, Perth, Western Australia 6000 ☎08/9322 5733, ⊛www.perthmap.com.au
Specialty Maps 46 Albert St, Auckland 1001 ☎09/307 2217, ⊛www.ubdonline.co.nz/maps

Arrival

Those traveling to Chicago by bus or train arrive just west of the Loop, within a stone's throw of public transportation and dozens of hotels. While flights touch down at O'Hare and Midway airports in Chicago's outlying areas, at least a dozen miles from the city center, efficient El trains will take you downtown within a half hour to 45 minutes. Taking a taxi from the airport won't save you much time and can be expensive, especially if you're going it alone. Alternatively, airport shuttles will cost less but tend to make multiple stops on the journey downtown.

By plane

If arriving by air, you'll most likely be coming into O'Hare International Airport on the city's northwest side, about seventeen miles outside the city center. There are several ways of getting into Chicago proper from here, the quickest and most reliable option being the forty-minute ride on the **Chicago Transit Authority (CTA) Blue Line El train**, which runs 24 hours and costs $1.50 one-way. You'll reach downtown from O'Hare in about 45 minutes, and just under half that time from Midway. The station is underneath the main parking garage, a short walk from most of the airport's terminals. From Terminal 5, though, you'll need to take the free Airport Transit System shuttle to Terminal 3 and follow the signs marked "City Transport."

Another option is taking one of the **airport shuttles**, which drop you off at your requested hotel for around $20, plus tip – half the equivalent taxi fare. Shuttles pull up in front of the main entrances of each terminal every five to ten minutes. Most of the

shuttle companies have information desks inside by the baggage claim area. Shuttles generally run between 6am and midnight. If you want to try and reserve ahead, call **Continental Airport Express** (☎312/454-7800 or 1-800/654-7871), one of the better shuttle services.

Taxis are your most expensive option, and you're at the whim of Chicago traffic – a single fare could run you anywhere from $35 and up, plus tip. Even in off-peak times, however, cabs are plentiful and can be found curbside at any terminal, outside of baggage claim. Usually the ride takes twenty minutes, but with traffic you could be looking at up to an hour. If you can find someone to split the fare, then a cab could be decent value.

From **Midway Airport**, on the southwest side of the city, the quickest and cheapest way to reach downtown is to take the **CTA Orange Line El train**, which departs every five minutes (off-peak, every 15min) and makes the ten-mile trip in just under half an hour. To find the El stop, follow the signs to the parking garage – the station is directly behind the garage. If you arrive at Midway late at night or very early in the morning, bear in mind that the Orange Line stops running between 1am and 4am Monday to Saturday, and between 1am and 7am on Sundays and holidays.

You can pick up a **taxi** just outside the baggage claim area. Fares are metered, and a ride into downtown will set you back about $20 (plus tip), taking anywhere from fifteen minutes to an hour, depending on traffic. If you're with other travelers, you might try the **shared ride service**, whereby passengers can share a cab for a flat rate of $19 per person; however, be sure to let the driver know beforehand that you want to do this.

Another option is taking the **Continental Airport Express shuttle** (6am–11.30pm; ☎312/454–7800 or 1-800/654-7871), which leaves from just outside the main terminal. Shuttles run every fifteen minutes between Midway and downtown Chicago (for $13), and also the northern suburbs.

By train and bus

Chicago is the hub of the nationwide Amtrak rail system, and almost every cross-country route passes through **Union Station** (☎312/558-1075), at Canal and Adams streets, just west of the Loop. The closest El stop is about four blocks away at Quincy and Wells streets, while cabs are available outside the station on both the upper and lower levels.

Greyhound and a couple of regional bus companies pull into the large modern terminal at 630 W Harrison St (☎312/408-5980 in Chicago, ⊛www.greyhound.com), between Des Plaines and Jefferson streets, a ten-minute walk from the Loop. The nearest El stop (Blue Line) is on Clinton Street, two blocks northeast of the terminal.

By car

When driving to Chicago you'll need to be aware of at least four major expressways feeding into downtown Chicago: **I-90/94** from the northwest and north; **I-290** from the west; **I-55** from the southwest; and **I-90/94** from the south.

Major expressways

I-55	Stevenson Expressway
I-90 East	Kennedy Expressway
I-94 North	Dan Ryan Expressway
I-290 East	Eisenhower Expressway

From O'Hare International Airport (on the northwest side), take I-90 East to Ohio Street, which will take you to Michigan Avenue, just north of the Loop. **From the northern suburbs**, take I-94 to the same Ohio Street exit. Alternatively, take the scenic route along **Lake Shore Drive** (Highway 41).

From the west, take I-290 East directly into downtown – it becomes Congress Parkway and runs along the Loop's southern edge.

Approaching the city **from the south** (from Indiana, near Lake Michigan), use I-90, following it over the Chicago Skyway's long bridge to merge onto I-94 North. Stay on this past the juncture with I-290, then exit at any of the next three streets and drive east to reach the heart of downtown. Alternatively, from Indiana via I-80/94, take the expressway to the Calumet Expressway, then to I-94 North and follow the directions from I-290, as given directly above.

From Midway Airport (and the southwest), take Cicero Avenue north to I-55. Take I-55 east to either I-94 North, past I-290 and exit east at any one of the streets thereafter, or simply stay on I-55 to Lake Shore Drive north and exit at Wacker Drive.

Leaving Chicago: reserving a shuttle seat

If you plan on taking a shuttle to either O'Hare or Midway, it's worth booking a seat in advance as vans can book up fast, especially around the holidays. Be sure to give yourself plenty of time to get to the airport.

Costs, money and banks

Chicago is relatively inexpensive compared to the major US cities: public transport is efficient and reliable enough in most instances, many of the museums are inexpensive (under $10) and offer free days, and unless you're intent on dining in high style, the food's relatively cheap too.

Average costs

Accommodation is likely to be your biggest single expense. The least expensive, reasonable double hotel rooms go from $90 a night, though you'll probably find some good deals on weekends and during Chicago's winter; see "Accommodation," Chapter 11, for more details. After accommodation, you could get by on $45–60 per day, which will buy you a basic diner breakfast, a fast-food lunch (pizza, burger, sandwich) and a budget sit-down dinner with beer, plus El fare. Beyond this, a little more luxury – such as fancier meals, taking taxis, going to a concert or play – will mean more like $70 a day. Bear in mind that sales tax is added to just about everything you buy in stores, except for certain groceries.

Bear in mind that **tipping** is customary and expected at restaurants (usually not less than 15 percent) and bars ($1–2 for a round of drinks), though you needn't feel pressure to leave a large tip if service is especially poor.

Banks and ATMs

With an **ATM card**, you'll be able to withdraw cash just about anywhere in Chicago, though you'll be charged a fee for using a different bank's network. If you have a foreign cash-dispensing card linked to an international network such as Cirrus or Plus – be sure to check with your home bank before you set off – you can make withdrawals from ATMs in the US. The flat transaction fee is usually quite small – your bank will be able to advise on this. Make sure you have a personal identification number (PIN) that's designed to work overseas. You may also be able to use your debit card for purchases, as you would at home.

Most **banks** in Chicago are open Monday to Friday, 9am–3pm, though a limited number have Saturday hours, usually open no later than 1pm. For a list of downtown banks, see p.224.

Travelers' checks

Travelers' checks **in US dollars** are widely accepted as cash in restaurants, stores and museums. The usual fee for travelers' check sales is one or two percent, though this fee may be waived if you buy the check through a bank where you have an account. It pays to get a selection of denominations so you'll have some flexibility. Make sure to keep the

Money: a note for foreign travelers

US currency comes in $1 bills and coins, bills of $5, $10, $20, $50 and $100, plus various larger (and rarer) denominations. All are the same size and same green color, making it necessary to check each bill carefully. The dollar is made up of 100 cents (¢) in coins of 1 cent (usually called a penny), 5 cents (a nickel), 10 cents (a dime) and 25 cents (a quarter). Fifty-cent and $1 coins are less frequently seen. Change – especially quarters – is needed for buses, vending machines and telephones, so always carry plenty, though automatic machines are increasingly fitted with slots for dollar bills.

Generally speaking, one pound sterling will buy $1.40, one Canadian dollar is worth around 64¢, one Australian dollar equals about 56¢ and one New Zealand dollar is equivalent to about 49¢. At the time of publication, the Euro equaled $1.

purchase agreement and a record of check serial numbers safe and separate from the checks themselves. In the event that checks are lost or stolen, the issuing company will expect you to report the loss immediately to their office; most companies claim to replace lost or stolen checks within 24 hours.

For a list of currency exchange offices, see p.224.

Credit and debit cards

Credit cards are a very handy backup source of funds, and can be used either in ATMs or over the counter. MasterCard, Visa and American Express are accepted just about everywhere, but other cards may not be recognized in the US. Remember that all cash advances are treated as loans, with interest accruing daily from the date of withdrawal; there may be a transaction fee on top of this.

A compromise between travelers' checks and plastic is **Visa TravelMoney**, a disposable pre-paid debit card with a PIN that works in all ATMs that take Visa cards. When your funds are depleted, you simply throw the card away. Since you can buy up to nine cards to access the same funds – useful for couples or families traveling together – it's a good idea to buy at least one extra as a back-up in case of loss or theft. You can call a 24hour toll-free customer service number in the US (☎1-800/847-2911); visit also the Visa TravelMoney website at ☜usa.visa.com/personal/cards/visa_travel_money.html. The card is available in most countries from branches of Thomas Cook and Citicorp.

Wiring money

Having money wired from home using one of the companies listed below is never convenient or cheap, and should be considered a last resort. It's also possible to have money wired directly from a bank in your home country to a bank in the US, although this is somewhat less reliable because it involves two separate institutions. If you go this route, your home bank will need the address of the branch bank where you want to pick up the money and the address and telex number of the bank's head office, which will act as the clearing house; money wired this way normally takes two working days to arrive, and costs around $40 per transaction. The quickest way to have money wired to you is to have someone take the cash to the nearest money-wiring company and have it wired to the office nearest you – a process that should take no longer than ten to fifteen minutes. The fee depends on the amount being sent, where it's being sent from and to, and how fast you need it. This service is offered by **Travelers' Express Moneygram** (also available at participating **Thomas Cook** branches) and **Western Union**. Travelers' Express only accepts cash, while the Western Union office sending the money will accept credit cards. The latter has slightly higher rates, and if a credit card is involved, they'll probably charge an extra fee.

If you have a few days' leeway, it's cheaper to send a postal money order through the mail; postal orders are exchangeable at any post office. The equivalent for foreign travelers is the **international money order**, but it may take up to seven days to arrive by mail. An ordinary check sent from overseas usually takes two to three weeks to clear.

Money-wiring companies

Thomas Cook Canada ☎1-888/823-4732, Republic of Ireland ☎01/677 1721, UK ☎01733/318 922, US ☎1-800/287-7362, ☜www.us.thomascook.com
Travelers' Express Moneygram Canada ☎1-800/933-3278, US ☎1-800/926-3947, ☜www.moneygram.com
Western Union Australia ☎1800/501 500, New Zealand ☎09/270 0050, Republic of Ireland ☎1800/395 395, UK ☎0800/833 833, US and Canada ☎1-800/325-6000, ☜www.westernunion.com

Phones, mail and email

As one of the country's major business hubs, it should go without saying that Chicago has a speedy and efficient communications infrastructure, so staying in touch shouldn't be a problem.

Telephones

All telephone numbers within Chicago use either the ☎312 or 773 area code, which you don't need to dial if you are calling from within the city. Outside Chicago, dial 1 before the area code and the seven-digit phone number. For detailed information about calls, area codes and rates in the Chicago area, consult the front of the telephone directory in the *White Pages*.

In general, calling from your **hotel room** will cost considerably more than if you use a pay phone, where you can make local calls for 35¢ for the first three or four minutes, 10¢ more for each additional two minutes. Hotels often charge a connection fee of at least $1 for all calls, even if they're local or toll-free, and international calls will cost a small fortune.

For overseas visitors, one of the most convenient ways of phoning home from abroad is via a **telephone charge card**, available from your phone company back home. Using access codes for the country you are in and a PIN number, you can make calls from most hotel, public and private phones that will bill to your own account. The benefit of calling cards is mainly one of convenience, as the rates aren't necessarily cheaper than calling from a public phone abroad and can't compete with discounted off-peak times many local companies offer. Since most major charge cards are free to obtain, however, it's certainly worth getting one at least for emergencies; contact your phone company for more details.

In the **US and Canada**, AT&T, MCI, Sprint, Canada Direct and other North American long-distance companies all enable their customers to make credit-card calls while overseas, billed to your home number. Call your company's customer service line to find out if they provide service from the US, and if so, what the toll-free access code is.

In the **UK and Ireland**, British Telecom (☎0800/345 144, ✆www.chargecard.bt.com) will issue free to all BT customers the BT Charge Card, which can be used in 116 countries; AT&T (dial ☎0800/890 011, then 1-888/641-6123 when you hear the AT&T prompt to be transferred to the Florida Call Centre, free 24 hours) has the Global Calling Card; while NTL (☎0500/100 505) issues its own Global Calling Card, which can be used in more than sixty countries abroad, though the fees cannot be charged to a normal phone bill.

To call **Australia and New Zealand** from overseas, telephone charge cards such as Telstra Telecard or Optus Calling Card in Australia and Telecom NZ's Calling Card can be used to make calls abroad, which are charged back to a domestic account or credit card. Apply to Telstra (☎1800/038 000), Optus (☎1300/300 937) or Telecom NZ (☎04/801 9000).

An alternative to telephone charge cards is cheap **pre-paid phone cards** offering cut-rate calls to virtually anywhere in the world. Various stores in Chicago sell them; look for signs posted in shop windows advertising rates.

A less well-known option is to call home through an Internet-phone service, usually available from one of the better cyber cafés. The audio quality isn't nearly as good as with a regular phone and there's usually a slight delay, but calling via the Internet ($5/30min) can work out to be cheaper than calling on a regular phone. Calls are patched through like any other phone call. (See p.224, for addresses.)

If you want to use your **cell phone**, you'll need to check with your phone provider whether it will work in Chicago, and what the call charges are. Many phones only work within the region designated by the area code in the phone number.

If you are visiting the US, your cell phone probably won't work unless you have a tri-band phone, for example. For details of which phones work in the US, contact your service provider. Should you have a phone that works in the US, you'll probably have to inform your service provider before going abroad to get international access switched on. You may get charged extra for this depending on your existing package and where you are traveling to. Tri-band phones will automatically switch to the US frequency, but these can be pricey, so you may want to rent a phone if you're traveling to the US. If you want to retrieve messages while you're away, you'll have to ask your provider for a new access code, as your home one is unlikely to work abroad. You are also likely to be charged extra for incoming calls when abroad, as the people calling you will be paying the usual rate. For further information about using your phone abroad, check out ⊛www.telecomsadvice.org.uk/features/using _your_mobile_abroad.htm

For time differences between the US and the rest of the world, see p.225.

Useful telephone numbers

Emergencies ☏911 for fire, police or ambulance
Directory inquiries for toll-free numbers ☏1-800/555-1212
Local and long-distance directory assistance information ☏411
Operator ☏0

International calls to Chicago:

Your country's international access code + 1 for the US + 312 or 773 for Chicago

International calls from Chicago:

Australia ☏011 + 61 + phone number
Canada ☏011 + 1 + phone number
New Zealand ☏011 + 64 + phone number
Republic of Ireland ☏011 + 353 + phone number
UK ☏011 + 44 + phone number

Mail

Ordinary mail sent within the US costs 37¢ (at press time) for letters weighing up to an ounce, while standard postcards cost 23¢. For anywhere outside the US, airmail letters cost 80¢ up to an ounce and 70¢ for postcards and aerogrammes. Airmail between the US and Europe may take a week and 12–14 days to Australasia.

You can have mail sent to you c/o **General Delivery** (known elsewhere as **post restante**), Chicago, IL 60601. Letters will end up at the post office at 200 E Randolph St (Mon–Fri 7.30am–5.30pm; ☏312/861-0473), which will only hold mail for thirty days before returning it to sender – so make sure the envelope has a return address. Alternatively, most hotels will accept and hold mail for guests.

Email

One of the best ways to keep in touch while traveling is to sign up for a free Internet email address that can be accessed from anywhere, for example YahooMail or Hotmail – accessible through ⊛www.yahoo.com and ⊛www.hotmail.com. Once you've set up an account, you can use these sites to pick up and send mail from any Internet café, or hotel with Internet access.

A useful website – ⊛www.kropla.com – has information on how to plug your laptop in when abroad, on phone country codes around the world and about electrical systems in different countries.

Finding an Internet outlet is fairly easy in Chicago – the city has numerous Internet cafés (see p.224) that charge, on average, $5 for half an hour's use. You're likely to spend twice as much ($5–10/hr) at the many business centers inside hotels. The hostels also have a few terminals (*Hostelling International – Chicago* has eight), though they charge the same as Internet cafés. Another option is to head to the Harold Washington Library in the Loop, where you can log on for free.

City transportation

For a city as spread out as Chicago, the public transportation system is extensive, and service is remarkably efficient. Most sights can be reached on the city's El train system, while buses, though slower, fill in the gaps. Other options include taking a taxi, or renting a car or bike.

CTA

The Chicago Transit Authority's **subway and elevated train system** – also known as the "El" – runs on seven lines that cover most downtown areas and neighborhoods, with the exception of parts of Lincoln Park toward Lake Michigan, the area east of Michigan Avenue toward Navy Pier, and Hyde Park. Each color-coded line (Blue, Brown, Green, Orange, Purple, Red and Yellow) radiates from the Loop. Trains are clean and run frequently during the day – roughly every fifteen minutes or so – though at night service on most lines is sporadic between 2am and 5am; the Red Line and Blue Line (between Forest Park and O'Hare), however, run 24 hours.

Fares are $1.50 a ride; you'll need to buy a **transit card** from a vending machine at El stations before you pass through the turnstiles. Cards will hold as little as $1.50 and as much as $100. Transfers deduct an additional 30¢, and are valid for two hours from the original fare.

Convenient **CTA Visitor Passes** allow unlimited travel for a set number of days; the one-day pass ($5) is good value, as are two-day ($9), three-day ($12) and five-day ($18) passes, which are valid for consecutive days of travel. You can buy passes at the airport on arrival, at any of the visitor information centers, as well as in Union Station and many of the currency exchange offices downtown.

The CTA also runs Chicago's **buses**, which accept Transit Cards, as well as coins and bills in exact change. Fares are the same as the El ($1.50), and for an extra 30¢ you can transfer between buses and trains within a two-hour window. Most bus lines operate daily; during rush hour and peak times, buses run every five minutes, every

Chicago Transit Authority

For route information and timetables, as well as disabled access, for CTA trains and buses call ☎312/836-7000 or log on to ⓦwww.transitchicago.com
For passes and other information call ☎1-888/968-7282 or visit the above website.

8–12 minutes during off-peak hours. Service is sporadic between midnight and 4am, but the major bus lines run all night.

Useful bus routes

#6 Jeffrey Express To get from downtown to Hyde Park.
#22 Clark Runs along Dearborn and Clark streets, and is one of the best buses for getting to Lincoln Park and the North Side.
#29 State Runs between the Loop and Navy Pier, on State St, Illinois St and Grand Ave.
#36 Broadway Similar to the #22, it runs along Clark between the Loop and Lakeview, then jumps to Broadway for its long slog north.
#72 North A good shuttle along North Ave, between the lake and Bucktown and Wicker Park.
#73 Armitage Runs parallel to the #72, but four blocks north on Armitage Ave.
#146 Marine-Michigan Runs between Museum Campus, the Loop (via State St) and to Andersonville (via Lake Shore Drive).
#151 Sheridan This Loop-Lincoln Park-Lakeview route runs along Michigan Ave, Stockton Ave (good for the Lincoln Park Zoo), and Sheridan Rd.

Metra

The commuter rail network run by **Metra** (information line: ☎312/836-7000, ⓦwww.metrarail.com) serves Chicago's suburbs, stopping at four main stations in the city:

Union Station, Ogilvie Transportation Center, LaSalle Street Station (LaSalle Street and Congress Parkway) and Randolph Street Station (where Randolph Street meets the northern tip of Grant Park). You're not likely to need Metra unless you want to visit Hyde Park (and the Museum of Science and Industry) or McCormick Place. (See individual chapters for details on getting to these locations.)

Fares start at $1.85 and go up to $6.95, depending on the distance traveled. Tickets can be bought from agents or vending machine at stations (or on the train if there's no ticket seller on duty at the station).

Taxis

Taxis are plentiful and are worth using if you're in a hurry or happen to be in areas that aren't well served by public transportation, especially late at night. If you know you'll be spending time in the more outlying areas like the South Side, it's a good idea to book a return cab in advance (see p.225 for a list of cab companies).

Fares are $1.90 to start the meter, $1.60 for each mile thereafter, or $2 for every six minutes in stopped or slow traffic. Most fares between the Loop and locations within a few miles of there (River North, N Michigan Avenue, the Gold Coast and Old Town, Museum Campus, Little Italy and Greektown) will run from $5 to $10. For points farther out (ie Andersonville and Hyde Park), expect to pay at least $12–15. Bear in mind that the tip should be 15 to 20 percent of the fare.

Taxis can be hailed on the streets or use the taxi stands outside train and bus stations, and hotels. Finally, when you arrive at your destination, ask the driver for a receipt – if ever you leave something in the taxi, you'll have a way to track it down.

Driving

There's not much reason to rent a **car** in Chicago, unless you want to explore outposts like Oak Park or admire the scenic route along Lake Shore Drive; public transportation will get you to most places fairly efficiently, while congestion and a dearth of

parking spaces, especially in the Loop and the surrounding areas, can make for a harrowing experience.

If you absolutely need a car (see p.15 for rental agencies), be prepared to pay hefty overnight parking charges ($20+) to park your car at a garage or lot, or else pay close attention to street parking signs to avoid being ticketed, which will cost you a minimum of $50 for even a minor parking offense.

During peak hours, **on-street parking** can be impossible, while streets in the residential areas either have two-hour ($2) parking meters or require resident permits. In most cases, you're better off putting your car in a parking lot or garage (from $9/hr to $20+/day). In the Loop, try the cheap underground garages on the north end of Grant Park (enter through Columbus or Michigan Avenue).

If your car is towed, expect to pay at least $150 to liberate it from the **City of Chicago Auto Pound Headquarters** (☎312/744-4444).

Bikes

Chicago is a bike-friendly city, with miles of bike lanes, plenty of bike racks, and some twenty El stations where riders can store their bikes indoors and hop on the train. Bikes are permitted on El trains, except during peak hours on weekdays (7–9am, and 4–6pm). The popular, lakefront path provides twenty-plus miles of uninterrupted cycling through well-tended parkland, with many sightseeing attractions, shopping districts and other diversions close by. For more information on biking in Chicago, visit **Chicagoland Bicycle Federation's** website at ⊛www.biketraffic.org

Of the main bike rental outfits, **Bike and Roll Chicago** has locations at 600 E Grand Ave, Navy Pier (☎312/595-9600) and North Avenue Beach (☎773/327-2706, ⊛www.bikerental.com), where you can rent bikes for $10 per hour or $40 per day. The Navy Pier store is open from April 1 to October 31; the North Avenue one from May 1 to September 30.

City tours

Most tours of Chicago deal with either architecture or the city's neighborhoods, though of course any number of smaller, specialized tours do exist, from ethnic food samplings and exploring financial exchanges to haunted house tours.

River tours and lakefront cruises are often the best way to get a feel for the city's size. There are a handful of companies that operate them, any of which will be sufficient, but the Architecture Foundation (see below) puts on the most detailed and comprehensive tours. For a more leisurely sightseeing at slightly more expense, you might try the cruise lines that offer lunch and dinner trips up and down the lake, the latter often around sunset.

Bicycle tours

Bike Chicago Rentals and Tours ☎ 1-800/915-2453. Free two-hour tours of the lakefront (June–Aug Mon–Fri).

Bike and Roll Tours ☎ 773/327-2706 (North Avenue Beach) or ☎ 312/595-9600 (Navy Pier), ⓦ www.bikeandroll.com. One- to three-hour guided tours covering the lakefront, Lincoln Park, Grant Park, Chinatown and Hyde Park's Osaka Garden. Free self-guided tour maps also available.

Bus and trolley tours

American Sightseeing Tours ☎ 312/251-3100, ⓦ www.americansightseeing.org/chicago.htm. Two- and four-hour bus tours ($15–30) of all the major neighborhoods; the Grand Tour takes in most of the city. Tours leave from the *Palmer House Hilton*, 17 E Monroe St. Courtesy pick-up service from all downtown and Near North hotels; reservations required.

Chicago Motor Coach Company ☎ 312/666-1000. Narrated double-decker bus tours (1hr+; $10) that cover the Historic Water Tower, Navy Pier and the Sears Tower, among other stops. Purchase tickets on the bus, or at the Sears Tower.

Chicago Trolley Company Tours ☎ 312/663-0260, ⓦ www.chicagotrolley.com. Hour-long tours (all-day pass $20, two-day pass $25) on motorized board-at-will trolleys (or double-decker buses), which make ten stops in the downtown area, including Sears Tower, Navy Pier, Museum Campus and the Historic Water Tower.

Gray Line Tours ☎ 312/251-3107, ⓦ www.grayline.com. One of the better bus-tour companies offering a good variety of tours, from the four-hour citywide "Inside Chicago" tour ($28) to the seven-hour ship and shore tour ($72) taking in the entire city by bus, plus lunch and a cruise on Lake Michigan. Tours leave from the *Palmer House Hilton*, 17 E Monroe St.

Cruises and river trips

Chicago Architecture Foundation ☎ 312/922-3432, ⓦ www.cruisechicago.com or ⓦ www.architecture.org. Intelligent, remarkably extensive list of tours, many with an architectural slant. Highly recommended. See box on p.41 for further details.

Chicago from the Lake ☎ 312/527-1977, ⓦ www.cfl81.com. Informative architectural river cruises and historical river/lake cruises operating from May through October. Tours leave from River East Plaza, 465 E Illinois St. Between May and November, tours leave almost every hour.

Metro Ducks ☎ 312/642-3825 or 1-800/298-1506, ⓦ www.metroducks.com/chicago.htm. Restored World War II amphibious landing vehicles first plunge into the Chicago River, then hit the city's roads for the usual sights. The ninety-minute tours leave from *Rock 'n' Roll McDonald's*, 600 N Clark St.

Odyssey Cruises ☎ 708/990-0800, ⓦ www.odysseycruises.com. Pricey brunch, lunch, dinner and romantic midnight cruises ($40–100 per person) on a huge, super-sleek yacht, departing from 600 E Grand Ave at Navy Pier. Reservations required.

Shoreline Sightseeing ☎ 312/222-9328, ⓦ www.shorelinesightseeing.com. Architecture cruises and thirty-minute sightseeing tours leaving from Shedd Aquarium, Buckingham Fountain and Navy Pier.

Spirit of Chicago ☎ 312/836-7888, ⓦ www.spiritofchicago.com. Swanky harbor cruises, with bar and live music. Lunch and dinner cruises from $37 and $73; sunset cruises $25. Boats depart from 600 E Grand Ave at Navy Pier. Year-round.

Wendella Boats ☏312/337-1446,
🖰www.wendellaboats.com. Well-run architecture
and sightseeing cruises ($17), leaving from the pier
near the Wrigley Building at 400 N Michigan Ave.
Summer only.

Specialist tours and activities

Chicago Blues Tour ☏773/772-5506,
🖰www.chicagobluestour.com. Twice-yearly tour
($25) of South Side blues clubs and the Blues
Heaven Foundation, formerly Chess Records.

Chicago Ethnic Grocery Store Tours
☏773/465-8064, 🖰ethnic-grocery-tours.com. Led
by a guide with an encyclopedic knowledge of the
city's ethnic food, these tours also offer the chance
to sample food along the way ($60).

Chicago Neighborhood Tours ☏312/742-1190,
🖰www.chgocitytours.com. Four- to five-hour
neighborhood ($25) and specialty tours ($45) given
year-round, though most are offered between May
and November. Themes include "The Chicago Fire,"
"Literary Chicago" and "Roots of Chicago Blues and
Gospel."

Loop Tour Train ☏ 1-877/244-2246. Free forty-
minute architecture and history tours co-sponsored
by the Chicago Architecture Foundation, Chicago
Office of Tourism, and the Chicago Transit Authority
(May 4 to Sept 28). Departs from the
Randolph/Wabash El station every Saturday at
11.35am, 12.15pm, 12.55pm, and 1.35pm. Pick up
tickets on the day of the tour at the Chicago Office of
Tourism Visitor Information Center (see p.20).

Not Your Mama's Bus Tour c/o StreetWise,
1331 S Michigan Ave (a block south of Roosevelt
Rd) ☏312/554-0060, 🖰www.streetwise.org.
Chicago as seen through the eyes of the
underprivileged. Tours led by formerly homeless
vendors of the *Streetwise* newspaper who give
personal reflections on life on the streets while you
ride a bus through Cabrini Green and the West Side,
covering roughly ten sights in over ninety minutes.
Tours offered on Fridays at 6pm, sometimes
Saturdays at 6pm (May–Nov, $20).

Untouchable Tours ☏773/881-1195,
🖰www.gangstertour.com. Guides dressed as
gangsters lead bus tours of Prohibition-era haunts
and hideouts of Chicago gangsters in Chinatown,
Pilsen, Little Italy, Greektown and Lincoln Park ($20,
children $15). Tours depart from the parking lot of
Rock 'n' Roll McDonald's, at 600 N Clark St.

Walking tours

Chicago Architecture Foundation (see under
"Cruises and river trips" above for contact details).
Offers by far the largest, most extensive list of
walking tours in Chicago, with well over fifty different
routes and themes.

Chicago Tour Guides Institute ☏773/276-
6683, 🖰www.chicagoguide.net. Three-hours
walking tours tailored for groups, offered in
numerous languages (starting from $40/hr). You'll
need to request transportation if you don't have your
own, and tours must be paid for at least seven days
in advance.

Opening hours and public holidays

We've noted specific opening and closing times for specific attractions throughout the guide, but given that opening hours can change, it's always a good idea to call ahead.

Opening hours

Office hours are generally 9am–5pm. Stores open as early as 8am and can close as late as 11pm on weeknights; on weekends, stores may open an hour later and close an hour earlier, especially on Sundays. Most **museums** follow roughly the same hours, though a few have extended hours (8–10pm) one day during the week and one on the weekend. Public spaces – plazas, monuments and such – are generally open 24 hours, but Chicago parks close around 11pm (or earlier, depending on the park) and reopen around 7am.

In the wake of the events of September 11, 2001, and subsequent security scares, some Chicago attractions – notably the Board of Trade and the Rookery – allow visitors only limited access. It's recommended that you call ahead before heading off for a tour of these destinations.

Public holidays

Chicago celebrates dozens of **national and local holidays**, but few – with the exception of New Year's Day, July 4, Thanksgiving, and Christmas – shut down the city completely. If you're in town on a holiday weekend other than the ones mentioned, it's safe to assume that stores, museums, and restaurants are operating as usual.

National holidays

January 1 New Year's Day; **3rd Monday** Dr Martin Luther King Jr's Birthday
February 3rd Monday President's Day
May Last Monday Memorial Day
July 4 Independence Day
September 1st Monday Labor Day
October 2nd Monday Columbus Day
November 11 Veterans' Day; **4th Thursday** Thanksgiving Day
December 25 Christmas Day

The media

By no means a news capital of the country, Chicago does have a nationally respected newspaper and television network, and is more or less the media center for most of the Midwest.

Newspapers and magazines

Chicago's **main newspaper**, the conservative *Chicago Tribune*, covers a mix of local, national and international news in a tone that's less staid and, at times, breezier than that of its East Coast counterparts, the influential *New York Times* and *Washington Post*. With the death of famed Chicago writer Mike Royko and the recent controversial ousting of columnist Bob Greene from his post at the *Trib* (as the paper is known), the paper lost its nationally known writers; the ageing Pulitzer-winner Studs Terkel has resumed the title of the town's best chronicler – any account from him is sure to be among the city's best writing.

The city's other major newspaper, *The Sun-Times*, tends to be more sensational in its coverage, focusing less on international news and more on local stories. The paper's lead film critic, Roger Ebert, is best known for his nationally aired TV show, *Siskel and Ebert*, on which he entertainingly sparred with *Tribune* film columnist Gene Siskel over the latest film releases for 23 years, until Siskel's death in 1999. Their signature thumbs up/thumbs down approach to movie viewing has survived relatively intact (though with a new co-host), as *Ebert and Roeper*, airing on WLS (Channel 7).

Besides the two major newspapers, there's the *Daily Herald*, Chicago's largest suburban daily paper – read mostly in the surrounding counties.

The **free weekly** *Chicago Reader* is indispensable for current arts and entertainment listings, and often has quirky editorials on a variety of topics. Other free papers have joined the scene but none comes close to cracking the *Reader*'s hold on the city. Chicago also has a few glossy monthlies, including the well-written and picture-heavy *Chicago* magazine. You can find these in most downtown bookstores, as well as in cafés and bars.

Most downtown **newsstands and bookstores** sell a huge variety of national and international newspapers, the best of which is probably Borders, 830 N Michigan Ave, at N Pearson Street (☎312/573-0564).

Newspaper and magazine websites

Chicago magazine ⊛ www.chicagomag.com
Chicago Reader ⊛ www.chireader.com
Chicago Sun-Times ⊛ www.suntimes.com
Chicago Tribune ⊛ www.chicagotribune.com
Daily Herald ⊛ www.dailyherald.com
New City ⊛ www.newcitychicago.com

TV and radio

Chicago seems to be in the middle of a television transformation: for a city that has been a fan of sports and local news, September 11, 2001, brought more sustained viewing interest in round-the-clock cable news than ever before, pushing local news stations behind worldwide cable TV in popularity. You can still catch offerings from the three major networks (NBC, ABC and CBS), as well as a respectable line-up of shows and news on the city's own two national channels – WGN

(Ch 9) and WTTW (Ch 11) – plus the low-budget Cable CLTV (Chicagoland TV). (Channel 11's homespun *Wild Chicago* show, airing every Sunday and Monday night, shouldn't be missed for its irreverent interviews and tours of Chicago's lesser-known areas.)

Admittedly, local news programming is almost completely US-centric, and Michael Jordan's scoring 50pts (despite his Chicago absence) will air over, say, any major happenings in Parliament. For international news, you'd be better off sticking with the national cable channels (Fox News Channel, CNN, MSNBC).

Radio is a significant part of most Chicagoans' daily routines, given the amount of time they wind up spending in traffic. There are plenty of radio options up and down the dial for news and entertainment; see below for a list of stations.

Broadcast TV stations

Channel 2 (WBBM/CBS)
Channel 5 (WMAQ/NBC)
Channel 7 (WLS/ABC)
Channel 9 (WGN)
Channel 11 (WTTW/Network Chicago)
Channel 32 (WFLD/FOX)
Cable CLTV/Chicagoland

Radio stations

Local AM stations

WMAQ (670) Sports
WGN (720) Talk
WBBM (780) News
WLS (890) Talk and news
WMVP (1000) Sports (including Notre Dame games)

Local FM stations

WBEZ (91.5) Talk, music and new (including National Public Radio programming)
WXRT (93.1) Adult album alternative
WNUA (95.5) Jazz
WBBM (96.3) R&B
WLUP (97.9) Rock
WFMT (98.7) Classical
WUSN (99.5) Country
WKQX (101.1) Contemporary pop and rock
WKSC (103.5) Mainstream top 40
WJMK (104.3) Oldies

Live talk shows

Chicago, unlike New York, is not somewhere you'd choose to seek out live talk shows, but a few such options do exist, if you want to be part of the studio audience. Oprah Winfrey, veritable queen of Chicago and national media personality, hosts **The Oprah Winfrey Show** from her West Side Harpo Studios, 1058 W Washington Ave. For more details, see p.106.

Known for his show's trashy brand of entertainment, **Jerry Springer** tapes his eponymous show here in Chicago at the NBC Tower, 454 N Columbus Drive, on the second floor (℡312/321-5365). Go if you must – it's sensational American TV at its worst.

In the same lurid vein, there's **The Jenny Jones Show**, also taped at the NBC Tower (℡312/836-9485). Shows tape twice a day on Tuesday, Thursday and Friday (9.30am–1pm, 1.30–4pm).

Crime, security and personal safety

For the most part, violent crime in Chicago is concentrated in a few areas, notably pockets of the South Side and West Side that see more homicides in a year than some US states. Tourists, however, have no real business venturing into these areas, and therefore shouldn't expect to encounter problems beyond what they would expect in any major city.

Overall, common sense should keep you out of trouble: stick to well-lit streets at night, and avoid parks, parking lots and alleys. Always lock your car, keep an eye on the kids at all times, and know where you're going or at least give the impression that you do. Don't have expensive jewelry on view and don't carry nice cameras, bags or any other items that might draw attention to you. Men should keep wallets in the front pocket, women should wear purses across the shoulder. When riding the subway at night (not advisable after midnight), have your wits about you and do not fall asleep – you'll be easy prey for any thief, or worse. Should you run into trouble and need emergency police assistance, find a phone and call ℡911 or hail a cab and ask the driver to take you to the nearest police station. (For non-emergencies, call ℡312/744-4000.)

If you're planning to explore Hyde Park, or others areas of the **South Side**, take special care: there are a few extremely dangerous sections sprinkled throughout – downtrodden communities where high-rise housing projects have become home base for gangs and drug trafficking. The same can be said of **Cabrini Green** just west of the Gold Coast, and larger stretches of the West Side, especially around the **United Center**. Never walk in these areas or drive through here at night.

Emergency numbers for lost cards and checks

American Express cards ℡1-800/528-4800
American Express checks ℡1-800/221-7282
Citicorp ℡1-800/645-6556
Diners Club ℡1-800/234-6377
MasterCard ℡1-800/826-2181
Thomas Cook/MasterCard ℡1-800/223-9920
Visa cards ℡1-800/847-2911
Visa checks ℡1-800/227-6811

Travelers with disabilities

Chicago is trying to be one of the better disabled-friendly cities in the US, but it still has a long way to go. Modernization issues plague many of Chicago's older buildings; however, ramps and other forms of access are being added to museums, sites and sports facilities, and the city's public transportation system has facilities such as station elevators and buses equipped with lifts and ramps.

Inquire with the CTA (☎312/836-7000) to find out which stops are wheelchair accessible; maps showing these stations are online at ⓦwww.transitchicago.com. For wheelchair accessible taxis, call ☎1-800/281-4466.

For general information on accessibility, contact the Mayor's Office for People with Disabilities, which has a hotline for travelers with disabilities (☎312/744-6673), the Department of Disabilities (☎312/744-2400) or the Department of Tourism (☎1-877/244-2246 or ☎312/201-8847, TTY number for the hearing impaired is ☎1-866/710-0294).

US and Canada

Access-Able ⓦwww.access-able.com. A one-stop shop for travelers with disabilities.
The Boulevard ⓦwww.blvd.com. Adaptive products, van rentals, accessible hotels worldwide, and many links.
Mobility International USA voice and TDD ☎541/343-1284, ⓦwww.miusa.org. Information and referral services, access guides, tours and exchange programs. Annual membership ($35) includes quarterly newsletter.
Society for the Advancement of Travelers with Handicaps (SATH) ☎212/447-7284, ⓦwww.sath.org. Travel-disabled information available to members ($45, students $30).

Wheels Up! ☎1-888/389-4335, ⓦwww.wheelsup.com. Provides discounted airfare, tour and cruise prices for disabled travelers; also publishes a free monthly newsletter.

UK and Ireland

Holiday Care UK ☎01293/773 535, Minicom ☎01293/776 943, ⓦwww.holidaycare.org.uk. Resource for travel and holiday information for people with disabilities, focusing on accessible hotels and attractions.
Irish Wheelchair Association Republic of Ireland ☎ 01/833 8241. Information about traveling abroad with a wheelchair.
Tripscope UK The Courtyard, Evelyn Rd, London W4 5JL ☎020/8994 9294, ☎8994 3618. National telephone information service offering free travel advice.

Australia and New Zealand

ACROD (Australian Council for Rehabilitation of the Disabled) ☎02/6282 4333. Provides lists of travel agencies and tour operators for people with disabilities.
Disabled Persons Assembly New Zealand ☎04/801 910. Provides lists of travel agencies and tour operators for people with disabilities.

The city

The City

The Loop

Roughly encompassing the tongue of land south and east of the Chicago River, **THE LOOP**'s pre-eminence in commerce, culture and city transport make it unmissable for all visitors and unassailable to most locals. The oldest official settlement, Fort Dearborn, once stood here – by the 1850s, the heart of Chicago's already thriving business district. Yet today, the city owes its spectacular downtown to a mix of luck, both bad (the disastrous great fire of 1871) and good (the arrival of rule-breaking, visionary architects in its wake). With the rabble of wooden buildings wiped away by the blaze, men like Louis Sullivan were able to stretch their considerable design skills and, in the process, usher in the modern architectural age. Chicago was the cradle of the skyscraper – the first was built here in 1885 – and the city's enthusiastic welcome of new and often unusual buildings has helped it amass one of the world's best collections of modern architecture, from the prototype skyscrapers of the 1880s to more recent, jaw-dropping achievements like the **Sears Tower**, for many years the tallest building in the world. (For more on architecture, see Contexts p.241.)

The north–south arteries of **State**, **LaSalle** and **Dearborn streets** more or less define the Loop. State Street is the commercial hub, filled with stores and thriving again after the city pumped substantial sums into a beautification project during the late 1990s: this is where you'll find the department store goliaths of Marshall Field's, Carson Pirie Scott and Sears. Dotted along Dearborn Street are impressive governmental offices, like the Federal Center Complex, alongside dramatic skyscrapers. LaSalle Street, meanwhile, is where the money's made – literally: the financial hub of the Midwest and home to the Board of Trade since Chicago's early days, it's here where you can really make, or lose, big money.

The Loop is also divided in another way: between ground-dwellers and office workers. At street level, standing under the rattling train tracks or zig-zagging through the hordes of people, it's easy to imagine Chicago in the nineteenth century, a bustling, no-nonsense place of factory hands and railroad workers. But looking out from the observatory deck of the Sears Tower, there's a sleek, silent grandeur to the city's skyscraper-packed skyline. The honking cars and rushing people are far away, and you'll be hurled ahead a hundred years into Chicago's future.

Though it's widely held that the Loop was named after the **elevated train lines** encircling the district, the nickname preceded the arrival of elevated cars by fifteen years. In the 1860s, a cable car line was set up to shuttle residents of the newly created suburbs on Chicago's South Side to and from downtown stores like Field, Palmer & Leiter (later Marshall Field's). The Loop name came from the circular turnaround where the cable car would reverse direction for the return journey.

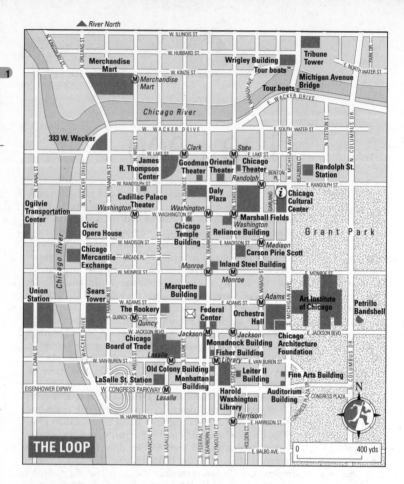

It should go without saying that the Loop is at its busiest and best during the working week (Mon–Fri, roughly 7am–6pm), when restaurants and attractions are open, and when it's easiest to peek inside the many architecturally impressive buildings. The one strip that still buzzes in the evening is **Randolph Street**, the hub of Chicago's theater district and a good place to grab a coffee or snack outside office hours; while on weekends, if you wander away from the revitalized State Street strip, the Loop can be majestically deserted.

In this chapter, we've highlighted many of downtown's most impressive buildings, and provided a rough walking tour to help guide you through them. Distances in the Loop are surprisingly modest, so even the laziest traveler can enjoy ambling in the area for an afternoon. The accounts that follow are by no means exhaustive, as almost every building downtown has some point of interest: whatever you do, be sure to look up at any building that catches your eye. It's often on the higher floors, or even the roof, that you'll find the most appealing architectural flourishes.

A good complement to any visit to the Loop (or a quick way to see it if you're short on time) is the exceptional ninety-minute **architectural river cruise** run by the Chicago Architecture Foundation (CAF), leaving several times daily from the *Chicago's First Lady* dock located at Michigan Avenue and Lower Wacker Drive (May–Oct Mon–Sat 3 trips, Sun 2 trips; $21; ☎312/922-3432, ⓦwww. architecture.org or www.cruisechicago.com). The knowledgeable docents explain the history, significance and architecture of all the riverfront buildings, the Sears Tower, 333 W Wacker, Merchandise Mart and the Wrigley Building among them.

The CAF also runs to intensive **walking tours** of the Loop: the "Historic Skyscrapers Tour" and the "Modern Skyscrapers Tour" ($10 each tour, $15 for both; 2hr). Although CAF has timed the tours so that you can do both in a single day, with the amount of walking you'll have to do, you're better off taking them over two days. Some docents also stray from the published routes to speak about buildings covered by the other tour, so you may luck out.

For more on tours of the Loop and the city beyond, see p.30.

Chicago Cultural Center

The area along Michigan Avenue immediately south of the river was, around a century ago, known as the city's prime entertainment district, and many of that era's grand structures preserve a sense of its unabashed artistic aspirations. Among the finest is the **Chicago Cultural Center**, 78 E Washington Blvd, at Michigan Avenue. An 1897 renaissance palace intended as the city's first permanent main library, the building now houses the **Chicago Office of Tourism** (details of which can be found on p.20), the **Museum of Broadcast Communications**, various galleries, touring exhibits, free lunchtime concerts and a café.

To explore the Cultural Center, either walk around yourself or take one of the **tours**, which meet in the Randolph Street lobby and last an hour (Wed, Fri & Sat, 1.15pm). Pick up a self-guided tour brochure at any of the first-floor welcome desks.

Museum of Broadcast Communications

The highlight of the Cultural Center is the fascinating **Museum of Broadcast Communications** (Mon–Sat 10am–4.30pm, Sun noon–5pm; free; ☎312/629-6000, ⓦwww.mbcnet.org), which holds more than 70,000 radio and television programs and commercials in its archives; you could easily while away a few hours (or much more) viewing old adverts, newsreels and sporting moments, in any number of screening rooms or special galleries.

The best of these is the MBC Television Center, which allows a peek at the on-air process – with you doing a star turn at the center. Next door, the AC Nielsen Research Center holds the lone camera used in the first televised presidential debate, between JFK and Richard Nixon. You need only to compare tapes here between that debate and more recent encounters to see how far production values have come, not to mention how much softer the camera treats its subjects. Also of interest is the Radio Hall of Fame, best for its displays on the early days of radio, when it was *the* broadcasting medium; sit down to listen to an installment of *War of the Worlds*, or an episode of *The Phantom*, to get a sense of its power. Temporary exhibits and a decent gift shop, with everything from Orphan Annie mugs to Seinfeld T-shirts, take up the rest of the space. The museum is scheduled to relocate to the corner of W Kinzie and N State streets in May 2004.

The rest of the Cultural Center has a few minor points of interest, including the **Landmark Chicago Gallery** along the center's western corridor, on the way to the Museum of Broadcast Communications, where black and white photographs of the city's landmarks evocatively trace the development of Chicago's architectural persona, from the Carson Pirie Scott building (the first steel-framed department store; see below) to the Union Stockyard Gate and beyond. You might also peek in the center's eastern corridor, which often showcases the work of local artists; like the Broadcast Museum it's free, and worth a quick poke around as long as you're here.

The upper floors of the center frequently host exhibits, screenings, lectures and concerts, but even if there's nothing going on it's worth a trip upstairs just for a look at the opulence of the spaces, notably Preston Bradley Hall, where you'll see intricate mosaic scrolls and rosettes spanning the arches under a stunning, 38-foot **Tiffany dome** – thought to be the world's largest.

Along State Street

Two blocks west you'll come upon the commercial corridor of **State Street**, coined "That Great Street" by Frank Sinatra, where the flagship location of **Marshall Field's and Co** can be found at no. 111 (Mon & Thurs 9.45am–7pm, Tues, Wed, Fri & Sat 9.45am–5.45pm; ☎312/781-1000, ⓦwww.marshallfields.com). This enormous department store, known for its lavish window dressings around the winter holidays, is housed in a nine-story Neoclassical building that was built in stages between 1892 and 1914 by Daniel Burnham (see boxes, pp.234 & 242). While the building itself isn't much to look at compared to other Loop architectural highlights, it is hard to miss; taking up an entire city block, it's flanked by two huge, bronze (now green) clocks, one of which has been keeping time for over a century. The clock at the corner of State and Washington streets cemented its status as a Chicago symbol when a painting of it by Norman Rockwell landed on the cover of the *Saturday Evening Post* in 1945 (in which a repairman sets the time on the big clock using his pocket watch). Even if you're not planning to shop, be sure to check out the glistening **Tiffany dome** inside the store – it's the first ever built of iridescent glass, and a nice complement to the one in the Cultural Center (see above).

Across the street from Marshall Field's, the thin, cream-colored **Reliance Building**, 32 N State St, is older and more architecturally important than it first appears. Often cited as the forerunner of the glass-and-steel skyscrapers that sprung up everywhere in the middle of the twentieth century, the building, which was begun in 1891 and completed in 1895 by Burnham, was the first entirely steel-framed building (which allowed the glass-heavy facade), preceding modern glass-and-steel towers by some sixty years. Today, it's the home of the chic *Hotel Burnham*; step inside for a look at the old-style lobby and decorative trimmings, even if you're not planning to stay. For a review of the rooms, see p.131.

Carson Pirie Scott, at 1 S State St, is a somewhat less glamorous sibling to Marshall Field's – your average department store, huge and soulless by today's-standards. Historically speaking, it is considered somewhat of a landmark, however, as a revolutionary melding of function and form, courtesy of Louis Sullivan – note the decorative cast-iron grill across the first two stories and the building's modular design and symmetrical facade. The entrance at the corner of Madison and State streets is the best vantage point for admiring the ironwork.

The Art Institute of Chicago

Back on Michigan Avenue, you'll come to the **Art Institute of Chicago**, 111 S Michigan Ave (Mon & Wed–Fri 10.30am–4.30pm; Tues 10.30am–8pm, Sat & Sun 10am–5pm; suggested donation $10, Tues free; ☎312/443-3600, ⓦ www.artic.edu), arguably one of the top museums in the country. Most famous for its collection of Impressionist and Post-Impressionist paintings, the museum can easily soak up an entire day.

Constructed for the World's Columbian Exposition between 1893 and 1916, the building oozes turn-of-the-century opulence, noticeable in its Corinthian columns, soaring archways and Neoclassical limestone facade. Guarding the grand entrance are two bronze lions, Chicago's mascots, which have been known to wear Bulls' jerseys and festive decorations to commemorate special events.

While most visitors, once inside, do head straight upstairs for the big money Impressionist works, there are rich works to be found nearly everywhere, and the museum has collections spanning a vast number of eras and artists. We've provided a room by room overview below. Be aware that the numerous wings (and the fact that the museum's bisected by the railway tracks) can make it tricky to find your way around, so do pick up a free map at the information desk in the main hall. There are unfortunately no audio tours, though a pocket guide to the museum is available for $3.95 in the bookstore: it's chatty and knowledgeable, but not laid out logically to follow the museum's displays so is of little help in actually navigating the collection.

School of the Art Institute of Chicago (SAIC)

The Art Institute of Chicago started life as the **Chicago Academy of Design**, a small art school founded in 1866 by a group of artists who wanted to provide top-notch education in studio arts and showcase student works. After outgrowing several rented facilities and losing its first permanent home to the Chicago Fire, the school changed its name to The Art Institute and eventually settled into its current location at 37 S Wabash Ave, in a modern building adjacent to the magnificent Beaux Arts pile that houses the school's now formidable art holdings.

Today, the SAIC is one of the largest independent accredited schools of art and design in the US, and its degree programs extend to creative writing, art education and arts administration; courses open to the public are offered through its Continuing Education and Special Courses Department (☎312/899-5130, 🖷899-1453, ⓦ www.artic.edu). Student works are also frequently on display in the school's galleries.

Second level: European and American Paintings, 1300–present day

Paintings are arranged in rough chronology, although confusingly this chronology starts at rooms 207–225 and then goes back through rooms 201–206 and 226. Twentieth-century pictures are split between the two wings, in two sequential arrangements, before continuing on to the first floor in rooms 134–139.

Main Hall (200)

Before diving into the galleries, pause in the stairwell as you enter: here there's a fine collection of architectural fragments, most of them salvaged from demolished buildings. There are chunks of cornices, and windows in frames: one of the most notable is Frank Lloyd Wright's **Avery Coonley Playhouse Window**, from the home he considered his masterpiece. Also stop by the ornately scrolled **Stock Exchange Elevator Grilles** by Adler & Sullivan – there's a full reconstruction in room 153 (see under "First level", below).

Renaissance (207–209)

There's a slew of early **Italian and Flemish paintings** here, though many are thoroughly missable: Rogier van der Weyden's spiritual, ethereal *Jean Gros* panel is worth checking out (207) as is Sandro Botticelli's predictably dreamy *Madonna and Child* in the same room. In room 209, have a look at Lucas Cranach the Elder's slender, tender *Adam and Eve*, as well as the creepy kissing babies by Joss van Cleve.

Mannerism and Baroque (211–215)

In room 211, Tintoretto's sensual *Tarquin and Lucretia* is a terrific example of Mannerism's obsession with distortion and contrapposto, although it's a pity that Jacopo Pontormo, one of the true masters of freaky, Mannerist exaggeration, is only represented by a pedestrian *Virgin and Child with Young St John the Baptist*. Guido Reni's Baroque *Salomé and John the Baptist* features a haughty, gorgeous and cruel Salome, and underscores the drama for which pictures of this period are most famous. Don't miss El Greco's *Assumption of the Virgin*: painted in 1577, it exemplifies El Greco's religious obsessions while also showcasing his unique, distended style.

Dutch paintings and Rococo (216–219)

The Golden Age of Dutch painting is the focus of room 216: it's rare to come across pictures by Rembrandt's talented pupil, Aert de Gelder, but the puffy, psychologically piercing painting here, *Portrait of a Young Woman*, is eye-catching. Rembrandt's own *Old Man with Gold Chain* contrasts the craggy sitter's furrowed face with his gleaming jewels: even so, the viewer's drawn first to the wrinkles around his eyes. El Greco has several canvases in room 217: his attenuated figures seem frighteningly modern. The four paintings in Giambatistta Tiepolo's sensual Torquato Tasso series exemplify his technique, where it often seems like he's painting with pastel-colored ice cream (218).

In the same room are several examples by Francesco Guardi of the veduta (meaning "view") style that was also popular at this time, showcasing detailed city scenes – there's even a small, albeit unremarkable Canaletto, the master of this genre. Fragonard's sketchlike *Portrait of a Man* (219) is arresting, as, with its reddish colors, the sitter's face looks almost like rotting meat.

Neo-Classicism, Romanticism and beyond (220–225)

Gainsborough's portrait of his elder sister, Mrs Philip Dupont, cleverly but kindly conveys her overwhelming properness (221A); there are also plenty of canvases by Delacroix, although little that's remarkable. Better is the curiously hard-staring, Neoclassical portrait of *Amédée-David, the Marquis de Pastoret* by Ingres (222). An exception to much of the unexciting mid-nineteenth-century work is Corot's *Interrupted Reading*, a melancholy study of a young girl reading, painted four years before the first Impressionist exhibition in 1874 (223).

Impressionism and Post-Impressionism (201–206; 226)

This collection, mostly purchased (then donated) by Bertha Honoré Palmer, is one of the finest Impressionist selections in the world, and undoubtedly the museum's best-known feature. In room 201, look for Gustave Caillebotte's masterpiece, *Paris Street, Rainy Day*, which plays with focus and perspective using his careful mathematical techniques; the shimmering cobblestones almost glisten with wetness. In the same room is Renoir's *Acrobats at Circus Fernando*, collector Bertha Palmer's favorite painting, and one she carried with her everywhere, even on trips abroad. You'll also see Rodin's pot-bellied, petulant nude study for his famed statue of Balzac, plus an early Monet from 1868, *On the Bank of the Seine, Bennecourt*, which has a free energy that his calculated later pictures can lack. Close by, Edgar Degas' *Millinery Shop* (202) looks oddly cropped, implying that the viewer is just a passer-by in front of the store window.

Room 203 is filled with Monet canvases, but the showstopper in this section is Georges Seurat's *La Grande Jatte* (205). It took Seurat two years to paint this pointilliste masterpiece, and that perfectionist instinct is evident even in the white frame, which he specially designed. Seurat's girlfriend was the model for many of the women depicted, including the bustle-sporting, immobile statue in the immediate foreground. In the same room, look for Henri de Toulouse-Lautrec's famed *At the Moulin Rouge* and its lurid greenish-yellow face of May Milton. Monet resurfaces with two sequences in room 206: his seemingly psychedelic London paintings of Waterloo Bridge, and a calmer Stack of Wheat series. Gustave Moreau's creepy, enigmatic picture *Hercules and the Lernaean Hydra* – a masterpiece of the aesthetic school of art for art's sake – dominates room 226, along with Dante Gabriel Rossetti's soft-focus *Beata Beatrix*.

Early twentieth century (230–235)

Amedeo Modigliani's sculptural, almond-shaped *Woman with Necklace* is in room 231; nearby are a few notables from a strong set of Brancusi sculptures: *2 Penguins* (232) resembles a crossed thumb and forefinger, while the serene, beheaded *Sleeping Muse* (233) is sleekly robotic like a figure from Fritz Lang's *Metropolis*. Note Georges Braque's brightly colored, convention-challenging canvas *Antwerp* (234A) as well as Picasso's famous *The Old Guitarist*, one of the best-known pictures from his Blue Period (234B). There are plenty of Gauguins from his time in Tahiti as well as Henri Matisse's first original sculpture, *The Serf* – if the paunchy, nude figure looks familiar, that's because Rodin used the same model for his Balzac study in room 201.

Surrealism and beyond (236–239)

The pranky pictures of Magritte are well represented, from the massive *On the Threshold of Liberty*, which features his signature ample nude (236) to a dusk

△ Spiral staircase, the Rookery

landscape that seems inspired by the scarlet sun of the Japanese flag, in *The Banquet* (237F). There are also a few canvases by Dali, plus some of the disturbingly erotic pictures of children for which Balthus was renowned, like *Solitaire* (236). Look also for works by Willem de Kooning, Robert Motherwell and Jackson Pollock (238–239), as well as three Mark Rothko colour fields.

Surrealism and beyond II (240–249)

Here you'll find yet more Brancusi, starting with his gleaming, ergonomic *Golden Bird* (240), plus Oskar Kokoschka's craggy *Commerce Counselor Ebenstein*: see how the painter emphasizes the hands of the Austro-Hungarian court tailor in this picture. There are several Mondrian paintings in room 241; alongside his better-known grid pictures is a mid-career landscape, *Farm Near Duivendrecht*, which makes clearer the evolution of those grids from his obsession with criss-crossing tree branches. Don't miss Man Ray's cute but unnerving *Puériculture* sculpture, in which a chubby, perfectly formed child's hand emerges from a tin can (242). Edward Hopper's lonely *Nighthawks*, depicting a low-rent diner and its patrons, is in room 244. Room 246 holds several of Giacometti's artistically anorexic sculptures, as well as his delightfully sketchy painting, *Caroline*; there's even a dark, brooding Francis Bacon picture, *Figure with Meat*, where a figure sits with a split carcass dangling either side of his head, echoing his most famous work. The wing's best-known image by far, though, is Grant Wood's *American Gothic*, where his sister and doctor posed with a pitchfork to create one of the most reproduced (and parodied) images in American art (247). Room 248 is dedicated to Georgia O'Keeffe; seek out her ominous *Black Cross, New Mexico*.

First level: Contemporary art, American decorative arts, arms and armor

The **Contemporary Art** collection (136–139) is stunning, from its massive David Hockney canvas *American Collectors*, all pinched profiles and pink kaftans (136) to the works of Cuban American conceptual artist Felix Gonzales-Torres: *Untitled (Last Light)* (138) and *Untitled (Portrait of Ross in LA)* (139) – help yourself to a candy from the latter as it's one of the artist's signature, self-renewing installations. The massive *Mao* by Andy Warhol (136) overlooks the collection of **Korean, Chinese and Japanese art** (102–109 and 131A–134), showcasing plenty of highly colored earthenware statuary and ornamental dishes, but little to hold your attention for long. War historians and enthusiasts might want to linger over the **arms and armor** displayed in massive room 140, but others should persevere on to the Rubloff building at the back. Here, in room 150, you'll find the site-specific **American Windows** by Marc Chagall: these six brightly colored stained-glass panels were produced by the artist in honor of America's bicentennial. On the other side of the courtyard, don't miss the painstaking reconstruction of a trading room from Adler & Sullivan's old **Chicago Stock Exchange**.

Elsewhere on this floor, you'll find a dull, chronological collection of American furniture (163–179), leavened with the occasional interesting painting – look for John Singer Sargent's sprightly *Mrs George Swinton* (175) and the five small but exquisite paintings by James McNeill Whistler (176). The other acknowledged oddity here is the creepy collection of ship figureheads in room 178, dating back more than three hundred years.

Lower level: European Decorative Arts

The bargain basement of the museum feels a bit like its forgotten attic, crammed with an unremarkable collection of European bric-a-brac, though it's worth seeking out real estate developer Arthur Rubloff's gaudy **paperweight collection**, that runs the gamut, from old doorknobs to the watermelon-sized Super Magnum paperweight. There's also an assortment of **twentieth-century furniture** – look for Mies van der Rohe's elegant *Barcelona* chair as well as poppy plastic designs from Italian firm Kartell.

Along Michigan Avenue

Immediately across the street from the Art Institute, two more culturally oriented buildings are worth closer inspection; as you make your way down **South Michigan Avenue** from there, you'll find numerous other examples of fine Chicago School buildings, many of them adding to the theme around the Institute and forming something of a cultural corridor in the lower Loop.

Orchestra Hall and Santa Fe Center

The 2600-seat **Orchestra Hall**, also known as Symphony Center, 220 S Michigan Ave, is a magnificent space that you can tour for free (for details call ☎312/294-3265) – or of course by purchasing a ticket to see the Chicago Symphony Orchestra (for details on that see p.189). Admire yet another early twentieth-century Burnham design, this one quite classical in nature, with a symmetrical brick-and-stone facade bearing the great composers' names – Beethoven, Bach, Mozart, Schubert and Wagner – and inside a soaring auditorium space recently spruced up by a multimillion-dollar renovation.

Right nearby, and easily recognized by its huge rooftop sign, the **Sante Fe Center**, 224 S Michigan Ave, houses the excellent **Chicago Architecture Foundation**, or CAF (Mon–Fri 9am–6pm, Sat 10am–6pm, Sun 10am–5pm; ☎312/922-3432, ⓦwww.architecture.org), which is also the site where Burnham hatched his groundbreaking plan for the city in 1909. Inside, a grand white-marble staircase descends into the elegant, skylit atrium where CAF has its office and tour center. The knowledgeable and enthusiastic staff can help you pick the right tour and direct you to the center's architecture exhibits; be sure to check out the impressive scale model of downtown Chicago.

Another historical building nearby, at 17 W Adams St, holds the storied **Berghoff Restaurant**, a Chicago favorite for its Old World atmosphere and hearty German American food (see p.143 for review).

Fine Arts Building

Heading south on Michigan Avenue, you'll come across the brownish-gray **Fine Arts Building**, at no. 410, a Neo-Romanesque structure built in 1885 by Solon S. Beman as a showroom for the Studebaker Company's carriages and wagons. A renovation in 1898 added several floors to the building and converted it into studio space, which fostered an artist's colony of sorts that included the likes of Frank Lloyd Wright (who had a drafting studio here) and Frank L. Baum (author of *The Wizard of Oz*). Little of the interior has changed since then – the spacious halls and open stairwells are still there, as are the original murals that grace the walls on the tenth floor. There's also a wonderful little gallery on the fourth floor showcasing mainly contemporary local artists (Wed–Sat noon–6pm; ☎312/913-0537, ⓦwww.fabgallery.com). Take a ride up in the hand-operated elevator for a whiff of the old Chicago.

Auditorium Building and Leiter Building II

The stately Chicago School **Auditorium Building**, 430 S Michigan Ave, now home to Roosevelt University, is best known for its 4000-seat **Auditorium Theatre**, whose entrance is at 50 E Congress Parkway (☎312/922-2110, ⓦwww.auditoriumtheater.org). The near-perfect acoustics and four massive, flamboyantly trimmed arches moved the modernist Frank Lloyd Wright to call it the "greatest room for music and opera in the world." The Auditorium Building itself was built by Sullivan and Adler in 1889 and included a hotel and office, but after less than a decade, the building had fallen into disrepair; at its low point it served as a recreation center for soldiers, who turned the stage into a makeshift bowling alley. Roosevelt University eventually bought the building in 1946, but it wasn't until the 1960s that the structure was fully restored and reopened. The Auditorium Building recently celebrated its 100th birthday with the opening of *Les Misérables* and has been undergoing an extensive cleanup to bring back the original color patterns, and uncover stenciling detail and a lovely mural that once graced the interior. Sullivan fans note: if you can't make a concert, then come for a tour (Mon–Fri, call for times; $5; ☎312/431-2354).

Heading two blocks west on Congress and turning right on S State Street, you'll come upon the blocky-looking **Leiter Building II** at no. 401, which was built in 1891 by William Le Baron Jenney (see box, p.243). The structure's skeletal exterior frame and spacious interior stories – with sixteen-foot ceilings and uncluttered by beams or fixed walls – were designed to maximize retail space, and this seemingly small advancement was ideal for the Chicago department store Sears, Roebuck and Co, which occupied the building for many decades. Incidentally, the more primitive Leiter Building I was at the corner of Monroe and Wells, and was demolished around thirty years ago.

Howard Washington Library

The nine-story, rust-colored building anchoring the lower Loop, at 400 S State St, is the **Harold Washington Library**, the city's main branch (Mon–Thurs 9am–7pm, Fri & Sat 9am–5pm, Sun 1–5pm; ☎773/542-7279, ⓦwww.chi publib.org). Its enormous granite slabs, five-story arched windows and brilliant green hat of iron helped put it in *The Guinness Book of World Records* as the largest public library building in the world. Indeed, all sorts of numbers could be tossed out to impress: over two million volumes, 71 miles of books and the largest **blues archive** in the country. Casual visitors, however, will be more drawn to the hundreds of paintings on display throughout as well as readings, book-signings and educational events.

Although it's designed in the Chicago School style of the late 1800s, the library was actually built in 1991 in honor of the city's first African American mayor, Harold Washington, who died while in office. In the lobby, look for the blue Jacob Lawrence mosaic mural depicting key moments from Washington's life. If you look down through the circular opening into the lower lobby, you'll see *DuSable's Journey*, a map that traces the routes of Jean-Baptiste Point du

Sable – Chicago's first settler – through the waters he navigated between his homeland of Haiti and Chicago; the quotations around the map's edges are taken from Harold Washington's inaugural speeches.

Along Dearborn Street

A block west of the library at **Dearborn Street** you'll find four more Chicago School buildings, each unassuming, but historic skyscrapers in Chicago's architectural development nonetheless. The bay-windowed **Manhattan Building** at 431 S Dearborn St, erected in 1891, is the world's first entirely iron-frame building and was briefly – at sixteen stories – its tallest. It's also the oldest surviving building by William Le Baron Jenney, the man responsible for the Leiter Building II and whose revolutionary designs paved the way for the dozens of skyscrapers that came thereafter.

Just to the north, the seventeen-story **Old Colony Building**, 407 S Dearborn St, was the first structure to use portal arches at its corners to combat the wind, which became increasingly problematic as buildings grew skyward. It's a narrow steel and glass frame, most eye-catching at those corners, where rounded bay windows preside rather than ninety-degree angles.

Across W Van Buren Street, the 1896 **Fisher Building**, at 343 S Dearborn St, isn't as monumental or groundbreaking as some of the other buildings in the Loop, but it does represent an aesthetic change – note the playful terracotta eagles, cupids, snakes and sea creatures that decorate the caramel-colored facade, not to mention the elaborate mosaic floors and rich mahogany woodwork inside. Originally designed as offices, it was recently converted for residential use.

Directly across the street, the hulking **Monadnock Building**, at 53 W Jackson St, embodies the shift from load-bearing masonry walls to skeletal steel frames. Built by Burnham and Root, the aptly named Monadnock (an Abenaki Indian term meaning a mountain standing alone) – was not only the tallest office building in the city when it was completed in 1891, but also one of the first commercial buildings with electricity, and at sixteen stories, the tallest building made entirely from stone – its walls are six feet thick to support the structure's immense weight. An addition, built two years later by Holabird and Root at 54 W Van Buren St, was constructed from steel frames that allowed thinner walls and created more room for glass windows.

Federal Center Complex

Between Jackson Boulevard and Adams Street, the triumvirate of black steel buildings that comprise the **Federal Center Complex** – a courthouse, government office building and single-story US post office – are the work of Ludwig Mies van der Rohe, founder of the International Style of modern architecture (see box, p.243). Austere in the extreme, these buildings are the best early examples of Chicago architecture's leap from the Chicago School to modernism; compare the federal buildings with neighboring Chicago School buildings like the Monadnock and Fisher, and you'll see the dramatic difference. All three governmental buildings are geometrically perfect and their steel frames brought to the surface, resulting in a highly linear and orderly construction that is beautiful in its simplicity. Stand in the plaza that joins them and the regularity of the steel and glass proportions will jump out at you. Even the grid lines cut into the plaza floor appear carefully designed to run into the buildings at precisely the points where they do, perhaps hardly surprising for an architect who is said to have stood over the architectural model for hours, as if in meditative trance, before moving something an eighth of an inch in a flash of recognition.

Looking a bit like a giraffe with its head stuck in the ground, the 53-foot vermillion sculpture in the plaza is the work of Alexander Calder, whose inexplicably named *Flamingo* "stabile" ("static" and "mobile") is a welcome splash of color among the sombre federal buildings.

From the Marquette Building to First National Plaza

The striking seventeen-story **Marquette Building**, a block north on Dearborn Street, was built in 1895 by Holabird & Roche. While it was a prototype of the tall office building (especially for the massive panes of the "Chicago style" windows), its decorative features set it apart from much of its progeny. The bronze reliefs over the main door depict scenes from the 1674 expedition of Chicago's European co-discoverer Jacques Marquette, from the launching of his canoe to his local burial (and for whom the building was named). But the exterior pales beside the glittering lobby, whose shimmering bronze fixtures are offset by a Tiffany glass mosaic, running around the atrium on the first floor. Designed by J.A. Holzer, it, too, retells the story of the French exploration of Illinois.

Some of the progress in office building can be charted as you continue on down the block. The **Inland Steel Building**, standing diagonally opposite at 30 W Monroe St, was completed in 1957 by Skidmore, Owings & Merrill. It was the first skyscraper built on pilings (steel columns), and the first to use external steel beams for structural support. Like the Leiter Building II (see p.49), the exterior frame freed the interior of beams and fixed walls, thereby allowing the maximum amount of rentable space. The building was also the first to have an underground parking garage, and the first to install air-conditioning.

Nearby, the rounded glass building at **55 W Monroe**, erected between 1977 and 1980, was the work of C.S. Murphy and Associates, including young architect Helmut Jahn (see box, p.242), who drew on everything from the Carson Pirie Scott Building, post-war modernism and the exterior frame innovations of the Inland Steel Building for inspiration. The result was a postmodern pastiche of a skyscraper – the first building to hide its structure with reflective glass; its surface, all aluminum and glass, curves sleekly round the corner of Dearborn and Monroe streets. There's not much to look at inside, except a handy branch of American Express (see "Currency exchange," p.224).

Walk north on Dearborn Street until you reach **First National Plaza** (on your left), between Monroe and Madison streets, where the sixty-story **Bank One Building** curves gracefully skyward at the plaza's north end. Though it's one of the most photographed edifices in the city, most people come here to see Chagall's *Four Seasons* mosaic, a 3000-square-foot wall of glass-and-stone tiles in 250 different shades, all painstakingly applied to give shape to whimsical dancers, musicians, animals and angels floating above cityscapes, as if carried by the wind. In 1994 a protective covering was applied to shield it from the elements.

Daley Plaza and around

Two blocks north, at the corner of Dearborn and Washington streets, you'll come upon **Richard J. Daley Plaza**, whose focal point is the untitled **Picasso sculpture**, which – depending your orientation – will look like a giant angry bird, a woman's face or, as one youngster told Chicago writer Studs Terkel, a giant red hot dog. The plaza was named for the father of current mayor Richard M. Daley. At times the space hosts performances, and around the winter holidays, an enormous twinkling Christmas tree.

Across Washington Street stands the **Chicago Temple Building**, home to First United Methodist Church of Chicago, among other tenants. Besides a French Gothic sanctuary on the ground floor, the building's main highlight is the **Chapel in the Sky**, located in the eight-story Gothic spire, which, from afar, looks like an elf's hat plopped onto a staid office tower. The chapel, which tops out at 568 feet above street level, is the world's tallest church; the only way to see inside it, however, is on one of the **free tours** leaving from the church's office on the second floor (Mon–Fri 2pm, Sun after services, usually 9.30am and noon; ☎312/236-4548).

Beneath the Chicago Temple Building, you'll spot yet another piece of public art, this one a sculpture by Picasso's contemporary, **Joan Miró**. This 39-foot *Chicago* statue, made of concrete, steel and ceramic tiles to represent a "great earth mother," will perhaps bring to mind other ideas; what passes for a head looks more like a pitchfork.

The theatre district and around

Since the relocation of the Goodman Theatre to Dearborn and Randolph streets, the city has been trying to recreate the theater culture that thrived here a century ago, refurbishing many of its early twentieth-century theaters and movie houses. All initial signs suggest success; the area immediately around the theaters is noticeably glitzy, with new hotels and restaurants springing up, each seemingly more expensive and crowded than the last. To see some of the grand interiors without catching a show, the Chicago Architecture Foundation offers an excellent ninety-minute **theatre district tour** ($10, students $5; ☎312/922-3432); for details on shows, see "Performing arts and film," p.185.

A quick look around might begin at the **Oriental Theatre/Ford Center for the Performing Arts**, 24 W Randolph St, which was built on the site once occupied by the Iroquois Theater, where in 1903 a deadly fire killed six hundred people. The Oriental Theatre then played for forty-odd years before closing down; fortunately, in 1996 a $34-million renovation restored the theater's famously bizarre interior – a riot of sculptured sea horses, goddesses and elephants, all designed to resemble, however obliquely, an Asian temple.

Nearby at 175 N State, the vertical "C-H-I-C-A-G-O" sign and marquee of the **Chicago Theatre** – the city's first movie palace (1926)- is all but impossible to miss, as is the facade, styled as it is after the Arc de Triomphe. The theater is better known, however, for its opulent interior – exquisite murals, crystal chandeliers and bronze light fixtures all modeled after Versailles. Forty-five-minute **tours** (by appointment only, Mon–Fri; $5; ☎312/263-1138), led by docents, cover all the highlights, including the theater's magnificent Wurlitzer pipe organ, as well as the stage and backstage dressing rooms.

One block west, at 170 N Dearborn St, the facade of the **Goodman Theatre**, lit up in rainbow-coloured lights, may bring to mind the flashiness of New York's Times Square. The state-of-the-art complex, which opened in 2000, puts on performances in its two auditoriums and outdoor amphitheater.

Back on Randolph Street and two blocks west of the Goodman is the **Cadillac Palace**, 151 W Randolph St, whose rather staid and unbecoming exterior hides a gemlike interior, in look and feel like that of a French palace, right down to the huge mirrors, crystal chandeliers and gold fixtures.

James R. Thompson Center

Diagonally opposite the Cadillac Palace, resembling an oversized slice of blue cake, is the **James R. Thompson Center**, 100 W Randolph St, the state's headquarters in Chicago. Helmut Jahn's design threw off more than a few people when it was completed in 1985, its bulging sides and exuberant color scheme standing out like a sore thumb amid the neighboring office towers. Inside, glass elevator shafts shuttle office workers to and from floors, past the silver-, red- and blue-toned interior. More than fifty state agencies are housed here, as well as an art gallery, three floors of restaurants and shops, and the expected parade of gawkers.

Aside from aesthetic concerns, the government workers found it to be too hot in summer and too cold in winter, thanks to the building's 400,000-square-foot glass shell. (In the end, the solution was to freeze eight 100,000-pound ice blocks every night and let them slowly melt the next day for use as coolant in the air-conditioning system.)

The sculpture standing in the building's foreground, looking like a cross between an iceberg and a ten-ton plaything, is Jean Dubuffet's *Monument with Standing Beast*. The mass of white fiberglass and black trim was taken from the artist's "art brute series," an attempt to divorce art from culture. According to Dubuffet, the piece contains four motifs: an animal, a tree, a portal and a Gothic church. Good luck finding them.

Along LaSalle Street

Chicago's Wall Street, the six blocks between Lake Street and Jackson Boulevard on LaSalle Street, won't take up much of your attention, unless you want to get inside the eye-catching **The Rookery** or peer into the frenzied trading pit at the **Board of Trade**. There's another Jahn building right here at **120 N LaSalle.** It's his last building to date, and though not nearly as wave-making as the Thompson Center, it definitely has some of his flashy style. The convex facade, covered in reflective glass, bulges out over the street, while above the main entrance you'll see Roger Brown's colorful mosaic *The Flight of Daedalus and Icarus*.

But the real postmodern sight is **190 S LaSalle**, Philip Johnson's only Chicago work, easily one of the more elegant and refined variations on that theme, best viewed from a few blocks away. Johnson teamed up with John Burgee Architects and built it during the late 1980s, almost completely mimicking the design of Root and Burnham's gorgeous 1892 Masonic Temple (demolished in 1939). This gives Johnson's masterpiece an opulent pre-1900 air; it appears like an all-masonry construction, a witty, postmodern architectural joke. Everything about it has a beautifully classic feel, from the five-story red granite base, to the thousands of thin, vertical windows rising to the exquisite gables some forty stories skyward. Similarly, the grand, seemingly endless lobby is rich in Gothic splendor; million of dollars' worth of gold leaf on the ceiling, individual elevator banks decorated in their own shades of marble and the intriguing bronze sculpture on the lobby's north end (Alfred Carel's *Fugue*) bring to mind a secular cathedral, complete with an altar of sorts manned by the security guard at the lobby's south end. Hanging in the adjoining side room is a tapestry of Daniel Burnham's 1909 plan of Chicago, perhaps one of the few chances you'll have of seeing the tremendous vision and plans he had for this city.

The Rookery

The Rookery, the massive red granite building at 209 S La Salle St, is the seminal work of two leading Chicago architects, Burnham and Root, and one of the city's most celebrated and photographed edifices. Its forbidding Moorish Gothic exterior, which looks as if it's been chiselled into a sophisticated office building, gives way to a wonderfully airy lobby, decked out in cool Italian marble and gold leaf in 1905 during a major remodeling by Frank Lloyd Wright and restored in 1992. The spiral cantilever staircase rising from the second floor must be seen to be appreciated. **Tours** of the building have been sporadic since September 11, 2001, so call the Chicago Architecture Foundation to check on their status.

Chicago Board of Trade

Half the world's wheat and corn (and, oddly pork belly) futures change hands here, at the world's busiest grain exchange amid the cacophonous roar of the **Chicago Board of Trade**, at 141 W Jackson Blvd at S LaSalle Street. Sadly, touring the building is no longer possible after the terrorist attacks of September 2001 – check in with the building's owners to see if and when tours are reinstated. If you do want to see the frenzied action on a trading floor up close, check out the Mercantile Exchange (see below).

The building itself is one of the rare examples of Art Deco anywhere in the city. Designed by Holabird & Root in 1930, the gorgeous monolithic tower is appropriately topped by a thirty-foot stainless steel statue of Ceres, Roman goddess of grain. The thirteen-foot clock on the facade, high above the main entrance, can be seen from almost fifteen blocks away on LaSalle Street.

The Sears Tower and the river

While the Loop proper is defined by the circle of El tracks, the blocks just beyond this core hold plenty of interest, chief among them the vertigo-inducing **Sears Tower**, visible from just about anywhere in the city. The broad, double-decked **Wacker Drive**, which follows the river northward and then west, was designed in 1909 by Daniel Burnham as an elegant promenade lined with benches and obelisk-shaped lanterns. Though it was never completed, and despite the almost constant intrusion of construction works, the promenade makes for a pleasant stroll, affording superb views of the river and downtown skyline (the State Street Bridge being an especially good vantage point). Above the Loop, along the river's south bank, you'll find several cafés beside the **river-**

walk between Lake Michigan and Michigan Avenue; further west, past the water taxis and tour boats, a recently resurrected stretch of the riverwalk follows the river's western bank, where you'll find more open-air cafés and some gardens.

The Sears Tower

East of the river, on S Wacker Drive at Adams Street, stands the 1468-foot **Sears Tower**, which was the tallest building in the world until 1997, when Malaysia's Petronas Towers controversially nudged it from the number one spot by the length of an antenna. Hair-splitting aside, the building has acquired a new poignancy since the terrorist attacks of September 2001 (as well as heavily heightened security).

The tower, finished in 1973 by Skidmore, Owings and Merrill, took only three years to build and was technologically innovative, especially in its step-back, framed-tube construction (allowing the wide base to support the narrower upper tower) and the heated walkway around its perimeter to help clear winter snow. The tower's vital statistics are staggering: more than 10,000 people work here, riding the more than one hundred elevators and looking out through 16,000 windows – all, thankfully, equipped with automatic window washers.

Enter on Jackson Street through the specially marked door and descend to the lower level to reach the ticket office. Feel free to skip the cursory eight-minute movie and head straight for the ear-popping elevator ride, which takes about seventy seconds to reach the **103rd-floor observatory** (daily: May–Sept 10am–10pm, Oct–April 10am–8pm, closed occasionally due to high winds; $9.50, seniors $7.75, children $6.75; ☎312/875-9696, ⓦwww. sears-tower.com). Once there, you'll have good views of the city's east and north sides, though even on a clear day you'll be squinting to see the neighboring four states (Michigan, Illinois, Indiana, Wisconsin), as touted in the tower's literature: call to check the visibility index before turning up – if it's under five miles, come another time. The handy touch-screen computers mounted on the rails will help identify what you see, and you can read fascinating stories from the city's history on the walls.

If the lines for the Skydeck are too long, keep in mind that you can get similar views atop the John Hancock Building in Near North (see p.61); in any case, the crowds typically thin out after 4pm.

The Chicago Mercantile Exchange

Three blocks north at 30 S Wacker Drive, you can watch precious metals, currencies and commodities bought and sold to the tune of some $50 billion a day at the **Chicago Mercantile Exchange** or "The Merc" (Mon–Fri 8.15am–3.15pm; free; ⓦwww.cme.com). The Merc floor is a dazzling throwback to pre-computer days, when Chicago was the hub of the railways – and so of the nation's trade. Head for the entrance on Monroe Street and be prepared for thorough security checks before you're escorted to the fourth-floor glass-enclosed viewing gallery. The frenzy of activity is breathtaking, as the staffers trade, record and arbitrate deals.

There's excellent on-site info to help you decode the goings-on. The different colored jackets signify different roles in the trading process: clerks sporting gold coats can't execute trades themselves, but administer everything from answering the phones to running errands; market reporters in blue report the price and quantity of trades as they happen; arbitrators in green are only called in when there's a dispute between buyers and sellers; and lastly there are the hardcore traders, who wear red (in fact, traders are allowed to wear any color or design they wish, so look out for a garish few who are more nattily dressed than their colleagues).

The four octagons on the floor are the trading hubs, and each red jacket uses a simple set of hand gestures to communicate above the throbbing noise of the floor. Palms inward indicate "I'm buying," palm outward, "I'm selling", while the number of fingers raised confirms the number of contracts he or she is trying to offload or purchase.

More than a million tons of trash are swept up every day, and the balletic cleaners who scamper round the frantic traders all day are also worth watching. The best time to visit the Merc is just before the close of trade, when the pressure's at its peak and tempers are most flared.

Civic Opera House and around

The massive **Civic Opera House**, at 20 N Wacker Drive, just below Washington Street, is another splendid venue for highbrow entertainment, home to the Lyric Opera. Conceived as a monument to culture and commerce and completed in 1929, the Neoclassical building was designed with a grand two-story portico running its entire length, making it look like a giant armchair when viewed from the river. While it's worth taking a tour of the opera house, they're only given in February and March and book up months in advance; at $30 they're also pricey (℡312/332-2244, ⓦwww.lyricopera.org).

Walking north from here to where the river bends eastward, you'll spot **333 W Wacker** on your right, a wafer-thin building covered in a skin of reflective green glass. Built in 1983, it was designed to mimic the contour and color of the Chicago River, and is best viewed from the opposite bank, which also has a few of its own notable buildings, namely the fortress-like **Merchandise Mart**, the twin corncob towers of **Marina City** and Mies van der Rohe's sleek, black **IBM Building** (for more on these, see "Near North," starting on p.57).

Near North

Despite the neighboring Loop's pre-eminence, Chicago's **Near North** has managed to become a center of attention itself, with its three, very different districts – **Michigan Avenue, Streeterville** and **River North** – each offering very different reasons to go. Transformed almost overnight from an industrial area of low-rent factories by the building of the Michigan Avenue Bridge in the early twentieth century, Near North is actually where most tourists spend the bulk of their visit, either enjoying the family entertainment at Navy Pier or, more likely, maxing out their credit cards at the megastores lining the Magnificent Mile.

The **Magnificent Mile**, along Michigan Avenue, is one of the most famous shopping strips in the world, and Chicago relentlessly pitches its glitzy selection of stores. As resistant as some visitors may be to buy into such hype, those who skip Michigan Avenue will miss out on one of Chicago's best attractions. The streets here are wide enough never to feel crowded (even during the holiday season), there are parks and benches for a pause between stores, and its expansive openness is refreshing after the canyons of buildings and low-flying trains in the Loop. Even those allergic to shopping should find something to buy, thanks to the enormous selection; if you're determined not to spend a dollar, it's still worth dawdling here to look at Neo-Gothic buildings like the **Tribune** and **Water Towers** as well as **Wrigley's** gleaming chewing gum headquarters that resembles a mammoth ivory wedding cake.

The glossy area sandwiched between Michigan Avenue and the lake is officially known as **Streeterville**, though few locals call it that. It was originally a dump (literally – see p.63 for more on its history) but is now one of the swankiest places in the city, home to high-rise, high-price condos and gleaming residential skyscrapers. There's not much other than homes and hotels here, save the corporate funland of **Navy Pier**, one of Chicago's top tourist attractions.

River North is one of the most schizophrenic districts in the city. On the one hand, it's crammed with theme restaurants like the *Rock 'n' Roll McDonald's* and the *Rainforest Café*, which cater to families and hapless tourists. On the other, it's Chicago's answer to New York's SoHo district: away from the main drags of Ontario and Ohio streets, you'll find a thriving, loft-heavy gallery district. The exhibits here on the whole are less avant-garde and more accessible than in similar neighborhoods in other cities – we've included our picks on p.68.

Be aware that away from Michigan Avenue, distances in Near North can be large, especially as you wander round River North: grab one of the free trolleys (see box on p.65) or head there on foot in comfortable shoes.

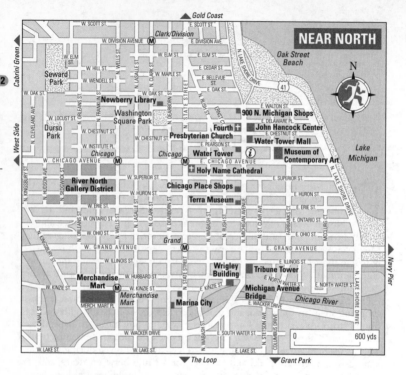

The Magnificent Mile

Walking along the wide swathe of Michigan Avenue is the one thing that almost every visitor to the city will do: at least according to the local business association, it's one of the top five shopping districts in the world. It's well stocked with mainstream retailers, from an enormous Virgin megastore to a Niketown, as well as every major department store from Saks to Neiman Marcus (for more information on these and other stores, see "Shopping," p.215). Equally as diverting perhaps are skyscrapers like the **Wrigley Building** and **Tribune Tower**, the fine collection of paintings at the **Terra Museum of American Art**, or the views from the **John Hancock Building**.

Although S Michigan Avenue was an early addition to the city plan (1836) and was soon crowded with museums and civic institutions, its northern stretches were only developed in the early twentieth century after the **Michigan Avenue Bridge** was finally constructed in 1920, allowing expansion across the Chicago River. Inspired by the Alexander III bridge in Paris, it's decorated with four forty-foot pylons, two at either end, each of which features a sumptuous relief depicting a key event in the city's history. This was also the first double roadway bridge ever built: the lower level was designed to service the *Chicago Sun-Times* and *Chicago Tribune* newspapers, which were originally both written and printed nearby, without disrupting commercial traffic flow. Note the two leaves that are raised to allow large boats to pass underneath: though the city took to the design quickly – it now has fifty such bridges – mastering them, apparently, took a little practice. On opening day, a bridge tender raised the bridge for a passing boat, unaware that four cars were parked on it and so gave them a forced bath in the river. If you'd rather cruise around the river than dive into it, the bridge is now the starting point for many **bus and boat tours** (see p.30).

Developers continued to lure business northward by renaming hardscrabble Pine Street – at that time, an unpaved road of soap factories, breweries and warehouses – as N Michigan Avenue to take advantage of existing Michigan Avenue's cachet. Next, they persuaded two local businesses to establish banner headquarters at the grand new avenue's southernmost end: Wrigley Building (1924) on the west, the Tribune Tower (1922) to the east. Still, it wasn't until real estate entrepreneur Arthur Rubloff christened the strip "The Magnificent Mile," then set about making good his claim in the 1960s, that the area truly came to life.

With the whole-hearted support of Richard Daley, Chicago's influential mayor at the time, the Magnificent Mile exploded with shops – and it hasn't looked back since. If you're interested in exploring that side of things, you may be drawn to any of the three major downtown malls: **900 N Michigan Ave, Chicago Place** and **Water Tower Place**. There isn't much to choose between them, although 900 N Michigan is probably the swankiest, and the Water Tower Place most notable architecturally. Begun in 1972, it was groundbreaking in its design, squeezing as it did a horizontal suburban-style mall into a tight urban corner, whose eight floors of retail space centered on an airy atrium. If you've kids in tow, stop off at **American Girl Place**, 111 E Chicago Ave, one block off the main drag (☎312/943-9400, ⓦwww.americangirlstore.com). It's somewhere between a toy shop and a doll museum, with theater performances thrown in for good measure, all catering to youngish girls. It's quite expensive (food events $20, theater performances from $26), but nonetheless manages to pull in the crowds.

The Wrigley Building and around

Flanking the southern entrance to the Mag Mile is the **Wrigley Building** at 400 N Michigan Ave, sometimes called the "Jewel of the Mile." The home of the Wrigley chewing gum company does indeed sparkle at night when hundreds of floodlights across the river bathe the creamy, glazed terra-cotta facade and huge clock tower, which are kept in tip-top shape by special cleaning crews. Modeled after the Giralda Tower of Seville's cathedral, the building has flourishes reminiscent of the French Renaissance.

Just north of the Wrigley building, looking a bit out of place among the drab office buildings, is the pensive-looking statue of **Benito Juarez**, president of Mexico from 1861 to 1872 and a contemporary of Abraham Lincoln. The two shared a famed correspondence and friendship, perhaps owing to their two similar paths to the presidency and their mutual respect for each other's pious outlook on life.

For a memorable bite to eat in the area, head down the stairs to the venerable grease pit, the **Billy Goat Tavern**, tucked away beneath the statue and Michigan Avenue. Immortalized by John Belushi's "cheezborger" skit on *Saturday Night Live*, this smoky, subterranean dive is where journalists have been scoffing down burgers since it opened in 1934 (for review, see p.151).

The Tribune Tower

Across the road from the Wrigley Building stands the **Tribune Tower**, 435 N Michigan Ave (Mon–Fri 8.30am–5pm; tours by appointment only; ☎312/222-

2116, ⓦ www.tribune.com); despite the dozens of skyscrapers crowding down-town's skyline now, it still stands out, thanks to the ornate, Neo-Gothic design. It's one of Chicago's signature structures and, along with the Wrigley Building, it was designed to act as a flashy anchor for the newly accessible Near North district.

The tower was built in 1925 as headquarters for the *Chicago Tribune*, support-ed by the deep pockets of the newspaper's eccentric editor-publisher Robert "The Colonel" McCormick. Dapper McCormick and his scruffy co-publish-er, Joseph Patterson, launched a contest in 1922 to mark the 75th anniversary of the founding of the *Chicago Tribune*, offering $100,000 in prizes to architects around the world willing to submit designs for a grand new headquarters. The winning entry was by Americans John Mead Howells and Raymond Hood (who beat out Fin Eliel Saarinen, whose sleek modernist design would prove far more influential across the world, and whose son was design legend Eero Saarinen). Admittedly, the lace-dipped-in-cement-style tower looks more Ghostbusters than Gothic to the modern eye, but The Colonel spared no expense on his masterpiece: it would cost a staggering $8.5 million to build.

Like Louis Sullivan, Howells and Hood were heavily influenced by Britain's Arts and Crafts movement, which rebelled against angular, mass-produced dec-oration; hence, most of the detailing features plants and animals, and likewise the figures from Aesop's fables, woven into the scrollwork in the stone screen above the main entranceway. Don't miss the **main lobby**, either, which has notable decorative features of its own: quotations serving as propaganda in sup-port of a free press are chiseled over almost every inch of marble. There's a mas-sive relief map of North America on the main wall; strangely, it's made from plaster mixed with old dollar bills, since tough currency paper helps with dura-bility. The planned image included much of South America, too; but then the slightly batty and very patriotic Colonel decided to make the United States more prominent by chopping two feet off the bottom of the design. Embedded in the building's base are some 120 fragments from brilliant struc-tures of the world – a stone from the Great Wall of China and one from Reims Cathedral among them.

Fragments of history

The most famous feature of the **Tribune Tower** is the fragments of famous buildings dotting the facade; they include rocks from the Houses of Parliament in London, St Peter's in Rome and the Forbidden City in Beijing. The tradition began with the Colonel himself who, while working as a war correspondent during World War I in France, grabbed a chunk of Ypres cathedral that had been knocked from the wall by German shells. Soon, the Colonel was instructing his far-flung network of news-hounds to gather other notable rocks (by honorable means) to create a display that would underscore his claim that the *Trib* was the "World's Greatest Newspaper." Of course, many reporters chose to risk the wrath of local lawmakers rather than the anger of their ornery boss, so no one can be sure how many of the souvenirs were purloined rather than purchased. Their activities became so well known that one journalist arrived in Reims, France, to see the local newspaper blaring warnings about his intentions across its front page.

These days, new (legal) acquisitions are set aside for ten years to gauge their true historic value before being mounted on the walls – exceptions include a piece of the Berlin Wall added in 1990, and the Moon rock on long-term loan from NASA that's displayed in its own glass case. To identify the fragments, pick up one of the superb free leaflets available inside the main lobby.

The *Chicago Tribune* is still housed here: look for the squat, later additions that were built to its north and east with the *Tribune*'s entry into radio and television. WGN radio (its call letters hark back to "World's Greatest Newspaper" – see box opposite) still broadcasts from here, and you can watch the deejays at work from the ground-level glass window on Michigan Avenue. Aside from that, there's also a fine, low-priced **café** on the tower's main floor, open to the public.

Terra Museum of American Art

Sandwiched between alluring stores at the heart of the Mag Mile and a short walk from the headline-grabbing Art Institute, the poor **Terra Museum of American Art**, 664 N Michigan Ave (Tues 10am–8pm, Wed–Sat 10am–6pm, Sun noon–5pm; tours daily at noon; free, suggested donation $5; ☎312/664-3939, ⓦwww.terramuseum.org), is often overlooked – a pity, as there are some fine pictures in the collection. Industrialist John Terra narrowed his early eclectic tastes to focus in on American art; the five-story building was specially built to house his stunning collection, and with its swooping ramps and fluid rooms, it's an especially user-friendly exhibition space. Displays change constantly: usually, at least two floors are set aside for rotating work from the permanent collection, while the rest house traveling exhibitions on an American theme.

The most iconic work in the collection is Samuel Morse's dapper, encyclopedic *Gallery of the Louvre*, a guidebook-style recap of the Louvre's greatest hits, all in thumbnails – look for his goofy Mona Lisa. Otherwise, most selections will include some canvases by Mary Cassatt, the only American to exhibit with the Impressionists in France: her daubed, gauzy pictures leave little impression, but graphic prints like *The Lamp* – heavily influenced by Japonisme – are stunning and unexpected. The radical turn-of-the-century painter Maurice Brazil Prendergast was one of Terra's favorites, and he's the artist most fully represented here, with more than eighty works; his style fuses smudgy Impressionist techniques with convention-breaking Modernism, angular figures covered with blobs of paint. There are also four delightful studies by John Singer Sargent for his famous painting *The Oyster Gatherers of Cancale*. Terra nabbed three at auction in 1971 but had to wait until just before his death 25 years later for the last (*Breton Woman with Basket*), which had come up for sale.

The John Hancock Building and around

Sleek and muscular, the **John Hancock Building**, 875 N Michigan Ave, is the street's dominant fixture, a quarter-mile-high construction of cross-braced steel, black aluminum skin and bronze-tinted windows that rises nearly out of sight, tapering upward to be capped, eventually, by two massive spires. Though it appears imposing from its base, viewed from afar it's beautifully austere, heavily influenced by the Miesian school – except for the colorful band of light at the top, visible at night.

Though shorter than both the Sears Tower and the Empire State Building, the Hancock building was for many years among the world's top ten tallest structures and offers – on a clear day – jaw-dropping 360-degree panoramic views of the city from its 94th-floor **observatory**. It also made history as the tallest mixed-use building in the world, its combining of commercial and office space with apartments being unusual for its time.

More than 1000 feet above Chicago, the observatory (daily 9am–11pm; last observatory ticket sold at 10.45pm; $9.50, children 5–12 $6; ☎312/751-3680,

ⓦ www.hancock-observatory.com) has an open-air viewing deck where winds can force the building to sway as much as ten inches from side to side, though you probably won't even notice. Don't let this, or the somewhat steep ticket price, prevent you from taking the elevator up to the observatory; the views are truly staggering – like the Sears Tower, you'll see as far as Indiana, Michigan and Wisconsin on a clear day. It's also open later than the Sears Tower, and the lines are less grueling. If the views alone aren't diverting enough, you can listen to an audio tour or check out one of the talking telescopes that point out what you're seeing. There's also a wall devoted to city history and a bit about the construction of the building itself. Those without kids in tow can check out the *Signature Room* bar and restaurant on the 95th floor, where – though the drinks are pricey – you'll get the fantastic view as well (for a review of the restaurant, see p.152).

At the base of the Hancock building, in a small store-lined courtyard, is a branch store of the **Chicago Architecture Foundation** (see p.41), which can set you up with tours and literature on Chicago's famed designs.

Opposite the John Hancock Center is the English Gothic **Fourth Presbyterian Church**, at 126 E Chestnut St, built in 1914. Peek inside for a look at the elegantly understated interior or stop by the fountain in the peaceful courtyard – a pleasant spot for a picnic.

Chicago Water Tower and Pumping Station

Across from the Water Tower Place mall stands the **Chicago Water Tower**, whose limestone cladding withstood the Great Fire that engulfed the rest of downtown and turned a clumsy example of Victorian Neo-Gothic into a stirring symbol of Chicago's survival.

Topped by a 100-foot tower that resembles a thick-stemmed tulip, the Water Tower was built in 1869 to house a standpipe that equalized the pressure of water from the Pumping Station across the street. Both were part of major sanitation projects undertaken by the city to supply safe drinking water to its swelling population, plans that centered on an ambitious tunnel that was built under Lake Michigan to tap into deeper, cleaner waters far from shore.

Today, the tiny interior of the Water Tower houses temporary exhibitions: you're more likely to dawdle in the grassy plaza to eat a sandwich or watch the endless stream of eager street performers. The Pumping Station houses the

Water Tower: a symbol of Chicago

For a city on the shores of one of the country's largest sources of fresh water, Chicago has a surprisingly long history with poor drinking water. The water quality was so bad, in fact, that it caused many outbreaks of disease, a pattern that forced the city to depend on bottled liquids. All that began to change, though, on March 25, 1867, when the city broke ground for the new water tower at Michigan and Chicago avenues, and two years later, the **Chicago Water Tower and Pumping Station** was up and running, a boon for the city's health. Though the water tower survived the devastating 1871 fire, its odd-looking appearance failed to impress Oscar Wilde, who visited Chicago in 1882 and described the tower as a "castellated monstrosity with pepper boxes stuck all over it." Though its looks have hardly improved over the years, and despite the efforts of local groups to replace it with more modern buildings, the homely tower has steadfastly held its ground – testament perhaps to its enduring legacy.

Chicago Water Works Visitor Center (☎1-877/CHICAGO; ⓦwww.choose chicago.com), whose knowledgeable staff can provide tons of maps and brochures, plus details on the latest cultural events in Near North. The store next door sells all the requisite local trinkets, and there's also a so-so café. Note that though the pumping equipment's still in operation today, there's no public access.

Streeterville

Stretching east of the Magnificent Mile to the lake, **Streeterville** was hardly a place to visit until the city revamped **Navy Pier** in 1995, creating the city's largest amusement park and one of its top attractions. The arrival of the **Museum of Contemporary Art** a year later helped raise the neighborhood's profile a notch, and nowadays even locals are likely to venture here for the swanky hotel bars and restaurants that dot the landscape. The lakefront makes for a pleasant stroll or a bike ride; the bike path running between Oak Street Beach and Olive Park (just north of Navy Pier) is accessible through tunnels at Oak Street, Chicago Avenue, Ontario Street and Ohio Street.

While Streeterville isn't known for its architecture, it does have the grandiose **Drake Hotel**, overlooking the lake on a prime piece of real estate. The hotel draws its share of celebrity guests with its sumptuous decor and gilt-edged service; take the time to soak in the ambience at the bar of the plush *Coq d'Or*. Three blocks east of the hotel, just before the lakefront, are two of Mies van der Rohe's more famous residential commissions, **860 and 880 N Lake Shore Drive**, completed in 1951. Known as the "glass houses," these solemn-looking towers aren't much to look at, but they're nonetheless partly responsible for the proliferation of glass-and-steel high-rises from the 1950s on.

George Wellington Streeter

More than any Chicago neighborhood, Streeterville had a shaky start. The land east of Michigan Avenue and north of the Chicago River came into being through a bizarre set of circumstances. On July 11, 1886, **George Wellington Streeter**, a captain and a spitfire of a man, ran his makeshift boat aground on a sandbar some four hundred feet offshore of today's Streeterville. After obtaining permission from one of the landowners to let him keep his boat there, he persuaded city contractors to dump refuse around his boat. In a short time, the rubbish had filled in the space between his boat and shore and could be called "land," a circumstance that Streeter would use to great advantage. He declared this previously nonexistent plot of over a hundred acres the "Free District of Lake Michigan," a territory independent of both Chicago and neighboring Illinois, and then sold chunks of it to unscrupulous buyers. For the next three decades, Streeter guarded this illegal shanty area with dubious legal claims and a shotgun. Somehow he survived through all of this, but the courts eventually overruled him in 1918, paving the way for development to begin in earnest west of his plot.

The Museum of Contemporary Art

The **Museum of Contemporary Art (MCA)**, 220 E Chicago Ave (Tues 10am–8pm, Wed–Sun 10am–5pm; suggested donation $10, students and seniors $6, free Tues; ☎312/280-2660, ⓦwww.mcachicago.org), is everything you might imagine to be "contemporary" – provocative, offbeat, seductive and divisive. Following a significant bequest in the will of a local art collector, the museum moved to its current quarters in 1997; the squat, boxy building lurking behind the Water Pumping Station was designed by German architect Josef Paul Kleihues and cost almost $50 million. The dominant feature of its facade is the steep, sweeping steps, which lead you up to the main entrance on the second floor.

The museum is on four levels: the ground floor is home to the shop and auditorium, while the main, second floor is where temporary exhibitions take place. Thanks to the museum's stated commitment to emerging artists, you'll often find intriguing unknowns showing alongside big names. But whether you enjoy the temporary exhibits or not, you're apt to find plenty of interest on the upper two floors, where a rotating selection of the permanent collection is on display.

Modern art stalwarts like Jasper Johns, Sol LeWitt, and even René Magritte, are represented in the museum's holdings, as are the modernist mobiles of **Alexander Calder**; a local art collector has lent the museum fifteen of his bobbing, abstract sculptures on indefinite loan, among them the monochromatic *Black 17 Dots* and *The Ghost*, especially eye-catching given the sculptor's penchant for using rainbow colors. **Jenny Holzer**'s scrolling LED signs are mesmerizing, as are **Bruce Nauman**'s flashing neon slogans like *Life Death Love Hate Pleasure Pain*. Contemporary art's king of kitsch, **Jeff Koons**, is also well represented – look for his shiny chrome *Rabbit* – as is the deadpan work of minimalist **Donald Judd**, who specializes in step-like sculptures. As for photography, the museum boasts an impressively wide-ranging collection of portraits by **Cindy Sherman** (in fact, MCA also owns a painting of Sherman by **Chuck Close**, in his customary passport-photo style), and works by the controversial **Andres Serrano** – the MCA has some of his *Morgue* series, in which deceased subjects are identified not by name but by the manner of death.

The chic on-site **café** is run by ubiquitous restaurateur Wolfgang Puck; it's best visited in summer when there's outdoor seating on the secluded terrace.

Navy Pier

Navy Pier may be Chicago's top tourist attraction, and is certainly family-friendly, but it has the feel of commercialism gone amok – everything in sight is sponsored to within an inch of its life, usually by *McDonald's*. (There's subtle McBranding everywhere – from the golden arches on the Ferris Wheel to the public spaces painted in red and yellow.) Navy Pier could also be anywhere – aside from one museum, which touts its local connection, this pier makes little reference to its hometown or its history. Built as Municipal Pier no. 2 in 1916 under Burnham's Chicago plan (see box p.234), it was quickly appropriated by the Navy during World War I, for which it was renamed in 1927. Navy Pier then served various civil and military purposes until the city decided to smarten up the ramshackle structure in the 1970s, and pumped massive investment into its refurbishment; it opened in its current incarnation in 1995. Note that it's immensely confusing to get around, thanks to the enormous concrete garage and convention center in its mid-section: stop at the information desk as soon as you enter through the main western doors and grab a **free map** – you'll need it.

Pier attractions

From the info desk, you can access the popular **Chicago Children's Museum** (Tues & Wed, Fri–Sun 10am–5pm, Thurs 10am–8pm; $7, free to 12 months and under; ☎312/527-1000; ⊛www.childrensmuseumchicago.org). This is a place that's heaven for little kids, but less interesting for older children. Exhibits include a large archeology pit, where would-be fossil hunters can dig for treasure; the city of Chicago, resized for toddlers, so little ones can drive a local bus; and even a fourteen-foot-high model of the Sears Tower made from more than 50,000 Lego bricks.

The next attraction, on the upper level, is the **Crystal Gardens**, a free giant hothouse filled with exotic plants and seating, as well as gravity-defying fountains that shoot semicircles of water into the air. It's pleasant enough and a good place for a picnic, but there's nothing especially compelling or unusual about any of the exhibits.

Continue on the upper level to **Pier Park**, where you'll find reach the 1500-foot Ferris Wheel (open during pier hours, weather permitting; $4). Sponsored by *McDonald's*, this soaring wheel offers views of downtown – though it adds nothing if you've already checked out the John Hancock tower (see p.61). Close by, there's an old-fashioned carousel, aimed at very young kids, with painted horses and the like (open weather permitting; $3).

Wedged into a tiny, seemingly impossible space by the monolithic parking lot, the **Chicago Shakespeare Theater** (☎312/595-5600 or 5635, ⓦwww.chicagoshakes.com) was ingeniously designed by its architects to host two terrific, intimate venues. The larger, with five hundred seats, has a thrust stage designed to replicate an Elizabethan set-up, while the smaller studio space upstairs is a flexible venue that can accommodate up to two hundred. For further details, see "Performing arts and film," p.186.

Tiring as it may be, don't give up walking yet – by far the best attraction on Navy Pier is unceremoniously stuck back in the corridors on the southern side of the two Exhibition Halls. The **Smith Museum of Stained Glass** (opening hours the same as Navy Pier; for tour information, call ☎312/595-5024) is an 800-foot-long gallery space that displays gorgeous stained-glass panels dating from 1870 to present day, grouped into four styles: Victorian, Prairie, Modern and Contemporary. You'll be able to guess the windows' original purpose and location by the subject matter – in fact, many of those on display were produced and installed locally. Look for Louis Sullivan's octagonal ceiling panels, rescued from the original Chicago Stock Exchange building before it was demolished, and Frank Lloyd Wright's *Avery Coonley Pool House Window*; it comes from the home that Wright considered the most successful of his Prairie designs. Other notable pieces include the darkly erotic and dreamlike *Queen of the Elves* by Marie Herndl and the startlingly modern *Round Headed Window* from a local church. That latter, produced in 1887, has poppy aquamarine circles ringed with honey and caramel rectangles that wouldn't look out of place in today's trendier interior design magazines.

Aside from the permanent attractions detailed above, much of what's on offer at Navy Pier changes seasonally – in summer, for instance, check the website or call for details on outdoor concerts at the **Skyline Stage**, while in winter, there's a free **skating rink** in Navy Pier Park. Otherwise, for our pick of the stores, bars and restaurants, see "Shopping," p.215, "Drinking," p.165 and "Eating," p.141.

River North

The once industrial wasteland of **River North** has seen its fortunes rise ever since the 1970s, when artists first recognized affordable studio space in its abandoned warehouses and factories. While the area around Michigan Avenue is heavily commercial and unappealing, you need only walk a few blocks west to where the art galleries take over and the crowds almost disappear for good. In the past fifteen years, the area has thrived, and nearly all of the streets – Chicago, Kinzie, Illinois notable among them – have benefited from the artistic spillover: you'll find everything here from art supply stores and antique furniture shops to trendy restaurants, while the preponderance of velvet-rope clubs turns the area after sundown into a throbbing nightlife scene.

Merchandise Mart

Though sights are thin on the ground, there are a few buildings worth noting along the north bank of the river. The monumental **Merchandise Mart**, 300 N Wells St at N Orleans Street (tours: Mon & Fri 1pm; 90min; ☎312/644-4664; call ahead to confirm times), houses six hundred showrooms of home furnishings, plus two floors of mall shops, all open to the public. Skip the building tour unless you're looking for interior design inspiration as the Mart's most impressive from the outside, where you can fully appreciate its enormity. With 4.2 million square feet of space, it's the largest building in the country besides the Pentagon and even has its own zip code. It was constructed for Marshall Field in 1931 as showroom and administrative headquarters. When the department store faced tough economic times after World War II, Kennedy patriarch Joe – who knew a good bargain when he saw one – snapped up the building for a fraction of its value simply by paying its back taxes. (The Mart's still owned by the Kennedys today and is the source of much of their wealth.) Joe's unmissable – if oddball – 1953 addition to the building was the **row of heads** on the plaza, grandly titled "the Merchandise Mart Hall of Fame" and paying tribute to the patron saints of shopping, including F.W. Woolworth, Edward A. Filene and, of course, Marshall Field himself.

Marina City and the IBM Building

Walking three blocks east to Dearborn Street, you'll see the twin corncob towers of **Marina City** (entrance at 300 N State St), a monument to the combined power of late 1960s paranoia and the Chicago winter. Architect Bertrand Goldberg designed the complex to be completely self-contained, offering everything you could need in your life (doctor, dentist, mall, even an undertaker) under one roof: in theory, you could be born, live and die here without ever leaving the building. Since most residents do need to get out and about once in a while, the bottom twenty stories are used as parking garages: the cars peeking out at the edge of each floor look surreal and not altogether secured hundreds of feet high in the air. Most visitors to the city, though, will only stop by to check out the *Chicago House of Blues* nightclub (see "Live music and clubs," p.179) which opened here as part of a massive modernization program in the late 1990s.

In contrast to the curvy Marina Towers, the **IBM Building** looming up behind them seems positively funereal. The near-black monolith was Mies van der Rohe's last American commission, and a variation of his seminal curtain-wall skyscraper – for better or for worse, the source of lesser imitations. You can ponder the building's aesthetic merits in the open forecourt at its base.

Chicago Sun-Times Building

The next building east is the **Chicago Sun-Times Building**, 401 N Wabash Ave (℡312/321-3000, ⊛www.suntimes.com). Crouched on the edge of the river, this chunky, low-lying office block was designed to look like a ship in full sail – although it's been derided as an eyesore since its construction. The *Sun-Times* has been in talks with billionaire real-estate magnate Donald Trump for the last few years, planning to tear down the current building and replace it with a skyscraper that would put both the Sears and John Hancock towers to shame. Since the terrorist attacks of September 2001, The Donald has scaled back his ambitions slightly, clipping the top fifteen floors off the plan (leaving a still-impressive 78); nonetheless, his projected tower would still stand 1073 feet, making it the fourth tallest in the city. At the time of writing, no final deal had been agreed, but *Sun-Times* management had given tenants in the building notice for summer 2003, so it's likely that groundbreaking will start soon after that – reason to catch the building while you can.

The River North gallery district

River North's **gallery district** doesn't generate quite the excitement that it did during its heyday in the 1980s, now that some galleries have had to pack up and move to cheaper neighborhoods, but it still accounts for a sizeable chunk of the city's art scene, notably around Huron and Superior streets, near Wells Street, where you'll find some well-established places.

Galleries usually host receptions for new shows on Friday evenings (5–8pm), and there are often plenty of Chicago glitterati on hand for great people-watching. Two openings are worth noting: the second or third Friday in September kicks off the Fall Gallery Season, while on the second Friday in January, all of the galleries have coinciding openings. For information on current events and occasional free trolleys that run between the River North galleries and the Michigan Avenue museums, pick up a copy of the free *Chicago Gallery News*, available from most hotels and galleries. The following are typically among the most interesting galleries; for additional reviews see "Shopping," p.215.

Ann Nathan Gallery 218 W Superior St (Tues–Fri 10am–5.30pm, Sat 11am–5pm; ☎312/664-6622, ⓦwww.annnathangallery.com). An eclectic assortment of paintings, sculpture and artfully decorated furniture by famous and not-so-famous artists, many from the Midwest.

Belloc Lowndes Fine Art 215 W Huron St (Tues–Sat 10am–6pm; ☎312/573-1157, ⓦwww.belloc lowndes.com). Run by two Englishmen, this tasteful gallery focuses mainly on contemporary British artists, with a few Americans occasionally thrown in. Especially cool (and extremely expensive) are a series of three-dimensional paintings by Patrick Hughes.

Primitive Art Works 706 N Wells St (Mon–Sat 11am–7pm; ☎312/943-3770, ⓦwwwprimitiveartworks.com). With more than one hundred cultures represented here, the four floors of jewelry, textiles and artifacts can certainly take up several hours of an afternoon. The knowledgeable staff can explain every piece in the house, from obscure and ancient Himalayan pieces to magical amulets worn by West African warriors.

Back on State Street, heading north for eight blocks or so will bring you to the **Holy Name Cathedral**, 735 N State St (tour information ☎312/787-8040), the epicenter of Chicago's Catholic community. Built in 1875, the Gothic church was designed by one Patrick Charles Keely, who, by that time, had a remarkable six hundred churches and sixteen cathedrals under his belt. Note the red decorations hanging high above the sanctuary – cardinals' hats (*galeros*), each one representing one of the city's past cardinals.

The Gold Coast and Old Town

T
he **GOLD COAST** is a hushed, moneyed enclave that sits at the northern end of the retail explosion of Michigan Avenue. It's one of the few snooty places in staunchly blue-collar Chicago, and for that reason alone seems almost refreshing – the empty back streets make a great haven from the crowds and noise of Near North. Though just as residential, adjacent **OLD TOWN** is somewhat livelier, a modestly charming area of historic wooden homes and hip restaurants and shops.

Soon after the Great Fire, the area now known as the Gold Coast became *the* place to live. Department store magnate Potter Palmer and his trendsetting wife Bertha made headlines in 1882 when they abandoned their swanky neighbors on the South Side to build a mansion in the middle of nowhere – on the site of the tower block at 1350 N Lake Shore Drive (sadly, Palmer's house was demolished in 1950). Soon, their fashionable friends followed and the neighborhood gained the standing it retains today: you can still see the mansions built by the likes of John Jacob Astor more than a hundred years ago, even if they're being crowded out by row upon row of high-rise door-manned buildings. Although there's little to do in the area other than shop, eat and drink, make sure to amble up **Astor Street** for its collection of eye-popping mansions – the swankiest are at its northern end. It's also worth spending a little time at the chic boutiques along **Oak Street**.

The Fire transformed Old Town, too, which was nothing but pasture for local cows until the blaze. Afterwards, thousands of German immigrants, displaced from their downtown homes, began to arrive, and the nickname "German Broadway" soon stuck. It was never a wealthy place - as is clear from the small houses everywhere – but the government's decision in the 1950s to sweep away a run-down section of what was, by then, known as Old Town, proved to have dire consequences. The city's misguided plans for housing projects in **Cabrini Green** turned the area, almost overnight, into a violent, no-go zone. The plummeting rents attracted hippies and their hangers-on who created a mini Haight-Ashbury in the late 1960s. Ironically, like their West Coast counterparts, they inadvertently started the process of gentrification that has peaked, along with the rents, here (except for the southwest corner around Cabrini Green) – some of the highest in the city.

Casual visitors to the area are most likely to take in a play at Chicago's most prestigious theatrical venue, the **Steppenwolf Theatre**, or a show at the legendary comedy club, **Second City**. Your best base for exploring is **Wells**

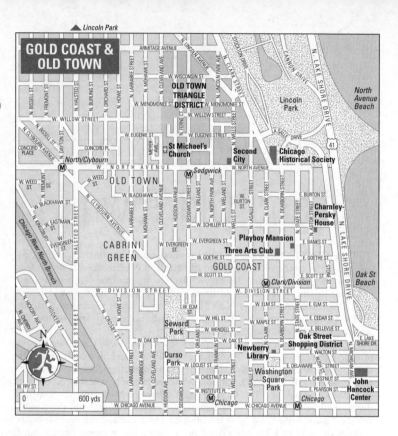

Street, the main drag: note that, even forty years after the hippies landed in the neighborhood, Old Town still has its share of dodgy streets. It's worth staying on the main thoroughfares, especially at night, and to skip anywhere close to Cabrini Green entirely.

The Gold Coast

Bounded by Chicago Avenue, North Avenue, Lake Shore Drive and LaSalle Street, the **Gold Coast** is focused during the day around the stylish boutiques along **Oak Street** and the eponymous beach on the lake – Chicago's most central (and style-conscious) patch of sand. After dark, the summertime crowds are apt to be found in the myriad bars of **Rush and Division streets**, where hordes of young singles congregate.

Above Division Street, the Gold Coast enters its most exclusive stretch; a stroll along Dearborn Street, State Street and North Astor Drive toward Lincoln Park will take you past some of the city's most palatial digs.

Chicago Avenue to Division Street

On the border between Near North and the Gold Coast, you'll find Chicago's swankiest shopping strip, **Oak Street** – a designer row filled with ultra-chic shops like Prada and Jil Sander as well as salons that cater to the local ladies who lunch. (For our pick of the shops here, see "Shopping," p.215.)

At its eastern reaches, you'll find the **Oak Street Beach**, a small stretch of sand that's packed on summer Sundays with residents from the high-rise condos along Lake Shore Drive. The beach evolved when this area was a resort – the famed **Drake** hotel (for review, see p.134) opened in 1920 as a beachfront property, where guests could wander from the changing rooms on the arcade level out onto the sands. Since the construction of Lake Shore Drive, however, the beach has been cut off from the *Drake* and other hotels; it's now reachable by a pedestrian tunnel beneath the road. There are full facilities by the water, including volleyball courts; expect to rub shoulders with women who bought their bikinis on Oak Street a few blocks to the west.

If you find the neighborhood's vanity a tad oppressive, there's relief nearby at the Romanesque **Newberry Library**, 60 W Walton St (Tues–Thurs 10am–6pm; Fri & Sat 9am–5pm, except before a Monday holiday; free tours Thurs 3pm, Sat 10.30am; ☎312/255–3595 or 943-9090, ⓦ www.newberry. org). This sumptuously appointed research library, whose wide-ranging collection covers western Europe and the Americas from the Middle Ages, includes a few oddities as well, such as the only bilingual text of *Popol Vuh*, the legend of an ancient Guatemalan tribe written down in 1515. The library often puts on exhibitions in the downstairs galleries, where you can linger over artifacts, photographs and paintings from its collection.

Across from the library, low-key **Washington Square Park** shows no signs of its colorful past. Once known as "Bughouse Square" for the neighboring flophouses, the park gained notoriety as a public forum where everyone from established writers and editors on down to struggling artists, hack writers and street performers had their say on the soapboxes. The park still sees the occasional speaker or two.

The street life picks up by several notches a couple of blocks west on **Rush Street**, a touristy strip of landmark restaurants, bars and shops, before reaching its culmination (or low point, depending on your view) with the testosterone-charged revelry of **Division Street**, home to a string of raucous bars vying for attention, notably *Mothers* and *Butch McGuire's* (for reviews of these and other bars in the area, see "Drinking," p.165).

North of Division Street

North of Division Street, it's best just to wander the side streets and take in the grandeur of one of Chicago's wealthiest and most desirable neighborhoods. The **Three Arts Club**, 1300 N Dearborn St (☎312/944-6250, ⓦ www. threearts.org), is as good a place to start as any. Founded in 1912 by a group of socially conscious women, including Jane Addams (see p.108), the residence has been housing women studying in the arts since it first opened in 1912, and the hefty brick and terra-cotta design by Holabird & Roche has artsy touches, like the colorful Byzantine-style mosaics in the arches above the main entrance (representing painting, music and drama) and classical sculpture set in the walls (note the replicas of the Jean Goujon panels of the Fontaine des Innocents in Paris). The pretty courtyard, where you can sit for a spell, hosts performances and art exhibits throughout the year.

A couple of blocks away (and if you're dressed the part), head to the **Pump Room**, in the *Ambassador East Hotel*, 1301 N State Parkway, for a taste of old-fashioned glamour. While the restaurant milks its movie-star associations for all they're worth – the foyer is covered with photos of celebrity patrons – it's still a fun place to linger over a drink and soak up the atmosphere.

Further up N State Parkway, the unassuming redbrick mansion at no. 1340 was once the famed **Playboy Mansion**, home and office of publisher and Chicago native Hugh Hefner, whose lavish parties for the glitterati were renowned. Hefner is long gone from here, as is the door plate inscribed "*Si non oscillas, noli tintinnare*" ("If you don't swing, don't ring"), and the mansion has since been converted into million-dollar apartments.

Charnley-Persky House and around

A right onto E Banks Street followed by a left on N Astor Street will bring you to the **Charnley–Persky House** at no. 1365, an austere three-story building of brick and limestone – easily identified by the wooden columned balcony on the second floor – considered a forerunner of modern residential architecture. Louis Sullivan and his assistant Frank Lloyd Wright built the house between 1891 and 1892, adopting the low-lying, symmetrical style that would later become the hallmark of Wright's Prairie School architecture and herald the move away from Victorian architecture trends. Inside, the stairwell and mantel-pieces feature beautifully carved woodwork, while the entrance is a skylit atrium panelled in burnished oak. The Society of Architectural Historians runs **free tours** on Wednesday at noon and on Saturday at 10am, with an additional tour offered from April to November on Saturday at 1pm. The latter includes a guided walk along Astor Street and a visit to the nearby **Madlener House**.

North of here, just below Lincoln Park, the conspicuous octagonal tower and nineteen chimneys mark the redbrick Roman Catholic **Archbishop's Residence** at 1555 N State Parkway.

Old Town

Old Town, spreading west of LaSalle Street to North Avenue, has a much more lived-in look than does the dandified Gold Coast. Originally a German immigrant community that sprang up around the 1873 St Michael's Church, the neighborhood boasts a broad ethnic and cultural mix – the result of the early immigrants moving onward and upward after World War II, and blacks and Italians moving in. While its refurbished century-old row houses and workers' cottages are prime real estate, as recently as thirty years ago its then shabby housing stock and derelict factories attracted a variety of creative types. Though **Wells Street**, the main drag, shows no signs of its hippie past, at least one survivor – the Second City comedy club – is still going strong. The rest of the neighborhood, which has benefited from the gentrification of neighboring Lincoln Park, is now crammed with some of the city's best bars, galleries and barbecue joints, and makes for a diverting afternoon's wander.

Summertime sees Old Town at its liveliest, particularly during the neighborhood's **Old Town Art Fair**, more a fun excuse to mingle with the crowds than for serious art buying.

Cabrini Green

The **Cabrini Green housing projects** have become synonymous in America with urban blight and gang violence – from the shooting of two police officers by a sniper in 1970 to the recent case of Girl X, a 9-year-old raped, abused and left for dead in a stairwell (she survived). Seventy-acre Cabrini Green is one of the saddest examples of misguided mid-twentieth-century urban planning, driven by the chronic housing shortage during World War II when returning veterans and new immigrants overwhelmed the city's housing market. The planned complex – named in honor of St Frances Xavier Cabrini, a nun who spent her life helping the poor – included suburban-style row houses, with small, neat yards and private entrances. For a while Cabrini Green seemed to be a success, providing affordable housing for low-income residents, but migration from the Deep South continued, and soon city housing was again under strain. In 1958, the Chicago Housing Authority added the Cabrini Extension, fifteen tower blocks nicknamed "The Reds" (after their color) and designed to house seven thousand people, and eight more high rises were added the following year – the William Green homes or "The Whites"; soon, however, like so many other urban high rises, the area was spiraling into decay.

Despite the lurid folklore about Cabrini Green (it's where the 1992 horror movie *Candyman* was set), it's no myth that the area remains a dangerous, no-go area, riven by gangs and drug problems. The city may be trying to encourage development in the area (including a newly built shopping center), but there's absolutely no reason for a casual visitor to Chicago to stray inside.

Wells Street and the Old Town Triangle

Old Town has little in the way of cultural sights, so a walk past the rows of Victorian homes and offbeat shops is the best approach. Especially noteworthy on Wells Street is the **House of Glunz**, 1206 N Wells St, a wine shop with an eclectic selection, dating to 1888. You can also poke around the local landmark **Barbara's Bookstore** up the street at no. 1350, an independent bookseller with a wide selection of fiction and children's books, and frequent author readings.

Farther up Wells Street, above North Avenue, begins the **Old Town Triangle**, a quaint little section of late-nineteenth-century cottages that have been preserved (to varying degrees of authenticity), thanks to an urban renewal project in the 1940s to protect the district's distinctive architecture. Since then, property values have climbed precipitously with the onslaught of gentrification, which has brought with it restaurants and shops. The neighborhood's chief claim to fame, however, is the vibrant **Second City comedy club**, 1616 N Wells St, which has been turning out stars since its doors opened in 1959 (see box overleaf; review on p.189). The grizzled **Old Town Ale House**, across the street at 219 W North Ave, sees a share of Second City comics at the bar, but it's also a Chicago institution in its own right (for review, see p.169).

St Michael's Church

Three blocks west, the massive **St Michael's Church**, 1660 N Hudson Ave, rises up, marking the center of the old German Catholic community that existed here during the mid to late 1800s. It was for years the tallest building in Chicago – even after the 1872 Fire that left only the charred walls and bell tower standing. Peek inside the Romanesque church built in its place for the pretty stained-glass windows.

The Second City

"To be, to be... sure beats the shit out of not to be."

John Belushi as Hamlet, Second City, Chicago, 1971

John Belushi may not have taken these words to heart, considering his premature end in 1982, but the **Second City improv club** that launched his career is still going strong, enjoying the kind of success expected of a First City venue. Taking its name from a biting *New Yorker* profile about Chicago's second-rung status, the club has been the last word on comedy in Chicago for forty-plus years, delivering a steady stream of quality acts on its cozy stage. Alan Alda, Alan Arkin and Ed Asner, followed by the likes of Bill Murray, Gilda Radner, Dan Aykroyd and Belushi in the 1970s, all had their start here, the latter becoming household names as the original cast of TV's long-running *Saturday Night Live*.

The Second City evolved from a drama troupe formed by students at the University of Chicago (Mike Nichols and Elaine May among them), becoming the improvisational Compass Players, who later settled into the club's present location in 1959.

Many of the club's alumni have gone on to star in feature films that have capitalized on the Second City's satirical humor: *National Lampoon's Animal House* (Belushi), *The Blues Brothers* (Aykroyd and Belushi), and *Caddyshack* (Murray) all have, for better or for worse, defined their careers, as have more recent vehicles starring Mike Myers and the late Chris Farley.

Though the Second City may have lost some of the manic energy of its heyday in the 1980s, it's still the best place to catch improv comedy in Chicago. For a review, see p.189.

South Loop and Near South

Much of South Chicago was built on two industries: railroads and printing. In the area immediately below the Loop it was printing presses that pushed growth; in fact, S Dearborn Street between Congress Parkway and Polk Street is known as **Printers Row**, after the massive printing works that hummed here in the late nineteenth century. Now, of course, the presses are long gone, replaced by automated, high-tech factories in the far suburbs, and the gigantic buildings that once housed them have been largely converted into condos, creating mini, self-contained communities dotted along the strip. The area's literary connections are still evident from the terrific **bookstores** here, as well as the numerous publishing offices (for a list of bookstores, see "Shopping," p.215).

The lakefront portion of the **South Loop** is one of the swishest parts of the city: there are massive greenspaces, with pockets of trees and the boastful **Buckingham Fountain**, bigger than the French original on which it's based. Often referred to as Chicago's front yard, **Grant Park** was built on landfill in the 1920s, a legacy of Daniel Burnham's revolutionary plans for Chicago, and is now used for many of the city's open-air festivals; there's also an extension – dubbed Millennium Park – that's due to open soon. The renamed **Museum Campus** to the south, which holds the Field Museum, Shedd Aquarium and the Adler Planetarium, was created in the late 1990s, when Chicago finally rerouted Lake Shore Drive to the west so that culture-hungry tourists wouldn't risk their lives scampering between these attractions.

The **Near South** is the first clear sign most visitors will see of Chicago's urban problems, thanks to the swaths of ill-kempt housing projects that begin here and continue on throughout the South Side. Aside from the historic **South Prairie Avenue district**, which preserves the palatial mansions of Chicago's former elite, the one safe, intriguing outpost out this way is Chicago's **Chinatown**, filled with markets and restaurants, and a great place for a cheap meal. Though the South Loop is safe for visitors, be aware that the area surrounding Chinatown is still rather iffy: take public transportation and you should be fine, but make sure not to wander outside the district's ten or so buzzing blocks.

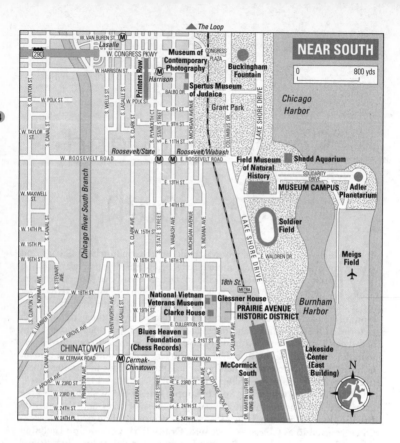

▲ The Loop

NEAR SOUTH

0   800 yds

Printers Row

Printers Row was for years an industrial wasteland, the last stop on most railroad lines and strewn with derelict warehouses and beer joints left over from its heyday as the center of the Midwestern printing industry. Like most other neighborhoods within a stone's throw of the Loop, however, it's been revitalized, and this short stretch manages to pull in more visitors with each passing year, especially in June during the lively **Printers Row Book Fair** (see p.209).

Dearborn Street Station

At the southern end of Printers Row, look out for the Romanesque Revival pile of **Dearborn Street Station**, a monument to Chicago's importance as the hub of the nation's railroad industry when the station was built in 1885. Where once thousands of the city's immigrants stepped off the trains, you'll now see a renovated office space; the station was closed in the 1970s after the declining railroad ceased to operate here.

Museum of Contemporary Photography

The blocks west of Printers Row, across from Grant Park, have a couple of small, noteworthy attractions. The **Museum of Contemporary Photography** at 600 S Michigan Ave on the Columbia College campus (Mon–Fri 10am–5pm, Thurs until 8pm, Sat noon–5pm; free; ☎312/663-5554, ⓦwww.mocp.org), is known for exhibits ranging from merely thought-provoking to flat-out weird. The museum has a rotating selection from its permanent collection on display that focuses on American photography since 1945, and it hosts temporary exhibits as well.

Spertus Museum

More cultural education awaits a few doors down, where the **Spertus Museum**, 618 S Michigan Ave (Mon–Wed & Sun 10am–5pm, Thurs 10am–8pm, Fri 10am–3pm; $5, students and seniors $3; ☎312/322-1747, ⓦwww.spertus.edu), houses the largest collection of Jewish art and artifacts in the Midwest, as well as consistently impressive temporary exhibits. Kids needn't feel left out: in the Rosenbaum ARTiFACT Center's archeological site, they can dig up dusty finds.

Grant Park

East of the Loop, **Grant Park** (daily 6am–11pm) provides a welcome but not entirely complete break from the downtown urban grid – wide strips of high-speed road and railroad slice through it, so casual rambling can be frustrating. The whole two-hundred-acre swath, stretching from Randolph Street south to Roosevelt Road, is sprinkled with sculptures and monuments, from a stern Lincoln to a proud Plains Indian on horseback.

The northern half of the park centers on the immense **Buckingham Fountain**, while close by, construction continues at a snail's pace on fifteen-acre **Millennium Park**, an ambitious plan for a 10,000-seat outdoor concert pavilion, outdoor ice-skating rink and lavish sculpture garden. Designed by Frank Gehry, the planned band shell is a flamboyant stainless-steel sculpture inspired by a "bouquet of flowers on the table" but closer in look to a fistful of steak knives. Millions of dollars over budget and years behind schedule, the park isn't likely to open before 2006.

The major attractions are gathered in the southern half of Grant Park, in something known as **Museum Campus** (☎312/409-4178, ⓦwww.museum campus.org), where three excellent museums are set among sculptures and terraced walkways.

As well, nearly every weekend in summer sees a musical festival here (be it gospel, blues, country, jazz or classical), held in the area around the Petrillo Music Shell. In early July the **Taste of Chicago** festival attracts some four million people to a week-long feeding frenzy, garnished with concerts and other live entertainment (for details on park events, see "Festivals and events" p.209).

Some history

During the late 1800s, the land that makes up today's Grant Park was being snapped up for rail expansion and future high rises, but two men – **Daniel**

Burnham and **Montgomery Ward**, the latter known for establishing the world's first mail-order business – were busy trying to protect the lakefront east of the Loop.Ward's prolonged battle to save the area from development actually had its roots as early as 1852, when the Illinois Central railroad built a trestle in Lake Michigan so that trains could reach the river. Ungainly as it was, the trestle buffered Michigan Avenue and its mansions from both floods and violent storm-driven waters, and over the years, the land between the rail tracks and the shore gradually began to fill in, especially after debris from the fire of 1871 was dumped here and the area named Lake Park. Its condition became so disgusting that Ward, nicknamed the "watchdog of the lakefront," began to fight for its renovation, much to the disbelief of local businessmen and city officials who considered the land fit for development and a source of revenue for the city.

Thanks to Ward's continuing legal fight, however, the land was left largely undeveloped (though McCormick Place did get built in the 1950s), and in 1901, the patch of green was renamed Grant Park. In time, Daniel Burnham's plan for the massive reconstruction of the city, which changed street grids and property lines, saved the lakefront "for the people." Though Burnham's ideas took decades to be fully realized, thanks to his initial plan the lakefront park now stretches some thirty miles from end to end.

Buckingham Fountain and around

Southeast of the Art Institute, **Buckingham Fountain** sits amid colonnades of trees and thousands of rose bushes. Donated to Grant Park in 1927 and modeled after a fountain at Versailles, this ornate pile of stacked pink marble provides a spectacle from May to October when it shoots more than a million gallons of water up to 150 feet in the air. It also plays host to popular light and water shows daily from dusk to 11pm. Strangely, the water circulation system is controlled by a computer more than seven hundred miles away in Atlanta, Georgia.

A few statues nearby are worth noting: across Columbus Avenue to the west of the fountain is the seated **Lincoln statue,** surveying the park from atop a pedestal. Like its counterpart in Lincoln Park, the statue was created by Augustus Saint-Gaudens, though it's more subdued. Flanking Congress Parkway near Michigan Avenue, **The Bowman and the Spearman** is an impressive pair of seventeen-foot-high bronze Indian warriors, created by Yugoslavian sculptor Ivan Mestrovic.

Field Museum of Natural History

Ten minutes' walk from Buckingham Fountain, the **Field Museum**, 1200 S Lake Shore Drive at Roosevelt Road (daily 9am–5pm; free tours Mon–Fri

11am & 2pm; $8; CTA bus #146; ☎312/922-9410, ⓦwww.fieldmuseum.org), is yet another legacy of the 1893 World's Columbian Exposition (although the current, updated building dates from 1921). The museum was created as a permanent home for many of the natural history exhibits that had been displayed at the exhibition and was endowed by millionaire Marshall Field, for whom it was named. These days, despite a few careworn exhibits, it's a fascinating museum collecting natural history's greatest hits, and vies with the more gimmicky Museum of Science and Industry in Hyde Park (see p.114) as the best way to captivate a child for an afternoon, if not longer.

The enormous, Greek-temple-like building is set on three floors, and is filled with over twenty million objects across six acres; don't let that daunt you, as with comfortable shoes and a plan of the museum (available at the information booth), it's easily navigable.

On the upper level, you'll find the best display of all, **Life Over Time**, which takes in 3.8 billion years of evolution – from the dawn of earth to the arrival of man – presented as a daily news show (there's even a jolly weatherman who, instead of offering weather forecasts, talks about environmental changes over thousands of years). Inside the exhibit, you'll find a large dinosaur display, including a full-size apatosaurus (once known as a brontosaurus) fossil plus an intriguing rundown of the effects of the Ice Age on earth. The only false note on this level is the **Plants of the World** exhibit, a fusty, cabinet-heavy slog through darkened rooms outlining the world's different ecosystems.

On the main floor, aside from Sue, the star attraction (see box below), stop by **Inside Ancient Egypt** for its tomb of Unis-ankh, son of a fifth-dynasty pharaoh; the limestone chunks were brought here and reassembled by the museum's first president, Edward Ayer. A dedicated Egypt enthusiast, he also purchased many of the mummies and coffins on display in the lower part of this exhibit; don't miss the marketplace at the end for its lively evocation of daily life in ancient Egypt.

Sue and Bushman

The *Tyrannosaurus rex* known as **Sue** is arguably the crown jewel of the Field Museum's collection: the most complete *T-rex* fossil ever found, missing only one foot, one "hand" and a few back bones. That she (actually, her gender is officially undetermined) was able to remain in such a preserved state is likely due to being killed by an avalanche or other such disaster that covered her corpse before predators could tear it apart and disperse the bones.

Sue was found on a South Dakota reservation by fossil hunter Susan Hendrickson in 1991, on the property of a Sioux Indian, Maurice Williams, who was paid $5000 from fossil hunters to renounce all claims. The government soon got wind of the discovery and impounded the *T-rex* skeleton pending a decision on ownership (the *T-rex* was found, after all, on government land). Eventually, after a court decided in Williams' favor, he auctioned off the bones to the highest bidder; thanks to the combined corporate muscle of *McDonald's* and Disney, the Field was able to outbid its rivals for the skeleton – for the staggering sum of $8.4 million.

Poor beloved **Bushman**, once one of the museum's most popular displays, is now housed downstairs and virtually forgotten thanks to the arrival of Sue. It's an ignominious fate for the massive gorilla from Lincoln Park Zoo who was so well known at his death in 1950 that he was laid in state for several days so that mourners could pay their respects. He looks faintly ridiculous now, trapped in an eternal glower inside a glass case that he would have shattered with one fist when alive.

On the ground level is the trippy **Underground Adventures** exhibit: upon entering, visitors are "shrunk" to one hundredth of their size and set on a pathway under the earth, surrounded by soil, giant roots and oversized, fiberglass insects, including a Cadillac-sized crayfish. Also on the floor is the preserved figure of **Bushman**, a six-foot lowland gorilla (see box above), as well as plenty of crowd-pleasing temporary exhibits.

Shedd Aquarium

On the shores of Lake Michigan, the **Shedd Aquarium** (summer, daily 9am–6pm; rest of year, Mon–Fri 9am-5pm, Sat & Sun 9am-6pm; $15, $7 on Mon, when Aquarium section only is free; ☏312/939-2438, ⓦ www.shedd.org), proclaims itself the largest indoor aquarium in the world. The 1920s structure is rather old-fashioned, but the lighthearted and tongue-in-cheek displays – some use *Far Side* cartoons – are informative and entertaining. The central exhibit, set in an octagonal space, is a 90,000-gallon re-creation of a Caribbean coral reef, complete with sharks (fed daily at 11am and 2pm), turtles and thousands of rainbow-colored tropical fish, surrounded by a hundred lesser tanks. Highlights include the sluggish and comical South American freckled sideneck turtles, housed across from a 250-pound alligator snapping turtle, which trundles to the surface to breathe every half-hour.

The recently added **Oceanarium** provides an enormous contrast, with its modern lake-view home for marine mammals such as Pacific dolphins and beluga whales (which consume nearly six hundred pounds of seafood daily). Designed to replicate a rocky Alaskan coastline, it's a carefully disguised amphitheater for demonstrations of the animals' "natural behavior," such as jumping out of the water and fetching plastic rings. Performances are four times daily and you need a ticket; at other times you can watch from underwater galleries as the animals cruise around the tank, and listen to the clicks, beeps and whistles they use to communicate with each other.

Eight years in the making, the aquarium's latest addition is set to open in the spring of 2003. The **Wild Reef – Sharks at Shedd** exhibit will feature an underwater coral garden consisting of 26 different habitats and teeming with hundreds of species of reef fish, many of them big enough to hold their own against the dozens of sharks.

Adler Planetarium

At the eastern end of the Museum Campus, and jutting out into Lake Michigan, is the expanded and renovated **Adler Planetarium** (daily 9.30am–4.30pm, first Fri of each month until 10pm; $10–15 for 1–2 shows, free Tues; ☏312/922-7827, ⓦ www.adlerplanetarium.org), whose excellent temporary exhibits tend to overshadow its more staid permanent collection – a rundown of everything you learned, and forgot, in high school science class. The nine permanent exhibits cover the usual topics ("Our Solar System," "The Milky Way Galaxy," "History of Astronomy"), but don't spend too much time here as the shows and temporary exhibits are usually more diverting.

The Adler houses two planetariums that put on half-hour shows several times daily. Recent shows at the more traditional planetarium – the **Sky Theater** – on the upper level, have looked at the story behind the Star of Bethlehem as well as photos taken by the Hubble Telescope; when there isn't a show on, it's cool for a look at the clear night sky projected on the dome by the Zeiss projector. On the lower level, the 360-degree **StarRider Theater** is an interactive digital movie theater that, like the Sky Theater, offers excellent shows of the explore-the-universe type, but with some added excitement; using "controls" in your armrest, you participate in flight-simulation shows.

Outside, by the planetarium's front steps is a nondescript, bronze sundial by Henry Moore, called *Man Enters the Cosmos*. From here, you'll have great views of the downtown skyline and, with the small Meigs Field Airport just to the south, don't be surprised if low-flying planes appear about to crash into the lake.

Soldier Field

Just south of Museum Campus, the 100-foot Doric colonnades of oversized **Soldier Field** mark it as a sports palace of a bygone age. Designed by Holabird & Roach, the seven-acre stadium was built in the 1920s as a memorial to American soldiers who died in the two world wars. Since then, the stadium has been the stage for many famous sporting events, including the 1927 heavyweight boxing rematch between Jack Dempsey and Gene Tunney that ended with the famously controversial "long count."

Home to the Chicago Bears for more than thirty years, Soldier Field has been closed for a $600-million facelift (to the chagrin of nearly all Chicago traditionalists), and is set to reopen in late 2003. When all is said and done, though, the Bears will remain, everyone will continue to get the name wrong (not Soldiers) and die-hard fans will keep braving the arctic winds off the lake (notice the teams of loud bare-chested men, seemingly numb to the sub-zero temperatures).

Prairie Avenue Historic District

The **Prairie Avenue Historic District** was the city's first elite neighborhood, and, for a brief time, the most expensive street in America outside New York's glitzy Fifth Avenue. Some of Chicago's first homes were built around Prairie Avenue in the mid-eighteenth century, and it came to be known as "Millionaire's Row" – the most coveted property in town – after George Pullman, creator of the Pullman railroad car, and some twenty industrial magnates settled here after the Chicago Fire, building extravagant mansions along S Prairie Avenue. Though a handful of their homes have survived, only **Glessner House** and **Clarke House** are open to the public, providing a glimpse of Chicago's Gilded Age.

By the beginning of the twentieth century, the rich had moved on to the lakefront north of the Loop to join millionaire Potter Palmer (see p.69), and the area around Prairie Avenue plunged into decades of seediness, helped along by the saloons and brothels that had sprung up nearby following the success of the railroads leading into the South Loop. In recent years, the city has tried to transform this now semi-industrial area into a fashionable loft neighborhood, but it's too early to tell whether the plan will be a success.

You're best off **getting here** by cab, bus or train, as the route is confusing and the streets are just not safe. It's about a $5 cab ride from the Loop, or a

△ Grant Park's Buckingham Fountain

Walking tours of Prairie Avenue, put on from June through October by Prairie Avenue House Museums, point out the avenue's prominent residents, the architecture of the homes and the history of the district's decline and renewal.

The only way to see inside **Clarke House** and **Glessner House** – the most visited of the bunch – is on a guided tour, which leaves from the Tour Center (the Glessners' former stables) on the 18th Street side of the house (Wed–Sun, tours of Clarke House at noon, 1pm and 2pm, tours of Glessner House, 1pm, 2pm and 3pm; $11 for both houses, $7 for one house; free Wed; ℡312/326-1480, ⓦwww.glesser house.org). Tours are on a first-come, first-served basis and are limited to twelve people for Glessner House, seven for Clarke House. To see both houses, be sure to show up at the Tour Center no later than 2pm.

short hop on the Michigan Avenue CTA buses (#1, #3 and #4), all of which stop at the corner of 18th Street and Michigan Avenue, in front of the Prairie Avenue House Museums (see box above).

Clarke House

Built in 1836, **Clarke House** at 1855 S Indiana Ave, is Chicago's oldest house and seems more suited to a New England town than a masonry-heavy city like Chicago. Even as far back as the 1850s, the house was reason to make an excursion here; city-dwellers used to come by carriage to see this white, timber-frame Greek Revival house with its white colonnade, built in what was then a forest. Later, the house spent many years as a community center before being gussied up as a minor museum of interior decor in the late 1970s.

Although the house has moved twice to avoid demolition (it's now just two blocks from its original location), the interior has faithfully recreated the Clarke family home, though with none of the original furnishings, which did not survive. Guided tours of the house amply evoke their pioneer existence during the early days of industrialization and the American migration west.

Glessner House Museum

One of the few structures to have survived the intervening years in this neighborhood is the Romanesque 1886 **Glessner House**, 1800 S Prairie Ave, Chicago's only remaining H.H. Richardson–designed house, standing sentry on the southwest corner of Prairie Avenue and 18th Street. Home to John and Frances Glessner, its unadorned structure was a departure from the more decorative traditional Victorian architecture, causing outrage among the neighbors, especially industrialist George Pullman. "I do not know what I have ever done," he reportedly said, "to have that thing staring at me in the face every time I go out my door." Behind the forbidding facade, the house opens onto a large garden court, its interior filled with Arts and Crafts furniture, and swathed in William Morris fabrics and wall coverings, and generously panelled in oak. Today, it exists almost entirely furnished as the Glessners left it, crammed with the family's collection of ceramics, delicate Art Nouveau and Venetian glass, plus intricate hand-carved furniture and ornamental pieces by Chicago artisan Isaac Scott.

Between Glessner House and Clarke House, the **Chicago Women's History Park** makes for a nice little walk along a curving path lined with a hundred plaques commemorating Chicago's famous women. Another worthy attraction around here is the **Woman Made Gallery** just south of Glessner House at 1900 S Prairie Ave (☎312/328-0038), which promotes the work of women artists with monthly exhibitions.

National Vietnam Veterans Art Museum

Next door to the Glessner House, the **National Vietnam Veterans Art Museum**, 1801 S Indiana Ave (Tues–Sun 11am–6pm, Wed until 9pm; $6; ☎312/326-0270, ⓦwww.nvvam.org), focuses on the war from a personal point of view. Displayed over three floors, the somber and, at times, wrenching exhibits include a mix of paintings, photographs, sculptures, drawings, diaries and other artifacts by American veterans of the war, and to a lesser extent, soldiers from Australia and North and South Vietnam.

One of the most powerful works hangs from the ceiling above the front desk: *Above and Beyond*, whose ten-foot by forty-foot sculpture consists of 58,000 dog tags representing Americans killed in the war, each stainless-steel tag imprinted with a soldier's name, branch of service and casualty date, and hung in chronological order, beginning with the first soldier killed in 1957 and ending with the last in 1975. The solitary black dog tag hangs in memory of soldiers who died from their injuries after the war.

Veterans are on hand to lead discussions for the visiting school groups; join one of these groups, if you can, and experience a powerful firsthand account.

South of Prairie Avenue

The rather cold-looking, steel-and-glass monstrosity southeast of the museum, at 2301 S Lake Shore Drive, is **McCormick Place**, a sprawling convention complex designed by Helmut Jahn. As there's really not much to see here, casual visitors are better off heading five blocks west to the **Blues Heaven Foundation** museum at 2120 S Michigan Ave, inside the building that once housed the legendary Chess Records, the greatest of all blues labels.

Started in 1957 by brothers Leonard and Phil Chess, the studio launched so many top blues musicians – everyone from Willie Dixon and Bo Diddley to Muddy Waters, Koko Taylor, and even Chuck Berry – that it became a shrine of sorts, nowadays run by the Willie Dixon Blues Heaven Foundation for the preservation of the blues. The Rolling Stones, who took their name from a Muddy Waters tune, even cut an album here and immortalized the place in their song "2120 South Michigan."

These days, you can take a **tour** of the renovated studio, though unless you're a blues aficionado or simply want to say you've been to the site, you're better off skipping it altogether – you won't see much beyond a sterile recording studio and there's little in the way of informed commentary by guides. Tours last a half-hour to 45 minutes (it's best if you call ahead to book a place) and end with a short "Keepin' the Blues Alive" video (daily noon–2pm; $10 donation; ☎312/808-1286). For more on Chicago blues music, see Contexts, p.248.

Chinatown

A mile west of McCormick Place, and best accessed on either the Red Line to Cermak-Chinatown or bus #24 to E Cermak Road and S Wentworth Avenue, the narrow, ten-block area of **Chinatown** has maintained its decidedly authentic feel. The distinctive green and red gate at Wentworth Avenue and Cermak Road marks the beginning of the district, and once through here you could just as well be in downtown Hong Kong as central Chicago.

Chicago's first Chinese immigrants began arriving in the 1870s, after the completion of the first transcontinental railroad when many of them found themselves out of work and without a place to live. They soon carved out an area around Cermak Road and Wentworth Avenue, two miles south of the Loop, though in time overcrowding threatened to strain the budding neighborhood's infrastructure and construction of city highways in the area restricted further growth. Even so, Chinatown has managed to survive and remains almost entirely Chinese.

There's nothing in the way of traditional sights around here, except the **On Leong Building**, 2216 S Wentworth Ave, easily identified by its large green and red pagodas – formerly the Chinese city hall and long the heart of the bustling commercial district. Today it houses, among other things, the only indigenous Chinese shrine in the Midwest. **Chinatown square** is an offshoot just to the northwest, with more shops, restaurants, plus the Chamber of Commerce. It's fun to poke around the little groceries filled with exotic spices, myriad teas, medicinal herbs and exotic-looking vegetables, but the real attraction here is the food: you'll be spoiled for choice among the more than forty **restaurants** serving inexpensive Mandarin, Szechuan, Shanghai and Cantonese cuisine; *Emperor's Choice* on Wentworth Ave and *Three Happiness* on W Cermak Road are among the best. For reviews of these and other restaurants in the area, see "Eating," p.141.

A few boisterous festivals also make the neighborhood worth checking out: July boasts the popular Lantern Festival, and February sees the vibrant Chinese New Year Festival take over the local streets (for more on these happenings, see "Festivals and events" p.209).

Bucktown, Wicker Park and around

The districts of **BUCKTOWN** and **WICKER PARK**, around three miles northwest of the Loop, are among Chicago's edgiest, home to a lively alternative music scene, numerous thrift stores and a fairly thriving café culture. The **UKRAINIAN VILLAGE,** the districts' younger sibling further south, is less affected: it's still dominated by the Eastern European immigrants who settled here a hundred years ago – you may hear it referred to by local Poles as *Helenowo*, after the area's sizeable Polish Roman Catholic parish.

Gentrification began in Bucktown, the northernmost of these three areas, and has gradually bled south over the past fifteen years. Largely ruled by Latino gangs, Wicker Park remained a staunch no-go zone until the housing prices in Bucktown skyrocketed; then, displaced artists made the leap south over the railroad tracks at North Avenue and established homes in Wicker Park, as well.

While there are no big-ticket sights in any of these locales, you'll find a couple of rewarding pockets, such as the quiet streets of the **Wicker Park historic district** (especially Hoyne and Pierce avenues) lined with some of the city's finest examples of Victorian-era architecture; many have been superbly, if a little self-consciously, restored. The best way to see these neighborhoods, however, is after dark: the nightlife here is hands down the best in the city, centered on the boisterous "six corners" intersection of **Milwaukee**, **North** and **Damen** avenues; there, you'll notice the contrast between the modern, concrete low rises on the main drags and the handsome Victorians dotting the back streets. The other commercial hubs – **North Avenue, Division Street** and **Chicago Avenue** – run east–west and serve as the informal dividing lines for Bucktown, Wicker Park and the Ukrainian Village, respectively. Although in general these neighborhoods are no longer as iffy as they were in the early 1990s, be on alert for some gang activity, especially in Wicker Park west of Western Avenue; stick to the main thoroughfares (and don't cross Western Avenue) and you should have few problems.

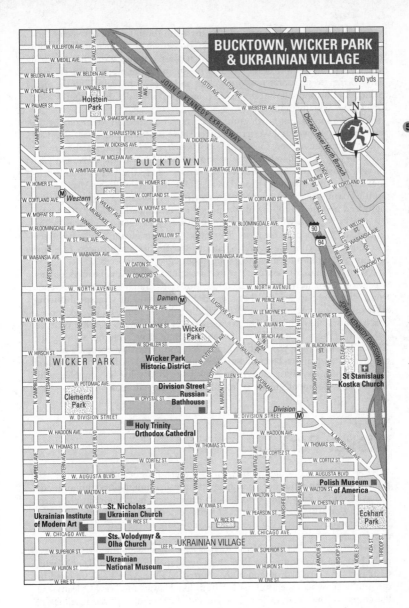

BUCKTOWN, WICKER PARK & UKRAINIAN VILLAGE

0   600 yds

Bucktown

Much like many of Chicago's inner suburbs, **Bucktown** began life as an immi-grant hub: Germans, Poles and other Eastern Europeans who arrived in the mid-nineteenth century settled on and around Milwaukee Avenue, an old

Native American trail that evolved into the main thoroughfare between farm-lands northwest of the city. By the 1980s, Bucktown was down and out, with correspondingly rock-bottom rents, and it wasn't long before hipsters had moved in, pushing most of the original Polish and more recent Hispanic residents further west. Soon low-fi rock clubs and cafés were reclaiming the area, making it clean and safe, but much less interesting culturally than either Wicker Park or the Ukrainian Village.

Bucktown spreads just north of the six corners, bounded on either side by the Kennedy Expressway and Western Avenue. Above this sprawling intersection are a bevy of restaurants and cafés (plus a few galleries); of special interest are the *Northside Café*, a bustling burger joint and bar at 1635 N Damen Ave, and *Club Lucky*, a short hop away at 1824 Wabansia Ave, where the former Polish banquet hall and bar has been restored to its 1930s glory. As well, the *Map Room* at 2100 W Armitage Ave is a terrific low-key café by day and a convivial pub by night, and be sure to stop by old-fashioned ice cream parlor *Margie's Candies*, a few blocks west on Western Avenue, which has been churning out delicious homemade concoctions for more than eighty years; its quaint booths have seen everybody from Al Capone and Sinatra to the Beatles and Princess Di – the Smashing Pumpkins even wrote a song about tables six and seven.

Restaurants and bars aside, it's worth a wander around Bucktown's quieter streets for a look at the variety of architecture. The stretch of Wabansia Avenue from Milwaukee to Ashland has a good representation of Chicago **housing styles** – be it contemporary or Victorian, single- or multi-family residences, coach houses, flats or lofts. The cornerstone of Bucktown's development sits just west of here at no. 2300. The rather nondescript building housing the **Clock Tower Lofts**, was built around 1900 and originally occupied by curtain makers and tailors. The building was entirely gutted in the early 1990s and converted into airy lofts, and within a few years their value had doubled, with waves of development spreading from here in all directions.

Wicker Park

Wicker Park remains slightly truer to its Eastern European roots than nearby Bucktown. Despite the encroaching gentrification, immigrant communities do still exist among artsy types who've been driven here by rising rents elsewhere in the city, creating an eclectic mix of artists, elderly women in babushkas and black-clad youth, all sharing the sidewalk en route to the café, deli or nearest poetry slam.

The latest band of hipsters to call Wicker Park home were the seven strangers picked to live in a house and have their lives taped for MTV's **Real World: Chicago**. The city had obsequiously courted MTV, having been snubbed by the producers who'd used funkier locations like Hawaii and New Orleans over the course of the previous ten years. But when the show arrived in Chicago, instead of fending off wide-eyed, autograph-hungry teens, producers found themselves protecting the cast from fire-spitting locals and occasional violence. Ironically, most of the protesters were MTV-generation artists and musicians, miffed that the network would dare share their favorite haunts with the world.

Though it's not much to look at, there is an eponymous park in Wicker Park, just south of the six corners, named for brothers Joel and Charles Wicker who donated it in 1870. The swan pond and park-front mansions are long gone,

The Wicker Park historic district

Chicago's architectural blockbusters, whether pioneering skyscrapers or modern engineering marvels, tend to be crammed into the Loop, but the northwest district of Wicker Park has its own immaculately maintained gems – nineteenth-century Victorians spared Chicago's wrecking ball to become a designated **historic district**.

This leafy area, bounded by N Damen Avenue and N Leavitt Street, stretching from Caton to Division streets (a sliver of it falls in neighboring Bucktown), is one of the most stringently gentrified segments of this up-and-coming area. Many of the buildings here were built from masonry after the 1871 Fire to meet new fireproofing codes, and exist under a slew of zoning laws, building codes and committees to ensure that local vistas can't be ruined by concrete tower blocks.

Start a walking tour of the area on **N Hoyne Avenue**, once known as "Beer Baron Row" for the number of brewing tycoons who built their homes here. Of the many eye-catching old buildings, the two most prominent are **nos. 1407** and **1521**. The former is set on the corner of Schiller Street, its onetime grandeur evident from the adjoining coach-house and enormous octagonal tower, though sadly, it's one of the least well preserved on the street. The latter (a block north) is in better condition: note the elaborate, wrought-iron scrollwork and table-leg columns, as well as the massive ornamental canopy over the entranceway. The Queen Anne period house, topped by a turret with a witch's hat roof, also preserves the expensive curved glass that was made possible late in the nineteenth century by industrial innovations. It's also worth stopping by **no. 1558**, at the junction with North Avenue, whose elaborately restored exterior features ironwork on its tower, leaded windows and lime paint with dark green contrasts.

Head back to **W Pierce Avenue** for more fine Victorian homes. The most famous is the **Paderewski House** (no. 2138), built in 1886 and onetime residence of the Polish consulate; the house was renamed in honor of the famed Polish pianist after he performed on its porch. Today, it's still one of the grandest in the area, a double-fronted mansion with a veranda even outside its dormer windows. Across the street is the unmistakable **Gingerbread House**, at 2137 W Pierce Ave, so named for the look of its intricate, machine-cut moldings. Built in 1888, this late Victorian masterpiece is painted in an eye-popping gold, ochre and blue color scheme – a far cry from the sober paint that would have graced it when it was built. **Nos. 2118** and **2046** farther down are also notable: the former for its faux-Gothic decorative elements above the upper windows, the latter for its rounded-glass bay windows.

Skip over North Avenue into Bucktown to **Concord Street** for the last of the important rows. Many of the houses on this stretch were built from stone by wealthy, late-nineteenth-century industrialists, and so have weathered well. The only thing disrupting the old world, suburban calm is the El, which now rumbles along the street's eastern reaches. Here, look out for the graphic, stained-glass features in the windows of **no. 2140**. Also note the houses that have suffered stylistic alterations, from the stone cladding that smothers **no. 2121** (the original detailing is still visible above the dormer window) to the Queen Anne mansion, **no. 2138**, whose rounded turret windows have been replaced by flat panes to save money.

Be sure not to miss the wonderful building at **2041 North Ave**, at Milwaukee, which once housed Turkish and Russian baths. This large but delicate white structure has been converted into a restaurant, but the fish reliefs above each window bear witness to its original use.

and there's just a plain-looking fountain breaking up this little patch of green. Writer Nelson Algren once lived in one of the pretty Victorian homes south of the park – but beware: after sundown it's best to steer clear of the park as it's known as a haven for drug dealers.

In a city full of ornate churches, the **St Stanislaus Kostka Church**, 1351 W Evergreen Ave (℡773/278-2470), west of Wicker Park, still stands out. Towering more than two hundred feet tall, the church has a stunning baroque interior, complete with chandeliers and stained-glass windows, which you can view by appointment. Built in 1876, the church was for many years the stronghold of the city's Polish Catholic community, once the heart of "Stanislawowo" and later "Kostkaville." As the area became increasingly gentrified and with the building of the Kennedy Expressway, much of the Polish community moved away; these days masses are given in English and Spanish as well as Polish, reflecting the area's changing make-up.

Just south of the church is **Division Street**, a once dangerous expressway made famous by Studs Terkel's *Division Street America*, a penetrating portrait of Chicago's hardscrabble urban life. In recent years, the street's rough reputation has been softened somewhat with the arrival of lounge-style restaurants and lower crime rates, but there's still enough grit left here to merit caution.

For a one-of-a-kind Chicago experience, head to the **Division Street Russian Bathhouse** at no. 1916 (Mon–Thurs 8am–10pm, Fri & Sat, 7am–10pm, Sun 6am–10pm; $22 for all-day admission, a towel, a locker key and soap, and massages start at $25 for 30min; ℡773/384-9671), a throwback to Chicago's stockyard days, when residential indoor plumbing wasn't as common as it is today. One of the few remaining *schvitz* (Yiddish for "sweat") places left in the country, the humble bathhouse has traditionally seen men from all walks of life unwind in its blistering 180°F steam rooms and ice-cold pools, including more than a few celebrities – check out the signed photos on the wall. (The owners have been leasing space to European Spa and Turkish Baths, ℡773/394-0500, which runs women-only steam rooms and saunas removed from the men's facilities and offers manicures, pedicures and facial treatments, too.)

Afterwards a stop at **Letizia's Natural Bakery**, just up Division at no. 2146, will replenish whatever you've sweated out. This tiny Italian-style bakery serves up good cappuccino and focaccia.

While the six corners area south of North Avenue has more commercial attractions than you'd ever visit, a few are worth noting for their lively scene or historic value. Along Milwaukee Avenue, south of North Avenue, look out for *Earwax*, 1564 N Milwaukee Ave, an enormous carnival-themed coffee-house-cum-video store; the hugely popular *Bongo Room*, 1470 N Milwaukee, known for its long waits and mouthwatering brunch menu. On a nice day, there aren't many better places to sip a beer and watch the Wicker Park street life go by than at the *Pontiac Café*, 1531 N Damen Ave, a former mechanic's garage.

Shoppers will find some good browsing around here, especially at Reckless Records, 1532 N Milwaukee Ave, and at vintage clothiers Recycle, 1474 N Milwaukee Ave, and Una Mae's Freak Boutique, 1422 N Milwaukee Ave – both as eclectic as they sound.

Ukrainian Village

The dominant feature of the low-rise skyline of the **Ukrainian Village** is the ornate, onion-domed roofs of **St Nicholas Ukrainian Catholic Cathedral**, 2238 W Rice St, at N Oakley Boulevard (tours by appointment, call

☎773/276-4537, ⓦwww.stnicholaseparchy.org), which was built in 1913 when the surrounding area was little but pasture. Almost one hundred years later, the church remains the hub of the local Ukrainian community and all services, except one on Sunday, are held in the native language.

The cathedral is a scaled-down model of St Sofia in Kiev, with 13 rather than the original's 32 domes, but it's a magnificent replica nonetheless, all beige brick and greenish copper. The mosaic in the main loggia above the entrance-way was installed in 1988 to commemorate the 1000th anniversary of Christianity's arrival in the Ukraine, and features the king who ushered in its acceptance, St Volodymyr (see below). It's well worth calling ahead to arrange a tour of the dazzling, Byzantine-style mosaics in the interior, as well as the largest chandelier in North America (holding a blinding 480 bulbs).

Two blocks south, at 739 Oakley Blvd, on the southeast corner of Chicago Avenue, stands **SS Volodymyr and Olha Ukrainian Catholic Church** (☎773/276-3990), whose squat, monumental structure is more modern but less intriguing than the neighboring cathedral. Its interior is appropriately fine, but the real reason to stop by is the enormous, glittering mosaic above the main entrance, which depicts the church's namesake saints, St Volodymyr and his mother St Olha, accepting Christianity into the Ukraine.

The Polish Museum of America

Preserving the heritage of the city's more than one million Poles, the long-standing **Polish Museum of America**, 984 Milwaukee Ave, at Augusta Boulevard (Mon–Wed & Fri–Sun 11am–4pm; $3 donation; ☎773/384-3352, ⓦpma. prcua. org),) has an eclectic mix of art and artifacts, mainly from Poland but relating to Polish Americans as well. Notable for its holdings of the personal effects of renowned pianist, statesman and former Polish prime minister Ignacy Paderewski, the collection also features several exhibits sent from Poland for the city's 1939 World's Fair but stranded here when the country was invaded during World War II.

Besides the displays of vibrant Polish folk costumes, military uniforms, hand-carved Easter eggs and religious relics, your eyes will be drawn to the huge painting in the Great Hall of Revolutionary War hero Casimir Pulaski, as well as the striking, thirty-foot-high stained-glass window made for the 1939 World's Fair.

Lincoln Park

Snooty hipsters deride **LINCOLN PARK** as a yuppie haven, filled with weekend rollerbladers working up a sweat before grabbing a latte. It's certainly true that the area is upscale, middle-class and rather mainstream, but its gorgeous namesake park is a powerful lure for any visitor, as are the leafy, tree-lined streets of the eponymous neighborhood. The one offbeat section exists in Lincoln Park's northern reaches around **DePaul University**: this enormous Catholic institution, better known for hard partying than devout prayers, has created a small but funky scene in the surrounding blocks.

Originally filled with orchards supplying produce to the city farther south, the Lincoln Park area was converted into Chicago's first cemetery in the mid-nineteenth century. The local dead rested in peace for only a few years before city bigwigs had their bodies moved elsewhere to make room for a massive,

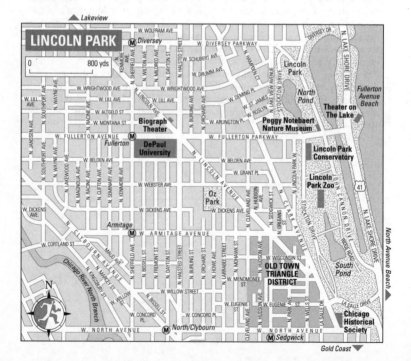

prairie-inspired greenspace fit for the unofficial capital of the Midwest. The park, established in 1864 and named in honor of president (and Illinois native) Abraham Lincoln, is a staggering slab of greenery, stretching more than 1200 acres and home to one of America's last free zoos. But it would be a hundred years before the surrounding neighborhood reached the same chic desirability of the park. An immigrant enclave that fell into disrepair through under-investment and lack of city interest, the Lincoln Park neighborhood was transformed in the 1970s after local institutions like DePaul University successfully agitated for attention (and dollars) – more than $300 million was pumped into a forcible gentrification project that's left the area as it is today: clean, green and just a tiny bit bland.

You'll find plenty of bars, clubs and restaurants here – especially along **N Halsted Street** and the diagonal arteries of **N Lincoln Avenue** and **N Clark Street**. Expect to rub shoulders with the Midwestern college graduates and upwardly mobile twentysomethings who've flocked here to nest alongside young families, despite the soaring rents. Not surprisingly, Lincoln Park is one of the safest places in the city – the biggest stress you're likely to face is finding a parking spot, so the best way to get here is by hopping on the Brown, Red or Purple El lines to the Fullerton stop.

The park

Extending some six miles from North Avenue to Foster Avenue along the lakefront, **Lincoln Park** (daily 7am–11pm) is lush and conspicuously devoid of commercial development, while offering some of the most dramatic views of the downtown skyline. The park's main tourist attractions are the **Lincoln Park Zoo** and the **Lincoln Park Conservatory**, but it's probably best experienced for its natural delights; thanks to the lake's natural regulation of air temperature, it makes for a comfortable place to laze through a hot summer's day, including the beaches, where throngs of locals come to sunbathe or play volleyball.

Running the length of the park is the scenic lakefront path, excellent for running, rollerblading and biking, and the easiest way to reach many of the park's beaches, playgrounds, tennis courts and ball fields. In fact, Chicago's reputation as one of the most bike-friendly cities in the country is due, in large part, to the extensive network of bike paths here. For details on rental outfits, see box below.

Although the wide streak of Lake Shore Drive cuts the park off from the water, you'll have plenty of chances to cross it via pedestrian tunnels and bridges.

Park practicalities

For **park programs and general information**, contact the Chicago Park District at ☎312/742-7529 or visit their website, ⊛www.chicagoparkdistrict.com

The **Bike Chicago** booth rents bikes for $8.75 per hour and $34 per day; they also rent in-line skates (see p.204). Between May and September, you can rent **paddleboats** on Lincoln Park's South Pond, outside *Café Brauer* (2021 N Stockton Drive, $10/half-hour or $15/hr). Boat rentals are from 10am to dusk. For more on these and other activities, see "Sports and outdoor activities," p.202.

Chicago Historical Society and around

At the park's southwest edge, the redbrick and glass **Chicago Historical Society**, 1601 N Clark St (Mon–Sat 9.30am–4.30pm, Sun noon–5pm; $6, free Mon; ☏312/642-4600, ⓦwww.chicagohs.org), holds an exhaustive record of the city's growth from its frontier days, either on display in its permanent and temporary exhibits or archived in its research center.

On the **first floor**, costumed staff bring to life Illinois pioneer days, demonstrating chores such as spinning flax and weaving yarn. A miniature Conestoga wagon is a minor highlight of the section devoted to the US garrison Fort Dearborn and Chicago's early days as a fur-trading center. Among the interactive exhibits, the one on the Chicago Fire stands out more than most (hours vary on weekdays, Sat 11am-4.30pm, Sun noon–4.30pm).

The bulk of the **second floor** is taken up by the American History wing. Many of Abraham Lincoln's personal effects can be viewed in the exhibit "A House Divided: America in the Age of Lincoln," a trenchant detailed look at slavery and the Civil War through a wealth of artifacts. Chief among these are Lincoln's famed correspondence with General Ulysses S. Grant, the table on which he wrote the Emancipation Proclamation, and his deathbed. Elsewhere on the floor, the "We the People" exhibit looks back at the American Revolution, focusing on the unsung heroes and lesser-known personalities who helped shape the nation between 1765 and 1820. As well, you can view pictures documenting Chicago history from 1803 to 1933.

Only serious history buffs should head up to the third-floor **research center**, which holds thousands of newspaper-clipping files and more than 1.5 million images of Chicago dating from the early nineteenth century, as well as paintings, sculptures, recordings and costumes. Noteworthy are the Studs Terkel Oral History Archives, where you can listen to fifty years' worth of radio interviews conducted by Chicago's renowned historian, and the Charles F. Murphy Architectural Study Center, a huge collection of drawings, photographs and models contributed by Chicago's major architects.

On a grassy flat, a few blocks east of the Historical Society, you'll find the white **Couch Mausoleum**, the last remaining sign of the park's past life as a cemetery. The Couch family refused to move the mausoleum to make room for the park, a court case that went all the way to the Supreme Court.

East of the Chicago Historical Society, Augustus Saint-Gaudens' **The Standing Lincoln** statue of the sixteenth president appears poised to address a congregation; the statue is considered the high point of Saint-Gaudens' career.

Two blocks east, volleyball tournaments and jugglers keep things lively at **North Avenue Beach**, a patch of sand where Chicagoans come to sun and be seen. If admiring the city skyline sounds more appealing, join the crowds for a drink at *Castaway's Bar & Grill* (see p.172), on the rooftop of the North Avenue beach house.

The Lincoln Park Zoo and around

In the heart of the park sits the venerable **Lincoln Park Zoo**, which you can enter at 2200 N Cannon Drive, Lake Shore Drive or Fullerton Parkway (Nov–March 8am–5pm, April–Oct 8am–6pm, Sat until 7pm in summer; free, parking $9; zoo grounds close one hour after last ticket sale; ☏312/742-2000, ⓦwww.lpzoo.com). The zoo is the oldest in the country, as well as one of Chicago's last major freebies – although the hefty parking charge tends to

△ Paddleboats in Licoln park

negate that deal somewhat. Opened in 1868 with the gift of two swans from New York's Central Park, Lincoln Park Zoo's 35-acre lakefront site is home to more than one thousand animals, divided between four trails, marked blue, red, gold and green, that snake through its grounds. The zoo itself is in a major state of flux, undergoing extensive construction work and renovation.

Though best known for its great apes, the zoo is currently refitting its **Great Ape House** and many of its residents are on loan to other zoos until 2005, as are the elephants and giraffes of the **African Journey** exhibit, set to reopen by mid-2003. In the meantime, monkey-lovers should check out the **Primate House** for the smaller lemurs and howler monkeys. Other highlights worth hitting are the **Kovler Lion House**, with its impressive collection of big cats and the **Farm-in-the-Zoo**, aimed squarely at little ones, a five-acre replica of a Midwestern farm.

Faintly reminiscent of London's famed Crystal Palace, and on a far smaller scale, the **Lincoln Park Conservatory** stands just south of Fullerton Parkway on Stockton Drive (daily 9am–5pm; free; ☎312/742-7736, ⊛www.chicago parkdistrict.com). Built in the early 1980s, this steamy indoor oasis is divided into five areas (Palm House, Show House, Orchid House and Fern Room), and has thousands of exotic plants on display. There's nothing spectacular in its collection, but at night the conservatory affords great views of the city.

Across Fullerton Parkway, you'll find the state-of-the-art **Peggy Notebaert Nature Museum**, 2430 N Cannon Drive (Mon–Fri 9am–4.30pm, Sat & Sun 10am–5pm; $6; ☎773/755-5100, ⊛www.nature-museum.org), which centers around an enormous glass enclosure housing an artificial rainforest full of hundreds of exotic **butterflies**; there's also an exhibit on the butterflies' life cycle and migration patterns, with knowledgeable staff on hand. Although the rest of the exhibits are better suited to school field trips, they're fairly informative, particularly "Wilderness Walk," which covers prairies and the city's environs in the 1800s, and the "Water Lab," a large-scale model of an urban river that explains how the rivers (eventually) end up inside each of us.

North of the zoo

Though attractions are thin on the ground in Lincoln Park's northern reaches, there are a few activities that can make a jaunt up here worthwhile. The narrow, sandy strip at **Fullerton Avenue Beach**, 2400 N Lake Shore Drive (daily from Memorial Day through Labor Day 9am–9.30pm) is less of a scene than the North Avenue and Oak Street beaches to the south. Nearby, the redbrick **Theater on the Lake** hosts annual summer performances by top local theater groups like Steppenwolf, Second City and the Chicago Theater Company (for more on these companies, see "Performing arts and film," p.185).

About two miles north of the theater, off Waveland Avenue, the crowded, nine-hole **Sydney R. Marovitz Golf Course** (see p.207) has good views of the city, but if you're looking to hit a few balls you're better off heading elsewhere. Beyond here, there's just more rolling park and little of interest, except a few outdoor pursuits, such as **archery** on Belmont Harbor Drive, and **birdwatching** at the Magic Hedge, an area of trees and shrubs at Montrose Point to the far north. The "hedge" sits at the tip of a curled sliver of land off the shores of Lake Michigan, on the site of a former missile base. The area lies in a migration corridor and sightings of more than three hundred species of birds have been recorded on this sandy hill. The best time to visit is during spring and fall migrations, but on any given day you're likely to spot up to fifty-odd species, including warblers, swallows and falcons; especially eye-catching are the thousands of purple martins that flock here in early August. The Magic Hedge is only accessible **by car**; from Montrose Avenue, east of Lake Shore Drive, take a right on Montrose Harbor Drive, then follow the first curve in the road to the small hill to the east.

Lincoln Park neighborhood

The best way to see the Lincoln Park neighborhood is to walk, and the streets around DePaul University are as good a place to start as any. On **Armitage** and **Webster** avenues, you'll pass upscale boutiques and shops of every kind, from women's fashion to outdoor-equipment stores, while **Halsted Street** is the focus of the area's nightlife. **Lincoln Avenue** and **Clark Street** – the two main commercial thoroughfares – cut diagonally through Lincoln Park and are dotted with secondhand bookstores, music shops and vintage-clothing stores, becoming more eclectic the further north you walk. Away from these streets, the area is pleasantly residential and tranquil.

While the neighborhood isn't known for any sight in particular, it is home to a notable institution or two. Below Fullerton Avenue, **DePaul University** begins its 36-acre sprawl, though its campus holds little of interest for casual visitors. Founded in 1898, the school's 20,000 students make it the largest Catholic university in the country, and a recent *Princeton Review* survey found them to be the "happiest" students in the country, though precisely what this is meant to indicate is really anyone's guess.

Just above Fullerton Avenue, at 2433 N Lincoln Ave, the 1915 **Biograph Theatre** marks the site where bank robber John Dillinger met his end in a shootout with the FBI in 1934. Dillinger was also known to frequent the back rooms of what's now the *John Barleycorn Memorial Pub*, just down the street (for a full review, see p.173). Besides its history, you won't find much reason to linger, unless you want to catch a movie inside.

Following N Lincoln Avenue south to Webster Avenue, you'll arrive at leafy **Oz Park**, replete with a yellow-brick road and shiny tin man. Named after Frank Baum's mythical land (Baum once lived in Lincoln Park), this thirteen-acre park is for anyone who wants to shoot hoops, play volleyball, or just take a break from shopping.

The St Valentine's Day Massacre

One of the bloodiest moments in Chicago's gangland history took place on February 14, 1929, when four men dressed as cops visited the garage of Al Capone's rival Bugs Moran, surprising seven of his henchmen. Announcing a bust, the men in uniform promptly gunned down Moran's men execution-style, an event that came to be known as the **St Valentine's Day Massacre**. The "cops" were widely believed to be Capone's men in disguise, sent to avenge the deaths of two of Capone's heavies as well as the theft of his booze shipments from Canada. Although Moran escaped unharmed, the massacre effectively put him out of business. While the police could never pin the deed on Capone, who was vacationing in Florida at the time, the FBI arrested him for tax evasion a few years later and shipped him off to Alcatraz. These days, there's just a patch of lawn where the garage once stood. For more on Capone, see p.237.

7

Lakeview, Wrigleyville and Andersonville

O ccupying Chicago's northernmost reaches, **LAKEVIEW** is little more than the poor man's Lincoln Park – though being slightly rougher around the edges is not necessarily a bad thing. And even if there isn't much to see or do here besides wander round, it's still pleasant to browse Clark Street, the main thoroughfare, on a Sunday afternoon or stroll along the lakefront parkway.

Lakeview was incorporated as a town in 1865 by a group of German celery-farmers, and takes its name from the long-vanished *Lakeview Inn*, a local hotel with sweeping vistas of Lake Michigan. The chunk of land north of Fullerton Avenue was a separate town (much like Hyde Park on the South Side, annexed by Chicago at around the same time) until 1889, when it was swallowed whole by the greedy city. As the settlement rapidly grew, its neighborhoods earned individual identities, none more so than **Wrigleyville**, which in 1914 became home to the newly built Wrigley Field, stadium of the Chicago Cubs. Sandwiching the ballpark are Chicago's two gay neighborhoods. To the south, the "pink triangle" of **Boystown** occupies the blocks between Halsted Street, Broadway and Belmont Avenue, while **Andersonville**, to the north, is a former Swedish settlement that has become a center for the city's lesbian community. If you do make a pilgrimage here, complete your trip by doubling back to Belmont Avenue and visiting the best-known Scandinavian shrine in the city, the *Ann Sather* restaurant, for a dish of lingonberry jelly and some pickled herring (for review see p.161).

Transport links here grow spottier the farther north you travel; the best option is to hop on the Red or Purple El lines that bisect the area. And remember to check the sports schedules before planning a trip – during home games, Wrigleyville transforms into a boozy, frat boy-packed nightmare, where it's often impossible to find parking or even grab a quiet coffee. Fine if that's what you're looking for, but for easy sightseeing skip those days.

Wrigleyville and around

Wrigleyville, the neighborhood surrounding Wrigley Field, got its name from savvy developers, hoping to trade on the park's immense popularity to sell the new houses they were building nearby. During baseball season, the area seems overrun by Cubs fans, loyally trailing blue and white team paraphernalia and crowding into the many local bars, often spilling out into the streets and even onto the rooftops. As there are no major highways around these parts, and virtually no parking to be found, the El trains to the Addison stop nearby become moving sardine cans.

At the center of it all, ivy-covered **Wrigley Field** itself remains one of the best places to get a real feel for baseball – the club is so traditional that it fought the installation of floodlights until 1988. Even if you know nothing about the baseball, there are few more pleasant and relaxing ways to spend an afternoon than drinking beer, eating hot dogs and watching the Cubs struggle to win a ball game (they haven't won a World Series since 1908).

Built in 1914 and named for Cubs owner and chewing-gum bigwig Philip Wrigley, the stadium has been extensively renovated in its 80-odd years, but some things haven't changed: the field is still the smallest in the league, the ivy planted by the outfield walls in 1937 is still there, and the scoreboard continues to be operated by hand. Equally enduring is the tenacious loyalty of its fans; despite heavy losses the Cubs manage to sell out every game. The "Bleacher Bums," a contingent of raucous fans, have been a fixture ever since they first staked their claim to the outfield bleachers back in 1966. They have the charming tradition of tossing back onto the field home-run balls hit by the opposing team.

If you can't make it to the ballpark during a game, there's a ninety-minute **tour** of the stadium that will take you through the clubhouses, suites, dugouts, press box, bleachers and playing field (call for schedule; tickets are $15 and must be purchased in advance; ☎773/404-2827).

Alta Vista Terrace

Nicknamed the "Street of 40 Doors," this charming oddity, tucked away northwest of the stadium, is well worth a detour. As the official story goes, after a trip to London, local real estate developer Samuel Eberly Gross wanted to create his own version of London's chic townhouses back home in Chicago. It took him four years to build his vision, **Alta Vista Terrace**, a single block of row houses wedged between N Sheridan Road and N Grace Street, but by 1904, they were complete and have remained refreshingly untouched ever since. Indeed, thanks to the old-fashioned architecture and wrought-iron benches on the sidewalk in front of many houses, it's all too easy to drift back a century.

Architecturally, the houses may seem eclectic and far from uniform at first glance, but as you wander down the street it's clear that Gross used several recurring motifs, often in houses that were diagonally opposite each other: heading north from Grace Street, notice how the garland molding above the bay windows of no. 3815 is repeated across the street in no. 3818 (and later in nos. 3831 and 3832). He seems not to have a set pattern, though: the curtain-like molding draped above the front door of no. 3808 doesn't recur until no. 3639 at the other end of the street; while the near-identical twins nos. 3823 and 3825 stand side by side, their ornate gables and massive fronts dominating the whole street.

Graceland Cemetery

The final resting place of Chicago's elite, lush **Graceland Cemetery** (8am–4.30pm) makes for a pleasant ramble across its 120 rolling acres, which spread from W Irving Park Road to Montrose Avenue. The main entrance is at Clark Street and Irving Park Road, where you can pick up a map as well as a copy of the Chicago Architecture Foundation's *A Walk Through Graceland Cemetery* ($9.95), though only fanatics looking to search out every marker might find need for this.

Opened in 1860, Graceland was created to replace the overcrowded municipal cemetery in what's now Lincoln Park (see p.93), a move brought on by fears that the lakeside cemetery posed a serious health risk. You'll spot a wide variety of memorials here, everything from fussy Gothic memorials to veritable temples. Socialites Potter and Bertha Palmer (see p.69) lie inside a massive Neoclassical mausoleum held up by sixteen columns. Less ostentatious is steel tycoon Henry Getty's grave – a subdued stone cube designed by Louis Sullivan – and the headstone of Daniel Burnham, which sits on a small island linked to the shore by a narrow walkway.

Two of Chicago's most influential architects have surprisingly unremarkable tombs: Ludwig Mies van der Rohe lies beneath a polished stone slab set into the ground, while Louis Sullivan's is only slightly more conspicuous. Sullivan, in fact, died in 1924 in poverty and lacked a gravestone for several years.

To get here, take the Red or Purple El line to the Sheridan stop.

Boystown

The buff bodies and fluttering rainbow flags lining the street let you know you're in **Boystown**, the thriving hub of Chicago's sizeable gay community. With its excellent restaurants and lively cafés, the street life buzzes mostly on Halsted Street and Broadway, between Belmont Avenue and Irving Park Road – among them tattoo parlors, rare-book stores and leather shops.

Most of the action centers around the long-standing bars here – *Sidetrack*, *Roscoes* and *Cocktail* – but throughout Boystown there's just about every type of gay bar conceivable, from country to Latin to biker. See "Gay and lesbian Chicago," p.196, for more.

North to Andersonville: Uptown

The curtain of nondescript high rises between Lakeview and Andersonville forms the backdrop for **Uptown**, once the playground of Prohibition-era mobsters and now home to Vietnamese, Chinese, Native Americans and even some migrants from Appalachia. The only reason it's on anyone's radar is because there are still musical remnants from the Jazz Age that swept through here.

Uptown's colorful past survives at *The Green Mill* (see p.180), once Al Capone's favorite watering hole and Chicago's best jazz club. Other historic venues include the *Aragon Ballroom*, 1106 W Lawrence Ave, and *The Riviera*, 4746 N Broadway (see p.181). As well, the *Old Town School of Folk Music*, at 4544 N Lincoln Ave, hosts hundreds of concerts a year, which reflect the school's exhaustive course offerings – everything from blues guitar to the Djembe and Aztec ceremonial dances. **To get here**, take the Ravenswood El line to Western Station, then walk east to Lincoln Avenue and turn south to the school or else catch the Lincoln (#11) or Western (#49) bus lines to their Wilson Avenue stops and from there walk south on Lincoln Avenue.

LAKEVIEW, WRIGLEYVILLE AND ANDERSONVILLE | Wrigleyville and around

Outside its specific neighborhoods, Lakeview holds a few pockets of interest along its commercial thoroughfares. What locals refer to as the **Southport Corridor**, along N Southport Avenue between Belmont Avenue and Irving Park Road, is not much more than shops, restaurants and bars, minus the crowds and sales gimmicks. One of the strip's long-standing novelties, however, is **Southport Lanes**, at no. 3325, a four-lane bowling alley that opened in 1922 and still uses human pinsetters to this day. Several blocks north, it's hard to miss the large pink neon sign and old-fashioned marquee of the **Music Box Theatre**, at no. 3733, a refurbished movie house built in 1929. Step inside to see the twinkling stars on the ceiling – worth a look (and accessible), even if there's not a show on (see p.192 for details).

Some of the **restaurants** around Belmont Avenue are worth going out of your way for. The Lakeview branch of *Ann Sather*, at 929 Belmont Ave, sells the chain's signature treats – gooey Swedish cinnamon rolls – while *Giordano's*, at no. 1040, is arguably the best place for Chicago-style deep-dish pizza. You'll also find a clutch of excellent dining options along N Clark Street, notably *Mia Francesca*, at 3311 N Clark St, which, serves some of the city's best Italian food (if you don't mind the long wait). There's also *El Jardin*, at no. 3335, where the food is merely a front for the potent margaritas.

Andersonville

Perched above Lakeview, **Andersonville** is as small-town as Chicago gets, and the few who bother to come are drawn by the promise of Swedish culture, specifically the food. Beginning in the 1840s, most of the Swedes who emigrated to Chicago settled here, transforming a cluster of celery farms into a bustling center. Although Swedes continued to emigrate here well into the twentieth century, by the 1960s their community had begun to disperse, returning to their homeland or moving to the suburbs. Despite the exodus, Andersonville still has one of the highest concentrations of Swedes in the US, though one that's struggling to preserve its identity in the face of a burgeoning lesbian community and a growing number of Middle Eastern businesses.

While public transportation to the area can be time-consuming, it's probably the best way to get here as taxi fares from neighboring Lakeview can be over $10. Take the CTA Red Line to Berwyn or Bryn Mawr or hop on bus #22 (Clark), #36 (Broadway) or #92 (Foster).

Everything worth visiting is on **Clark Street** or nearby in the few blocks north of Foster Avenue. Chief among these is the engaging **Swedish American Museum Center**, 5211 N Clark St (Tues–Fri 10am–4pm, Sat & Sun 10am–3pm; ☎773/728-8111, ⓦwww.samac.org), devoted mainly to Chicago's Swedish American heritage but with enough broad appeal to please anyone interested in the immigrant experience. Two floors of exhibits, mostly artifacts and folk crafts, give a sense of the daily life the early transplants led, with the second floor taken up by hands-on exhibits aimed at kids.

During the winter holidays, residents of nearby states make the pilgrimage to Andersonville for the **Swedish food**: traditional rosette and spritz cookies, Swedish meatballs, Göteborg sausage and pickled herring. Any of the handful of establishments devoted to Swedish cuisine are worth a try. For warm, sticky cinnamon rolls, try *Ann Sather*, at 5207 N Clark St, or *Svea*, 5236 N Clark St, for some down-home Swedish cooking (open till 4pm). If you're after lingonberries, Swedish meatballs or pickled herring, there's *Erickson's Delicatessen & Fish Market* at no. 5250, whose owner is also a trove of neighborhood information. Across the street, *Wikstrom's*, no. 5247, is a good alternative, as is *The Swedish Bakery* at no. 5348. And though it's anything but Swedish, the Indonesian-flavored *Kopi A Travelers Café* is good for a cup of espresso and a browse through their travel books.

You'll get a different side of Andersonville's past across the street at *Simon's Tavern*, at 5210 N Clark St. (Notice the double entendre in the neon sign and chances are you belong here anyway.) One of the last great **city taverns**, *Simon's* is thick with atmosphere, helped along by the worn mahogany bar, the steamship motif and the Viking paraphernalia. During the 1930s, the original owner began a free check-cashing service for Swedish laborers, throwing in free sandwiches to boot – an ingenious idea, as most of the money he doled out to laborers never left the bar. If you're lucky, the present owner will show you the bullet-proof check-cashing station under the stairs or the original basement door to the speakeasy.

8

West Side

Chicago's **WEST SIDE** was the port of entry for Chicago's myriad ethnic groups, among them Greeks, Italians and Eastern Europeans who flocked to the city during its late-nineteenth-century boom years and congregated in its now distinct neighborhoods. Since then, many of the residents have moved to the suburbs or been displaced by large-scale development (notably the campus of the University of Illinois-Chicago), a shift that's especially evident in **Greektown**, where these days you'll struggle to find many Greek Americans other than those running the local restaurants. **Little Italy**, on the other hand, is one of the few immigrant communities that is still flourishing, as young hipsters move in alongside older residents. Oddly, given its far distance from Mexico, Chicago has one of the largest Mexican and Mexican American populations in the country: that community is clustered in the old Eastern European neighborhood of **Pilsen**, evidenced by the colorful murals on many buildings.

Between these residential areas and downtown stands the **West Loop**, where warehouses thrown up in the nineteenth century were converted into trendy loft apartments a hundred years later. Aside from these and the trendy restaurant row along W Randolph Street, the West Side is a solid, working-class area with few official sights – a visit here is more about soaking up ethnic flavors (and sampling a few at local restaurants, too), than hopping between museums.

The best **public transport** option to reach these neighborhoods is the El Blue Line, which hugs the Congress Expressway; but make sure to stick to main streets, especially at night. Pilsen especially is a safe enclave stuck amid blocks of urban blight, so get off at the 18th Street stop or just grab a cab.

West Loop

Crossing the Chicago River into the **West Loop**, the first thing you'll notice is gleaming new office towers and the tips of construction cranes poking into the sky, all signs of economic spillover from the Loop. Beyond here West Side proper begins, a sprawl of tired-looking low rises that continues on, flat and unchanging, for miles.

Close to the river are the city's two main train stations. You can get a whiff of the grand days of train travel inside **Union Station**, at 500 W Adams St, where almost every cross-country Amtrak train passes through. During the 1940s and 1950s, more than 100,000 people filed across the pink marble floors of the Great Hall daily or sat under its airy, vaulted ceilings on the wooden benches; now that number has been halved, and most travelers bypass the hall

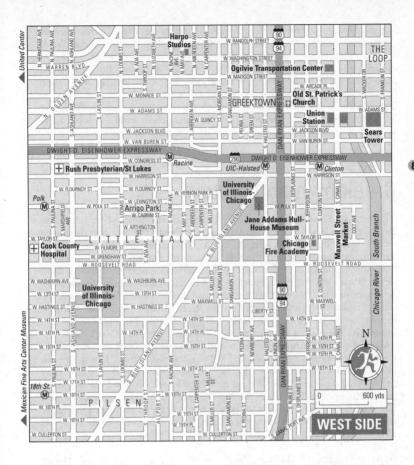

and buy their tickets on board the trains instead. The climactic baby carriage scene in the movie *The Untouchables* was shot on the marble steps.

The more contemporary **Ogilvie Transportation Center**, also known as North Western Station, services the Metra commuter rail network three blocks north at 500 W Madison St. The train station is housed beneath the striking Citicorp Center tower – the blue glass of Helmut Jahn's postmodern skyscraper cascades down its north and south sides like a waterfall. Other notable Chicago projects by the architect have included the United Terminal at O'Hare Airport and the James R. Thompson Center (see p.53).

Around the train stations, you'll find a few points of interest. The city's oldest church stands a couple of blocks west of Union Station at 700 W Adams St. Completed in 1856, **Old Saint Patrick's** has fifteen magnificent stained-glass windows inspired by Celtic art from the Columbian Exposition and the *Book of Kells*. Each July, the restored Romanesque building hosts the "World's Largest Block Party," a fundraiser that doubles as a singles' event (see p.212). Just west of North Western Station you'll find Claes Oldenburg's playful *Batcolumn*, a slender 100-foot cage shaped to resemble an oversized baseball bat planted in front of the Social Security Administration Building, at 600 W Madison St.

A short walk northwest of here will bring you to the area's top **restaurants** – *Blackbird, Marche, Red Light* – who've set up shop on arty-industrial W Randolph Street; for reviews, see "Eating", p.141. The only other place of note around here is **Harpo Studios**, at 1058 W Washington Blvd (Mon–Fri 9am–5pm; ☎312/591-9222, a former armory where the enterprising Oprah Winfrey tapes her phenomenally popular talk shows. Tickets to the shows are free, but you'll need to book them up to a month in advance (seats are not assigned). Keep in mind that you'll have to stand outside until the doors open, and it will likely be cold, given that the show usually takes the summer off.

Greektown and around

The original **Greektown** grew up around Halsted Street where it used to intersect Blue Island Avenue. Known as "the Delta," the area had developed into a bustling little community by the 1950s, but the building of the Eisenhower Expressway and the UIC campus eventually pushed Greektown out to its present location, centered on the intersection of Halsted and Madison streets. What's left of the neighborhood is a clutch of restaurants, cafés (*tavernas*) and shops on Halsted Street between Madison and Van Buren streets. While the tacky Greek temples and pavilions on the street corners – misguided attempts to beautify the neighborhood for the 1996 Democratic National Convention – may give the place a gimmicky feel, it does have excellent Greek food.

Most of the **restaurants** along Halsted Street are cut from the same cloth; menus may vary somewhat, but seafood is a common thread. Cheap options like *Greektown Gyros*, at no. 239, are almost always crowded, while cozy neighborhood places like *Rodity's*, at no. 222, offer reliably good Greek food at reasonable prices. (Wherever you go, be sure to try the *saganaki*, a local Greektown spectacle that calls for fried kasseri cheese to be doused in brandy and set aflame.) Delicious baklava and other Greek desserts can be found at *Pan Hellenic Pastry Shop*, at no. 322. For more on the area's dining scene, see "Eating", p.141.

The highlights of the neighborhood calendar are the annual **Greek Independence Day Parade** in March and three days in August when the tempting aromas of the **Taste of Greece** festival fill the air.

United Center

The swish **United Center**, at 1901 W Madison St, replaced the old Chicago Stadium in 1995, a famously loud space that saw just about every kind of event, from hockey and basketball to Elvis concerts and speeches by Franklin D. Roosevelt (the phrase "New Deal" was first uttered here). Home to the Bulls and the Blackhawks, the new stadium has been called "the House that Michael Built," after the Bulls' Michael Jordan, who led his team to dominate the NBA during the 1990s. While both the Bulls and the Hawks have seen better days, watching a game here is still a fun way to experience Chicago's raucous sports scene. (For more about the sports teams, see pp.203 and 204.)

There's nothing special about the stadium to make the one-hour backstage tour worthwhile (for groups of 15–40 only, by reservation; $20, includes lunch; ☎312/455-4500), but if you're here for a game or a concert, you might sup-plicate by the **bronze statue** of Jordan out front. Bear in mind that the surrounding neighborhood is gang-ridden and dangerous, so take a cab there. If you have a car, the stadium has plenty of monitored parking.

Garfield Park Conservatory

One of Chicago's least-known and most underrated attractions is the **Garfield Park Conservatory**, 300 N Central Park Ave (9am–5pm; $3 suggested donation; ⊤312/746-5100, ⓦwww.garfield-conservatory.org; Green Line to Conservatory–Central Park), sister to the Lincoln Park Conservatory but the bigger and better of the two. Billing itself as "landscape art under glass," the current conservatory sits in the eponymous 184-acre park. It was built between 1906 and 1907 to replace the original glasshouse designed by William Le Baron Jenney (see box, p.243), which fell into disrepair and was demolished.

You could spend a few hours here, wending your way through various rooms devoted to plant groups, past primeval-looking fern and mosses, giant agave (the source of tequila) and other striking cacti, towering banana trees and waterfalls. Kids will enjoy the hands-on displays in the children's garden, turning a crank to guide a giant "bee" into a flower, among other things. There's also an outdoor sensory garden where you can hold and smell fragrant flowers and fruits. Visitors can take a self-guided tour (guided tours are for members only) through the well-marked and easily navigable gardens, which are almost never crowded.

Garfield Park itself unfolds across 185 acres interrupted by flower gardens and a lagoon, as well as facilities for all kinds of sports (tennis, basketball, soccer, baseball), a playground and also a pool.

Little Italy and around

Many of the first Italian immigrants came to the city in the 1890s as temporary workers, intending to return home with money earned from hard graft on the railways, but those who settled in this poor enclave quickly turned it into **Little Italy**, a vibrant, restaurant-packed community. Now, the charming old row houses that fill most of the back streets have seduced young professionals into moving here. As well, the one troublesome hiccup in the district's upswing was recently condemned: the run-down housing projects at the corner of Taylor Street and Racine Avenue, which, sandwiched between older Italian settlements to the west and newer, funkier outposts to the east, had bisected the neighborhood.

To catch the full flavor of Little Italy, you'll need to amble down Taylor Street, from Halsted to Ashland. Look out for *Mario's Italian Lemonade,* the little red, green and white shack at 1068 W Taylor St, which has been selling delectable Italian ices and lemonade for more than thirty years. The last of Little Italy's old-style businesses, *Mario's* draws long lines in summer that give the place a friendly, block-party atmosphere. Across the street at no. 1079, *Al's Number 1 Italian Beef* has been doing similarly brisk business since 1938, with faded photos of its celebrity clientele on the walls. For pure Chicago-style gluttony, their "dipped" Italian beef sandwiches are hard to beat (see p.162).

If you're here during the day, the neighboring streets can make for a pleasant stroll; head for the blocks around **Arrigo Park**, a patch of green just north of where Taylor and Loomis streets meet, which has some lovely townhouses at its northern end.

Maxwell Street Market

Maxwell Street Market was a local legend for years, a sprawling square mile of assorted stalls that brought the different local ethnic groups – white, black, Latino, Italian, Jewish – together on a Sunday to haggle and gossip.

The market began as a collection of stalls set up by Jewish immigrants who had fled the pogroms of Eastern Europe and settled around Maxwell Street, where they opened kosher meat markets and used pushcarts to sell their goods, much as they had in their homeland. By the 1880s, other ethnic groups in the area – especially Poles and Greeks – had adopted the pushcart idea and set up shop themselves, and in 1912 the area was officially given its name. With the mass migration from the South after World War I, the area adjusted, absorbing African Americans as well. The market became a once-weekly affair and was known for its outdoor entertainment, especially the "blues" that blacks brought with them from the Delta. Musicians met here and jammed for decades, drawing appreciative crowds, at least until 1994, when the city turned its attentions to "fixing up" Maxwell Street.

The market was, in effect, forced out by the local government, which quietly stopped collecting trash each week after the market and then accused the stalls of being a nuisance and a health hazard. Officials then evicted the squatting stalls and gave them a new, albeit soulless home on Canal Street. Meanwhile, UIC swarmed over the coveted previous location and threw up buildings, renaming the area University Village. The eviction and subsequent regeneration were both controversial moves, which still rankle almost a decade later.

For the record, the place where Mrs O'Leary's poor cow supposedly kicked over a lantern and started the massive fire of 1871 was in a barn at what's now the intersection of Jefferson and Taylor streets, just short of a mile from the center of Little Italy, and east of the John F. Kennedy Expressway. There's really nothing to see here, other than the **Chicago Fire Academy**, where trainee firefighters learn to extinguish smaller blazes.

Maxwell Street Market

If you're in Little Italy on a Sunday, you could poke around the **Maxwell Street Market**, a couple of blocks away at the intersection of Roosevelt Road and Canal Street. This giant open-air flea market has food, drink and live blues music from 8am to 2pm each Sunday, no matter how cold the weather. Locals may moan that it's only a shadow of the original Maxwell Street Market (see box above) – and they're right – but you can still come away with a bargain or two, or sample from the wide variety of food stalls that sell everything from Polish sausages to Salvadoran *pupusas*.

Jane Addams Hull-House Museum

Just west of Little Italy, you'll run smack into a concrete sprawl, known as the campus of the 25,000-strong **University of Illinois–Chicago** (UIC). The university, which made headlines in the 1960s when it started building locally, brought much-needed money into the area, but at the same time displacing many of the residents and altering the West Side's landscape for good. You will, however, find a piece of the area's history preserved in the form of the **Jane Addams Hull-House Museum**, 800 S Halsted St, at Harrison Street (Mon–Sat 10am–4pm, Sun noon–5pm; free; ☎312/413-5353), which makes for a rewarding visit if you're in the area.

Hull-House was an innovative settlement house (or neighborhood social welfare agency) that provided much-needed services to children, women and immigrants on Chicago's struggling West Side, where they lived in appalling conditions. Jane Addams, a social reformer who went on to co-win the Nobel Peace Prize, founded the house in 1889 with fellow reformer Ellen Gates Starr after being inspired by a visit to Toynbee Hall, an influential settlement house in London's East End. By 1907, Hull-House had grown to fill several buildings, with day-care centers for the children of working mothers, employment centers for immigrants, an art studio and gallery, a labor museum, a public kitchen and even a coffeehouse.

Owned and run by the university, only two of the original Hull-House buildings have survived: both Hull Mansion and the dining hall have been restored to their original appearance. Inside Hull Mansion, you'll see some of Addams' original furniture, paintings and photographs, plus rotating exhibits and memorabilia from famous supporters and Hull-House visitors such as Carl Sandburg, Ida B. Wells, Frank Lloyd Wright, W.E.B. Dubois, Clarence Darrow, Gertrude Stein, and William Butler Yeats, among others. On the second floor of the dining hall, a fifteen-minute slide explains how Hull-House tackled the West Side's deplorable social problems.

For an excellent firsthand account of Hull-House, read Addams' *Twenty Years at Hull-House*; see p.258 for a review.

Pilsen

The bustling center of **Pilsen**, home to the city's large Latino community, is focused along 18th Street, west of Racine Avenue. In summer especially, you could easily mistake it for a neighborhood on the outskirts of Mexico City, with radios blaring salsa music from apartment windows and residents congregating around the *fruiterias*, *panaderias* and Mexican restaurants. The authentic **Mexican cuisine** to be found in these restaurants is reason enough to come here, as is the **Mexican Fine Arts Center Museum**, the largest Latino cultural institution in the US.

The first Mexican immigrants began arriving here in the mid-1800s, their numbers growing steadily until World War I, when labor shortages in the US brought thousands of Mexicans to Chicago seeking work. Many found jobs in the steel mills, railyards and stockyards, and settled on the near West Side, where the immigration services of Hull-House (see above) did much to ease their way. Like the West Side's Greek and Italian communities, however, urban renewal and the building of expressways eventually forced the immigrants to settle in nearby Pilsen, a neighborhood that had originally been settled by Bohemians who named it after the town of Plzen in West Bohemia. Today, roughly one million Mexicans live in Chicago, and census figures estimate that by 2010, Mexicans will be the largest ethnic group in Chicago.

Getting here on public transportation is possible, though in most cases time-consuming. On weekdays, take the Cermak Branch of the Blue El Line to the 18th Street stop; bear in mind that this branch doesn't run on weekends. Your best bet on weekends is to take a taxi. The buses that run frequently along Halsted Street, Blue Island Avenue and the other main streets into Pilsen can be painfully slow, even with a bit of traffic.

Mexican Fine Arts Center Museum

Pilsen's main attraction is the engaging **Mexican Fine Arts Center Museum**, at 1852 W 19th St and Wolcott Avenue (Tues–Sun 10am–5pm; admission free, plus separate fee for some exhibits; ☎312/738-1503, Ⓦwww.mfacmchicago.org), dedicated to the arts of Mexico as well as US Mexican communities. The small, but wide-ranging exhibits are displayed in five rotating galleries, with thoughtful captions in both Spanish and English. On display is a history of Mexican art from ancient times to the present day, shown through Pre-Columbian artifacts, charming Talavera de Puebla pottery (glazed Spanish-influenced earthenware) and contemporary photos of the Mexican experience in Chicago. You might also spot a few sketches by famed muralist Diego Rivera, as well as etchings by Jose Clemente Orozco and the politically charged work of David Alfaro Siqueiros.

Free guided **tours** of the Main Gallery are offered each Sunday (in English, noon–1pm, in Spanish 1–2pm). There's also a giftshop stocked with distinctive black Oaxacan pottery and hand-woven rugs, silver jewelry and a good selection of books. The museum, which is known locally for its annual **Day of the Dead exhibit** (for more on the festival, see p.213), also puts on performing arts festivals twice a year, in the spring and fall.

The museum's only drawback is its somewhat remote location on the lower West Side; you could make a day of it by combining a visit here with a trip to Chinatown or to the historic homes further east on S Prairie Avenue.

9

South Side and Hyde Park

No neighborhood in the city better illustrates the issues facing modern Chicago than the **SOUTH SIDE**. On the one hand, you can wander through the hushed, Neo-Gothic quadrangles of the University of Chicago, famous for its aptitude for snagging Nobel Prizes. On the other, mere blocks away, you'll find yourself in the most dangerous and run-down districts of the city, swaths of low-rise streets where windows are boarded up and check-cashing and convenience stores proliferate.

The story of **Hyde Park**, the main target for most visitors heading to the South Side, is intertwined with Chicago's apogee in the 1890s, when it was the

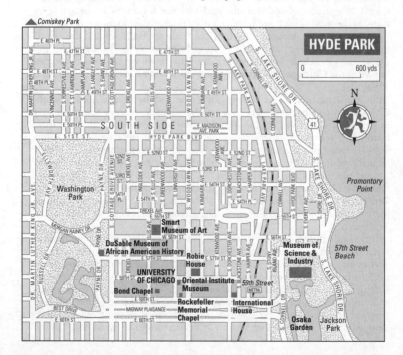

site of the city's two greatest civic projects. The first was the **University of Chicago**, which was grafted onto the newly annexed area of Hyde Park by the city in 1892 and quickly achieved academic fame; it's perhaps best known as the site of the first nuclear reaction (for more on this, see "Enrico Fermi," p.238). A year after the university was founded, Hyde Park was selected as the site of the **World's Columbian Exposition**, a mammoth civic scheme that was arguably Chicago's finest moment: remnants from that spectacular success include the building that houses the **Museum of Science and Industry** and the Midway Plaisance greenspace. Hyde Park also holds one of the hands-down most important (and most intriguing) structures in the city, Frank Lloyd Wright's **Robie House**.

Outside Hyde Park, the South Side is a predominantly African American neighborhood, and one all but forgotten by the city's (largely white) government: racial tensions run high and many locals feel that the area's been unfairly left to decay while white districts like Lincoln Park have been aggressively smartened up.

Sadly, the danger from that urban blight is still all too real: straying past Cottage Grove Avenue to the west, 51st Street to the north and the southern boundary of the Midway Plaisance is inadvisable, especially at night. To reach Hyde Park on **public transportation**, take the Metra to 55th-56th-57th or 59th street stations or the #6 Jeffrey Express bus; avoid the Green Line El. For the South Side sights and entertainment we've highlighted outside Hyde Park, the safest option is to **take a cab**.

Some history

The South Side has see-sawed between swanky mansions and gritty industry since Chicago first exploded in the mid-nineteenth century. It was home to many of the local railway and manufacturing magnates for many years – at least until Potter Palmer decamped to the Gold Coast in the 1880s and the rest of the elite followed (see "The Gold Coast and Old Town," p.69). It was also the site of the city's heavy industry, including the monumental slaughterhouses known as the **Chicago Stockyards**, whose stink wafted over the area until the 1950s.

But the South Side is best known as the crossroads between black and white Chicago. When labor shortages in the early twentieth century forced owners to look to newly arrived African American workers from the South to fill their factories, it was natural for those employees to settle close by on the South Side. This tendency was compounded by the city's **segregation policy**, which sequestered most African Americans along a southerly strip of State Street. Isolated geographically, politically and culturally from the city as a whole, Chicago's black community developed a singular identity – that's when its association with blues music and jazz clubs was truly cemented, especially in the entertainment district known as **The Stroll**, which began at S State and 31st streets.

At the same time a distinct African American culture was developing here, so was a simmering resentment at their treatment by local whites – there were six days of race riots across the city as early as 1919. This anger only worsened as the largely white local government paid little attention to the economic impact Chicago's crumbling industrial backbone had on the South Side. It has never truly recovered, and a casual trip by car down S Stony Island Drive will take you past low-rise buildings covered in barbed wire, piles of old furniture dumped on the streets and heavy iron grilles on most shop windows.

△ Rockefeller Memorial Chapel, University of Chicago

Comiskey Park and the 1919 World Series

The most famous scandal in baseball history happened at **Comiskey Park**, the non-descript stadium perched beside the Ryan Expressway. Home to the **Chicago White Sox**, the lesser-known of the city's two baseball teams, the original "baseball palace of the world" was razed in 1990 to make way for the modern facility that stands in its place.

Despite having some of the best players ever assembled on one team – one that outclassed the rest of the league in regular season, en route to a 110-win season – the White Sox played uncharacteristically sloppily in the final game of the 1919 World Series, which they were heavily favored to win, losing 10–5 to the Cincinnati Reds. Shortly after, suspicion fell on eight White Sox players who were accused of throwing the game in exchange for cash. Although all eight players, notable among them star Shoeless Joe Jackson, were ultimately acquitted of criminal activity after a lengthy investigation, they were banned from baseball for life, and the team itself disgraced with the name "the Black Sox." John Sayles' evocative film *Eight Men Out* (1988) makes a good introduction to the incident.

Hyde Park

Seven miles south of downtown, **Hyde Park** is an island of middle-class prosperity surrounded by urban poverty, the most attractive and sophisticated South Side neighborhood. Fitting into less than two square miles between 47th Street and 61st Street and from S Cottage Grove Avenue to the lake, it's also one of the most racially integrated areas of the city, strikingly evident in its array of ethnic eateries and its mix of low-income housing and mansions. It's also among the more erudite, with the **University of Chicago** at its center and the popular **Museum of Science and Industry** in Jackson Park.

For a glimpse of collegiate Hyde Park – and a smattering of terrific second-hand bookstores (see box on p.119) – head for **57th Street**: it bisects the main campus and passes the Robie House on the way. Otherwise, Hyde Park's commercial hub is **53rd Street**, where there's greater evidence of the urban blight that looms outside the area's boundaries, with cheap cafeterias standing alongside chic houseware shops.

Though the area is mostly safe, crime rates are still somewhat high, and you should try not to walk alone during the day and never at night, especially along the main drags of 53rd, 55th and 57th streets, where racial tensions are still palpable.

Museum of Science and Industry

The monumental **Museum of Science and Industry**, 57th Street and Lake Shore Drive (Mon–Sat 9.30am-4pm, Sun 11am-4pm; $9, $15 includes admission to one IMAX film, free Tues; ☎773/684-1414; ⊕www.msichicago.org), is a textbook example of how terrific fun can be integrated with higher learning; it will entrance even the most reluctant child, mostly thanks to the genuinely enthusiastic and question-friendly staff. The Beaux Arts building itself was originally designed as the Palace of Fine Arts for the World's Columbian Exposition in 1893; the only temporary structure salvaged at the exhibition's end, it was painstakingly dismantled before a stone frame was rebuilt around its steel skeleton. A massive refurbishment in 1997 has made the place more

Avoid the overpriced dining options at the museum and instead try one of the small, friendly ethnic **restaurants** – Thai, Middle Eastern, Korean – on 55th Street, just a five-minute walk away. Overall, they offer better-quality food than their American neighbors. Be a bit adventurous with your food choices – the servers are almost always willing to offer a suggestion or explanation. *Snail Thai Cuisine*, 1649 E 55th St, serves large portions of delicious, authentic Thai food; the popular noodle dish *pad thai* is always freshly made, and all of the curries are superb. Keep in mind, though, that many dishes can be quite spicy.

Just a few blocks away at no. 1611, *The Nile Restaurant* offers good, reasonably priced Middle Eastern food – the sandwiches, especially the *kifta kebab*, are large enough to be a meal in themselves.

navigable: visitors now enter through the subterranean entrance hall, surfacing under the main rotunda, and can plan a visit from there. You'll still need a map, though, to get around the three sprawling levels.

On the main floor, whatever you do, don't miss the **Coal Mine**: here, hard-hat sporting staffers take you through a thirty-minute coal miner training session, which includes a rickety ride on an underground trolley. Close by, there's also the mesmerizing **Chick Hatchery**, divided into two habitats. In one, you can watch fluffy chicks running around and eating; in the other, you can witness the damp, awkward-footed baby birds pecking their way out of a shell and then slumping down to rest after all the exhaustion.

Other popular stop-offs on the ground floor include the enormous, exhaustively detailed dollhouse known as the **Fairy Castle**, and the **U-505 Submarine**, captured from Germany in 1944 by forces led by a Chicago native. These days, you can take free, twenty-minute tours, "captained" by a staff member decked out in navy regalia – though claustrophobics should steer clear.

Upstairs on the balcony, check out the **HIV exhibit**, which explains the virus in easy-to-understand, comic-book style, and the walk-through **human heart.** As you make your way through the museum, make sure to take the **blue stairs** at least once, which hold perhaps the most startling exhibit of all – a pickled human being, sliced into wafer-thin sections and wedged between sheets of glass.

The most disappointing part of the museum is the **Henry Crown Space Center**: despite the presence of a real space suit and the Apollo 8 command module, it feels rather dated and nothing more than promotion for the nearby IMAX cinema ($9/one film; $13/two films).

The Robie House

Perched on the edge of the University of Chicago, the **Robie House**, 5757 S Woodlawn Ave (access by tour only, $9; ☎708/848-1976, ⓦwww.wright plus.org), is one of architect Frank Lloyd Wright's masterpieces, and its location in Hyde Park makes it a more convenient alternative to better-known Oak Park north of Chicago (see p.120). Commissioned by local businessman Frederick Robie in 1908, the redbrick Robie House is a prime example of Wright's **Prairie School style**, a deliberate attempt to pull away from the English-inspired Victorian houses in the surrounding areas of the growing city. Drawing inspiration from the flat Midwestern prairie, and attempting to carve out a distinctly American style, Wright gave Robie an overwhelmingly horizontal house. Sacrificing practicality to achieve aesthetic consistency, he didn't even include downspouts in the building's drainage system, and ninety years' worth of water damage to the pavements was the result. Wright wanted every element unified – which meant that he wanted to design everything: building, plants, light fittings, chairs, even the clothes the Robies' two children would wear – and was known to show up unannounced at any time to make sure that all the furniture was still in its proper place. (The Robies learned to hold him off at the door, rearrange the rooms and then invite him in.)

The house passed through several families' hands in quick succession after the Robie family lost its fortune; in 1926, the house was bought by the Chicago Theological Seminary, which promptly converted it into student accommodation. As if the damage this caused wasn't enough, by 1957 the Seminary had raised enough money to carry out its original plan of demolishing the building completely. It took the philanthropy of another businessman, William Zeckendorff, to save the house, which he then donated to the University of Chicago in 1963.

At the moment, it's midway through a massive restoration (set to end in 2007) that's already brightened up the outside; work on interior is scheduled to begin soon. If you want to take a look inside, join one of the regular **tours** – although most of the house's impressive exterior features are visible from the sidewalk.

The University of Chicago

The **University of Chicago** is perhaps the top institution in the Midwest, and interested in proving itself worthy compared to the East Coast Ivy League crew: the intensely studious 13,000-strong student body is one unfortunate symptom, as are T-shirts sold in the campus bookstore that read "The U of C: Where Fun Comes to Die." The soaring, perpendicular Gothic buildings are better evidence of its grand ambitions. For the most impressive introduction to the university, either walk or drive west down the **Midway Plaisance**, a long green strip that was the site of the World's Columbian Exposition. The Midway was then filled with full-sized model villages from around the globe, including an Irish market town and a mock-up of Cairo complete with belly dancers. These day, it's used mainly by joggers and students tossing Frisbees. At its far west end, you'll find Lorado Taft's 1922 **Fountain of Time** sculpture and reflecting pool, a somewhat overwrought memorial commemorating one hundred years of peace between the US and England (under renovation at the time of publication).

To explore the campus, consider taking one of the student-led **tours** that depart from the Office of College Admissions, 1116 E 59th St (Mon–Fri 10.30am year-round, plus 1.30pm March–Nov). Intended primarily for prospective students and their parents, these one-hour walking tours cover the entire campus and offer some campus history and architectural commentary, as well as some quirky anecdotes.

Rockefeller Memorial Chapel

If you'd rather see things on your own, a good place to start is the **Rockefeller Memorial Chapel**, at 5850 Woodlawn Ave, philanthropist John D. Rockefeller's last, and major architectural contribution to the university. Dedicated in 1928, the austere limestone chapel's most impressive feature is its tremendous size, which you can take in by walking its length all the way to the altar, taking in the stained-glass windows and numerous religious figurines.

The chapel is, fittingly, home to the world's second largest musical instrument – the tuned bells of **Laura Spelman Rockefeller Carillon**. If you have the time and the gumption to climb the 274 steps of the stone spiral staircase for the complete carillon tour, you will be rewarded with a spectacular view of the city and Lake Michigan, plus the chance to stand inside one of the larger bronze bells and even pound out a couple of notes on the keyboard that will be heard for blocks. A single person controls the carillon's 72 bells by pressing large oak keys with his or her fists, as well as using foot pedals. Tours are offered during the academic year, starting from the base of the tower on weekdays at 5.30pm.

Across the street from the chapel's entrance, book lovers cherish the **Seminary Co-op Bookstore**, housed in the cozy basement of the Chicago Theological Seminary at 5757 S University Ave. Reminiscent of an over-crowed small-town library, the store has over 100,000 volumes of academic and mainstream books on religion crammed in its cellar (see p.217 for other Hyde Park bookstores).

Oriental Institute

Just north of the chapel, the **Oriental Institute**, 1155 E 58th St (free admission, suggested donation $5; ☏773/702-9514, ⓦwww-oi.uchicago.edu), is well worth an hour's visit for its superb collection of artifacts from the ancient Near East, notably Egypt, Mesopotamia, Iran and Anatolia. It's not a museum in the traditional sense, but a research institute that shows off just a fraction of its world-class holdings. In the midst of a $10-million renovation, only two of the five galleries have been reopened (check the website for updated info), but both are rewarding. Especially good is the **Egyptian gallery**, where the most impressive piece is the "Colossal Statue of King Tutankhamun," which dates from 1334 BC (though it's hardly colossal, it's still pretty tall at seventeen feet). Look out also for vivid colors on the elaborately decorated "Mummy and Coffin of Meresamun," which shows scenes of the hoped-for afterlife. Many of the artifacts in the **Persian room** were excavated by the Oriental Institute itself during the 1930s when U of C was at its peak in the field of archeology. Among the highlights is the robust-looking "Colossal Bull Head" from Iran, one of a pair of beautifully carved stone statues dating from 486 to 424 BC.

The Quads

At the heart of the university, between 57th and 59th streets and Ellis and University avenues is the **Main Quadrangle**, or "The Quads." Surrounded by Neo-Gothic offices and libraries, its footpaths and lawns are the busiest part of campus, usually buzzing with students heading to and from classes. The best ways to enter the quadrangle are from the east at the intersection of 58th Street and University Avenue or through the gate directly across from Regenstein Library on 59th Street. In the southeast corner, you'll find the peaceful **Social Science Quad**, which makes for a good spot to contemplate the periodic sounding of the bells (see above).

Lying in the shadow of the much grander Rockefeller Chapel is the quaint but unremarkable **Bond Chapel**, in the Classics Quadrangle in the southwest corner of The Quads. The chapel is frequently the site of small weddings, perhaps owing to the rather high marriage rate among its alumni.

If only for its sheer oddity, pass by Henry Moore's bronze *Nuclear Energy* sculpture, located on the east side of S Ellis Avenue between 56th and 57th streets. The university was the site of the Manhattan Project research, and the heavy, mushroom-shaped work commemorates the moment that "...man achieved here the first self-sustaining chain reaction and thereby initiated the controlled release of nuclear energy."

The small, scholarly collection at the **Smart Museum of Art**, 5550 S Greenwood Ave (☎773/702-0200), is where the majority of the U of C's art collection is stored and displayed. Perhaps because of the museum's size, there's a lot of attention paid to detail, from the impeccable displays and unique themes down to thoughtful captions and quotes from artists. Though you'll find a little bit of everything here – Chinese bronzes, Old Master paintings, Frank Lloyd Wright's dining room furniture and sculptures by Rodin, Degas and Henry Moore, among others – the museum is perhaps best known for its works by the **Chicago Imagists**, whose playful, cartoon-like art emerged from Hyde Park during the 1960s. Interesting in its concept is the exhibit "Sacred Fragments: Magic, Mystery and Religion in the Ancient World," which examines religious artifacts from the Mediterranean region through modern interpretations.

To round out your U of C tour, grab a beer or a greasy lunch just north of campus at **Jimmy's Woodlawn Tap**, at 1172 E 55th St, a shabby, 50-year-old local bar that has seen the likes of Dylan Thomas, Margaret Mead and Saul Bellow.

DuSable Museum of African American History

On the west edge of Hyde Park and a ten-minute walk from the center of the U of C campus, the **DuSable Museum of African American History**, 740 E 56th Place (daily 10am–5pm, Sun from noon; ☎773/947-0600, ⓦwww.dusablemuseum.org), is the oldest American institution devoted to collecting and preserving the heritage of Africans and African Americans. With such an ambitious mission, it's almost impossible for the museum not to fall short – which it does on several fronts – but there's still enough here to make a visit worthwhile if you're in the area, if not necessarily something you'd journey out specifically for.

Start by picking up a map at the entrance and head past the bust of Jean-Baptiste Point du Sable (see p.229), the museum's namesake, to reach *The Ames Mural* (also known as *The Roots Mural*) – Robert Ames' mural of carved oak (1965), which

---

Hyde Park parakeets

Perhaps the neighborhood's most unique populace is the local flock of some hundred *Myiopsitta monachus* – better known hereabouts as **Hyde Park parakeets**. Native to Argentina and Brazil, these bright-green monk parakeets, sporting gray underbellies and blue wing feathers, were first sighted in the area in the 1970s nesting in huge tangles of twigs in the treetops or electrical poles. Unlike their South American counterparts, the Hyde Park parakeets aren't considered agricultural pests and are more known for their loud, high-pitched squawking.

How these tropical birds came to trade their sultry southern homeland for Hyde Park is not known, though it's commonly thought that the birds escaped from a cage at a Chicago airport. Despite the bitingly cold winters here, they have managed to thrive; threats of elimination by the US Department of Agriculture in the late 1980s eventually faded after local protests.

Nicknamed "Parrot Park," the corner of **Harold Washington Park** at Lake Shore Drive and 53rd Street is the most popular nesting site for the birds.

If the Seminary Co-op whets your appetite, Hyde Park supports several other unique bookstores. Dating back to 1937, **O'Gara & Wilson, Ltd**, 1448 E 57th St, offers a rich selection of rare, used and unusual books, perfect for the avid book collector or anyone who enjoys the musty scent of antique texts. Farther down on 55th Street, **Powell's Bookstore**, 1501 E 57th St, also specializes in used books, but with a more recent selection. Each morning, employees place a cardboard box of free used books outside the store. Stop by early, before it's picked over.

powerfully brings to life the African American struggle by way of key scenes and figures from history, from Harriet Tubman to Civil Rights marches on Washington.

In a small corridor in the main leg of the museum, you'll find traditional African art displayed in the **Africa Speaks** exhibit, mostly carved pieces such as stools, dolls and combs from early West African kingdoms; the Mossi dance masks are especially playful and ornate. The nearby **Trial to Triumph** exhibit, however, is disappointing: the news clippings, pictures of lynchings, and the meager display of handcuffs don't pack as much of a wallop as they could. Things pick up across the hall in a room devoted to the **first African Americans in aviation**. Of special interest are the pilot license issued to the first African American pilot, Bessie Coleman, and a photographic tribute to the Tuskegee Airmen, an all-black US Air Force team who distinguished themselves in combat during World War II.

The **main hall**, the largest space of all, is usually reserved for upbeat temporary exhibits; beyond here is a re-creation of the office of Harold Washington, Chicago's first black mayor.

Promontory Point

For a change from Hyde Park's busy storefronts and crowded sidewalks, you can visit the small headland at the east end of 55th Street, **Promontory Point**. This open, grassy spot on the rocky shores of Lake Michigan usually teems in summertime with picnicking families, sunbathers and joggers, all of whom come for the spectacular view northward to downtown Chicago. (The view south of industrial Indiana is much less appealing.) A dip in the lake around the Point is refreshing, but take care to avoid swimming in the generally unclean and crowded 57th Street Beach to the south.

Oak Park

eafy **OAK PARK**, ten miles west of the Loop, is the prime excursion in the outlying area, famous for its all-American architecture: there are dozens of buildings designed by **Frank Lloyd Wright** here, as well as his own home and studio. In fact, it's a throwback suburb, with tree-lined streets and cobwebby boutiques sitting alongside manicured parks and prettified Victorian homes: Oak Park feels like Main Street USA, a safe, oldfashioned place filled with wholesome families. It should come as no surprise then that Ray Kroc, who founded *McDonald's*, lived here from the age of 5.

It's a pleasant place to spend the day, wandering round the squirrel-filled backstreets and popping into interesting buildings like the **Unity Temple** or **Pleasant Home**. There are definitely a few signs of creeping modernization now: amid the Mock Tudor tearooms and winding alleys in downtown's shopping district, there's now a branch of Benetton and a large concrete parking garage, for instance – but by and large this twitchy-curtained community looks much as it did one hundred years ago. Though it's fine for a day trip, there isn't much reason to spend the evening – nightlife largely comprises upscale, unexciting restaurants aimed at the well-heeled, slightly older locals.

Some history

Oak Park was founded by an Englishman, Joseph Kettlestrings, who arrived here with his wife and children in 1832. He bought much of what's now the downtown and worked in a sawmill, running an inn with his wife for travelers. The town stayed a smallish settlement of around five hundred for almost twenty years; first known as Kettlestrings Grove, it was then nicknamed Oak Ridge, thanks to the high ground covered with oak trees nearby.

But when the **railroad** arrived in 1848, everything changed: the train allowed people to live locally but commute to jobs in the grimy city and the town became known as Oak Park in the 1860s, when a developer tweaked its name to help lure middle-class refugees. He needn't have bothered, as many fearful Chicagoans decamped to the suburbs, especially swanky neighborhoods like Oak Park, after the Great Fire in 1871. One of those newer arrivals was Frank Lloyd Wright, who moved here in 1887 with his mother, after she separated from her husband; her inspired son wanted to launch his architectural career and rapidly-rebuilding Chicago was at that time a town of opportunity (for more on Wright, see pp.244–246). He began building locally soon after moving here and was commissioned by many wealthy suburban businessmen to construct houses for them.

Those wealthy clients were typical local residents and by the turn of the century the town was a prosperous, churchy enclave, where alcohol was banned for many years and movies weren't shown on Sundays until the early 1930s.

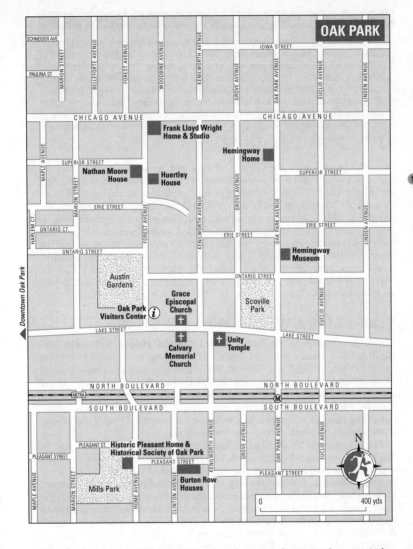

The town has resisted Chicago's advances for years, determined to stay independent and with enough local wealth to ensure it can. In fact, Oak Park has changed little in a hundred years, thanks to a combination of those conservative residents and stringent zoning laws – it's effectively an architectural time capsule. Rest assured, though, at least now you can buy a beer or two.

Arrival and information

To reach Oak Park by **car**, take the Eisenhower Expressway (I-290) west from downtown to Harlem Avenue and exit north. If you don't have a car, don't worry as the town's well served by public transportation. Both the Green and

While Oak Park isn't exactly overflowing with restaurants, there are a few spots that deserve mention. **Marion Street Grille**, 189 N Marion St (℡708/383-1551) serves straightfaced French bistro fare in a small, cozy setting. There's contemporary American cuisine (and fondue, oddly enough) at the popular **Café Winberie**, 151 N Oak Park Ave (℡708/386-2600), and **Geppetto's**, 113 N Oak Park Ave (℡708/386-9200) serves an excellent stuffed pizza. On the lighter side, **Buzz Café**, 905 S Lombard Ave (℡708/524-2899) is an excellent local coffee shop and **Petersen's**, 1100 W Chicago Ave (℡708/386-6131) has been serving fans of their homemade ice cream since 1919.

Blue **El** lines stop here: the Green Oak Park stop is marginally more convenient, as it lets you off closer to downtown and the **visitors center**. You'll find the latter at 158 N Forest Ave, hidden next to a massive concrete car park (daily Oct–April 10am–4pm, May–Sept 10am–5pm; ℡708/848-1500 or 1-888/OAK-PARK, ⓦwww.visitoakpark.com). Free maps are available here, as well as an exhaustively informative **self-guided audio tour** round town that takes approximately two hours ($6). Illogically, it's more efficient to reverse the itinerary and work backwards if you want to see inside most sights (descriptions can be programmed in any order); the Pleasant Home (see p.124) has fewer tours available than the Frank Lloyd Wright Home & Studio and it's better to hit that first.

Frank Lloyd Wright Home & Studio

The slick operation at the **Frank Lloyd Wright Home & Studio**, 951 Chicago Ave (tours only, Mon–Fri 11am, 1pm & 3pm, Sat & Sun 11am–3.30pm; $9; ℡708/848-1976, ⓦwww.wrightplus.org), seems inspired by its control freak former owner: the paranoid, officious approach, where tourists are constantly warned to touch nothing and check all bags, makes this a less than welcoming place to visit. But if you think you're able to tour without giving into the temptation to touch, you'll be rewarded with a trip around a sumptuously restored turn-of-the-century home.

Wright borrowed $5000 from his boss Louis Sullivan to build the house in 1889, on his marriage to Kitty Tobin. This was Wright's first chance to put into unfettered practice his theories that a building should not just be a shell, but an environment, and to start opening up traditionally boxy Victorian interiors. It reads somewhat like an intriguing footnote to his mature work in the Prairie style; in itself, it only hints at his later, more beautiful designs. Notice the earthy tones, wide verandas and the tree growing through the passageway to his studio – all signs of his obsession with blurring the boundaries between man and nature, outside and inside. Despite its early date, the house was pre-wired for electricity, even though there was no power line extending to Oak Park; Wright, commuting to work in downtown Chicago, knew that the revolutionary new power source would soon stretch out to the suburbs and wanted his house to be ready when it arrived.

The Home & Studio is worth stopping by as part of a larger tour of Oak Park, but given that the building shows only flashes of Wright's later genius (not to mention the horribly schoolmarmish approach of those running the show), you're better off spending longer at the nearby Unity Temple (see below); for a stunning, mature example of residential architecture by Wright, head over to the Robie House in Hyde Park (see p.115).

South along N Forest Avenue, which is filled with gaudily restored Victorian mansions, there are two buildings by Wright that contrast his pre- and post-Prairie styles: the **Huertley House** (1902), at no. 318, and the **Nathan Moore House** (1895; rebuilt 1923), directly opposite on the corner of Superior Street. The former, a low-slung, heavily horizontal, brown brick home is a proto-Prairie building. The latter, a mustard-colored Mock Tudor monstrosity, is a rare instance of the ornery architect following a client's brief rather than his own whims (hardly surprising, as it was one of Wright's first independent commissions and he couldn't kick and scream to get his way as he later would).

Hemingway Home and Hemingway Museum

Brawny outdoorsman Ernest Hemingway seems out of place in manicured Oak Park, but it's here at **Hemingway Home**, 339 N Oak Park Ave (home and museum Thurs, Fri & Sun 1–5pm, Sat 10am–5pm; $7 combined ticket; T708/848-2222, Wwww.hemingway.org), that he was born and lived until the age of 20; his grandfather's house, where he stayed until the age of 6, has been lovingly transformed into a period shrine to the writer. It's taken ten years and more than $1million (plus lengthy interviews about the house's decor with a 90-something woman in Texas whose family bought the property after grandpa Hemingway's death) to create the authentic Hemingway Home. The attention to detail is extraordinary: bald cypress from Florida and Louisiana was originally used throughout the house for skirting boards and doorframes, but much had been torn out when the building was converted into apartments. So restorers traveled to Florida, where modern salvage teams were rescuing cypress logs lost during river transports a hundred years ago; they bought this salvaged wood (well preserved thanks to the excessive oils in cypress) and used it to refit the house. There are few family possessions here – a notable exception is the taxidermied animals on the first floor – but it's an evocative recreation of a Victorian house even so.

The **museum**, two blocks south at 200 N Oak Park Ave, is housed in an old Christian Science church. The exhibits inside are excellent: picture-heavy panels trace Hemingway's life from birth to Paris to Havana, and there's a rotating temporary space for themed shows. The photographs from the Hemingway family album are especially revealing – look for the 1910 image of 11-year-old Ernest showing his nature-loving disposition by feeding a nut to a squirrel (look closer, and you'll notice the squirrel's stuffed). The one missed opportunity is that Hemingway's notoriously awkward relationship with Oak Park (a place with "wide lawns and narrow minds," as he once said) isn't addressed at all.

Unity Temple and around

The **Unity Temple**, 875 Lake St (Mon–Fri 10.30am–4.30pm, Sat & Sun 1–4pm, guided tours Sat & Sun 1pm, 2pm & 3pm; $4, $6 for guided tour; T 708/383-8873, Wwww.unitytemple-utrf.org), marks one of Frank Lloyd Wright's lesser-known masterpieces. Though Wright himself wasn't especially religious, his mother was a Unitarian, a splinter Christian group that approaches religion through the natural world and emphasizes the wonders of nature (Small wonder, then, that Wright's Prairie style evolved as it did, focusing on organic forms and the natural world). She was friends with the local minister and helped her son snag the commission to build this church for the Unitarian congregation in Oak Park.

From the outside, the temple resembles a forbidding, column-covered concrete box; Wright deliberately made it hard to find an entrance, so that worshippers would have to "interact" with the building as soon as they arrived. Slipping through the doors on Kenilworth Avenue, you find yourself in an atrium that leads, through a low-ceilinged passageway, into the main auditorium. Painted in ochre and muddy greens, with dark wood detailing, the church is both cozy and airy. Wright created a recessed oasis in the center of the square room, filled with pews; each of the two balconies overlooks this area and creates a sense of intimate community, despite a seating capacity of more than four hundred. In order to maintain this privacy, there are no windows at eye level, but the ceiling is a massive, leaded glass skylight that floods the room with light. Another feature that fosters community is the placement of the exit doors. Unlike most traditional churches, where the congregation turns its back on the pastor to leave, Wright wanted worshippers to pass the pastor as they left (and so chat with him) – hence the hidden doors either side of the pulpit through which you must leave.

If the clunky pews seem out of place, that's not surprising – Wright designed his own, but as the cost of the building spiraled to one and half times its projected budget, the congregation opted for cheaper alternatives. Note, too, the radiators everywhere: Wright's ingenious but inept forced-air heating system broke down almost as soon as the building was put to use and these radiators had to be grafted onto the building to keep worshippers warm. One feature that still functions beautifully is the boxy auditorium's superb acoustics: fundraising concerts are regularly held here – check the website for details.

There are several other churches clustered west along **Lake Street**, underscoring Oak Park's religious origins – from the freshly scrubbed Neo-Gothic **Grace Episcopal Church** (no. 924) to the squat and dingy, Romanesque revival **Calvary Memorial Church** (no. 931).

Historic Pleasant Home and south Oak Park

It's a shame that poor, neglected **Pleasant Home**, 217 S Home Ave, is so often eclipsed by its starry neighbor, Wright's Home & Studio (see above), as a visit here is every bit as interesting, helped by the friendly, passionate docents (tours only, March–Nov Thurs–Sun 12.30pm, 1.30pm & 2.30pm, Dec–Feb 12.30pm & 1.30pm; $5; ☎708/383-2654, ⓦwww.oprf.com/phf).

The enormous building was designed by Prairie School architect **George Maher** in 1897 for investment banker and philanthropist John Farson. Farson died soon after in 1910, and the house was sold to Herbert Mills, the inventor of vending and slot machines; in turn it was sold to the local park service in 1939 for use as a community center. Recently, though, the home's been reclaimed and slow restoration has begun.

There's not much furniture inside yet, other than the monolithic dining table Maher designed and that was too heavy to ever move, but the rooms themselves are an intriguing early hint of how the Prairie style would evolve. The rooms bleed into one another (a signature Prairie motif), while the huge windows open onto a wraparound porch (blurring indoors and outside). In the library, the gigantic, curved-glass sash windows - which recede six feet into the wall above when lifted - underline the money-is-no-object opulence of the place. Maher was also determined to achieve balance in design, whatever the obstacle: see how the door to the left of the onyx fireplace in the Great Hall is a sham, only there to even out the entranceway to the right. If the docent's willing, ask to stop by the women's bathroom on the first floor, which contains one of Maher's original marble sink designs, complete with in-built, shell-shaped soap dish.

Tours spend time on the second floor at the small, ragtag museum of the **Historical Society of Oak Park**: it's small, but there's a detailed room dedicated to the history of the area and filled with old photographs.

The final architectural pit stop on a tour round Oak Park is just east of here, where you'll find the heaviest concentration of preserved **Victorians** in town, along Pleasant Street between Clinton and Oak Park avenues. The five **Burton Row Houses**, on the corner of Pleasant and Clinton, show how developers here were anxious to offer affordable housing to middle-class refugees from the city: the shared partition walls lessen privacy as well as price.

Listings

Listings

Accommodation

With more than thirty million visitors passing through Chicago each year, the city needs to maintain an abundance of **accommodation**; indeed, there are around 82,000 rooms in the metropolitan area, though in truth many of these are in large, rather anonymous hotels catering to business travelers and conventioneers. Even so, you shouldn't have too hard a time finding reasonable and affordable, if often unexciting, options in the city center. Most basic accommodation (save hostels and perhaps B&Bs) will run you a minimum of $100 a night, especially if you need a room at the last minute.

A preponderance of hotels are concentrated in just a few pockets around downtown, the largest of which is **Near North**, where several dozen expensive hotels cluster in River North and around N Michigan Avenue. The more business-oriented **Loop** has a few pricey hotels, but also the city's best hostel, as well as some mid-range boutique options. Besides being close to many of the downtown attractions, the Loop offers easy access to O'Hare International Airport (40min by El train) – a cumbersome trip from other parts of the city unless you're willing to shell out $35 for a taxi.

Outside the most central areas, accommodation choices thin out considerably, though there's more variety in terms of B&Bs versus business hotels, and rates are generally lower. Most of the city's B&Bs and guest houses are located in **Old Town** and **Lincoln Park**, while **Lakeview** has some budget options and arty-boutique hotels, though staying this far north may not be practical for extended downtown exploration – but all will do if you want to get a better feel for the city's residential neighborhoods. **West and south of the Loop**, you'll find few big-name chains, but again, these aren't areas where you'd choose to stay unless you're planning to spend most of your time in Greektown or Little Italy, or at McCormick Place or Hyde Park. We've also included a list of **airport hotels**, which are worth considering only if you need to catch an early-morning flight.

Even in a major city like Chicago, where you'll find some of the top hotels in the country, it's still possible to find excellent rooms at drastically reduced prices, either through one of the popular **booking agencies** like Hot Rooms (☎773/468-7666 or 1-800/468-3500) or one of the **Internet search sites** (Ⓦwww.orbitz.com or Ⓦwww.expedia.com, to name two). In fact, unless you want to stay at a B&B or one of the hostels, you should do your pre-trip bargain hunting

> ## Rough Guide favorites
>
> **Rooms with a view**
> The Drake (p.134)
> Park Hyatt Chicago (p.135)
> Ritz-Carlton (p.135)
> Swissotel Chicago (p.133)
> W Chicago Lakeshore (p.136)

Lincoln Park

N

W. ELM ST.
W. HILL ST.
W. ELM ST.
E. ELM ST.
E. CEDAR ST.
W. MAPLE ST.
W. WENDELL ST.
E. BELLEVUE ST.
E. OAK ST.
W. OAK ST.
W. LOCUST ST.
E. WALTON ST.
W. CHESTNUT ST.
E. DELAWARE PL.
W. INSTITUTE PL.
E. CHESTNUT ST.
E. PEARSON ST.

Lake Michigan

W. CHICAGO AVENUE
E. CHICAGO AVENUE
W. SUPERIOR ST.
E. SUPERIOR ST.
W. HURON ST.
E. HURON ST.
W. ERIE ST.
E. ERIE ST.
W. ONTARIO ST.
E. ONTARIO ST.
W. OHIO ST.
E. OHIO ST.
W. GRAND AVENUE
E. GRAND AVENUE
W. ILLINOIS ST.
E. ILLINOIS ST.
W. HUBBARD ST.
E. HUBBARD ST.
W. KINZIE ST.
E. KINZIE ST.

Chicago River

Navy Pier

MERCH. MART PL.

E. SOUTH WATER ST.
E. WACKER DRIVE
W. FULTON ST.
W. WACKER DRIVE
W. LAKE STREET
W. LAKE STREET
E. LAKE ST.
W. RANDOLPH ST.
W. RANDOLPH ST.
E. RANDOLPH ST.

W. WASHINGTON ST.
W. MADISON ST.
E. MADISON ST.
W. MONROE ST.
E. MONROE ST.
W. ADAMS ST.
E. ADAMS ST.
QUINCY ST.
W. JACKSON BLVD.
E. JACKSON BLVD.
W. VAN BUREN ST.
E. VAN BUREN ST.

EISENHOWER EXPWY
W. CONGRESS PKWY.

Greyhound Bus Terminal

W. HARRISON ST.
E. HARRISON ST.

W. POLK ST.
E. BALBO DR.

E. 8TH ST.
W. TAYLOR ST.
E. 9TH ST.
E. 11TH ST.
W. ROOSEVELT ROAD
E. ROOSEVELT ROAD

E. 13TH ST.
E. 14TH ST.

0   800 yds

CENTRAL CHICAGO
ACCOMMODATION

W. 15TH ST.

Hyde Park   McCormick Place

Best Western Grant Park	36
Best Western Inn of Chicago	16
Best Western River North	17
Cass Hotel	12
Comfort Inn	18
Congress Plaza Hotel	32
Crowne Plaza	28
Drake Hotel	1
Fairmont Hotel	25
Fitzpatrick Hotel	11
Four Seasons Hotel	2
Hampton Inn and Suites	20
Hilton Chicago and Towers	35
Holiday Inn and Suites Downtown	33
Holiday Inn (Mart Plaza)	22
Hostelling International–Chicago	31
Hotel Allegro	26
Hotel Burnham	27
The Hotel Monaco	24
Hotel Inter-Continental Chicago	19
House of Blues Hotel	21
Ohio House Motel	15
The Palmer House Hilton	29
Park Hyatt Chicago	9
Peninsula Chicago Hotel	10
The Raphael	6
Red Roof Inn Chicago	13
Ritz-Carlton	8
Seneca Hotel	7
Sofitel Chicago Water Tower	4
Swissotel Chicago	23
Travelodge	34
Tremont Hotel	5
W Chicago City Center	30
W Chicago Lakeshore	14
Whitehall Hotel	3

online – because there are so many hotels in the city, even the top hotels are forced to slash rates during the week and at off-peak times – it's easy to find a $450 room at luxury places like the *W* hotels or the *Drake* for under $200.

Alternatively, going through a **B&B service** like Chicago Bed and Breakfast (see box below) will get you a room, or a full apartment, in a private residence or guest house, priced from around $85 to usually not more than $160, unless the B&B is exceedingly precious, historic or otherwise. Corporate **discounts** and those for AAA (American Automobile Association) members can bring down the price significantly, so make sure to inquire about them before making your reservation. Keep in mind, however, that all Chicago hotels will add a 14.9 percent room tax to your bill. It's also wise to arrange for a room ahead of your visit, especially around holidays and in spring and summer; note that Chicago can also get overrun by conventions, some of them big enough to fill every available room in the city.

If you're arriving by car, **parking** at the Loop and Near North hotels will be unavoidable and costly ($20–30 per night).

The Loop

Allegro 171 W Randolph St, at N LaSalle St ☎312/236-0123 or 1-866/672-6143, ℱ312/236-0917, ⓦwww.allegrochicago.com; all lines to Clark St. This chic, recently restored 1920s business hotel, right in the theater district, has 483 brightly colored and comfortable rooms, with down comforters and amenities like CD players and data ports. The staff's professionalism is a selling point and there's a free wine hour every evening (5–6pm), as well as an on-site fitness center and access to a nearby pool. ④–⑤

Hotel Burnham 1 W Washington St, at S State St ☎312/782-1111 or 1-866/690-1986, ℱ312/782-0899, ⓦwww.burnhamhotel.com; Red or Blue Line to Washington; Brown, Green, Orange or Purple Line to State/Lake. Set in one of the world's first glass-and-steel skyscrapers, the *Burnham* is an intimate boutique hotel where everything – from the romantic ambience and exemplary service down to the metal elevator grilles and the indigo velvet headboards – strives to create a luxurious oasis amid the heavily trafficked business hotels of downtown. The one hundred rooms and twenty-odd suites all come with turn-down service and twice-daily housekeeping, and there's a free wine reception in the lobby (daily 5–6pm), plus free coffee and tea (6–9.30am). Prices fluctuate wildly depending on availability, but Internet prices, last-minute and package deals (dinners, tours) can make this place affordable even if it's out of your immediate range. The excellent *Atwood Café* is on the first floor (see p.143). ④–⑤

Congress Plaza Hotel 520 S Michigan Ave, at W Congress Parkway ☎312/427-3800 or 1-800/635-1666, ⓦwww.congresshotel.com; Red Line to Harrison; Blue Line to La Salle; Brown or

Orange Line to Library-State/Van Buren. Huge hotel (823 rooms) and convention center that was built for the 1893 World's Columbian Exposition and has seen better days. Many of the rooms – which tend toward the small and are sometimes rough around the edges – have great views of Buckingham Fountain and Lake Michigan, though, and the hotel is a decent alternative to some of the better-restored and modern boutique hotels in the Loop, many of which fill up. ❹–❺

Crowne Plaza 10 S Wabash Ave, at W Madison St ☎312/372-7696, ☏372-7320, ⓦwww.crowneplaza.com; Blue or Red Line to Monroe, all other lines to Madison. This recently remodeled, ten-story business hotel, inside the landmark Silversmith building, has 143 simple but tasteful rooms. The bright, cheery (though sometimes small, given the hotel's age) rooms come with a CD player and coffeemaker, and there's also a fitness center. Within a stone's throw of the Loop sights and a few blocks from the river and the Mag Mile. ❹–❺

Fairmont 200 N Columbus Drive, at E Lake St ☎312/565-8000, ☏856-1032, ⓦwww.fairmont .com; Red Line to Lake; Brown, Green, Orange or Purple Line to Randolph/Wabash. In addition to luxurious rooms and suites, there's a pleasant art-filled lobby, two swank ballrooms and a fitness club. The food and service is top-notch and while not as splashy as the *Peninsula* or the *Park Hyatt*, it's just as plush and provides a somewhat more personalized touch. ❺–❻

Hostelling International – Chicago (J. Ira and Nikki Harris Family Hostel) 24 E Congress Parkway, at S Wabash Ave ☎312/360-0300 or 1-800/909-4776, ☏312/360-0313, ⓦwww.hichicago.org. Red Line to Harrison; Blue Line to La Salle; Brown or Orange Line to Library-State/Van Buren. Well run and meticulously clean, this modern, 500-bed hostel on the Loop's southern edge has dorms sleeping six to ten ($25 per bed, $3 extra for nonmembers per night), most of which have adjoining bathrooms. Close to all El lines and within walking distance of Loop attractions, the lake, Grant Park and Museum Campus. Facilities include a full-service kitchen, laundry room and luggage storage, plus Internet access, Ping-Pong tables and even a library. Open 24hr. Accepts cash, travelers' checks, Visa and MasterCard. ❶

Hyatt on Printers Row 500 S Dearborn St, at W Congress Parkway ☎312/986-1234, ⓦwww .printersrow.hyatt.com; Red Line to Harrison; Blue Line to La Salle; Brown or Orange Line to Library-State/Van Buren. A small (161 rooms) but beautiful chain located in a National Historic Landmark building that's often overlooked by visitors because it's primarily a business hotel. There's an exercise center and complimentary morning paper. The popular restaurant, *Prairie*, has Frank Lloyd Wright-inspired decor and serves gourmet-inflected seasonal American fare. ❻–❽

Monaco 225 N Wabash Ave, at E Lake St ☎312/960-8500, ☏960-1883, ⓦwww.monaco -chicago.com; Red Line to Lake; Brown, Green, Orange or Purple Line to State/Lake. Plush boutique hotel decorated in French Art Deco style and close to the Mag Mile. Though some of the amenities like the "companion" goldfish – which guests missing their pets can take to their rooms – are gimmicky, the hotel itself is far nicer than any of the nearby business hotels charging similar prices. The rooms, some of which come with Jacuzzis, are stylish, and there are even some special "Tall" rooms, with longer-than-average beds and raised showerheads. Prices vary widely depending on availability; your best bet is to check their website for promotions and last-minute discounts. ④–⑤

The Palmer House Hilton 17 E Monroe St ☎312/726-7500, ⓕ917-1779; Red or Blue Line to Monroe, all other lines to Adams/Wabash. The oldest continuously operating hotel in the US and the sister hotel to New York's famed *Waldorf-Astoria*, the *Palmer* is a good bet if you want to be in the Loop but close to the Mag Mile. There is an enclosed shopping arcade, a health club and small indoor pool and four restaurants, including *Trader Vic's*, an iconic Tiki bar-restaurant (see p.166). The rooms are generally smallish, but kept to Hilton standards. Though the larger rooms and suites can be pricey, it's possible to book one of the smaller rooms at highly discounted rates (as low as $120) that can work out to be cheaper than some budget chains. Free morning paper delivered to your door. ④–⑥

Swissotel Chicago 323 E Wacker Drive, at N Columbia Drive ☎312/565-0565, ⓕ565-0540, ⓦwwwswissotel.com; Red Line to Lake; Brown, Green, Orange or Purple Line to Randolph/Wabash. Stylish and better run than most other business hotels in town, the towering 632-room *Swissotel* has superb city views from its location on the Chicago River and Michigan Ave, and a 42nd-floor health club with pool. All rooms have marble bathrooms and are pretty spacious. There's also a nine-hole golf course next door. Rooms with the better views cost $10–30 more, and like other business-minded hotels, rates tend to go down on weekends. ⑥–⑦

Travelodge 65 E Harrison St, at S Wabash Ave ☎312/427-8008, ⓕ427-8261 ⓦwww.travelodge .com; Red Line to Harrison. No-frills chain in the South Loop near Grant Park that's clean and has comfortable enough beds and bathroom furnishings, but overall a bit lackluster. ③–④

W Chicago City Center 172 W Adams St ☎312/332-1200 or 1-877/946-8357, ⓕ312/ 917-5771, ⓦwww.whotels.com; Red or Blue Line to Jackson; Brown, Orange or Purple Line to Quincy. Ultra-chic chain hotel in the heart of the Loop, with beautifully decorated and comfortable rooms. The lobby – a two-story space called The Living Room – is sumptuously ornate and equipped with its own DJ. Best to ignore published prices and instead search for deals online. The *Whiskey Blue* is a slick, retro after-work hotspot (see review) while the *We Restaurant* is a popular French bistro. ⑥–⑦

Airport hotels

Hilton O'Hare Airport O'Hare International Airport, directly across from the terminals ☎773/686-8000, ⓕ312/917-1707, ⓦwww.hilton.com/ hotels/CHIOHHH; Blue Line to O'Hare. This busy, 900-room hotel is nice enough and reasonably priced, though you'll walk farther to your room than you did from the main terminal to the hotel. Facilities include restaurants, a sports bar and a health club. ④–⑥

Hyatt Regency O'Hare 9300 W Bryn Mawr Ave ☎847/696-1234, ⓕ698-0139, ⓦhttp://ohare.hyatt.com; take the free hotel shuttle from baggage claim at O'Hare. The most likely reason you'd stay here is if you're stranded at O'Hare and the comparable, but slightly less expensive *Hilton* is full. The hotel has a pool and fitness center. ⑤–⑥

Radisson Hotel O'Hare 6810 N Mannheim Rd ☎847/297-1234 or 1-800/333-3333, ⓕ847/297-5287, ⓦwww.radisson.com/rosemontil; take the 24hr shuttle from baggage claim at O'Hare. Two miles from O'Hare, the *Radisson* is the best value among the airport hotels, with basic rooms, indoor and outdoor pools, plus a small fitness center. ③–④

Sofitel O'Hare 5550 N River Rd ☎847/678-4488, ⓕ678-9756, ⓦwww.sofitelchicagoohare.com; take the free hotel shuttle from O'Hare. Three miles from O'Hare, this plush hotel, with 300 immaculate rooms, includes a superb restaurant, a pool, sauna and fitness center (all with 24hr access), a good bakery, cheap parking ($12/night) and free shuttles to the airport every 20 minutes, 24 hours a day. Rates are almost always cheaper on weekends. ④–⑥

Near North

Best Western River North 125 W Ohio St, at N LaSalle Blvd ☎312/467-0800 or 1-800/780-723, ℻312/467-1665, ⊛www.bestwestern.com/rivernorthhotel; Red Line to Grand; Brown or Purple Line to Merchandise Mart. This refurbished *Best Western*, in a great River North location close to many attractions but off the main tourist drag, is the only downtown hotel that provides guests with free parking. Rooms are spacious, while facilities include a fitness center and an indoor pool on the roof. Close to transportation. A good deal all around. ❹–❺

Cass Hotel 640 N Wabash Ave, at E Ontario St ☎312/787-4030 or 1-800/227-7850, ℻312/787-8544; Red Line to Grand. No-frills budget hotel that gets by on its low rates and central Near North location. Rooms are a bit blah, and not especially clean, the lobby usually thick with smoke, and the *Sea of Happiness* hotel bar is a true, wonderful tacky dive. Tends to book up on weekends. ❸

Comfort Inn 15 E Ohio St, at N State St ☎312/894-0900 or 1-888/775-4111, ℻312/894/0999, ⊛www.chicagocomfortinn.com; Red Line to Grand. Basic high-rise budget chain hotel – though with a more glamorous-looking lobby than most – but with amenities such as a fitness room, whirlpool and sauna, and free local calls. Suites feature wet bar, microwave and refrigerator and extra sleeping area for kids. ❹

The Drake 140 E Walton St, at N Michigan Ave ☎312/787-2200, ℻787-2549, ⊛www.thedrakehotel.com; Red Line to Chicago. If it didn't occupy the most coveted piece of property in the city and have such history, Chicago's elegant *Drake* might have been surpassed years ago by its high-powered competitors. Across from Oak Street Beach and with outstanding views of Lake Shore Drive and Lake Michigan, the hotel has 535 renovated rooms, which still feel a bit aged and are smallish, especially compared to some of the newer hotels in the area. Some rooms start from $400 a night, but most cost half that, and a few rooms even less. ❺–❽

Fitzpatrick Hotel 166 E Superior St, at N Michigan Ave ☎312/787-6000 or 1-800/367-7701, ⊛www.fitzpatrickhotels.com; Red Line to Chicago. Sumptuous hotel with a subtle Irish theme (think mini shamrocks and expat staff). The rooms, converted from apartments, are huge and well designed, with comfortable beds. The location in Streeterville, one block east of Michigan Ave, is a major plus. ❹

Four Seasons Hotel 120 E Delaware Place, at N Michigan Ave ☎312/280-8800 or 1-800/819-5053, ℻312/280-7585, ⊛www.fourseason.com; Red Line to Chicago. The service is unbeatable at this majestic 343-room hotel, which offers sumptuous rooms with superb views, a spa, fitness club and skylit pool, and top-notch restaurants and lounges. You pay for what you get, and you'll rarely find a reduced rate here. ❽

Hotel Inter-Continental Chicago 505 N Michigan Ave, at E Illinois St ☎312/944-4100 or 1-800/465-4329, ℻312/944-1320, ⊛http://chicago.intercontinental.com; Red Line to Grand. Originally built in 1929 as a luxury men's club, this classic hotel features 844 festively decorated rooms on 42 floors, as well as a junior Olympic pool. Best to stay in the Tower as opposed to the lower floors, despite the slight extra cost, as the views are impressive. The recently renovated rooms are impressively modern, with minibar, coffeemaker, and terry bathrobes. Hotel amentites include laundry valet service and a gorgeous, Olympic-sized swimming pool. ❺–❼

Ohio House Motel 600 N LaSalle St, at W Ohio St ☎312/943-6000, ℻943-6063; Red Line to Grand; Brown or Purple Line to Merchandise Mart. If you're on a tight budget, this two-floor roadside motel is usually available, though its down-at-the-heels air makes it a last-resort budget option. That said, it's probably the best cheap hotel in the downtown area. ❸

Omni 676 N Michigan Ave, at E Erie St ☎312/944-6664, ⊛www.omnihotels.com; Red Line to Grand. The spiffier, newer cousin to the *Omni Ambassador East* (see p.136), the *Omni* (used by the Oprah Winfrey show for its guests) is pricey but worth the money. Each of the rooms features complimentary Internet access, two TVs, and plush terry robes. Health-conscious travelers can check into one of their Get Fit Rooms which feature a treadmill, dumbbells and healthy snacks. There's also an indoor heated pool and two sundecks. ❼–❽

Park Hyatt Chicago 800 N Michigan Ave, at Chicago Ave ⊤312/335-1234, Ⓕ239-4000, Ⓦwww.parkchicago.hyatt.com; Red Line to Chicago. Professional but not obstrusive, sophisticated and perhaps a touch arrogant, the *Park Hyatt* is the newest entry to vie for the title of top Chicago luxury hotel. The list of amenities goes overboard – each room has CD and DVD players, four phones and Mies van der Rohe-designed chairs – and the prices tend to as well. Hard to find reduced rates here as occupancy remains high in its 203 rooms. Has a magnificient gourmet restaurant, *NoMi* (see p.152) and faces onto Water Tower Park. ⑧

Peninsula Chicago Hotel 108 E Superior St, at N Michigan Ave ⊤312/337-2888, Ⓕ751-2888, Ⓦwww.fasttrack.peninsula.chicago.com; Red Line to Chicago. Everything you've ever wanted from a hotel and then some, this hip, new luxury hotel has 339 plush guest rooms with every conceivable amenity, including TVs beside the bathtubs. The well-equipped spa on the 19th and 20th floors offers spectacular views of Lake Michigan and N Michigan Ave, while the hotel bar is popular with the martini-drinking set. ⑦–⑧

The Raphael 201 E Delaware Place, at N Mies van der Rohe Way ⊤312/943-5000 or 1-800/983-7870, Ⓕ312/943-9483; Red Line to Chicago. Just behind the John Hancock building in Streeterville, this superbly located boutique hotel offers nice, larger-than-average affordable rates (including continental breakfast) and very friendly service. Much better value than the more well-known hotel chains, and sister to the *Tremont* (see below). ④–⑤

Red Roof Inn Chicago 162 E Ontario St, at N St Clair St ⊤312/787-3580, Ⓕ787-1299; Red Line to Grand. Better than you might expect from a budget motel chain, the *Red Roof*'s clean, comfortable rooms are close to the Mag Mile, the River North galleries and restaurants. Though slightly worn, the motel is good value for the area, often going for $100 or less. Weekends generally see rates go up a few dollars. ③

Ritz-Carlton 160 E Pearson St, between N Michigan Ave and N Mies van der Rohe Way ⊤312/266-1000, Ⓕ266-1194, Ⓦwww .fourseasons.com/chicagorc; Red Line to Chicago. The place to stay if you want to feel like royalty, with giant and richly appointed

rooms, several top-notch restaurants, a health club, lap pool and spa. Connected to Water Tower Place and a block from the Mag Mile. The airy café off the lobby makes for a great place to soak up the luxurious atmosphere. ⑦–⑧

Seneca 200 E Chestnut St, at N Mies van der Rohe Way ⊤312/787-8900 or 1-800/800-6261, Ⓕ312/988-4438, Ⓦwww.senecahotel.com; Red Line to Chicago. Plush boutique hotel, next to the John Hancock building, with spacious rooms for those wanting to stay near N Michigan Ave, but away from the crowds. Frequent special deals (standard room, full breakfast included) make this a good-value option (full-price rates are somewhat inflated) but service can be lackluster. ④–⑤

Sofitel Chicago Water Tower 20 E Chestnut St, at N Rush St ⊤312/324-4000, Ⓕ324-4025, Ⓦwww.sofitelchicago.com; Red Line to Chicago. This sleek glass tower is one of the more striking hotels in Chicago. The 400-plus rooms are minimally decorated yet comfortably chic, the service is impeccable, and many of the rooms – especially the suites – have lake views. Equally stylish is the street-level bar, *Le Bar*. Rarely do you come across a hotel this well appointed without paying over $250. ⑤–⑦

The Talbott 20 E Delaware Place, at N State St ⊤312/944-4970, Ⓦwww.talbotthotel.com; Red Line to Chicago. Striving for (and mostly achieving) old English country club style, the *Talbott* is a small Gold Coast boutique hotel built in 1927. The rooms are small but comfortable, the service impeccable, and the lobby with its leather armchairs and dark-wood walls a wonderful escape. Just steps off Michigan Ave but utterly relaxing. ⑤

Three Arts Club 1300 N Dearborn St, at E Goethe St ⊤312/944-6250, Ⓕ944-6284, Ⓦwww.threearts.org; Red Line to Clark/Division. Residence serving women working in the arts, catering mainly to long stays (over 4 months) but with rooms for shorter visits (minimum 3 days, $52 per person/per day, $294 per week or $960 a month), though you must apply in advance (membership not necessary). Housed in an old Gold Coast mansion, the club has sunny, comfortable rooms with twin beds and shared baths, plus a gorgeous living room and gallery, several pianos, a laundry room and a delightful courtyard. Rates include breakfast and dinner year-round, and guests can take advantage of frequent free arts programs. Note for the summertime: they do not have air-conditioning. ❸

Tremont Hotel 100 E Chestnut St, at N Rush St ☎312/751-1900, ℉751-9253; Red Line to Chicago. Conveniently located on a quiet little side street, one block from N Michigan Ave and the Water Tower area. Though rooms tend to be small and a little worn, they're in good enough shape, the staff is attentive and the hotel has some charm. ❹–❺

W Chicago Lakeshore 644 N Lake Shore Drive, at E Ontario St ☎312/943-9200 or 1-888/W-HOTELS, ⓦwww.starwood.com; Red Line to Grand. The lakefront location is this chic hotel's biggest asset, followed by well-appointed rooms with down-stuffed beds and high-end amenities. The luxurious first-floor lounge and bar are immensely popular with Chicago's crowd, as is the rooftop bar, *Whiskey Sky*. One of the closest hotels to Navy Pier and an infinitely more relaxed setting than its sibling in the Loop (see above). ❺–❼

Gold Coast and Old Town

The Claridge 1244 N Dearborn Parkway, at W Goethe St ☎312/787-4980 or 1-800/245-1258, ℉312/266-0978, ⓦwww.claridgehotel.com; Red Line to Clark/Division. Excellent value in one of the city's most expensive neighborhoods, with amenities you'd expect from a more expensive hotel. This determinedly old-fashioned boutique hotel, geared more toward business commuters than tourists, offers a morning paper and complimentary continental breakfast, as well as bathrobes and use of the fitness center and spa. Very central – a few blocks from the lake and near the Mag Mile, as well as dozens of restaurants and bars. Rooms are well appointed but on the small side. ❹–❺

The Gold Coast Guest House 113 W Elm St, at N Clark St ☎312/337-0361, ℉337-0362, ⓦwww.bbchicago.com; Red Line to Clark/Division. This converted 1873 row house, run by a wonderful host, includes continental breakfast and evening refreshments in their rates and usually requires a two-night stay on weekends. Each of the four guest rooms comes with air-conditioning and private bath – a couple even have a whirlpool – and bed sizes vary by room. There's also a charming garden out-

Westin 909 N Michigan Ave, at W Delaware Place ☎312/943-7200, ℉397-5580, ⓦwww.westinmichiganave.com; Red Line to Chicago. Over 700 rooms in this large chain luxury hotel right across from the John Hancock. Recently renovated rooms are plush, with great beds, and mostly good views of the area. Has a pricey and excellent steakhouse ("The Grill") on the first floor. Can't beat it for location and they often have discounted rates, especially in winter. ❺–❻

Whitehall 105 E Delaware Place, between N Rush St and N Michigan Ave ☎312/944-6300, ℉944-8552, ⓦwww.thewhitehallhotel.com; Red Line to Chicago. Boutique hotel just off Mag Mile that strives for, and mostly achieves, a sort of non-snooty European ambience. Guests have use of the fitness center as well as complimentary car service within a two-mile radius of the hotel. One of the top choices for those who want to stay in the area but try to avoid the chains. ❻

side and the lake is just a ten-minute walk away. No smoking. ❹

Old Town Chicago B&B Inn 1442 North Park Ave, at Schiller St ☎312/440-9268, ℉440-2378, ⓦwww.oldtownchicago.com; Brown or Purple Line to Sedgwick. Lavishly decorated wing of a multimillion-dollar Art Deco town house in Old Town. The four guest rooms, all suites with luxurious queen beds, each come with private bath and cable TV, and breakfast as well as 24hr snacks are included in rates. There's also a nice roofdeck. A three-night minimum stay is generally required for weekend stays reserved more than a week in advance. One of the nicer B&B options in the city. ❺–❻

Omni Ambassador East Hotel 1301 N State Pkwy, at W Goethe St ☎312/787-7200 or 1-800/842-6664, ℉312/787-4760, ⓦwww.omnihotels.com; Red Line to Clark/Division. Great hotel in a prime Gold Coast location, offering surprisingly affordable room rates for the area. Considering its age, the 285 rooms are very spacious, comfortable and well kept-up. It's better than staying in the Loop if you want to explore Old Town, Lincoln Park and beyond, or simply stay in this affluent neighborhood. Built in the

1920s, the *Ambassador* was a favorite haunt of Frank Sinatra and the Rat Pack during the 1950s, and its famed *Pump* Room bar is still here, worth a visit just to see the cream of Chicago society. ❹–❺

South Loop and Near South

Best Western Grant Park 1100 S Michigan Ave, at E 11 St ☎312/922-2900 or 1-800/472-6875, ⓕ312/922-0134, ⓦwww.bestwestern.com/grantparkhotel; Green, Orange or Red Line to Roosevelt. Located in the South Loop near the Museum Campus, this recently renovated chain hotel has 173 rooms – all free from any sort of style, yet clean enough – an outdoor pool and sundeck, and complimentary coffee and newspapers. Popular with convention and tour groups; weekends tend to book up. Lake-view rooms fetch $10–20 more. ❹

Essex Inn 800 S Michigan Ave, at E 8th St ☎312/939-2800; Red Line to Harrison. 15-story, 255-room South Loop hotel that's favored by many travelers for its cheap rates, clean, if somewhat spartan rooms and convenient location to Loop attractions. ❸–❹

Hilton Chicago and Towers 720 S Michigan Ave, at E Balbo Drive ☎312/922-4400, ⓕ922-5240, ⓦwww.chicagohilton.com; Red Line to Harrison. Unless you need too be here for a convention or want to stay near Grant Park, you might not find too much need to stay at this 1500-room hotel. Still, the rooms are kept up well enough, there are huge lakefront views, and prices aren't bad, There's an indoor pool, fitness room and all the business-traveler amenities you'd expect. ❺–❻

Holiday Inn & Suites Downtown Chicago 506 W Harrison St, at S Canal St ☎312/957-9100, ⓕ957-0474, ⓦwww.hidowntown.com; Blue Line to Clinton (right underneath the inn). A good, but not great, value chain hotel just southwest of the Loop, near the Sears Tower, the two main Metra train stations, and Greektown and Little Italy. Rooms are spacious, staff are pleasant, and there's a small restaurant on site, as well as a fitness room and outdoor pool. ❸–❺

Hyatt Regency McCormick Place 2233 S King Drive, at E Cermak Rd ☎312/567-1234, ⓦwww.mccormickplace.hyatt.com; bus #35. This handsome hotel towers incongruously over the empty acres just west of the convention center, which provides pretty much all of its guests. Although it's a bit isolated, it's possible to find some good deals here when there's not a huge convention in town. The 800 rooms are colorfully decorated and each offers complimentary high-speed Internet access. There is also an impressive array of on-site services like printing, shipping and computer workstations. ❺–❽

Wheeler Mansion 2020 S Calumet Ave, at E 18th St ☎312/945-2020, ⓕ945-2021, ⓦwww.wheelermansion.com; Metra: 18th St. Probably the city's most luxurious B&B, housed in a beautifully restored 1870s mansion, with the amenities of a small luxury hotel (Egyptian cotton sheets, towels and robes, turn-down service). Popular with conventioneers meeting at McCormick Place, the B&B is also just a block from the historic Glessner House (see p.83) and the rest of S Prairie Ave. Rates include breakfast, and there's a classy first-floor dining room where you can order in food and dine in the evening. Minimum stays usually apply on weekends, and you can choose from standard rooms ($230–285), and junior and master suites ($265–365); prices include tax. ❻–❽

Wicker Park

House of Two Urns 1239 N Greenview Ave, at W Division St ☎773/235-1408 or 1-877/896-8767, ⓕ773/235-1410, ⓦwww.twourns.com; Blue Line to Division/Milwaukee. Charming, quiet B&B in Wicker Park with five creatively decorated and unusual rooms (the Alice room has a Lewis Carroll vibe, while the Alcove offers great views and a reading nook). Amenities go beyond the usual B&B offerings to include DVD rental, private phone lines and answering machines, and you'll also get good views of the downtown skyline from the roof deck. The only drawback is that most guest rooms share a bathroom with another guest room. Advance bookings usually require a minimum three-night stay. A 10–15 percent discount is usually offered in January and February. ❸–❹

The Wicker Park Inn 1329 N Wicker Park Ave, at N Wood St ☏ 773/486-2743, ℱ 486-3228, ⓦ www.wickerparkinn.com; Blue Line to Damen. Three-room B&B in a two-story 1890s row house, a few blocks from the El. It's nothing

extraordinary, and not as quaint as *Two Urns* (see above), but it does book up quickly – for weekend stays, call ahead two months. Rooms are bright but small – think your first post-college apartment. Breakfast is included and is served daily in the small dining area. Smoking is not permitted, and cats are on the premises. The inn charges a flat rate ($115–$150) and accepts most major credit cards as well as travelers' checks. Check-out time is 11am, but the owners don't mind storing your luggage throughout the day. ❹

Lincoln Park

Arlington House International Hostel 616 W Arlington Place, at N Geneva Terrace ☏ 773/929-5380 or 1-800/467-8355, ℱ 773/665-5485, ⓦ www.arlingtonhouse.com; Red, Brown or Purple Line to Fullerton. Lincoln Park's only hostel is basic and not much else. Stay only if you can't afford anything else. Dorms have up to seven beds ($22 per bed) and private rooms are available (from $50 per room). Within walking distance of the Lincoln Park Zoo and Conservatory and the neighborhood's nightlife, and close to public transportation. As thefts have been reported, be sure to use the safe-box rentals and luggage storage. Unlike many hostels, it's open 24hr, with no curfew. ❶

Centennial House 1020 W Altgeld St, at W Fullerton Ave and N Sheffield Ave ☏ 773/871-6020, ℱ 871-0412; Red, Brown or Purple Line to Fullerton. A very small and cute B&B consisting of two apartments furnished in nineteenth-century European antiques – ideal for large groups (up to 15) – plus a double and a single room, and an extra room in the owners' home. A two-night minimum stay is required and the apartments tend to book up well in advance. Prices range from $100 to $175 for rooms, while the apartments go for more (rates vary widely, call well in advance); they all include breakfast and free local phone calls. ❸–❹.

Comfort Inn 601 W Diversey Parkway, at N Clark St ☏ 773/348-2810, ℱ 348-1912, ⓦ www .comfortinn.com; Brown or Purple Line to Diversey. This hotel (one of the first Comfort Inns), has clean, basic rooms and is kept very clean by the excellent staff. Rooms

vary in size and price, but overall it's good value for the area. There's a small parking lot and free continental breakfast and cable TV. You're also a quick cab ride from most of the area's nightlife and within walking distance of the lake. Money-back guarantee if you're unhappy with your stay. ❸–❹

Days Inn Lincoln Park-North 644 W Diversey Parkway, at N Clark St ☏ 773/525-7010, ℱ 525-6998, ⓦ www.lpndaysinn.com; Brown or Purple Line to Diversey. A decent place to crash in accommodation-starved Lincoln Park. Not necessarily the most inspired atmosphere, but rooms are bright and clean, and rates include complimentary continental breakfast (6.30–11am), as well as passes to Bally's health club next door, which has an indoor track, lap pool, sauna, whirlpool and cheap parking (from $8). ❸–❹

Windy City Urban Inn 607 W Deming Place, at N Clark St ☏ 773/248-7058 or 1-800/375-7084, ℱ 773/529-4180, ⓦ www.windycityinn.com; Red, Brown or Purple Line to Fullerton. Cozy and friendly B&B in a restored Victorian mansion, with charmingly decorated rooms named after local literary lights (Saul Bellow, Studs Terkel, Hemingway), none of which seem to have much to do with the author chosen. All have private bath and rates include a breakfast buffet. Note that rooms vary in price quite a bit, from $145 to $225, while the Coach House apartment-suites are $185–325 for two people. Children welcome. Credit cards are accepted, and weekends tend to book up quickly. Recommended. ❹–❽

Lakeview and the North Lakefront

Best Western Hawthorne Terrace 3434 N Broadway St, at W Hawthorne Place ☎773/244-3434, ℱ244-3435, ⓦwww.hawthorne terrace.com; Red Line to Addison; Red, Brown or Purple Line to Belmont. Located in Boystown, one block from the Lincoln Park lakefront, this good-value budget option – formerly a hotel for transients, though you'd never know it – has 59 clean rooms (including some junior suites) that come with complimentary continental breakfast and newspaper. Facilities include a fitness center with a sauna and whirlpool. ❸–❹

Chicago International Hostel 6318 N Winthrop Ave, at W Rosemont Ave ☎773/262-1011, ℱ262-3673, ⓦwww.chicagointernationalhostel.com; Red Line to Granville or Loyola. You'll almost always find a spot at this very basic 125-bed hostel near Loyola University. Beds cost $20 per night, with dorms sleeping four to eight and sharing two unisex bathrooms. A few private doubles ($48) and triples ($69) – with bath – are also available, and stays of ten days get one night free. The hostel, recently renovated and under new management, has a kitchen, laundry, free parking and luggage storage, and closes between 3am and 6am. Accepts travelers' checks, Visa and MasterCard, and requires a photo ID showing permanent residence outside Chicago. ❶

City Suites 933 W Belmont Ave, at N Willow Ave ☎773/404-3400 or 1-800/248-9108, ℱ773/404-3405, ⓦwww.cityinns.com; Red, Brown or Purple Line to Belmont. A smallish, old-fashioned hotel on busy Belmont Ave, perfect for younger people who want to explore the area's bars and stagger home or to just walk around some of the city's less-explored neighborhoods. Rooms (double rooms and office suites) are basic but clean, and It's a dependable option in a non-touristy location. ❹

Majestic 528 W Brompton Ave, at N Lake Shore Drive ☎773/404-3499 or 1-800/727-5108, ⓦwww.cityinns.com; Red Line to Addison. This old business hotel in Wrigleyville, with country manor decor, has charming features like vintage elevators and radiators. Good value in an area not exactly overflowing with hotels and close to Lakeview's nightlife. Note, however, that it's a bit of a hike from downtown. ❸–❹

The Willows 555 W Surf St, at N Broadway St, ☎773/528-8400 or 1-800/787-3108, ⓦwww.cityinns.com; Brown or Purple Line to Diversey. Well-kept and affordable boutique hotel, located in a border zone between Lincoln Park and Lakeview, and just two blocks from Lake Michigan. Recently renovated in French country style, *The Willows* has decent-sized rooms and suites and complimentary breakfast is included in rates. Sister to the *Majestic* and *City Suites* hotels (see above), the *Willows* is the most romantic of the three. ❸–❹

West Side

Quality Inn Downtown 1 S Halsted St, at W Madison St ☎312/829-5000 or 1-800/228-2222, ⓦwww.qualityinnchicago.com; Green Line to Clinton; Blue Line to UIC/Halsted. Close to Greektown and not far from the Sears Tower, this basic chain hotel is a good option for those wanting to be near the Loop and the West Side, but not wanting to pay Loop prices. The 400 rooms, almost unchanged since the place began as a *Holiday Inn* in 1969, are very dated but reasonably clean, and there's also a café, bar and grill. ❸

South Side

International House of Chicago 1414 E 59th
St, at Blackstone St ☎773/753-2270, ℱ753-
1227, ⊕http://ihouse.uchicago.edu; **Metra: 59th
St.** Not a hostel per se, but simple housing
for University of Chicago students that's
open to the public ($50 per day for a pri-
vate single room with shared bath). Right
on campus and a block from the Metra
University of Chicago/59th St train station,
the 100-room building also has a little café,
open on weekdays. The front desk is
staffed 7am–11pm, and check-in is not
possible after 11pm; there is, however, no
curfew. Discounts are available on stays of
a month ($30 per day), and double rooms
($83 per day). Accepts travelers' checks
and credit cards – you'll need the latter to
make a reservation. ❸

Ramada Inn Lakeshore 4900 S Lake Shore
Drive, at E 51st St ☎773/288-5800 or 1-
888/298-2054, ℱ773/288-5745. Four-story
no-frills motel in Hyde Park, with an outdoor
pool and sweeping views of the lake. A
good bet – affordable and good-sized
rooms – if you're visiting the University of
Chicago and one of the only hotels in the
area. Direct shuttle to airports, a lifesaver
for a hotel this far south. ❸

Oak Park

Wright's Cheney House B&B 520 N East Ave,
at Oak Park Ave ☎708/524-2067, ⊕www
.oakparknet.com; **Green Line to Oak Park.** Frank
Lloyd Wright designed this Prairie-style
house in 1904 and most of the furnishings
and fabrics in the two suites ($155 per
night) as well. The simply adorned suites,
which are usually booked a month in
advance, have kitchenettes stocked with
food, as well as large bathrooms with
Jacuzzis. There's usually a two-night minimum stay on weekends, with May and
October being especially hard to book. Just
six blocks from the El, the B&B is close to
five other Wright-designed homes. ❺

Eating

I f there's something that Chicago does with aplomb it's food. **Dining out** is a huge part of the city's culture – more relaxed and down-to-earth than in other major US cities, something reflected in the proliferation of good, reasonably priced restaurants. That's not saying there aren't plenty of world-class establishments here to give New York a run for its money, where you could easily spend a hundred dollars a head. At the other extreme, some of things Chicago does best (pizza, hot dogs and the like) can be had for less than $5. Sampling something from each part of the spectrum is ideal.

The city built itself around a century ago as the focal point for distribution and packaging of foodstuffs, quite possibly the reason local portions tend to be not just sizable, but extreme. Servers at many Italian restaurants will make sure to ask you, "Did you want the *full* portion, or just the half?" When in doubt, go with the half, as many times a full portion could feed a family of three. Steaks are typically gargantuan, the **deep-dish pizzas** (see box below) can easily defeat even the most dedicated trenchermen, and Italian beef sandwiches are piled high and slopping out all over the place: it's a rare Chicago diner who thinks they didn't get their money's worth.

Upton Sinclair's 1906 *The Jungle* memorably exposed the disgusting condi-
tions at the mythically vast slaughterhouses and meatpacking facilities that sprawled over the South Side. While conditions are much more hygienic these days, that industry's legacy meant Chicago had an awful lot of meat around and a large immigrant population to feed. Thus the proliferation of **hot dog stands** like *The Wiener's Circle*, *Portillo's*, *Superdawg* and others (don't even try the sacri-
lege of putting ketchup on your hot dog here; most dog stands refuse to stock it), as well as numerous **Italian beef** joints and the ability to get a Polish sausage just about anywhere. Not to mention, of course, giant juicy **steaks**, several outstanding barbecue and ribs joints and a number of incredible burger places.

Deep-dish pizza

This kind of pie is not the flat, thin entity most people are familiar with. Instead, it's a mountainous agglomeration of chunky tomato sauce, layer upon layer of gooey cheese and thick chunks of sausage and pepperoni. Brave souls eat with their hands, many resort to fork and knife. If you're looking for an argument with a Chicagoan, make an offhand comment about what you think is the best deep dish in the city; odds are, they'll have an opinion. A strong – and different – one. See the "Restaurants and dining by cuisine" box on p.147 for a quick rundown of your pizza options.

Not that everything else isn't available too: you'll of course be able to get vegetarian meals, along with all sorts of New American fusion cuisine, plenty of Asian offerings, and anything in between you may desire. Close to the city center most everything is available; for the high points in **ethnic cuisines**, you may have to venture further afield.

Most visitors stay in the **River North/Magnificent Mile** area, where a great number of the city's finest restaurants are located, like

Frontera Grill (thought to be the best Mexican food in the United States), *Gino's East Pizzeria* and the *Chicago Chop House*. Right nearby are the packed restaurant rows on Rush Street in the **Gold Coast**, Wells Street in **Old Town** and (a little further north) Halsted Street in **Lincoln Park**. But it would be a shame to limit your dining to these few square miles. While the **Loop** has relatively few restaurants worth seeking out – most people eat dinner elsewhere if they are coming in for some evening entertainment – several of them, like *Everest* and *Lou Mitchell's* (with its excellent breakfast) are some of the best in the city. In general, the further you venture from the tourist spots and into the neighborhoods, the better, more local and more interesting your culinary experience will be.

Quick jaunts to **Greektown**, around Halsted Street and Jackson Boulevard, and **Little Italy**'s Taylor Street, are relatively easy and more than worthwhile, though recent decades have seen them grow more commercial and less authentic; further out, **Pilsen** on the southwest side has some excellent **Mexican** fare and a few **Chinatown** restaurants that are the only reason most Chicagoans ever make the journey to that part of town. **Wrigleyville** and **Lakeview** have perhaps the most Chicago-style eateries, which is to say, odd combinations of sausages, ribs, and other anomalous greasebombs. The **Hyde Park** area is your best bet for southern soul food.

Relaxed weekend **brunches** are something else the city does well; the best places (like *Bongo Room* in Wicker Park and *Original Pancake House,* off Rush) will have lines out the door and down the block, but there's any number of spots that will do in a pinch.

The listings in this chapter are arranged **geographically** and correspond more or less to the breakdowns in the guide. Each neighborhood is in turn split into two divisions: **Cafés, snacks and light meals**, which emphasizes spots for breakfast, lunch or a quick bite any other time; and **Restaurants**, for slightly more formal dining, typically at dinner. However, there is certainly crossover between the two, and many diner-type places, found in the first category, can be useful for inexpensive meals at dinnertime too. And numerous upscale restaurants also serve lunch, often at a lower price than dinner menus. Note too that it's always good to have a **reservation** at the pricier joints; if it's essential, we've said so in the review.

For listings **by cuisine**, turn to the box on pp.146–148. We've given each restaurant a **price category** (see box above), rather loosely structured as a benchmark for the average meal of two courses plus a drink, but it's easy to overshoot the category by factoring in multiple drinks, coffee and desserts, and so on.

The Loop

Corner Bakery

It's getting so that you can barely turn a corner in downtown Chicago – especially the Loop – without running into a Corner Bakery. Forgive the faux-homey look and the often infuriatingly slow and confusing lines and focus instead on the baked, buttery panini, gooey desserts, great coffee and plethora of fresh-baked breads. Listed below are a few of their Loop locations (for a full list see ⊛ www.cornerbakery .com): 360 N Michigan at Wacker ⊤312/236-2400; 35 E Monroe at Michigan ⊤312/372-0072; 120 S LaSalle at Adams ⊤312/269-9100; 188 W Washington at Wells ⊤312/263-4258.

Cafés, snacks and light meals

Lou Mitchell's 565 W Jackson Blvd, at Clinton; ⊤312/939-3111; Red Line to Jackson; Blue Line to Clinton. Started in 1923, this is Chicago's first diner, one block from Union Station, and while the menu hardly seems to have changed, it's still worth it to the businessmen who dutifully wait as long as it takes. Those in line get donut holes to tide them over. Inexpensive.

Restaurants

Atwood Café 1 W Washington St, at State ⊤312/368-1900; Brown Line to Washington. Snazzy contemporary American café in the *Burnham hotel* that serves everything from braised shortribs to cavatappi pasta. Giant windows face the street for great people-watching. Expensive.

Bacino's 118 S Clinton, at Monroe ⊤312/876-1188; Blue Line to Clinton. Thin- and stuffed-crust pizzas that have a more gourmet take on the topic than most of the local chains. They make a big deal of their "healthy" mushroom and spinach pie, which would be healthy but for all that wonderful cheese. Worth checking out. Inexpensive.

Berghoff 17 W Adams St, at State ⊤312/427-3170; Brown Line to Jackson. Century-old tavern that survived Prohibition by selling food and root beer. Unbeatably nostalgic scene, especially the oak-paneled walls and attentive, veteran waitstaff. The satisfying, if heavy, food is of the Wiener schnitzel variety and they serve their own, decent, beers. Octoberfest here is not to be missed. Moderate.

Catch-35 35 W Wacker, at Dearborn ⊤312/346-3500; Brown, Green, Orange or Purple Line to State; Red Line to Lake. A serious power lunch and dinner spot for financial and advertising types that features dozens of daily seafood specials and live jazz. Leave the tourist togs at the hotel. Expensive.

Giordano's 28 E Jackson Blvd, at State ⊤312/939-4646; Brown Line to Jackson; 130 E Randolph St, at Michigan ⊤312/616-1200; Brown, Green, Orange or Purple Line to Randolph. Some consider this the town's best deep-dish pizza. While it's definitely a contender, the sheer number of locations has helped dilute this brand's consistency, especially in the Loop. Inexpensive.

Miller's Pub 134 S Wabash, at Monroe ⊤312/645-5377; Brown, Green, Orange or Purple Line to Adams. Within these walls – covered in autographed celebrity photos – you can find some of the best ribs in town, as well as excellent steaks and seafood at unbeatable prices. The atmosphere is welcoming and the charm undeniable. Moderate.

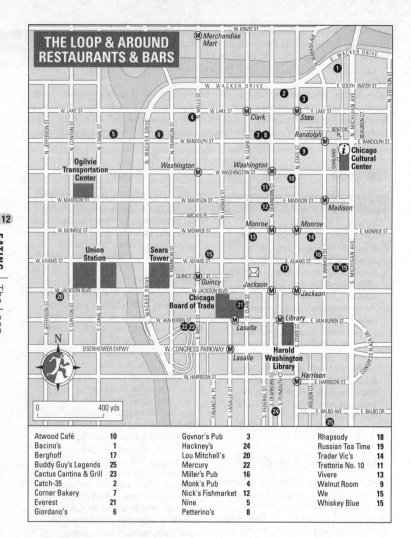

THE LOOP & AROUND RESTAURANTS & BARS

0   400 yds

Atwood Café	10	Govnor's Pub	3	Rhapsody	18
Bacino's	1	Hackney's	24	Russian Tea Time	19
Berghoff	17	Lou Mitchell's	20	Trader Vic's	14
Buddy Guy's Legends	25	Mercury	22	Trattoria No. 10	11
Cactus Cantina & Grill	23	Miller's Pub	16	Vivere	13
Catch-35	2	Monk's Pub	4	Walnut Room	9
Corner Bakery	7	Nick's Fishmarket	12	We	15
Everest	21	Nine	5	Whiskey Blue	15
Giordano's	6	Petterino's	8		

Nick's Fishmarket 2 S Dearborn St, at One First National Plaza ☎312/621-0200; Brown Line to Monroe. Popular with pre-theater crowds and one of the few decent seafood options in the Loop. A lot has been said about Chef Jose Bernal's Asian flavoring of the menu – especially items like black and blue ahi – which adds a welcome dash of excitement and without straying too far from traditional menu offerings. Expensive. *Nick's Grill* upstairs has a more casual menu.
Nine 440 W Randolph St, at Canal ☎312/277-0207, ⓦwww.n9ne.com; Green Line to Clinton;

Brown, Orange or Purple Line to Washington. Sleek steakhouse serving prime cuts and contemporary American fare. Tempura rock shrimp with Asian dipping sauces, and the trio of caviar cones are the signature appetizers. If you didn't go broke ordering dinner, have a pricey martini at the popular and ultra-moderne *Ghost Bar* upstairs. Expensive.
Petterino's 150 N Dearborn St, at Randolph ☎312/422-0150; Brown Line to Washington; Brown, Green, Orange or Purple Line to State. There's not much terribly exciting about this bright, straight-arrow Italian steak-

house, but its location on the first floor of the new Goodman Theatre building makes it a perfect dining spot for those attending a show at the Goodman or nearby Chicago Theatre or Gene Siskel Film Center. Steaks and pasta dishes, mostly. Moderate to expensive.

Rhapsody 65 E Adams, at Wabash; ☎312/786-9911; Brown, Green, Orange or Purple Line to Adams. Elegant but affordable spot perfectly located for those going to the Art Institute or Symphony Center, which are just around the corner. The airy and plant-filled space is flooded with sunlight during the day while the New American dishes are delicious and tangy; heavy on the seafood. Moderate.

Russian Tea Time 77 E Adams, at Wabash; ☎312/360-0000; Brown, Green, Orange or Purple Line to Adams. Very affordable, popular and cozy spot near the Art Institute for all your caviar, vodka and blini needs. Moderate.

Trattoria No. 10 10 N Dearborn St, at Madison ☎312/984-1718, ⓦwww.trattoriaten.com; Brown Line to Washington. Classic but not stuffy Italian fare at this homey local favorite. Menu items include homemade ravioli, farfalle with confit of duck and fresh risottos. Moderate.

Vivere 71 W Monroe, at Wabash ☎312/332-4040; Brown Line to Monroe. Perfect for a pre-theater repast (it's right by the Shubert), *Vivere* is the most worthwhile of the three family-owned restaurants in the Italian Village mini-complex here. The others (*La Cantina Enoteca* and *Village*) are dull and downright touristy, while *Vivere*'s colorful decor and lighter, snazzier take on Italian fare attracts more of a local crowd. Moderate.

Walnut Room 111 N State St, at Washington, 7th floor ☎312/781-3125; Brown Line to Washington. Though Marshall Field's department store dining room is rather touristy, the decor – high ceilings, chandeliers and dark wood – the elegantly simple food and the simply elegant service make this a classy spot for a downtown lunch. Moderate.

We 172 W Adams St, at Wells ☎312/917-5608; Brown, Orange or Purple Line to Quincy. Just as utterly hip and plush as you would expect from the *W* hotel, this bar-like French restaurant serves things like foie gras and ahi tuna with a soy glaze in a design-your-own-meal manner (match meat from column A to sauce from column B, etc). Expensive.

River North

Cafés, snacks and light meals

Ed Debevic's 640 N Wells St, at Ontario ☎312/664-1707; Brown or Purple Line to Chicago. Sure, it's one of those wacky, 1950s-style diners where the waitstaff sings and serves up malts, burgers and fries, but the catch here is that the staff is also insulting, obnoxious and just plain rude. Not for masochists only, the food is actually quite good, and kids love the chance to yell back at adults in public. Inexpensive.

Mr. Beef 666 N Orleans St, at Erie ☎312/337-8500; Brown or Purple Line to Chicago. The little shack looks ready to fall over, held together only by will and the love of the diet-hating locals and celebrities who trek here for the giant Italian beef sandwiches, dripping with juice and peppers. Inexpensive.

Portillo's Hot Dogs 100 W Ontario St, at N LaSalle ☎312/587-8910; Red Line to Chicago. One-of-a-kind Chicago establishment, somewhere between a fast-food place and a tacky novelty restaurant. Their Italian beef (thin-sliced beef piled into a hoagy and slathered with gravy and peppers) is a tangy delight, while the hot dogs can't be beat. There's a *Barnelli's Pasta* in this same building, but who cares? Inexpensive.

Restaurants

Ben Pao 55 W Illinois St, at Dearborn ☎312/222-1888; Red Line to Grand. Dark, romantic decor mixed with a good pan-Asian menu that's got a little more pop to it than you'd expect for a non-Chinatown spot. Great bar and a good pre-theater menu. Moderate to expensive.

Bin 36 339 N Dearborn St, at Kinzie ☎312/755-9463; Red Line to Grand. *Wine for Dummies* in restaurant form, this bright little café in the House of Blues complex serves tart dishes like wild mushroom risotto and lobster salad and has a staff that specializes in helping educate first-time wine connoisseurs. Moderate.

Restaurants and dining by cuisine

12

EATING

Continues over

Brasserie Jo 59 W Hubbard St, at Clark
☏312/595-0800; Red Line to Grand. Upscale
French brasserie, notable for its rather
striking giant clock, the authentic zinc bar
imported from France and good fish and
steak dishes. The menu here emphasizes
more rustic French fare like steak *frites* and
onion tarts but alternates them with original
dishes like shrimp and vegetables served
inside a phyllo-dough pouch. Wonderful
service. Moderate to expensive.

Café Iberico 739 N La Salle St, at W Chicago
Ave ☏312/573-1510. Considered one of the
best places for tapas in town, *Iberico* is
usually packed full with families and gangs
of co-workers or friends all passing their
small dishes back and forth and pounding
drinks. On weekend nights they serve sangria from big jugs and have traditional
Spanish bands. Moderate.

Carson's 612 N Wells St, at Ohio ☏312/280-
9200, ⓦwww.ribs.com. Homesick ex-
Chicagoans get ribs from *Carson's* shipped
to them all over the world. This location –
there are several in the area – is pretty plain
to look at, but the babyback ribs, drenched
in the sweet house sauce (tasting like
molasses), keep the place packed, especially on weekends. A tough call between
this and *Twin Anchors* as for who has the
better ribs. Expensive.

Chicago Chop House 60 W Ontario St, between
N Dearborn and N Clark streets ☏866/831-
5330; Red Line to Chicago. Housed in an old
brownstone right near *the Hard Rock
Café/Excalibur* tourist nexus, this steak-

house is heavy on Chicago memorabilia and
crowds. It remains, however, an excellent
spot to get one of the best cuts of steak in
town. Casual attire and attitude. Expensive.

Chilipancingo 358 W Ontario St, at Orleans
☏312/266-6428; Brown or Purple Line to
Chicago. Named for the capital of the chef's
home state back in Mexico, this festive yet
subdued Mexican spot is deservedly
famous for its *mole* dishes. Always doing
steady business, it's still usually easy to get
a table. The *carne asada* goes down especially well with one of their chilly, perfect
martinis. Moderate to expensive.

Coco Pazzo 300 W Hubbard St ☏312/836-0900;
Red Line to Grand. Authentic Tuscan-style
roasted meats and delicious pasta dishes
served in classy surroundings – the rabbit
ragout pasta is superb. The restaurant's little
sister, *Coco Pazzo Café* in Streeterville (636
N St Clair St), offers much the same quality
at half the price. Moderate.

Erawan 729 N Clark St, at Chicago ☏312/642-
6888; Brown or Purple Line to Chicago. While
the service can be erratic, this pricey
gourmet Indian restaurant has a strong
band of followers who crave its delicately
presented dishes like satay of venison tenderloin. Expensive.

Fogo de Chão 661 N LaSalle St, at W Erie St
☏312/932-9330; Brown or Purple Line to
Chicago. All-you-can-eat Brazilian restaurant
where the servers wander the dining room
wielding giant skewers of succulent meat,
and slice up the ones you choose. At $40 a
head, it's only good value if you have a

NEAR NORTH & AROUND RESTAURANTS

N

0   600 yds

Lake Michigan

Chicago River

Chicago River North Branch

Ashkenaz Delicatessan	7
Ben Pao	42
Big Bowl	6
Billy Goat Tavern	47
Bin 36	53
Boston Blackies	40
Brasserie Jo	48
Café Iberico	24
Café Spiaggia	12
Cape Cod Room	14
Carson's the Place for Ribs	32
Cheesecake Factory	20
Chicago Chop House	35
Chilpancingo	31
Coco Pazzo	44
Dillon's	5
Dragonfly Mandarin	3
Ed Debevic's	32
Edwardo's	2
Eli's the Place for Steak	23
Erawan	25
Five Faces	4
Fogo De Chao	28
Frontera Grill and Topolobampo	21
foodlife	45
Gibson's	9
Gino's East	33
Green Door Tavern	26
Harry Caray's	52
Heaven on Seven	37
House of Blues	54
Iron Mike's Grille	19
Keefer's	51
Kiki's Bistro	16
Kinzie Chop House	50
Klay Oven	49
Lawry's	13
Le Colonial	41
Maggiano's	17
MK	11
Morton's of Chicago	18
Mr. Beef	30
Nacional	27
Naha	43

NoMi	22
Original Pancake House	10
Palagi's Ristorante	46
Park Avenue Café	15
Pizzeria Uno	39
Portillo's Hot Dogs	34
Salpicón	1
The Signature Room	20
Tavern on Rush	8
Tempo	18
Tizi Melloul	38
Tru	29
Vong's Thai Kitchen	43

149

huge appetite. It's all best washed down with refreshing, but lethal, *caipirinhas*, Brazil's signature mixed drink. Expensive.

Frontera Grill and Topolobampo 445 N Clark St, at W Illinois St ☎312/661-1434; Red Line to Grand. Two top Mexican restaurants under one roof – overseen by master chef Rick Bayless – deservedly considered the best in the country. The better-value *Frontera Grill* is more casual but constantly packed due to its no-reservation policy (the snazzier *Topolobampo* grills a mean ostrich but is almost impossible to get into with less than a couple weeks' notice). There's so much to choose from that the five-course tasting menu is the best bet for first-timers. Very expensive.

Gino's East 633 N Wells St, at Ontario ☎312/943-1124; Brown or Purple Line to Chicago. *Gino's* new location (incongruously packed into an ex-Planet Hollywood) manages to maintain the tacky but homey, graffitti-strewn interior of the cramped old spot over on Ontario. Avoid the house beer but dive into a hefty deep-dish pie: with its slightly sweet, polenta crust loaded up with spicy sauce and gooey cheese, it's just short of divine. Inexpensive.

Green Door Tavern 678 N Orleans St, at Erie ☎312/664-5496; Brown or Purple Line to Chicago. A former speakeasy built in 1872, this rather precariously tilted structure is now home to a wonderfully comfortable tavern that serves over a dozen varieties of the best burgers in town and at least 30 beers. Inexpensive.

Harry Caray's 33 W Kinzie St, at N Dearborn St ☎312/828-0966; Red Line to Grand. The legendary former announcer for the Cubs lives on in his Italian-styled steakhouse that has weathered the years and turned out, unlike most sports-personality-run joints, to actually be a really good spot to have a steak – splurge for the Vesuvio pan-searing treatment – and watch a game. Chock-full of sports memorabilia. Expensive.

House of Blues 329 N Dearborn St, at Kinzie ☎312/923-2000; Red Line to Grand. The dark, colorful interior lends a dramatic tint to an otherwise serviceable Southern menu. A lot depends on the choir performing that day, but the Sunday Gospel Brunch (usually 9.30am, noon and 2.30pm; $35 per person; reserve in advance) can be one of the best in town, heavy on the seafood, jambalaya, etouffee and soul food. Moderate.

Keefer's 20 W Kinzie St, at Dearborn

☎312/467-9525; Red Line to Grand. While the look of this sleek place, anchoring a sparkling new Dearborn office building, is more suburban office park than big city, the offerings are nothing to scoff at. The high-cholesterol appetizers, half-dozen types of sizzling steaks and attentive service are clearly meant to appeal to the corporate fat cat in all. Expensive.

Kiki's Bistro 900 N Franklin St, at W Chicago Ave ☎312/335-5454; Brown or Purple Line to Chicago. Laid-back, classic French bistro catering to an older crowd, especially standards like *coq au vin* and steak *au poivre*. Food is delicious and not as overpriced as many bistros. Moderate to expensive.

Kinzie Chop House 400 N Wells St, at Kinzie ☎312/822-0191; Brown or Purple Line to Merchandise Mart. Foot traffic from nearby Merchandise Mart keeps this steakhouse – hunkered right under the El – hopping, especially at lunch, when it's a cheaper, but usually just as good, less crowded alternative to the pricier steakhouses. There's also plenty of other dishes on tap, from peppercorn halibut to rock shrimp risotto. Moderate to expensive.

Klay Oven 414 N Orleans St, at Kinzie ☎312/527-3999; Brown or Purple Line to Merchandise Mart. More menu items than you'll know what to do with at this popular, classy – both in the service and the decor – Indian restaurant. The wide selection of tandoori and vindaloo should satisfy any palate. The restaurant's signature oven cooks up eight tempting varieties of their delicious breads. Moderate.

Maggiano's 516 N Clark St, at W Grand Ave ☎312/644-7700; Red Line to Grand. Grand Italian family-style restaurant serving basic Italian fare but known more for its portions – massive even by Chicago standards, get the half-order unless you're planning on sharing. Although many locals decry it as inauthentic, its flavorful pastas and juicy steaks are more than capable of standing against most contenders. Reservations recommended. Moderate.

MK 868 N Franklin St, at W Chestnut ☎1-866/ 235-6440, ⊚www.mkchicago.com; Brown or Purple Line to Chicago. Trendy, upscale place that looks almost more like your rich friend's amazing loft (with a skylight no less), offering New American and continental cuisine alongside a great wine list and an imaginative dessert selection (like a pear crisp with cinnamon ice cream and port wine cream sauce). Reservations are a must. Jackets recommended for men. Very expensive.

Nacional 27 325 W Huron St, at Orleans ☏ 312/664-2727; Brown or Purple Line to Chicago. This Nuevo Latino restaurant is named for the 27 nations of Latin America and its menu makes a valiant and exciting effort to include each and every one of them. You can have Cuban stuffed potatoes, empanadas and chimichurris for dinner and then hang around for when the place transforms into a lively dance party after around 11pm. Moderate to expensive.

Naha 500 N Clark St, at Illinois ☏ 312/321-6242. Exciting, high-end dining that takes an American-Mediterranean menu and gives it a seasonal twist. The owners are veterans on the local restaurant scene and it shows, from the minimal, natural beauty of the interior to the always intriguing menu. Very expensive.

Palaggi's Ristorante 10 W Hubbard St, at State ☏ 312/527-1010; Red Line to Grand. Striking the right balance between retro and gourmet Italian, this is a casual but stylish eatery with a large, exciting menu – excellent calamari and mouthwatering sauces – that

always satisfies. Moderate.

Pizzeria Uno 29 E Ohio St, at N Wabash Ave ☏ 312/321-1000; Red Line to Grand. *Uno's* reputation as the birthplace of deep-dish pizza keeps the crowds coming to the original location of this long-standing Chicago-based (now nationwide) chain, despite long lines and poor service. To handle the overflow, they opened up a twin, *Pizzeria Due*, around the corner at 619 N Wabash. Generally not worth it. Inexpensive.

Tizi Melloul 531 N Wells St, at Grand ☏ 312/670-4338; Brown or Purple Line to Merchandise Mart. Opulently decorated Mediterranean resto that focuses on lavish Moroccan dishes and has large round tables for sizable parties to more easily sample from the delectable dishes. There's belly dancing on Sunday nights. Expensive.

Vong's Thai Kitchen 6 W Hubbard St, at State ☏ 312/644-8664; Red Line to Grand. Formerly known as *Vong*, this is the Chicago outpost of chef Jean-Georges Vongerichten's noted Manhattan eatery, this time with a delectable French-Thai menu and lazy, opium-den ambience paired with more reasonable prices. Moderate.

Magnificent Mile and Streeterville

All restaurants in this section can be easily reached on the Red Line at either Chicago or Grand Avenue stops.

Cafés, snacks and light meals

Cheesecake Factory 875 N Michigan Ave (underneath the John Hancock building), at E Chestnut St ☏ 312/337-1101. Tourists regularly flood this chain outpost decked out in luxuriant belle epoque decor (waits are frequently over an hour long). The mostly American menu is as long as some phone books, the portions are uniformly massive (go at lunchtime to avoid overeating) and not too exciting, but it's the 30-odd flavors of mouthwatering cheesecake that you go here for. Get a couple of slices to go and eat them by the lake instead. Moderate.

foodlife 835 N Michigan Ave, at Pearson (inside Water Tower) ☏ 312/335-3663. While it's essentially just an overblown food court decorated like an outdoor market in Water Tower Place, this does offer a good option for relatively cheap dining on the Mile. Go from station to station, selecting from ribs

and chicken, pastas, Mexican, gourmet soups and thick pizza slices; pay on your way out. Inexpensive to moderate.

Tempo 6 E Chestnut St, at State ☏ 312/943-4373. Though the staff at this 24-hour breakfast spot clearly hasn't been to charm school, it doesn't matter, as long as you're in the mood for their fluffy, fully stuffed omelets. Inexpensive.

Restaurants

Billy Goat Tavern 430 N Michigan Ave, at Kinzie ☏ 312/222-1525. Dingy and beloved bar/grill, lurking in the shadows underneath Michigan Ave, with dangerously greasy burgers. No fries (potato chips only), a minimal beer selection, and wood panelling reminiscent of a 1970s rec room – either great atmosphere or none at all, depending on your view. *Tribune* scribes (the late Mike Royko was one of them) regularly inhabit the grimy old stools. Thursdays: half-price double cheeseburgers. Inexpensive.

Boston Blackies 164 E Grand Ave, at N St Clair St ☎312/938-8700. The Art Deco look and retro film posters on the walls are incongruous for such a bare-bones menu but their signature half-pound burgers are excellent (some claim the best in the city) and service is passable. Inexpensive.

Café Spiagga 980 N Michigan Ave, at E Oak St, ☎312/280-2755. Unlike its namesake next door (*Spiagga* restaurant), the café offers excellent Italian-French food without the stuffiness or the high prices – though to be sure, the food there is impeccable, too. Moderate.

Cape Cod Room in the *Drake Hotel*, 140 E Walton St, at N Michigan Ave ☎312/787-2200. Yankee-style seafaring decor, dark wood walls and a splendid lakeview set the tone for this classic seafood restaurant that dates to the 1930s. There's sea fare from both oceans and freshwater as well, some of the uniformly excellent offerings including shrimp with shallots, Maine lobster and Cajun-style swordfish. Jacket required. Very expensive.

Eli's the Place for Steak 215 E Chicago Ave, at Michigan ☎312/642-1393. The decor at this celebrity haunt across the street from the Museum of Contemporary Art is nothing to shout about, but everything else is just perfect. Steaks are large, charred and delicious, while the creamy, signature cheesecake is a must for dessert. Service is abnormally friendly. Expensive.

Heaven on Seven 600 N Michigan Ave ☎312/280-7774; also at 111 N Wabash Ave ☎312/263-6443. Just downstairs from the Loews movie theater, this Cajun joint is always jumping with loud music and exuberant service. The Creole fare, including etouffee and andouille sausage, is spicy and authentic for the most part, though you may have to shout over the zydeco for the waiter to hear you. Moderate.

Iron Mike's Grille 100 E Chestnut St, at Michigan ☎312/587-8989, @www.mikeditkaschicago.com. Carnivorous football fans worship at this ultra-masculine altar to seared meats and sports run by Chicago Bears legend Mike Ditka. Besides steaks and babyback ribs, there are more refined offerings like wasabi crusted salmon and

fusilli with smoked pork. Good place to catch the game, too. Expensive.

Lawry's 100 E Ontario St, at Michigan ☎312/787-5000. Yes, the same Lawry's that produces those bottles of seasoned salt available in supermarkets, but the best prime-rib in town, a big juicy, savory slab served from a rolling cart. The restaurant itself is something of an institution, located in a grand old mansion built roughly a century ago by the McCormick family. Great lunch menu with made-to-order prime rib, corned beef, and turkey sandwiches. Expensive.

NoMi (in the *Park Hyatt*), 800 N Michigan Ave, at Chicago ☎312/239-4030. *NoMi*'s 7th-floor views of Streeterville and the lake beyond alone are worth the visit (especially from the small outdoor terrace), but fans swear by the menu which seems French-inspired, but jumps all over the place with sushi, sashimi, risotto and lobster for the taking. Very Expensive.

Park Avenue Café 199 E Walton St, at Mies van der Rohe ☎312/944-4414. In the *DoubleTree* next to the John Hancock, here's a solid, upscale bet for delicious American dishes like lobster and tuna steaks. The Sunday brunch (served dim sum style) is a local favorite and needs reservations. Very expensive.

Signature Room at the 95th 875 N Michigan Ave, at E Chestnut St (in the John Hancock) ☎312/787-9596. Though food may be just okay and somewhat pricey, and the service often limp, the wraparound view of the city from the Hancock's 95th floor is nothing short of spectacular. Best enjoyed over brunch or just a drink in the bar. A popular spot for romantic dinners; be prepared to wait. Expensive.

Tru 676 N St Clair St, at E Huron St ☎312/202-0001. If you've got the patience and the bank account to handle the long, prix-fixe-style experience and skyscraper-high prices, this is consistently one of the top fine-dining options in this part of the country. Chefs Rick Tramonto and Gale Gand serve up dazzling gourmet dishes such as the galaxy of intriguing mousses and the caviar staircase (has to be seen to be believed) in an impeccably white, minimalist decor. Gand's desserts are the stuff dreams are made of. Very expensive.

Gold Coast and Old Town

Unless otherwise noted, the closest train stop is Red Line to Clark/Division and closest bus is #22 and #36.

Cafés, snacks and light meals

Ashkenaz Delicatessen 12 E Cedar St, at State ☏312/944-5006. It's about as bare-bones as you can get, just a counter and a couple tables, but the serious kosher food – one of the only good delis in this part of town – is worth going for. Corned beef sandwiches are lean and huge, the rugelach (small rolled pastries) a sweet finish, and the staff chatty. Inexpensive.

Dillon's 1157 N State St, at Division ☏312/654-0495. The cheery service and bright decor set the tone for this hole-in-the-wall frozen custard shop. Get yours with hot fudge, nuts, chunks of toffee or just plain, it's all creamy deliciousness. Inexpensive.

Five Faces 10 W Division St, at State ☏312/642-7837. The food might not be that good when you're sober, but for everyone stumbling out of Division/Rush bars, this late-night hole in the wall serves up the best, greasiest fries and cheeseburgers in the city. Inexpensive.

Original Pancake House 22 E Bellevue Place, at N Rush ☏312/642-7917. Old-fashioned, ultra-casual breakfast joint, always good for just about everything on the menu. Egg dishes are hot and fresh, while the pancakes are fluffy and the coffee surprisingly full-bodied for a diner. Another location at 2020 N Lincoln Park. Inexpensive.

Restaurants

Adobo Grill 1610 N Wells St, at North ☏312/266-7999. Next door to the Second City comedy club, this upscale Mexican place is known for excellent guacamole – mixed at your table to taste – and strong margaritas (made from any of 80 tequilas). The dishes include baby octopus and snapper Veracruzana and pretty much all of them pack a kick. Arrive early as service is far from swift. Moderate.

Big Bowl 6 E Cedar St, at State ☏312/644-8888. One of the most spacious and enjoyable of this local chain's several locations. Competent menu serves up a pan-Asian mix (heavy on the noodle dishes) in plush,

gold-toned surroundings. Inexpensive to moderate.

Dinotto Ristorante 163 W North Ave, at Wells ☏312/787-3345, ⊛www.dinotto.com. Little brother to larger, busier *Café Dinotto* around the corner, has a cozy air with indifferent service, but the pastas – especially a tricolor rotollo in a cream tomato sauce – and desserts are outstanding. Good dinner spot after a movie or live show at *Piper's Alley* across the street. Moderate.

Don Juan on Halsted 1729 N Halsted St, between Willow and North ☏312/981-4000; **Red Line to North/Clybourn.** Casual Mexican place that serves traditional dishes like rellenos and burritos along with outré entries like venison fajitas and sesame-chipotle chicken wings. The colorful, hacienda-like interior makes it more fun than its romantic moniker would have you believe. Expensive.

Dragonfly Mandarin 1206 N State St, at Division ☏312/787-7600; ⊛www .dragonflymandarin.com. Loungey Asian restaurant with dance club tunes. The dishes are mostly variations on standards – potstickers and Mongolian steak – but its one of the only stylish non-steakhouse restaurants in the area. Moderate to expensive.

Edwardo's Natural Pizza 1212 N Dearborn St, at E Division St ☏312/337-4490. Just a takeout joint with a few booths, but this local chain's deep-dish pizza is something to behold. Their claim of fresh ingredients is underscored by the taste, from crispy crust to spicy sausage and crunchy vegetable toppings. Good lunch specials. Inexpensive.

The Fireplace Inn 1448 N Wells St, at W North Ave ☏312/664-5264. Great babyback ribs, dripping with sweet sweet red sauce and served in a dim, piney establishment. The steaks are killer, too, and the prices pretty good, considering what you get. Moderate.

Flat Top Grill 319 W North Ave, at Orleans ☏312/787-7676. No-frills Mongolian-style barbecue where you choose the ingredients – rice, noodles, meats, fish and veggies. All you can eat and cheap. Inexpensive.

Freddy's Ribhouse 1555 N Sheffield Ave, at North ☏312/377-7427; **Red Line to North/Clybourn.** Even though it can occasionally feel like a soulless chain, *Freddy's* actually delivers with some knock-your-socks-off ribs, chicken and an assortment of other BBQ stomach-stuffers. Moderate.

Gibson's 1028 N Rush St, at Bellevue Place ☎312/266-8999. This loud steakhouse offers excellent cuts and impeccable service; the waitstaff even brings your pre-cooked steak to the table for inspection. The bar is something of a scene and popular with a 40s-and-over crowd – local wags call it a "Viagra bar." Favored by movie and theater celebrities working in town. Reserve well in advance. Very expensive.

Kamehachi of Tokyo 1400 N Wells St, at Schiller ☎ 312/664-3663; ⓦwww.kamehachi.com. Opened in 1967 and the first Japanese restaurant in Chicago, this *Kamehachi* (and its two other locations, one at 240 E Ontario and another at 1320 Shermer in Northbrook) continues to offer some of the most supremely fresh and delightful sushi in town, especially the dragon rolls and Chicago crazy rolls (tuna, yellowtail, salmon and crab). Moderate.

Le Colonial 937 N Rush St, at Walton ☎312/255-0088. The atmosphere is delectably retro colonial, all airy white space, palm trees and rattan furniture, while the menu gives gourmet zing to tasty Vietnamese dishes like wok-seared monkfish. Incredibly romantic. Expensive.

Mitchell's Restaurant 101 W North Ave, at N Clark St ☎312/642-5246. A good cheap standby, and a long-standing favorite, serving all-day breakfast specials. Worthwhile for its location – near Old Town and Piper's Alley – and 24-hour status, and not too much else. Inexpensive.

Morton's of Chicago 1050 N State St, at Maple St ☎312/266-4820; ⓦwww.mortons.com. The original location of this upscale steakhouse chain serving perhaps the best steak in town. The waiters are dressed to the nines, while the steaks are described in such delectable detail that you can't decide between the 20oz New York sirloin or the 24oz porterhouse. Even if you don't think it's the best steak in Chicago, it's an unforgettable, classic dining experience. Very expensive.

O'Brien's Restaurant 1528 N Wells St, at North ☎312/787-3131; ⓦwww.obriensrestaurant.com. Irish-American neighborhood standby right in the middle of Old Town bustle. Menu features meat and seafood items like Lake Superior whitefish and pork chops Louisiana

(Cajun rice and bourbon sauce). Also good for just a drink, especially in their often-packed outdoor beer garden. Moderate to expensive.

Old Jerusalem 1411 N Wells St ☎312/944-3304. The hummus, served with piping hot pita bread, is to die for at this cheap, bare-bones eatery that thrives on its takeout business, while the rest of the standard Middle Eastern offerings (tabouli, *baba ganoush*) are good value. The falafel, especially, has character, served hot and crispy with garlicky tahini. Inexpensive.

Salpicón 1252 N Wells St, at W Scott St ☎312/988-7715. Authentic but original Mexican haute cuisine served in a funky, colorful interior; smaller and mellower than *Adobo*. The menu ranges from tequila-marinated halibut to chile-infused chicken and cool, sweet desserts like *naranjas en dulce* (boiled orange quarters in a cinammon-orange syrup). Expensive.

Tavern on Rush 1031 N Rush St, at Bellevue ☎312/664-9600. Airy, spacious restaurant and lounge catering to a young, trendy crowd. The menu is nothing exciting – ideally, stick to drinks – but the surroundings are made for young bright things and the tall windows ideal for people-watching. Moderate.

Topo Gigio Ristorante 1516 N Wells St, at Schiller ☎312/266-9355. Always crowded Italian hotspot in Old Town, with relaxed outdoor seating and cheap and wonderful dishes like chicken cacciatore and escolar tuna. Moderate.

Twin Anchors 1655 N Sedgwick St, at W Concord ☎312/266-1616. The long waits and dive-bar environs only seem to enhance the reputation of this decades-old institution (a speakeasy once upon a time), where the delicious barbecue meat slides off the bone. Loud, crowded and delicious, there's also steaks and fried chicken offered up. Moderate.

Uncle Julio's Hacienda 855 W North Ave, at N Halsted ☎312/266-4222; Red Line to North/Clybourn. Tried and true Tex-Mex fare – a cut above the suburban chains but still very familiar stuff – with terribly tacky decor that seems merely kitschy after a few margaritas. Outdoor seating is available and recommended. Moderate.

Vinci 1732 N Halsted St, between North and Willow ☎312/266-1199, ⓦwww.vinci-group.com; Red Line to North/Clybourn. Warm and inviting place serving up sizable, but not monstrous, portions of rustic Italian fare just up the street

from Steppenwolf Theatre (the troupe of actors has their own table here). Moderate.

South Loop, Chinatown and Near South

Cafés, snacks and light meals

Manny's Deli 1141 S Jefferson St, at W Roosevelt Rd ☎312/939-2855; Green, Red or Orange Line to Roosevelt. One of Chicago's only New York-style delis – and definitely one of the best in the city – with everything from matzo ball soup and giant corned beef sandwiches to cheese blintzes and tongue sandwiches, served up cafeteria-style. Next to the University of Illinois at Chicago, so it draws a studenty crowd, along with some grizzled locals. Inexpensive.

Restaurants

Chicago Firehouse 1401 S Michigan Ave, at 13th St ☎312/786-1401; Green, Red or Orange Line to Roosevelt. Charming restaurant in a historic South Loop building that used to be, big surprise, a firehouse. While the four-square food (meatloaf, steaks, variations on the potato) here can be inconsistent, this is one of the few dining options in the area and very convenient to some South Loop bars and nightclubs. Moderate.

Emperor's Choice 2238 S Wentworth Ave, at W 22nd Place ☎312/225-8800; Red Line to Cermak/Chinatown. Chinatown's most famous restaurant, this place offers excellent seafood, with some unusual items on the side for adventurous eaters, like the soft-shell crab with red peppers and jalapeno. Service is attentive, but not aggressively so. Moderate.

Everest 440 S LaSalle St, at W Van Buren ☎312/663-8920; Brown or Orange Line to LaSalle. It's a dizzying view from this high-flying, exclusive French restaurant located on the 40th floor of a Loop skyscraper and the food is no less dazzling. There's

pheasant-filled beignet, wild hare hamburger and roasted chestnut soup among the delectable offerings. Very expensive.

Gioco 1312 S Wabash Ave, at 13th ☎312/939-3870; Green, Red or Orange Line to Roosevelt. Stylish, white-tablecloth Italian that has been bringing in a hip South Loop crowd by virtue of its simple but never-dull dishes like hand-rolled penne in cream sauce and rabbit with pureed fava beans. Expensive.

Hackney's 733 S Dearborn St, at W Harrison ☎312/461-1116, ⊛www.hackneys.net; Red Line to Harrison. Beloved local burger chain – which started in Glenview in 1939 – serving plenty of solid comfort food from its beautiful Printers Row building, and known for its lean and wonderful Hackneyburger (get it on dark rye, with blue cheese) and French-fried onion loaves. Inexpensive.

Hong Min 221 W Cermak, at S Wentworth Ave ☎312/842-5026; Red Line to Cermak/Chinatown. Hands down one of the least attractive restaurants in the city, but the food — whole pike, Mongolian shrimp and massive, delectable potstickers – makes you forget all about it. Inexpensive.

Penang 2201 S Wentworth Ave, at W 22nd Place ☎312/326-6888; Red Line to Cermak/Chinatown. More upscale and stylish than your average Chinatown place, *Penang* specializes in Malay cuisine. The menu has over 100 dishes on it – including char-grilled beef satay – and dozens of sushi offerings to boot. Inexpensive to moderate.

Won Kow 2237 S Wentworth Ave, at W 22nd Place ☎312/842-7500; Red Line to Cermak/Chinatown. Established in 1927, it's the oldest restaurant in Chinatown, serving dim sum until 3pm, lobster, crab and Cantonese-based noodle and rice dishes. Inexpensive.

Bucktown and Wicker Park

Cafés, snacks and light meals

Bongo Room 1470 N Milwaukee Ave, between Evergreen Ave and Honore St ☎773/489-0690. Hip brunch spot – stroller yuppies start lining up early – with long waits and a slightly overpriced menu, but the food is worth it. Moderate.

Earwax Café 1564 N Milwaukee Ave, at North ☎773/772-4019; Blue Line to Damen. Excellent coffeehouse that serves plenty of satisfying vegetarian fare. Has a fun, hip and colorful atmosphere pitched at the area's hipster residents. There's a few sandwich items for meat eaters. You can rent videos here, too. Inexpensive.

Hilary's Urban Eatery 1500 W Division St, at N Milwaukee Ave ☎773/235-4327; Blue Line to Division. Great breakfast spot where scruffy romantics canoodle over dishes as disparate as pancakes and salmon cakes. Try the excellent daily specials, like the *huevos rancheros*. Moderate.

Iggy's 700 N Milwaukee Ave, at W Huron St ☎312/829-4449; Blue Line to Chicago. A good after-hours diner with the usual greasy-spoon menu (kitchen open till 4am). The rooftop beer garden is a pleasant place for a drink. Moderate.

Letizia's Natural Bakery 2144 W Division St, at Hoyne Ave ☎773/342-1011; Blue Line to Damen. Delicious paninis, coffees and pastries are on offer at this tiny café – all of them made on site and without bleached flour. Inexpensive.

Margie's Candies 1960 N Western Ave, at W Armitage Ave ☎773/384-1035; Blue Line to Western. Famous neighborood ice-cream parlor (it opened in 1921) that serves a cavity-inducing array of homemade candies and deliciously creamy shakes and malts. Inexpensive.

Toast 2046 N Damen Ave, at W Armitage Ave ☎773/772-5600; Blue Line to Damen. Delicious omelets, stuffed French toast and other breakfast staples, but with long waits – up to an hour on weekends. Popular with yuppified, beautiful young things from Lincoln Park who come to scope each other out. Inexpensive.

Vienna Beef Factory Store & Deli 2501 N Damen Ave, between Fullerton and Diversey avenues ☎773/235-6652. Sit elbow to elbow with the factory workers having their breakfast or lunch, munching on steaming hot dogs right off the assembly line, along with the many other fine Vienna meat products available, including corned beef, pastrami and Polish sausages. Inexpensive.

Restaurants

Café Absinthe 1954 W North Ave, at N Milwaukee Ave ☎773/278-4488; Blue Line to Damen. You pay for the atmosphere at this trendy North Avenue restaurant – a dark, curtained haunt for beautiful people. The wine list is decent, and the food, a tasty blend of nouveau American and French (Baileys chicken au jus), has some imaginative touches. Expensive.

Club Lucky 1824 W Wabansia Ave, at N Honore St ☎773/ 227-2300; Blue Line to Damen. Retro Rat Pack-styled joint, where the drinks are strong (some of the best martinis in town) and the food straightforward and satisfying (fettucine scampi, breaded eggplant, and the like). Moderate.

Fortunato 2005 W Division St, at N Damen Ave ☎773/645-7200; bus #70. Authentic Italian food on Division Street's burgeoning restaurant row in Wicker Park. Really cool room, open kitchen. The focus here is on the food's source: the pasta (including ravioli with oxtail and tagliatelle with mushrooms) is made by hand and the produce all organic. Expensive.

Hacienda Tecalitlan 820 N Ashland Ave, at Chicago ☎312/243-1166; bus #66. A giant restaurant on an otherwise desolate stretch of road that looks on the inside to be an actual hacienda. Pitch-perfect decor aside, the Mexican standards are excellently done. Try for a weekend night, when there's usually live music. They also serve excellent, huge burritos out of a storefront around the corner at 1814 W Chicago, at N Wood (☎773/384-4285). Moderate.

Hi Ricky Asia Noodle Shop and Satay Bar 1852 W North Ave, at N Wolcott Ave ☎773/276-8300; Blue Line to Damen; 3730 N Southport Ave, at W Waveland ☎773/388-0000; Brown Line to Southport. Good value at this popular, chic pan-Asian chainlet serving noodle bowls and satays influenced by Burmese, Vietnamese and Thai cuisine. The veggie dumplings are a treat, as are the curried Malay Indian noodles. Inexpensive to moderate.

BUCKTOWN, WICKER PARK
& AROUND RESTAURANTS & BARS

Bongo Room	21	Holiday Club	20	Pontiac Café	17
Café Absinthe	12	Le Bouchon	6	Quencher's	1
Club Lucky	10	Leopard Lounge	8	Rainbo Club	31
Earwax Café	18	Letizia's Natural Bakery	22	Smoke Daddy	23
Fortunato	25	Map Room	5	Soul Kitchen	16
Gold Star Bar	26	Margie's Candies	4	Spring	14
Hacienda Tecalitlan	29	Marie's Rip-Tide Lounge	7	Subterranean	15
Hi Ricky Asia Noodle Shop and Satay Bar	13	Meritage Café and Wine Bar	2	Ten 56	28
Hideout	9	Nick's Beergarden	19	Toast	3
Hilary's Urban Eatery	24	Northside Café	11	Tuman's Alcohol Abuse Center	30

Ixcapuzalco 2919 N Milwaukee Ave, at N Allen
Ⓣ773/486-7340; bus #56. From the same
people who run *Chilipancingo* (see p.148)
comes this elegant Logan Square/West
Bucktown eatery. The walls are covered in
festive folk art and the *moles* bring serious
gourmands from all over the city. Moderate
to expensive.

Le Bouchon 1958 N Damen Ave, at W Armitage
Ave ⓉTel773/862-6600; Blue Line to Damen. As
authentic as French bistros come. Tiny and
romantic, with inexpensive entrees like frog
legs and steamed mussels (about $12).
Hard to get in past the cadre of die-hard
Bucktown fans. Moderate.

Meritage Café and Wine Bar 2118 N Damen
Ave, at W Dickens Ave ⓉTel773/235-6434; bus
#50, #73. Bold and innovative fusion cuisine
– foie gras on cornbread, elk with shiitake
mushrooms – that rotates seasonally keeps
this tight space perennially-crowded.
Expensive.

Smoke Daddy 1804 W Division St, at N Wood
St ⓉTel773/772-6656. For most people, the
nightly live music is the only attraction here,
but the restaurant serves up some great
barbecue. Moderate.

Soul Kitchen 1576 N Milwaukee Ave, at North
ⓉTel773/342-9742; Blue Line to Damen. A grati-
fying mix of soul food (black-eyed peas and
all) and lots of spicy Creole and Caribbean
offerings in a characterful Wicker Park setting. Moderate.

Spring 2039 W North Ave, at N Damen Ave
ⓉTel773/395-7100; Blue Line to Damen. New
American food with an Asian twist (and
even some Middle Eastern accents) in one
of Chicago's top restaurants. Decor is
clean and peaceful, like a rock garden-
turned-restaurant, and the menu features
interesting flavor minglings like cod with
oxtail and red grouper with couscous.
Expensive.

Lincoln Park

Cafés, snacks and light meals

Bourgeois Pig 738 W Fullerton Ave, at N
Burling St ⓉTel773/883-5282; Brown or Purple
Line to Fullerton. Around forty different teas
are available at this coffeeshop though
some may gripe about the small portions of
coffee. Still, the atmosphere is appropriately
dark and literary, even if Marxists may be
hard to find here these days. Inexpensive.

Cameron's Delight Ice Cream 500 W
Diversey, at N Pine Grove ⓉTel773/472-4200. The
decor strives for an old-timey feel and the
30-plus flavors of uniformly excellent ice
cream make sure that everyone walks away
happy. Inexpensive.

Chicago Pizza and Oven Grinder 2121 N
Clark St, at W Dickens Ave ⓉTel773/248-2570.
Trademark grinders (Italian sausage sandwiches), a limited selection of pizzas, and
excellent salads; waits can be long – plenty
of time for you to check out the site of the
St Valentine's Day Massacre across the
street (see p.97). Inexpensive.

Demon Dogs 944 W Fullerton Ave, at Sheffield
ⓉTel773/281-2001. Hidden right under the El
and across the street from DePaul, this is a
classic old hot dog joint that serves them
up good and cheap; note the 1980s rock
memorabilia on the wall. Inexpensive.

Potbelly Sandwich Works 2264 N Lincoln Ave,
at W Webster Ave ⓉTel773/528-1405, Ⓦwww
.potbelly.com. The original location of this
popular, no-frills sandwich shop with decor
dating from its days as an antique shop
(selling potbelly stoves, naturally). The lines
are always long and the sandwiches themselves are good and fresh-tasting on crispy
Italian rolls. Try the Wreck (salami, roast
beef, turkey and ham with Swiss) to get
your $4 worth. Around fifteen branches
scattered throughout Chicago. Inexpensive.

Ranalli's on Lincoln 1925 N Lincoln Ave, at W
Armitage Ave ⓉTel312/642-4700. The pizza,
pasta, sandwiches and salads are more
than adequate, but still secondary to the
spacious and fun outdoor patio/beer
garden. Ask about the drink specials.
Inexpensive.

Restaurants

Ambria 2300 N Lincoln Park W, at Belden Ave
ⓉTel773/472-5959. Excellent French cuisine
served in a quiet, dim, romantic setting, and
priced accordingly, though the degustation
menus – petit, vegetable, shellfish or the
eight-course "grand" menu – are a better
deal. Risotto with rabbit is especially memorable. Very expensive.

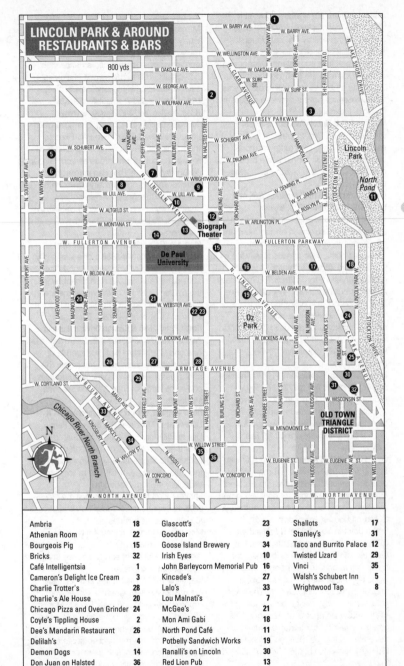

LINCOLN PARK & AROUND
RESTAURANTS & BARS

Lincoln Park
North Pond
De Paul University
Biograph Theater
Oz Park
OLD TOWN TRIANGLE DISTRICT

Ambria	18	Glascott's	23	Shallots	17
Athenian Room	22	Goodbar	9	Stanley's	31
Bourgeois Pig	15	Goose Island Brewery	34	Taco and Burrito Palace	12
Bricks	32	Irish Eyes	10	Twisted Lizard	29
Café Intelligentsia	1	John Barleycorn Memorial Pub	16	Vinci	35
Cameron's Delight Ice Cream	3	Kincade's	27	Walsh's Schubert Inn	5
Charlie Trotter's	28	Lalo's	33	Wrightwood Tap	8
Charlie's Ale House	20	Lou Malnati's	7		
Chicago Pizza and Oven Grinder	24	McGee's	21		
Coyle's Tippling House	2	Mon Ami Gabi	18		
Dee's Mandarin Restaurant	26	North Pond Café	11		
Delilah's	4	Potbelly Sandwich Works	19		
Demon Dogs	14	Ranalli's on Lincoln	30		
Don Juan on Halsted	36	Red Lion Pub	13		
Geja's Café	25	Rose Angelis	6		

Athenian Room 807 W Webster Ave, at N Halsted Ave, near Oz Park ☎773/348-5155. Students from nearby DePaul University flock to this Greek diner for the cheap, tasty gyros, Greek fries and salads. Decent and cheap if you're in the area looking for a quick bite, but not worth going out of your way for. Service hovers between casual and invisible. Inexpensive.

Bricks 1909 N Lincoln Ave, at Wisconsin ☎773/255-0581. Snazzy pizzeria that eschews the deep-dish route for more selective, thin-crust toppings like prosciutto and fontina. Over two dozen beers available. Inexpensive.

Charlie Trotter's 816 W Armitage Ave, at N Halsted St ☎773/248-6228, ⊛www .charlietrotters.com. Superlative American and continental cuisine in elegant surroundings from one of the country's most renowned chefs, with an extensive wine list and attentive service to match. If you can't get a reservation, try *Trotter's To Go*, mostly a takeout business (1337 W Fullerton Ave, at N Lakewood ☎773/868-6510), which has two small tables, plus divine spit-roasted chickens (for about $12) and fabulous beef tenderloin for not much more. Restaurant: Very expensive; To Go: Moderate.

Dee's Mandarin Restaurant 1114 W Armitage Ave, at N Sheffield Ave ☎773/477-1500. Probably the best Chinese food outside Chinatown, this upscale restaurant offers delectable sesame chicken, wonderfully fresh shrimp, and refreshing Mai Tais. Inexpensive.

Geja's Café 340 W Armitage Ave, at N Orleans St ☎773/281-9101. Perfectly romantic and popular restaurant that serves up excellent fondue along with oodles of dark wood and candlelit atmosphere. Try for one of the curtained-off booths. Expensive.

Green Dolphin Street 2200 N Ashland Ave ☎773/395-0066, ⊛www.jazzitup.com. Hip west Lincoln Park supper club where the menu caters both to meat-and-potato types and those with a taste for foie gras, brioche and succulent seafood. The quiet reflection-inducing sea-green interior and black-and-white photos of jazz and blues greats make for a comfortable setting, and the adjoining jazz bar puts on a variety of live music (see also p.180). Recommended. Expensive.

Lalo's 1960 N Clybourn Ave, at W Armitage Ave

☎773/880-5256. Hearty portions of regional Mexican cuisine, accompanied by ridiculously large margaritas and live mariachi music. Nothing special but always reliable and affordable. There's also a dance club downstairs. This family-owned chain has several locations in the city. Inexpensive.

Lou Malnati's 958 W Wrightwood Ave, at N Lincoln Ave ☎773/832-4030, ⊛www .loumalnatis.com. Ex-Chicagoans have been known to have a pie or two Fed-Exed to them in times of need. The deep-dish here is perhaps not as monstrous as from *Gino's* or *Giordano's*, but it's a densely packed, tastebud-delighting extravaganza nonetheless (with extra-crispy, ever-so buttery crust). They also make a mean not-so-thin crust pie. 20 locations in Chicago. Inexpensive.

Mon Ami Gabi 2300 N Lincoln Park W, at Belden Ave ☎773/348-8886. For a less stuffy, more affordable alternative to *Ambria* (see above), try this bistro, across the lobby in the *Belden-Stratford* hotel, where the steak *frites* is the highlight. Great views of Lincoln Park and a superb wine list. Expensive.

North Pond 2610 N Cannon Drive, in Lincoln Park ☎773/477-5845; bus #22. Charming little Arts and Crafts-style park cottage fills up quick with brunchers ready to sample the chef's wares – hazelnut pancakes, boneless pheasant – that change with the seasons. Moderate.

Rose Angelis 1314 W Wrightwood Ave, at N Lakewood ☎773/296-0081; Brown or Purple Line to Fullerton. Homey, off-the-beaten-path spot that serves mostly vegetarian variations on traditional Italian cooking (there's a few meat dishes, as well); the raviolis are especially inviting. Moderate.

Shallots 2324 N Clark St, at Belden ☎773/755-5205. Kosher cooking doesn't always have to mean deli, as this upscale Mediterranean-style restaurant goes to show, with a menu of enticing gourmet dishes like ribeye filet and Moroccan-style duck breast. Expensive.

Stanley's 1970 N Lincoln Ave, at W Armitage Ave ☎312/642-0007. Country kitchen with superb breakfasts and tasty Bloody Marys. The fun and nostalgic bar area leads into a cozy eating section that's never too crowded. The free mashed potatoes are an odd, but nice, touch, and there's a $10.95 all-you-can-eat brunch buffet on the weekends. Inexpensive.

Taco and Burrito Palace 2441 N Halsted St, at Fullerton ☎773/248-0740. This late-night Mexican joint doles out chimichangas, tacos and exceptional burritos. The line snakes out the door late Friday and Saturday nights; play the ancient video games while you wait. Inexpensive.
Twisted Lizard 1964 N Sheffield Ave, at W Armitage Ave ☎773/929-1414. Given the small size of this restaurant's bar and the basement location, the usually long wait can seem even longer. Still, this is a good spot for filling and tasty Mexican standards and pitchers of margaritas, in one of Lincoln Park's trendiest areas. Inexpensive.

Lakeview, Wrigleyville and the North Lakefront

Cafés, snacks and light meals

Harmony Grill 3159 N Southport Ave, at W Belmont Ave ☎773/525-2508; Red Line to Belmont. Serving food until well after midnight, this dining room addition to *Schubas Tavern* (see p.175) features a tasty menu of overstuffed sandwiches, barbecue and all types of filling comfort food. Their weekend brunches are deservedly popular, especially in the summer. Expensive.
Intelligentsia 3123 N Broadway St, at W Barry ☎773/348-4522. While its coffee, though good, may not be the Starbucks-killing super-brew that its proponents claim, there's no doubt that this is a choice spot to kill a few hours with a cup of joe, a pastry and a *Reader*. The hum of quiet conversation is always present, though never loud enough to break your concentration. Inexpensive.
Salt and Pepper Diner 3537 N Clark St, at Addison ☎773/883-9800; Red Line to Addison. The design is standard 1950s diner, but this is more of a crowded (and justifiably so) basic breakfast joint than another burgers and malt dive. Inexpensive.
Swedish Bakery 5348 N Clark St, at W Summerdale ☎773/561-8919. This old-fashioned 1920s bakery serves delicious marzipan cake and custard cup sweet rolls, among other sugary offerings, but the long lines and small, easily crowded space can be annoying. Inexpensive.
The Wiener's Circle 2622 N Clark St, at W Wrightwood Ave ☎773/477-7444; bus #22. Whether the staff is arguing amongst themselves or verbally assaulting you (in what appears to be good fun), you'll enjoy some of the best hot dogs in town, best eaten loaded up with all the pickles, peppers, onions and tomatoes you can get. Inexpensive.

Restaurants

Arco de Cuchileros 3445 N Halsted St, at W Cornelia ☎773/296-6046. Excellent tapas bar on the north end of Boystown that provides dozens of tasty possibilities in a no-frills but comfortable setting. Stay awhile with a pitcher of delectable sangria. Moderate.
Cousin's Turkish and Mediterranean 2833 N Broadway St, at W Surf ☎773/880-0063. Bustling little Turkish joint where you can opt for floor cushions for the full effect. Good seafood dishes and traditional Middle-Eastern cuisine, with most meals under $10. Inexpensive.

Ann Sather

Scattered all over the city's North Side, **Ann Sather** is a chain of charming Swedish diners that's become Chicago's most popular breakfast spot. The cinnamon rolls are legendary, while the Swedish pancakes with lingonberries are almost as good. Stick with the Swedish items on the increasingly American menu. Inexpensive. ⓦwww.annsather.com. 5207 N Clark St, at Foster ☎773/271-6677; 3416 N Southport Ave, at Roscoe ☎773/404-4475; 3411 N Broadway St, at Roscoe ☎773/305-0018; 929 W Belmont Ave, at Sheffield ☎773/348-2378; 2665 N Clark St, at W Drummond ☎773/327-9522; 1448 N Milwaukee Ave, at N Honore ☎773/394-1812.

El Jardin 3335 N Clark St, at W Belmont Ave
℡773/528-6775; Brown or Purple Line to
Belmont. Decent Mexican food very popular
with the Wrigleyville crowd, but the strong
margaritas and animated crowd are the real
draw. Moderate.

Penny's Noodle Shop 3400 N Sheffield Ave, at
N Clark ℡773/281-8222. Cheap, quality and
usually packed noodle joint that spans
Asian cuisines, with good outdoor dining –
especially the numerous curries and
amazing spring rolls – during the warmer
months. BYOB. Inexpensive.

Strega Nona 3747 N Southport Ave, at W Grace

St ℡773/244-0990; Brown Line to Southport.
Decent Italian restaurant serving traditional
fare, very convenient if you're in the area for
a movie at the Music Box Theater or a
show but a worthwhile dinner destination
regardless. There's also pleasant sidewalk
seating in the summer. Moderate.

Tango Sur 3763 N Southport Ave, at W Grace
℡773/477-5466. Small, family-run restaurant
specializing in charred Argentinian-style
steaks and ribs along with parrillada (short
ribs, beef, sweet bread and black sausage);
not much in the way of sides. For the brave
and ravenous. Moderate.

West Side

Cafés, snacks and light meals

Al's Number 1 Italian Beef 1079 W Taylor St, at
Aberdeen St ℡312/226-4017; bus #37, #60.
Takeout joint that was once the king of Italian
beef before numerous copies began arriving
– and still turns out a tasty sandwich (around
$5), especially the "dipped" varieties. There's
another one in River North at 169 W Ontario
(℡312/943-3222). Inexpensive.

Restaurants

Blackbird 619 W Randolph St, at S Jefferson St
℡312/715-0708; ⓦwww.tribads.com/blackbird/;
Green Line to Clinton. Marvelous and innovative New American fare in a super-trendy
setting, though often overcrowded and a bit
pricey. Try the signature appetizer – braised
rabbit in curry sauce – followed by the
superb sturgeon with braised oxtail. Very
expensive.

Café Jumping Bean 1439 W 18th St, at S
Loomis St ℡312/455-0019; bus #9. Popular
Pilsen hangout for local artists with funky
decor – the furniture and walls covered in
bright, expressionistic swatches of color –
that mixes a coffeehouse groove with
Latino café fare. Inexpensive.

Costa's 340 S Halsted St, at W Van Buren
℡312/263-9700; Blue Line to UIC/Halsted; bus
#8, #126. Spacious south Greektown joint
with live music, large portions of traditional
Greek fare – the Athenian chicken, mussels Salonika and *saganaki* (fried cheese)
are especially good. Moderate.

Francesca's on Taylor 1400 W Taylor St, at S
Loomis St ℡312/829-2828,
ⓦwww.miafrancesca.com; Blue Line to Polk.
Among the best Italian places in Little Italy,
and also the city, *Francesca's* serves up
authentic food with zing and verve (including
a heavenly carpaccio) in a lively and fun
atmosphere. Unlike the other *Francesca*
restaurants in Chicago, this one happily
takes reservations. Moderate.

Greek Islands 200 S Halsted St, at W Adams St
℡312/782-9855; Blue Line to UIC/Halsted; bus
#8, #126. Greek and Middle Eastern food, a
cut above most other restaurants in the
area, with a huge, colorful dining room, an
open kitchen and the sumptuous Spartan
Warrior Feast. Crowded all week long and
justifiably so. Moderate.

Marche 833 W Randolph St, at Green ℡312/
226-8399, ⓦwww.marche-chicago.com; bus
#131. One of the highlights of the West
Randolph restaurant row, this French bistro
packs them in every night with its bally-
hooed cuisine – including wonderful
bacon-wrapped sea scallops and some
amazing desserts – and nightclub-style
atmosphere. Expensive.

Nuevo Leon 1515 W 18th St, at Ashland Ave
℡312/421-1517; Blue Line to 18th St.
Excellent traditional Mexican food – among
the best in Chicago – served since 1962 in
a colorful family-style restaurant in the
Pilsen neighborhood, especially lively after
Sunday morning mass. Combine a trip out
here with a visit to the nearby Mexican Fine
Arts Center Museum (see p.110) and bring

your own alcohol; they'll supply a bucket and ice. Moderate.

Parthenon 314 S Halsted St, at W Jackson Blvd ⓣ312/726-2407; ⓦwww.theparthenon.com; Blue Line to UIC/Halsted; bus #8, #126. Greektown standby that claims to have invented flaming *saganaki* (fried cheese doused with Metaxa brandy). Regardless of the claim's merit, they do serve up tasty gyros and various well-priced kabob platters, not to mention a whole roasted suckling pig that can feed a dozen or more. Moderate.

Red Light 820 W Randolph St, at S Green St ⓣ312/733-8880; bus #8, #131. Dark, upscale West Side pan-Asian restaurant, popular with a young, sleek crowd that comes to munch on the Taiwanese catfish and grilled quail. Expensive.

Rodity's 222 S Halsted St, at W Adams St ⓣ312/454-0800; Blue Line to UIC/Halsted; bus #8, 126. Inexpensive and friendly mom-and-pop place serving first-rate Greek chicken, avgolemono (egg-lemon) soup and *saganaki*. The attentive waitstaff won't rush you, either. Inexpensive.

Rosebud 1500 W Taylor St, at Ashland Ave ⓣ312/942-1117; Blue Line to Polk. Expensive and cozy Little Italy institution that may have lost some of its sheen, but it's still an excellent place for large (very large) portions of satisfying Italian staples like veal francese and chicken Vesuvio. The original location,

with some offshoots throughout the city. Also has an excellent bar in front. Moderate to expensive.

Santorini 800 W Adams St, at S Halsted ⓣ312/829-8820; Blue Line to UIC/Halsted; bus #8, #126. Styled as a Greek taverna, with an inviting wood-burning fireplace, *Santorini* offers good shellfish and lamb dishes. Moderate.

Taqueria El Milagro 1923 S Blue Island Ave, at W 19th St ⓣ312/433-7620; Blue Line to18th St. Expect some lines at this Pilsen favorite – while you wait, you can sample warm tortillas from the tortilla factory next door. Inexpensive.

Twisted Spoke 501 N Ogden Ave, at W Grand Ave ⓣ312/666-1500; ⓦwww.twistedspoke.com; bus #65. Out-of-the-way restaurant/bar with rooftop dining and somewhat affected biker atmosphere. You can't go wrong with the half-pound Fatboy burger and the margaritas. If you find yourself here around midnight, a dicey proposition at best, you'll experience "Smut and Eggs," when porn goes up on the screens. Moderate.

Wishbone 1001 W Washington Blvd, at N Morgan St ⓣ312/850-2663; bus #131. Tasty Southern homestyle cooking – try the cornbread muffins, fried chicken and mashed potatoes – and a top spot for a filling Sunday brunch, though you should expect a wait. Right around the corner from Oprah's Harpo Studios. Moderate.

South Side/Hyde Park

Cafés, snacks and light meals

Caffé Florian 1450 E 57th St, at S Blackstone Ave ⓣ773/752-4100; bus #6. Good coffee joint – also serving pizza and sandwiches heavy on the vegetarian side of things – where University of Chicago students and locals split apart radical issues. Inexpensive.

Medici on 57th 1327 E 57th St, at S Kenwood Ave ⓣ773/667-7394; bus #6. Typical college hangout, with two levels of graffiti-covered tables, good pizza, decent burgers, and lots of smoke; not to mention the stained-glass windows downstairs. "The Med"'s high point is Sunday brunch, particularly the fresh-squeezed orange juice. Inexpensive.

Valois 1518 E 53rd St ⓣ773/667-0647; bus #171. You can get breakfast until 4pm every

day at this classic cafeteria-style eatery that's been serving sandwiches and meat-and-potatoes fare like pork chops and Swiss steak since the 1930s. Popularized in a recent book, *Slim's Table*. Inexpensive.

Restaurants

Army and Lou's 422 E 75th St, at S Martin Luther King ⓣ773/483-3100. This South Side institution has a good selection of satisying soul food for the choosing: short ribs, cornbread, chitterlings and sweet potatoes have been bringing its regular customers in from all over the city for decades. Inexpensive.

Calypso Café 5211 S Harper St, at 52nd St ⓣ773/955-0229; bus #6. Festive island-

themed decor and decent, spicy Caribbean and Jamaican fare. The conch chowder and plantains are recommended. Moderate.
Dixie Kitchen & Bait Shop 5225 S Harper Ave, at 53rd St ☎773/363-4943; Metra to 53rd. Delicious Southern cooking at good prices, served in a room with playful 1930s decor. The menu ranges from delicious Southern BBQ to hot Cajun and Creole gumbos and jambalayas. The fried green tomato appetizer is a must and the service simply wonderful. Inexpensive.
La Petite Folie 1504 E 55th St, at Lake Park Blvd ☎773/493-1394; bus #6. Hyde Park's only upscale (in the menu and decor, not the price) French restaurant, tucked away in a tiny mall beside *Walgreen*'s. This little bistro's reasonably priced, classic French cuisine (like roulade of sole and a tasty foie gras variation) is uniformly good; the prix-fixe menu is often the best deal. Moderate.
Piccolo Mondo 1642 E 56th, at S Hyde Park Blvd ☎773/643-1106. Situated in the ground floor of the old *Windmere* hotel (now luxury condos), just across the street from the Museum of Science and Industry campus (see p.114). One of the few Italian restaurants on the South Side, serving basic fare like rigatoni gregorio and rottolo rossini. There's a deli counter up front. Moderate.
Pizza by Capri 1501 E 53rd St at S Harper Ave ☎773/324-7777. Hyde Park pizza parlor that serves both thin and deep-dish pies as well as pastas, many of the vegetarian variety, such as the Popeye Romano (fettucine with spinach). Several locations in the city. Inexpensive.
Ribs 'n' Bibs 5300 S Dorchester Ave, at E 53rd St ☎773/493-0400. For no-frills takeout ribs, this Hyde Park institution is the place to go. Go for the Lil' Bronco, half a slab of their dripping-with-sauce ribs and fries. Wear an old shirt, as this food splatters. Inexpensive to moderate.

Further out

While there's plenty to choose from in the areas discussed in this chapter, there are still several notable restaurants that, while they might be tricky to get to, are worth the effort. A trio of **North Side Indian** restaurants are especially praiseworthy: **Arun's** (4156 N Kedzie Ave, at W Warner Ave; ☎773/539-1909) has for years set the standard for impeccable, high-class service and unbeatable gourmet fare; **Viceroy of India** (2516 W Devon Ave, at N Campbell Ave ☎773/743-4100) is a huge and always dependable eating palace in the heart of Devon's Indian community; **Hema's Kitchen** (6406 N Oakley, at W Devon Ave ☎773/338-1627) is a cosy little unsung hero that serves cheap and scrumptious Indian/Pakistani dishes. If your hot dog cravings are still not sated (and you've got a car) head out to **Fluky's** (6821 N Western Ave, at W Pratt Blvd ☎773/274-3652) for a great dog and even better milkshake, or to **Gene & Jude's Red Hot Stand** (2720 River Rd, at W Grand Ave ☎708/452-7634) where the fries are skin-on and outstanding, the dogs snap with flavor and the tamales melt in your mouth.

13

Drinking

C hicago has been defined by its boisterous **drinking scene** since at least the early 1900s, when Schlitz, a major local brewery, owned more land than anyone else in town, save another pillar of the community, the Catholic Church. Muckraking journalist George Turner estimated in 1907 that in some "wards" (neighborhoods) there was roughly one bar per 150 residents (of course, the same writer also referred to immigrants as "rough and hairy tribes," so his math may be suspect).

The city's hard-drinking reputation was cemented during the Prohibition era of the 1920s and 1930s, when the need for beer and bathtub gin consumed Chicago in the gangland violence that some still associate with the city more than eighty years on. These days, drinking is still a serious business, if usually less dangerous. You'll find more **sports bars** here than in New York and Los Angeles combined, while only slightly less ubiquitous are the city's popular **beer gardens** – casual outdoor patios that teem in summer with people who've made up ingenious excuses to skip out of work early. As well, just about every kind of bar imaginable exists, from Irish bars and chic velvet-rope places to movie houses and bowling alleys that double as drinking establishments.

While every neighborhood has its own cluster of bars, **Near North** has more per square mile than anywhere else in Chicago, with most of them concentrated around the raucous intersection of **Rush** and **Division** streets.

River North has some fancy places for cocktails, as does the Mag Mile, where luxury hotel chains have poured tons of money into their sumptuous lounges. Conservative, collegiate **Lincoln Park** is known for its dozens of sports bars, but also has a number of quality lounges and pubs, and nearby **Lakeview** has perhaps the best mix of types of bars, despite the clutch of Cubs bars around Wrigley Field. Some of the best hunting grounds are in **Bucktown**, **Wicker Park** and the **Ukrainian Village**, which have an eclectic mix of bars ranging from grungy saloons with beer-soaked floors to sleek lounges with exotic fish tanks.

The **Loop** mostly caters to an after-work office crowd and theatergoers, though there are a couple excellent taverns in the more isolated **South Loop**.

There isn't much in the way of destination drinking on the South Side, with the exception of the traditionally Irish neighborhood of **Beverly** and **Hyde Park**. If you happen to be around during one of its **street festivals** (see pp.209–214), though, there's plenty of drinking to be found, usually accompanied by live music.

Bear in mind, too, that many places double as bar and restaurant; see Chapter 12 for more potential listings.

Chicago's bar scene tends to be quiet early week, picking up on Wednesday and through the weekend. Long weekend brunches are prime drinking times as there's always some game on the big TVs at most bars. Late-night drinking is also a hallmark of the city's bar scene: the average 2am weekday closing time extends to 5am on Saturdays in some places. Bars are packed right up to closing time, and late-night bars often have lines at 2am that are longer than the ones you'll see earlier in the night.

Remember to carry **photo ID** or your passport with you; many bars won't let you in without it. You have to be 21 to drink in Illinois.

Drink prices are fairly reasonable compared to other major US cities, except in the most upscale bars. **Beer** is usually cheap, between $3 and $5 a pint, and many bars have happy hours (roughly 4–8pm) featuring drink specials, usually half-price drafts of domestic beers, or a bucket of six bottles for the price of five. Local favorites include **Old Style**, a mass-produced lager brewed in Milwaukee, and the many varieties of **Goose Island**, a robust Chicago beer from a brewery that runs a few of its own bars in the city.

Mixed drinks and **wine** are more expensive, typically from $5 to $10, depending on the fanciness of the establishment. A few odd cocktail combinations have persisted here, like the brutal but effective **Car Bombs** – a shot of whiskey dropped into a full pint of Guinness and downed in one swoop. And, with the exception of some swankier lounges, you are practically guaranteed to find a **Golden Tee** – a phenomenally popular golf arcade game developed by a Chicago area company – somewhere in each and every bar in this city, usually played by one frantic guy surrounded by two or three of his buddies, cheering or razzing him.

The Loop

Berghoff 17 W Adams St, at State ☎312/427-3170; Brown Line to Jackson. Though known primarily for its food, this German American institution also serves its own beer and root beer in the atmospheric *Stand Up Bar* upstairs, amid aging woodwork and antique fixtures.

Govnor's Pub 207 N State St, at Lake ☎312/236-3696; Red Line to State/Lake. Irish sports pub that has its share of devotees and is a perennially-packed after-work spot due more to its location than the airport-bar ambience.

Monk's Pub 205 W Lake St, at Wells St ☎312/357-6665; Blue Line to Clark. Noisy neighborhood dive bar with a good selection of beers and popular with the lunchtime and after-work crowd. Serves great burgers and chili, along with the usual pub fare.

Trader Vic's *Palmer House Hilton* 17 E Monroe St, at State St ☎312/726-7500; Brown Line to Monroe. One of the last surviving branches of this dwindling (and gloriously tacky) Polynesian tiki bar and restaurant chain,

Trader Vic's is good for those looking for something different. Four-dollar Mai Tais and free hors d'oeuvres on Thursdays.
Whiskey Blue 172 W Adams St, at Wells St ☏ 312/782-4933; Brown, Orange or Purple Line to Quincy. One of the few spots in the Loop – located in the *W* hotel – for upscale drinking ($10 martinis). The leggy waitresses are a trademark of restaurateur Rande Gerber's establishments while the decor is sleek and sexy.

Near North

The Bar at the Peninsula Chicago 108 E Superior St, at N Michigan Ave ☏ 312/337-2888; Red Line to Chicago. Reminiscent of a men's club, with leather armchairs wherever you look, this plush lounge attracts a well-heeled crowd with its extensive array of high-priced cocktails and cigars, not to mention the stunning view of the city.
Bar Louie 226 W Chicago Ave, at N Franklin St ☏ 312/337-3313; Brown or Purple Line to Chicago. The first in a growing bar chain, this one serves drinks and food late (until 4am on weekends). Loud and unromantic, it's very Chicago, and the walls are covered with murals and colorful mosaics. The crowd, despite a fair number of business people, is mixed. The bar food is a cut above average, with some tasty sandwiches and salads in addition to the usual fried appetizers.
Billy Goat Tavern 430 N Michigan Ave, at W Kinzie St ☏ 312/222-1525; Red Line to Grand. The *Billy Goat* is in a class by itself – an institution that has become a tourist destination without losing any of its character. The tavern, a journalists' hangout for more than half a century, also serves cheap beers and burgers. See also review in "Eating," p.151.
Blue Frog 676 N LaSalle St, at W Erie St ☏ 312/943-8900; Red Line to Chicago. An almost-hidden dive bar in River North, this very casual joint has shelves of near-complete board games, various karaoke nights and patrons trying to get away from all the Hard Rock Cafe-type places in the area.
Brehon Pub 731 N Wells St, at W Superior St ☏ 312/642-1071; Brown or Purple Line to Chicago. Family-owned *Brehon* (Gaelic for lawyer) is a casual Irish-American pub, with a wonderfully hospitable staff, that's been here for twenty years. There's an adequate beer garden, plus a pool table and dart board, and a jukebox playing the latest tunes. Draws a mixed after-work crowd. On St Patrick's Day, just about every pub crawl gang makes a pit stop here.
Celtic Crossings 751 N Clark St, at W Chicago Ave ☏ 312/337-1005; Red Line to Chicago. One of Chicago's more authentic Irish joints. With no TVs, it's best suited for a pint and good conversation. The bar, which offers a dozen beers on tap, draws a mature crowd and often has live music on Saturday nights and Sunday afternoons.
Charlie's Ale House 700 E Grand Ave, on Navy Pier ☏ 312/595-1440. A branch of the original Lincoln Park ale house and the best of the Navy Pier restaurant/bars, serving more than forty types of beers, along with liquor. The patio is a great place to sidestep the Navy Pier throngs in summer, while the restaurant serves a tasty meatloaf and chicken pot pie. Open year-round.
Clark Street Ale House 742 N Clark St, just south of Chicago Ave ☏ 312/642-9253; Red Line to Chicago. Relax at the handsome cherrywood bar with one of the vast selection of domestic beers (including a couple of good house brews), scotches and cigars. There's also a pleasant outdoor beer garden in summer.
Coq d'Or in the *Drake Hotel*, 140 E Walton St, at N Michigan Ave ☏ 312/787-2200; Red Line to Chicago. Smoky Prohibition-era speakeasy-style environs popular with suits at lunch and the after-work martini crowd. Elegant cabaret tunes complete the atmosphere of rare sophistication. Choice burgers and what may be the finest club sandwich in the city.
Cru Café 888 N Wabash Ave, at E Chestnut St ☏ 312/337-4078; Red Line to Chicago. Great people-watching at this corner wine bar just south of the Rush corridor. Order one of the hundreds of wonderful and surprisingly affordable wines offered and relax in the muted candlelight.
ESPN Zone 43 E Ohio St, at Rush St ☏ 312/644-3776. You'll find TVs even in the bathrooms

at this sports addict's playpen where the food portions are massive and the company of women a faint memory. The weekend crowds come here to drink beer, overload on televised sports (especially from one of the armchairs in front of the main wall-size TV screen) or try their hand at the many interactive video games.

Harry's Velvet Room 56 W Illinois St, at N Dearborn St ☎ 312/527-5600; Red Line to Grand. Super-snazzy underground River North lounge that's replete with leather booths, dim lighting, swank DJ tunes and martinis to die for.

Kaz Bar 329 N Dearborn St, at W Kinzie St ☎ 312/527-2583 or 923-2000; Red Line to Grand. This Moroccan-styled lounge in the lobby of the *House of Blues Hotel*, takes pseudo-Arabic ornate to another level, with its tents and draped fabrics everywhere. They serve inventive martinis and there's occasional live music on weekend nights.

Le Colonial 937 N Rush St, at W Walton St ☎ 312/255-0088; Red Line to Clark/Division. The lounge above the well-regarded *Le Colonial* French-Vietnamese restaurant (see p.154) is one of the sexiest in town, a bit like an attic with a terrace overlooking the city, where the vibe reeks of elegantly divine ennui. You can order from the restaurant menu, languish on a sofa or smoke cigars in the designated smoking section.

Martini Ranch 311 W Chicago Ave, at N Franklin St ☎ 312/335-9500. It's all about the martinis – all shapes and varieties, some of the best in the city – at this swanky little place near the gallery district that usually has standing-room only.

O'Callaghan's 29 W Hubbard St ☎ 312/670-4371. Down-to-earth River North after-work bar, with a vaguely Irish pub feel, that attracts a mixed crowd. The drinks are nothing special, but the welcoming staff keeps regulars coming back for more.

Pippin's Tavern 806 N Rush St, at E Chicago Ave ☎ 312/787-5435; Red Line to Chicago. An actual hole-in-the-wall, this bar is a tiny oasis of dark wood, holiday lights and good beer. Perfect for an afternoon drink.

The Redhead Piano Bar 16 W Ontario St, at N State St ☎ 312/ 640-1000; Red Line to Grand. Known for its cabaret acts, this bar also serves excellent martinis – thirty types in all. Usually draws a mature singles crowd, though it's not uncommon for crooners better suited to the karaoke circuit to start belting them out.

Underground Wonder Bar 10 E Walton St ☎ 312/266-7761; Red Line to Chicago. Cramped subterranean drinkers' bar (not for lightweights) with live music 365 days a year, performed well into the wee small hours. A bit dark and louche, in a good way.

Whiskey Sky 644 N Lake Shore Drive, at E Erie St ☎ 312/255-4463. The views of Lake Michigan from this 33rd-floor lounge in the Lake Shore Drive *W* hotel are great, but the place is so popular that you have to put your name on the guest list in advance if you hope to even drink here on a Friday or Saturday night. A haven for models, sports figures and business types, none of whom blinks at the $11 martinis.

Gold Coast and Old Town

All bars here are accessible by the Red Line to Clark/Division or #22 and #36 buses.

Butch McGuire's 20 W Division St, at N Dearborn St ☎ 312/337-9080. *Butch's* has the best reputation of all the Division Street bars, a dubious award which means that on Friday and Saturday nights it's almost impossible to get in, and filled with aging singles once you do. The Christmas tinsel, stuffed animals and motorized trains add to the suffocation.

Hotsie Totsie 8 E Division St ☎ 312/337-9128. Smoky, nautical-themed bar where those in

the know go to escape the long lines at the other bars on Division Street. It's seedier and less of a pickup joint, which can seem comforting some nights.

The Leg Room 7 W Division St, at N State St ☎ 312/337-2583. Sandwiched in between the crowded Division Street drinkeries, this velvety little lounge is a delightful breath of calm, with ice-cold martinis and perfectly tacky leopard-print decor.

The Lodge 21 W Division St, at N State St

☎312/642-4406. Strong drinks, a good beer selection and friendly bar staff make the shellacked pine walls less oppressive than they ought to be. Another good Division Street hideaway.

Melvin B's Truck Stop 1114 N State St ☎312/751-9897. In summer, the huge outdoor patio teems with a mix of joggers, rollerbladers and business types who come to drink like fish and munch on the decent bar food. Come winter the menu slims down to just the staples (pizza, hot dogs, chili) and a tamer indoor scene.

Mother's 26 W Division St ☎312/642-7251, ⓦwww.originalmothers.com. Providing the quintessential Division Street experience – a frenzied singles scene, loud and sweaty with bodies.

Old Town Ale House 219 W North Ave, at N Wieland St ☎312/ 944-7020. This dark, smoky dive, with its antique decor and book-lending library, has character to spare; check out the mural behind the bar that honors long-standing regulars. A favorite with artists, photographers and literary types since it opened in 1958, it's also seen numerous Second City comics tie the knot. Open late.

P.J. Clarke's 1204 N State Parkway, at E Division St ☎312/664-1650. The two-story sibling of the famed New York City burger joint, this *P.J.'s* serves a good brunch and some legendary burgers, but is still more known as a drinking establishment. The friendly bar is definitely a pickup scene, but still fun and not oppressive.

Weed's Tavern 1555 N Dayton St, at W Weed St ☎312/943-7815. Depending on your tastes, either inviting or disgusting, with bras strung from the ceiling and a relentlessly rowdy attitude. *Weed's* is the type of place where you'd get a free round of tequila shots just because you've never been there.

Whiskey Bar and Grill 21 E Bellevue Place, at N Rush St ☎312/475-0300. The local branch of this chainlet of style bars run by Cindy Crawford's husband should not be confused with *Whiskey Blue* at the *W*. It's still a scenemaker type of place, with beautiful people elbowing their way toward the more beautiful bartenders, but a little easier to get into.

Zebra Lounge 1220 N State Parkway, just north of W Division St ☎312/642-5140. Lounge singers, middle-aged swingers, transvestites and young preppies all mix at this tiny Gold Coast neighborhood bar, whose bad keyboardist only enhances its corny appeal.

South Loop and Near South

Alcock's Bar 411 S Wells St, at W Congress Parkway ☎312/922-1778, ⓦwww.alcocks.com; **Brown, Orange or Purple Line to LaSalle.** This bar overflows with Bears fans whenever the team plays at home, and financial types from the nearby Board of Trade during the week. Otherwise it's a low-key joint with rock 'n' roll blaring from the jukebox, bottled beers and sandwiches and hot dogs at lunch. Closed Sundays.

Cactus Cantina & Grill 404 S Wells St, at W Congress Parkway ☎312/ 922-3830; **Brown, Orange or Purple Line to LaSalle.** Strong, inexpensive drinks (with dancing to work them off) are the draw at this after-work hangout – a popular pickup scene in summer, especially with traders from the nearby exchanges. Closed weekends.

Kitty O'Shea's 720 S Michigan Ave, at E Balbo Drive ☎312/922-4400; **Red Line to Harrison.** This passable Irish pub, inside the massive *Hilton*, caters mainly to the hotel's guests. Though it's normally not a place you'd go out of your way for (although it is one of the few decent bars near the Michigan Ave hotels), they do serve a good Guinness and pub staples like shepherd's pie, and have live Irish music every night.

Mercury 221 W Van Buren St, at S Wells St ☎312/427-1774; **Brown Orange or Purple Line to LaSalle.** The mostly empty South Loop neighborhood can't diminish the attractions of this back-to-basics bar that features nightly DJs, couches, well-made martinis and not much else, thankfully.

Tantrum 1023 S State St, at E 11th St ☎312/939-9160; **Red Line to Roosevelt.** Slick, new little lounge in a mostly drink-free South Loop zone. Step up to the gorgeous mahogany bar for one of their 30 ingenious martinis and let time slip away.

△ Celtic Crossings bar, Near North

Bucktown, Wicker Park and Ukrainian Village

California Clipper 1002 N California Ave, at W Augusta Blvd ☎773/384-2547, ⓦwww .californiaclipper.com. This Prohibition-era bar near Humboldt Park has vintage booths and low lighting to add to the retro feel (plus pictures and models of the old plane which gave the bar its name). Frequent free live music, and Monday is bingo night.

Gold Star Bar 1755 W Division St, at N Wood St ☎773/227-8700; Blue Line to Division. All-business, old-fashioned Ukrainian Village bar where the focus is on drinking cheap beer in strictly blue-collar surroundings with a great classic and alt-rock jukebox.

Hideout 1354 W Wabansia Ave, at W Willow St ☎773/227-4433, ⓦwww.hideoutchicago.com; bus #72. The *Hideout*, tucked away among the warehouses between Old Town and Bucktown, is a low-key bar that just happens to be the center of Chicago's growing alternative country music scene. It attracts an interesting crowd for the almost nightly shows (which range to readings and video screenings).

Holiday Club 1471 N Milwaukee Ave, at N Honore St ☎773/486-0686, ⓦwww.swingersmecca.com. Recreating a Vegas-style lounge from the 1950s and 1960s, *Holiday* is one of Wicker Park's more popular joints and a self-proclaimed "Swingers mecca" (you can judge for yourself the veracity of this statement). There's good bar food, drink specials several nights a week and pool tables as well.

Leopard Lounge 1645 W Cortland Ave, at N Ashland Ave ☎773/862-7877; bus #73. Clubby lounge bar that sees mainly Lincoln Park and Bucktown residents, who dress up a little to match the cool environs (like the big fish tank behind the bar) and for a chance to hook up. There's an outdoor garden and pool table, as well, but be warned: this is pretty heavy on the pickup-joint vibe.

Map Room 1949 N Hoyne Ave, at W Armitage Ave ☎773/252-7636; Blue Line to Western. One of Bucktown's best bars, the *Map Room* offers a wide selection of beers (over two dozen kinds, in constant rotation) in a travel-themed setting – bookshelves lined with *National Geographics*, guidebooks and such, as well as Internet terminals. Crowded every night (there's usually some drink special on tap), the friendly and family-owned bar has live music on the

weekend and a popular International Night on Tuesday – a buffet focusing on a single country's cuisine.

Marie's Rip-Tide Lounge 1745 W Armitage Ave, at N Hermitage Ave ☎773/278-7317; bus #73. A small, late-night tavern between Lincoln Park and Bucktown that serves a mixed crowd – everyone from yuppies to blue-collar types to artist-wannabes and determined bar-crawlers who've been tossed out of every other tavern in the area; the staff – especially the adorably testy and cantankerous Marie herself – is part of its appeal. Have a beer or a straightforward mixed drink: this is far from trendy cocktail country.

Nick's Beergarden 1516 N Milwaukee Ave, at W North Ave ☎773/252-1155; Blue Line to Damen. Right under the El tracks, the rather slovenly *Nick's* succeeds largely because it's one of the few late-night bars in Wicker Park (open till 4am Sun–Fri, 5am on Sat). That said, it's a congenial place with a beer garden (open May–Nov) and live music (usually blues) on weekends. Most people don't start arriving until midnight, when the unusually large space fills up fast.

Northside Café 1635 N Damen Ave, at W Wabansia Ave ☎773/384-3555; Blue Line to Damen. While bars come and go in trendy Wicker Park and Bucktown, the *Northside* has carved a lasting place for itself with its huge, mouthwatering burgers, year-round outdoor patio, and unbuttoned atmosphere.

Pontiac Café 1531 N Damen Ave ☎773/252-7767. In warm weather, this former garage becomes the center of Wicker Park's outdoor drinking and singles scene. A great place for a post-work beer, getting loaded before a show at the nearby *Double Door* (see p.181) or a spot of people-watching on weekends. The beer is all bottled – Bud and other basics – and the sandwiches and burgers are better than they have any right to be.

Quencher's 2401 N Western Ave, at W Fullerton Ave ☎773/276-9730, ⓦwww.quenchers.com; bus #49, #74. This hip microbrewery in the northern reaches of Bucktown has been around since 1979, long before the trend hit the mainstream. There's an astonishing array of more than 200 beers (including everything from New Hampshire's Smuttynose Old Brown Dog Ale to the

Brazillian brew Xingu Black), a good enough reason to brave the bar's semi-obnoxious party-hearty attitude.

Rainbo Club 1150 N Damen Ave, at W Division St ☎773/489-5999; bus #50. An old neighborhood standby that's become chic by virtue of its trendy Ukrainian Village location. The authentically retro feel to the place (pinball machine, photo booth) is complemented by both the above-average music that spans all genres and the inexpensive beers that satisfy all tastes.

(Slow Down) Life's Too Short 1177 N Elston Ave, at W Division St ☎773/384-1040; bus #70. Self-consciously gaudy (holiday lights and beach-bar-style paraphenalia everywhere) in a fun sort of way, this riverside bar offers great views of the sun setting over the city. There's a bar menu, as well as various games (Ping-Pong, pool, air hockey, horseshoes) and the crowd is surprisingly diverse for the Division Street area. The beer garden out back often hosts reggae bands.

Subterranean 2011 W North Ave, at N Damen Ave ☎773/278-6600, ⓦwww.subt.net; Blue Line to Damen. One of the best bars around the six-corner intersection of N Milwaukee, W North and N Damen avenues, this onetime

brothel and gambling house (thus the chandelier and ornate woodwork) is now a three-floor cabaret, lounge and dance club, housed in a nineteenth-century building. The first floor, The Lounge, achieves a sexy, red-light-district, loungey vibe, while the two-floor Cabaret upstairs is a decent live-music venue.

Ten 56 1056 N Damen Ave, at W Cortez St ☎773/227-4906. This former speakeasy reopened as a hip bar in the late 1990s, suited for fast-gentrifying Ukrainian Village. It's bathed in seamy red light and shows an endless procession of kung fu flicks on TVs scattered around the place, which become even more entertaining after a few of their signature 10oz martinis.

Tuman's Alcohol Abuse Center 2201 W Chicago Ave, at N Leavitt St; no phone; bus #66. A fantastically nasty dump of a bar. Order a drink that's even remotely trendy and you could well be asked to leave. The crowd (which can look rough but is more bark than bite) comes for the cheap drinks and gritty atmosphere (excellent punk rock on the jukebox), but that could change, now that folks come here from fashionable Bucktown and Lincoln Park.

Lincoln Park

Castaway's Bar & Grill 1501 N Lake Shore Drive, at N LaSalle St ☎773/281-1200. Miami's South Beach meets Chicago at this seasonal bar and restaurant, upstairs in the gaudy boathouse at North Avenue Beach. In summer, the place fills with patrons in bikinis (and even shoulder-riding iguanas), drawn by the relaxed Margaritaville ambience as well as priceless views.

Charlie's Ale House 1224 W Webster Ave ☎773/871-1440; Brown or Purple Line to Fullerton. Although the crowd can be a bit J Crew, Charlie's is still a great place to kick back with a few pints in the popular, vine-covered outdoor garden-patio after a walk through Lincoln Park.

Coyle's Tippling House 2843 N Halsted St, at W George St ☎773/528-7569; Brown Line to Diversey. Tons of beers, TVs and a long menu of standard grubbing items, Coyle's is a reliable, no-pretense hangout that's at its best when a football game is on (especially a Bears or Iowa Hawkeyes one).

Delilah's 2771 N Lincoln Ave, at at W Diversey Parkway ☎773/472-2771; Brown Line to Diversey. Delilah's is out of place in sedate Lincoln Park, with all the punk rock on the jukebox and the cult movies that screen here on weekends. Featuring an extensive selection of whiskeys and over 150 beers, this neighborhood favorite also features excellent DJs spinning everything from classic punk to alt-country and R&B. Upstairs, there's a pool room that's usually less crowded than the bar.

Glascott's 2158 N Halsted St, at W Dickens Ave ☎773/281-1205; Brown or Purple Line to Fullerton. Also known as Glascott's Groggery, this friendly neighborhood pub has been around since 1937, run by a family that's been in the business since the 1800s. Popular with baseball-cap-wearing, barhopping types.

Goodbar 2512 N Halsted St, at W Fullerton Ave ☎773/296-9700; Brown or Purple Line to Fullerton. The young, good-looking staff are well matched by the clientele at this funky tavern, which also has an upstairs lounge and rooftop beer garden. Alternative pop and rock gets spun in the back of the bar during the week and the DJs prefer hip-hop and house on the weekend.

Goose Island 1800 N Clybourn Ave, near N Sheffield Ave ☎312/915-0071, ⓦwww .gooseisland.com; Red Line to North/Clybourn. The rare case of a successful Chicago microbrewery – a huge, multileveled space that was once a warehouse, serving dozens of fabulous home brews (especially their crisp India pale ale) along with delicious burgers, steaks, seafood, beer-battered fries and salads. They also have a Wrigleyville location at 3535 N Clark (☎773/832-9040).

Hog Head McDunna's 1505 W Fullerton Ave, at N Greenview Ave ☎773/929-0944; Brown or Purple Line to Fullerton. Off the main Lincoln Park bar drags, this is a cool neighborhood joint where the music is never too loud and the TV plays the *Simpsons*.

Irish Eyes 2519 N Lincoln Ave, at W Lili Ave ☎773/348-9548; Brown or Purple Line to Fullerton. This little Irish dive pours a fair Guinness, and people pack the place every single night to hear – and sing along to – old Irish drinking tunes with regulars like Whitey O'Day.

John Barleycorn Memorial Pub 658 W Belden Ave, at N Lincoln Ave ☎773/348-8899, ⓦwww.johnbarleycorn.com; Brown or Purple Line to Fullerton. One of the city's most popular bar and beer gardens, this former speakeasy draws on a nautical theme to attract a mix of students from nearby DePaul University, young couples and families and beer lovers (more than 30 brews to choose from). Though it can get crowded on weekends, it's not uncomfortably so. There's another location near Wrigley at 3454 N Clark (☎773/549-6000).

Kincade's 950 W Armitage Ave, at N Sheffield Ave ☎773/348-0010; Brown or Purple Line to Armitage. The bachelorette parties, drink specials, rude staff and huge crowds will make *Kincade's* a nightmare for some, and simply the beginning of a rowdy night for others. For the serious traveling sports fan:

The three-level bar also has 38 TVs and extremely cheap food buffets.

Liar's Club 1665 W Fullerton Ave, at N Clybourn Ave ☎773/665-1110; bus #73. Located in an industrial no-man's-land, the dark and decaying *Liar's Club* is a singles bar verging on a dance club, bathed in red lights, with everyone grooving to the Ramones or drum 'n' bass, with the pretense meter sitting at zero.

McGee's 950 W Webster Ave, at N Sheffield Ave ☎773/549-8200; Brown or Purple Line to Fullerton. Beneath the El tracks, this yuppie Irish sports bar has cheap, cheap drinks and serves excellent pub food, but it's an overwhelmingly college/sports kind of place.

Red Lion Pub 2446 N Lincoln Ave, at W Montana St ☎773/348-2695; Brown or Purple Line to Fullerton. A friendly English pub where you'd be comfortable dropping by solo. Claiming to be haunted, the pub has a host of dedicated regulars (many UK expats) and features a series of weekly readings (usually in the fantasy vein).

Walsh's Schubert Inn 1301 W Schubert Ave, at N Lakewood Ave ☎773/472-7738; bus #11. This fine northside neighborhood tavern – located in a two-story house – has a facade typical of the homes in this area and so is easy to walk right by. *Schubert's* boasts a convivial mix of young locals, business folk, and old-timers, and also has one of the nicer beer gardens in the city (walk through the service entrance, down the metal ramp).

Webster's Wine Bar 1480 W Webster Ave, at N Clybourn Ave ☎773/868-0608. This quiet, candlelit bar is a nice spot for a drink, popular with young couples who pair off in the dim lighting among the book-covered walls. The staff is knowledgeable and helpful, serving up some better-than-average appetizers, like the exceptional pear and brie quesadilla.

Wrightwood Tap 1059 W Wrightwood Ave, at N Seminary Ave ☎773/549-4949; Brown or Purple Line to Fullerton. Secluded little spot that's definitely more of a neighborhood hangout but worth finding on karaoke night.

Cubby Bear 1059 W Addison St, at N Clark St ⊤773/327-1662; Red Line to Addison. Spacious, crowded and loud, *Cubby Bear* would be just another sports bar if it weren't for Wrigley Field across the street. When the Cubs are in town, the one hundred TVs turn on and the crowds squeeze in to down $2 drafts and graze at the $3 taco bar. They also have a decent lineup of live touring rock and hip-hop groups.

Cullen's Bar & Grill 3741 N Southport Ave, at W Waveland Ave ⊤773/975-0600; Brown Line to Southport. The top night spot in the burgeoning Southport Avenue corridor, this authentic Irish pub is among the best of its kind in Chicago, with a welcoming staff, above-average pub food (try the delectable mashed potatoes) and live Celtic music several nights a week. There's also outdoor seating In warm weather.

Duke of Perth 2913 N Clark St, at W Oakdale Ave ⊤773/477-1741; bus #22. The city's only Scottish pub, with more than seventy kinds of single-malt scotch whiskey, all-you-can-eat fish and chips on Wednesday and Friday ($8), and a full lineup of Scots delicacies like leek pie and Scotch eggs.

Ginger Man 3740 N Clark St, at N Racine Ave ⊤773/549-2050; Red Line to Addison. One of the only defiantly non-sports-related drinking establishments in Wrigleyville, this bar has pool tables, no screaming Cubs fans, over 50 bottled beers and a cool, rocker vibe.

Green Mill 4802 N Broadway St, at N Racine Ave ⊤773/878-5552; Red Line to Lawrence. This onetime speakeasy was Al Capone's favorite bar; today it's the best jazz club in the city (see review in "Live music and clubs," on p.180). It's also one of the best bars in the city, with good conversationalists for bartenders and a great Jazz Age air about it. Just about every movie filmed in Chicago seems to set at least one scene in here. Worth the long train ride up north and conveniently located near to Aragon and Riviera concert halls in a defiantly non-yuppified part of town.

Hi-Tops 3551 N Sheffield Ave, at N Halsted St ⊤773/348-0009, ⓦwww.hi-topsusa.com; Red Line to Addison. Right down the street from Wrigley Field and with TVs just about everywhere, *Hi-Tops* is a mess of sports, booze and drunken buffoonery come game day.

All other times just an above-average sports bar with an unusual dedication to televised games and DJs on weekend nights.

Hopleaf Bar 5148 N Clark St ⊤773/334-9851. If you happen to be in Uptown or Andersonville, be sure to stop by this undiscovered treat, one of the best beer selections in Chicago (over 150 to choose from, many of them Belgian). The decor is old-style German and there's even a good selection of magazines for those drinking alone.

Hye Bar 3707 N Southport Ave, at W Waveland Ave ⊤773/244-4102; Brown Line to Southport. A neighborhood bar given a slightly Irish flavor by the Irish beers on tap and friendly Irish bartenders. Mainly a yuppie hangout, the place gets a more mixed crowd from nearby Wrigleyville as well. "Car bombs" (a whiskey shot in a pint of Guinness) are so popular here that the staff may even join you for one.

The Irish Oak 3511 N Clark St ⊤773/935-6669. A relative newcomer to the Chicago bar scene, this Irish bar has quickly become a favorite. Located near Wrigley Field, it's a pleasant alternative to the raucous sports bars on game days, and features live music on Wednesday and Thursday, plus all-you-can-eat fish and chips on Wednesday and Friday, like the *Duke of Perth* (see above).

Moody's Pub 5910 N Broadway St, at W Rosedale Ave ⊤773/275-2696; Red Line to Thorndale. Far up north lies this little gem, a dim-lit bar with some of the best burgers in the city and a beer garden that has been known to suck people in for entire lost afternoons.

Murphy's Bleachers 3655 N Sheffield Ave, at W Waveland Ave ⊤773/281-5356; Red Line to Addison. Even with the wall-to-wall Cubs fans, substandard food (don't bother) and overpriced drinks, *Murphy's* is a traditional and fun pre- or post-game stop for all Wrigley attendees. If it's not game day, though, remember that there are plenty of other bars in the neighborhood.

Nick's Uptown 4015-17 N Sheridan Rd, at W Irving Park Rd ⊤773/ 975-1155; Red Line to Sheridan. With little competition this far north, *Nick's Uptown* gets huge crowds after the other bars close down. The crowd at this late-night joint – characterized by garish lighting and an inexplicable pineapple decorating scheme – tends to be young and rowdy (fights are common). Fortunately, there's plenty of room for everyone – there are some seventy stools along the bar and a separate room with pool tables if the main room is too crowded.

Pops For Champagne 2934 N Sheffield Ave, at W Oakdale Ave ☎773/472-1000, ⓦwww .popschampagne.com; Red Line to Belmont. This sophisticated jazz bar – a destination on special occasions – has been pouring more than a hundred kinds of champagnes, and liquor, too, for more than twenty years. Prices range from modest ($8 per glass) to sky-high, and while there's not an official dress code, leave the jeans and sandals behind.

Redmond's 3358 N Sheffield Ave, at W Roscoe St ☎773/404-2151; Red Line to Belmont. Unusually classy sports bar that offers a full menu of middling-to-great American dishes, plush booths, and 30-some beers (everything from Labatts to Boddington's).

Resi's Bierstube 2034 W Irving Park, at N Lincoln and N Damen aves ☎773/472-1749. Located beyond Lakeview's northern reaches, *Resi's* may hard to get to, but if you're looking to soak in some German ambience this atmospheric bar is hard to beat. Choose from more than thirty Bavarian beers on tap, plus a sausage-heavy menu, while surrounded by Oktoberfest posters and souvenirs put up by the German owners. There's also a pleasant beer garden out back.

Schubas Tavern 3159 N Southport Ave, at W Belmont Ave ☎773/525-2508; Red Line to Belmont. The front half of this combo concert space/restaurant is a decent no-frills drinking space. Over a dozen good tap beers ensure a regular flow of drinkers, many of them oblivious of the concerts being performed in the back hall, along with serious alt-rock fans. Get late-night eats in the attached *Harmony Grill* (see "Eating," p.161).

Sheffield's Wine and Beer Garden 3258 N Sheffield Ave, at W Belmont Ave ☎773/281-4989; Red Line to Belmont. When the weather's warm, lines wrap around the entrance of this leafy outdoor beer garden for the fine assortment of wines and beers (20 drafts, plus bottles). The indoor bar is cozy, with lots of nooks and crannies in which to hide away.

Simon's Tavern 5210 N Clark St, at W Foster Ave ☎773/878-0894; bus #22. This former speakeasy, now an aged Swedish bar (dig the Viking-style decorations), has a beautiful long wooden bar and good Andersonville neighborhood cred. The friendly staff, full of historical info, tend to a crowd that's a mix of Swedes, gays and lesbians, and people who come for a slice of laid-back Chicago style.

The Vic 3145 N Sheffield Ave ☎312/618-8439. On Brew & View nights, the theater opens its bar during screenings of current and classic movies. For details, see review on p.192.

Village Tap 2055 W Roscoe St, at N Seeley Ave ☎773/883-0817; Brown Line to Addison. West of Lakeview, in Roscoe Village, you'll find a massive and appealing beer selection which draws curious out-of-towners and artsy locals alike to this long, skinny, usually-packed bar. Try to go during the week, as it can be a madhouse on the weekend.

Will's Northwoods Inn 3032 N Racine Ave, at W Nelson St ☎773/528-4400, ⓦwww .willsnorthwoodsinn.com; Brown Line to Wellington. Modeled after a northwoods angler's lodge, this well-worn, laid-back sports bar does actually sponsor Muskie fishing and canoe trips to Wisconsin. Even if it's all a little too cheesehead, there aren't a lot of places this relaxed, with Leinenkeugel and Pabst Blue Ribbon to drink, not to mention complimentary cheese curds and brats during Packers games.

West Side

Betty's Blue Star Lounge 1600 W Grand Ave, at N Ashland Ave ☎312/243-8778; Green Line to Ashland. A bare-bones, late-night bar that brings in a low-key crowd for the cheap beers ($2 Old Style on tap) and the lack of pretense. Weekend nights it rocks until early morning with DJs and revelers.

Jaks Tap 901 W Jackson Blvd, at S Peoria St ☎312/666-1700; Blue Line to UIC/Halsted. Forty draft beers (Bellhaven to Warsteiner) and a decent brewpub menu are the highlights of this University of Illinois-Chicago area bar run by the same people as operate the *Village Tap* (see above). Atmosphere runs to exposed brick walls and lots of gleaming wood.

Matchbox 770 N Milwaukee Ave, at N Ogden Ave ⊤312/666-9292. This slender bar is one of the more intriguing places in the city for cocktails, and the very tight space, excellent martinis and friendly atmosphere make for a fun, communal experience.

Tasting Room 1415 W Randolph St, at N Ogden Ave ⊤312/942-1212. A two-story, tastefully decorated wine bar that's more about the wine than the ambience, *The Tasting Room* employs several sommeliers to help visitors

with their choices. There's plenty of tasty appetizers (from cheese selections to meat and seafood plates) to sample with the wine (available for purchase also in the Randolph Wine Cellars, attached to the bar).

Twisted Spoke 501 N Ogden Ave, at W Grand Ave ⊤312/666-1500, ⊛www.twistedspoke.com; bus #65. Despite the tough-looking biker decor, everyone's welcome at this charming bar/restaurant. For more details, see "Eating," p.163.

South Side/Hyde Park

The Cove Lounge 1750 E 55th St, at S Everell Ave ⊤773/684-1013. A Hyde Park hole-in-the-wall that caters mainly to a handful of regulars, except on Thursday night when crowds of UC students take full advantage of the $4 pitchers. Not the best, but a decent option in a surprisingly bar-free zone.

Jimbo's 3258 S Princeton Ave, at W 33rd St ⊤312/326-3253; Red Line to Sox/35th. A no-frills neighborhood bar that succeeds because of its proximity to Comiskey Park. It's usually packed with Sox fans before and after games as it's one of the only places to drink near the park.

Keegan's Pub 10618 S Western Ave, at W 106th St ⊤773/233-6829. Wood-paneled walls,

Guinness, a fireplace and fervor for the White Sox are the name of the game at this classic neighborhood joint in Beverly. Friendly enough even if they're not overly excited to wait on a new face.

Woodlawn Tap 1172 E 55th St, at S Woodlawn Ave ⊤773/643-5516. Referred to strictly as "Jimmy's" after the bar's late owner, this dimly lit bar is an oasis for locals and students alike, who love its bookish airs and cheap drinks and burgers. With just three smoky, unadorned rooms, two bars carrying a modest selection of beer and liquor, and a lone pinball machine, it's the kind of place to "hear and be heard."

14

Live music and clubs

Being the crossroads that it is, Chicago has one of the best **music scenes** in the US, often reflecting the changing musical landscape of the country as a whole. From the early days of jazz and blues to the rise of alternative rock in the mainstream, Chicago has made its mark, albeit in its characteristically down-to-earth way.

Although Louis Armstrong and scores of other top musicians brought jazz from New Orleans nearly 75 years ago, Chicago's musical identity is rooted in the **blues**; indeed, Chicago is considered the capital of modern electric blues. During the genre's heyday in the mid-twentieth century, blues clubs lined the streets of Chicago's South Side around the influential Chess Records studio, where blues legends Muddy Waters, Willie Dixon, Junior Wells and Koko Taylor all recorded. Economic forces have more or less pushed – or pulled – blues clubs from the South Side to the city's more accessible north side, and on an average weeknight, you'll find five or six different blues acts performing in Near North and Lincoln Park alone.

Besides blues, Chicago has a burgeoning **alternative rock** scene that came of age in the 1990s, with breakthroughs early in the decade by the Smashing Pumpkins and Liz Phair, followed more recently by Wilco. As well, **alternative country** (or "alt country") has been steadily gaining in popularity, while as far as dance music goes, **house** and **techno** basically started in Chicago, so that's all you're likely to hear in the dance clubs. One would think **jazz** would be bigger in Chicago than it is; that said, finding live jazz on any night of the week won't be hard – a visit to premier jazz club *Green Mill* deserves at least a night (see p.180).

The venues in Chicago are another distinction: the city has some of the country's best **rock halls** (former movie palaces and theaters converted into concert spaces). Just about every major American band, it seems, includes the city on their itineraries, and you'll be able to hear them here for not much more than $25 a ticket.

As for a sampling of where to go: **Near North**, **Lincoln Park** and **Lakeview** have the highest concentration of blues and dance clubs; **Bucktown** and **Wicker Park** cater to alternative and indie rockers, while rock 'n' roll can be heard just about anywhere there's a stage and a tap. Some of the more ethnic and world music get their due, as do gospel, hip-hop, reggae, samba, punk and country.

For **current music listings**, pick up the excellent free weekly *Chicago Reader* – copies come out Thursday afternoon and are usually all gone by Saturday. Other good sources include the weekly *New City* and the gay and lesbian *Windy City Times*. Full listings also appear in the Friday issues of the *Chicago Sun-Times* and the *Chicago Tribune*, and *Chicago* magazine has useful arts and restaurant listings. The Gramaphone Ltd record store, at 2663 N Clark St (℡773/472-3683), is the best place for details of one-off **dance** nights.

The most convenient way to buy **tickets** is through a ticket agency like Ticketmaster (℡312/559-1212, ⓦwww.ticketmaster.com), though be prepared to pay a fee on top of the ticket price. You can also go to the venue's box office and save yourself the fee.

Expect to pay $5–12 for tickets to shows at small clubs like the *Double Door* and *Schubas*; $15–35 at mid-sized venues like *Metro*, The Vic, The Aragon, and $30 and up at stadiums like the United Center and the Allstate Arena. Bear in mind that bars and clubs strictly enforce the legal **drinking age** (21), and you won't be admitted without **proper ID** (a driver's license or passport).

Major concert venues

Allstate Arena 6920 N Mannheim Rd, Rosemont ℡847/635-6601; Blue Line to River Road, transfer to Regional Transportation Authority (RTA) bus #221 or #222. Soulless, out-of-the-way stadium pulling in big-name concerts, with seating for 18,000-plus.

Petrillo Music Shell Columbus Drive and Jackson Blvd, in Grant Park; Red Line to Jackson. Multi-purpose outdoor stage and lawn in the Loop, often used for free summer concerts – notably the Chicago Blues Festival (see p.211). If you want to see the performers, get a seat near the stage, otherwise just camp out on the lawn with a blanket.

Ravinia Festival Ravinia Park Road, Highland Park ℡312/836-7000; reachable via Metra train (Union Pacific North Line). Board at Ogilvie Transportation Center, get off at the Ravinia Park stop, which is right at the Festival's West Gate. A Chicago gem, this performance complex is located on the North Shore about 25 miles north of the Loop. Just a fifteen-minute ride on the Metra commuter train, the pavilion makes for the most intimate outdoor music venue in summer, featuring top acts of nearly every musical genre, with numerous performances by the Chicago Symphony Orchestra. Bring a picnic and sit on the lawn or buy a ticket for a seat in the pavilion (there are also concerts in the two small theaters). Ticket prices vary, though usually not less than $15. Highly recommended.

United Center 1901 W Madison St ℡312/455-4500; public transportation not recommended. Home to the Chicago Bulls and Blackhawks, this stadium on the West Side also draws superstar music acts. Not the best place to hear music by any stretch, but if you want to see the top performers, you'll go.

Blues

Some sixty **blues clubs** are scattered throughout the city, most of them small, loud, smoky and adorned with all manner of blues memorabilia. Chicago blues was born on the South Side, and for true aficionados, a visit to one of the few remaining clubs there is almost mandatory – though take care, as the area can be dodgy, especially after dark. That said, excellent blues can also be heard in any number of clubs right in the heart of the city, and many bars and clubs include live blues acts in their lineups. Names to watch out for include Son Seals, Vance Kelly, Melvin Taylor and Buddy Guy – any one of these bluesmen can put on a powerhouse show.

Cover charges range from next to nothing to about $25, depending, usually, on the club's proximity to the tourist circuit, and some require a two-drink

LIVE MUSIC AND CLUBS | Major concert venues • Blues

minimum. If you happen to be around in the summer, there are plenty of outdoor music concerts to be had, including the massive Chicago Blues Festival (see p.211). The city also runs neighborhood blues and gospel **tours** from time to time; see p.31 for details. (For more on blues history, see Contexts, p.248.)

Blue Chicago 536 N Clark St, at W Ohio St ☎312/661-0100 and 736 N Clark St, at Superior St ☎312/642-6261; Red Line to Grand. Touristy blues joints featuring mostly female vocalists, though they won't disappoint if you're looking for a blues scene close to the Near North hotels – there's almost always one loud, audience-involved rendition of "Sweet Home Chicago." The $7 cover charge gets you into both clubs, the smaller of which (no. 536) is not much bigger than a closet.

B.L.U.E.S. 2519 N Halsted St ☎773/528-1012; Brown or Red Line to Fullerton. Open since the 1970s, this intimate club in Lincoln Park has hosted all the greats, and has live blues every night of the week. They sometimes have deals with *Kingston Mines* across the street (see below). The cover on weekends is around $10, less on weekdays.

Buddy Guy's Legends 754 S Wabash Ave ☎312/427-0333; Red Line to Harrison. This large South Loop club, owned by the veteran guitarist and vocalist, has great acoustics and atmosphere, and live blues every night (Guy himself has an extended stint each January). The roster features new talent and established greats, and though somewhat touristy it's worth dropping by. Monday nights are jam nights. Covers range from $8 to $12 during the week, $15 to $25 on weekends.

Checkerboard Lounge 423 E 43rd St ☎773/624-3240. A Chicago blues landmark on the South Side that features the best in local acts, along with some big national names. Despite the fact that it's a dive, out of the way in an unsafe neighborhood and patronized by the shot-and-beer crowd, it's well worth a visit. Take a taxi there and back (you may need to call one for the return trip). Not recommended for single women. Cover $5–7.

House of Blues 329 N Dearborn St ☎312/527-2583; Red Line to Grand. Despite its name, this swish Near North concert venue puts

on all kinds of music, including blues. The acoustics are phenomenal and the waitstaff attentive. Its popular Sunday Gospel Brunch ($35) sells out quickly (see p.150). Concert tickets start around $17.

Kingston Mines 2548 N Halsted St ☎773/472-2031; Brown or Red Line to Fullerton. Opened in 1968, this Lincoln Park staple is one of Chicago's oldest blues clubs, appropriately dark, loud and smoke-filled. It's packed every night and consistently delivers some of the finest blues around. Bands alternate on two stages, keeping up a constant stream of music throughout the evening; big names perform till 5am on Saturdays. Cover $12–15.

Lee's Unleaded Blues 7401 S Chicago Ave ☎773/493-3477. Small, friendly juke joint way down on the South Side, in one of the most rough-and-tumble parts of the city. About twenty blocks south of the University of Chicago, *Lee's* does attract a student or two, but mostly it's a staple of locals who come for the nightly blues. Best to come here by car or taxi.

Reservation Blues 1566 N Milwaukee Ave ☎773/645-5200; Blue Line to Damen. Relative newcomer to the city's blues scene, this Wicker Park club feels more like a commercial venture than a true, gritty blues joint, but it does have a decent list of local blues acts – Vance Kelly, Melvin Taylor, or the man himself, Eddy "The Chief" Clearwater, would make for a great night here.

Rosa's Lounge 3420 W Armitage Ave ☎773/342-0452. Run by an Italian mother-and-son duo on the West Side, *Rosa's* is a soulful, welcoming and excellent blues club, with a solid calendar of shows (Tues–Sat). The only drawback is the location: it's about thirty blocks west of downtown, so you'll need a taxi. Tuesdays with Melvin Taylor, one of Chicago's unsung guitar virtuosos, are a highlight. Covers vary ($5–15).

Jazz

Jazz clubs are, by no means, as abundant in Chicago as they are in New York, and a good portion of the jazz that Chicago hears happens in bars not entirely devoted to jazz. On the other hand, two clubs easily hold their own against the country's best: the historic *Green Mill* in Uptown and *Jazz Showcase*, in Near North, the spot for renowned jazz artists passing through town.

Andy's 11 E Hubbard St ☎312/642-6805; **Red Line to Grand.** A casual fixture on Chicago's jazz scene, popular for its lunchtime concerts and Monday night improv jam sessions. While many Chicago bars offer occasional "jazz" trios and such, *Andy's*, in Near North, is devoted entirely to jazz – traditional, mainstream and be-bop. The crowd is mix of drinkers, jazz lovers and those who come to dine off the decent menu. Mon–Fri 6.30pm–midnight, Sat till 1am. Cover $5–10.

Chicago Cultural Center 78 E Washington St ☎312/346-3278; **Red Line to Washington.** Home to the city's main visitor center (see p.20), this splendid old building in the Loop also has gallery spaces where classical and jazz groups often host free lunchtime and evening concerts. The crowd is a real mix – suits on lunchbreak, travelers and music lovers in the know.

The Cotton Club 1710 S Michigan Ave ☎312/341-9787; **Green or Red Line to Roosevelt.** South Loop venue that attracts two crowds: a mellow, well-dressed set (in the Cab Calloway front room), and a younger, hip-hop group (in the Gray room in the back). Not a club you'd seek out unless you happen to be in the area. Modest cover. Mon–Fri till 4am, Sat till 5am.

Green Dolphin Street 2200 N Ashland Ave ☎773/395-0066. This sophisticated and casually elegant restaurant and jazz bar attracts a mixed crowd to its location in industrial west Lincoln Park. The music, depending on the night, could be anything from Afro-Cuban to big band. Kick back with a cigar from the floor-to-ceiling humidor or tuck into the eclectic menu (see p.160).

Green Mill 4802 N Broadway St ☎773/878-5552; **Red Line to Lawrence.** This former Uptown speakeasy and Al Capone haunt is pure Chicago and should not be missed. Though far from downtown, it's the most revered jazz club in the city, both for its acts and atmosphere – the beautiful interior still retains its period charm. Open till 4am. Cover varies, usually around $5.

Jazz Showcase 59 W Grand Ave ☎312/670-BIRD; **Red Line to Grand.** If you're looking for top talent and are willing to pay a hefty cover ($15–25), then Chicago music mogul Joe Segal's place in Near North might be for you. Since 1947, it's been the venue of choice for mainstream jazz artists, from Hargrove to Brubeck. Shows at 8pm and 10pm Tues–Thurs, 9pm and 11pm on Fri and Sat; and 4pm, 8pm and 10pm on Sun. Students get a discount. Cash only.

Velvet Lounge 2128 1/2 S Indiana Ave ☎312/791-9050. This low-key tavern run by Chicago jazz institution Fred Anderson has live jazz five nights a week, and is a good place to catch the more exploratory side of recent Chi-town jazz. Open-mic nights on Sundays 5–9pm.

Rock

One look at the music listings in The *Reader* will reveal that there are dozens of **rock bands** performing any night of the week, mostly on the city's north side in Lincoln Park, Lakeview and Wicker Park. Catching a show in one of the rock halls is a quintessential Chicago experience and shouldn't be missed, especially at venues like *Metro*, The Riviera or The Vic. For smaller shows in more down-to-earth surroundings, Wicker Park's *Double Door* and *The Empty Bottle* in the Ukrainian Village offer some of the best in the city, but keep in mind that the often raucous crowds are more prone to stage-diving than sitting back and listening.

Bigger venues

The Aragon Ballroom 1106 W Lawrence Ave, at N Broadway; ☎773/561-9500; Red Line to Lawrence. The acoustics may be wanting at this 5000-seat behemoth in Uptown, but the ornate decor and size (room for 4000+) keep it on Chicago's short list of top, mid-sized concert venues.

The Congress Theatre 2135 N Milwaukee Ave ☎773/252-4000; Blue Line to Western. This former Bucktown movie palace, with Gothic trimmings, now attracts mainly indie and punk acts, popular deejays and a smattering of up-and-coming rock acts. Cover charges vary.

Metro 3730 N Clark St ☎773/549-0203, ⊛www.metrochicago.com; Red Line to Addison. This Lakeview club's excellent acoustics and reputation as a top venue for national and local indie acts pull in Chicago's party crowds. The *Smart Bar*, in the same building, is a dance club (see p.184).

Park West 322 W Armitage Ave, at N Clark St; ☎773/929-5959. Spacious Lincoln Park standby that tends to host softer, college-band types, and the crowds who follow them.

The Riviera Theatre 4746 N Racine Ave ☎773/275-6800; Red Line to Lawrence. Part of Uptown's music triumvirate (joining the Aragon and the *Green Mill*), the aging but characterful Riviera hosts major rock acts. Always nice to catch some jazz at the *Green Mill* after a concert here.

The Vic 3145 N Sheffield Ave ☎773/472-0449; Brown or Red Line to Belmont. Huge former vaudeville theater in Lakeview that now sees a steady flow of popular rock bands. A great place to catch a show – the acoustics are good and there's ample space to stand (on the floor) or sit (in the balcony). The only drawback is its tendency to be loud and sweatier than most other venues. Also hosts "Brew & View," (see p.192) when there's not a concert on.

Smaller clubs

Cubby Bear 1059 W Addison St, at N Clark St ☎773/327-1662; Red Line to Addison. Busy by day with crowds from neighboring Wrigley Field, this boisterous sports bar features alternative rock bands after dark (Wed–Sat), though music takes a backseat to the sports scene. Cover $5–7.

The Double Door 1572 N Milwaukee Ave ☎773/489-3160; Blue Line to Damen. Right on the border of Wicker Park and Bucktown, this club has been on top of the alternative music scene for decades. There's usually some indie band playing on most nights, while Sundays are usually reserved for Liquid Soul's acid jazz. The crowd is very Wicker Park (unshaven, consignment-store dress, messy hair), and there are pool tables downstairs if the music gets too loud. Covers vary, though it's usually half what the big north side music venues charge. Recommended.

Elbo Room 2871 N Lincoln Ave ☎773/549-5549; Brown Line to Diversey. Known around Chicago as the place where band Liquid Soul got their start, this easygoing Lakeview venue has lost a bit of its edge over the years, though it still puts on music most nights of the week, from ska and alternative rock to funk and acid jazz.

The Empty Bottle 1035 N Western Ave, at W Cortez St ☎773/276-3600; Blue Line to Division. A hole-in-the-wall club in the Ukrainian Village that showcases some top talent, ranging from up-and-coming indie bands to avant-garde jazz and progressive country. Truly loud (earplugs sold at the bar), though rarely overfilled and always enjoyable.

Fireside Bowl 2646 W Fullerton Ave ☎773/486-2700; Blue Line to California. This all-ages music venue on the north end of Bucktown puts on a few punk and ska shows a week, draws a young crowd and is rarely filled to its capacity of 800. Opens at 6pm, closes at 2am; cover is usually about $5.

The Note 1565 N Milwaukee Ave ☎773/489-0011; Blue Line to Damen. Music venue that survives more on its Wicker Park location than from the talent performing on its stages, which is a bit of everything, including jazz, reggae, hip-hop, funk and salsa (Tues–Sat). There's pool in the front room if you want to cool down between sets.

Schubas Tavern 3159 N Southport Ave ☎773/525-2508; Brown Line to Belmont. A small Lakeview mainstay booking an impressive roster of rock and alternative country and roots revival bands, all in all a great place to see a show. The bar in front is very popular between sets and on weekends. Fri till 2am, Sat till 3am. Cover varies.

Folk, country and world music

Chicago's **world music** scene is surprisingly healthy, with Irish and rootsy folk music leading the list. Almost any of the neighborhood taverns will have Irish or Celtic music come weekends, especially on Sundays, while a smaller number put on some form of country or folk music. The Old Town School of Folk Music, northwest of Lakeview (see below), is perhaps the city's best venue for world-music lovers, with its diverse concert offerings.

While we've listed some excellent venues below, note that many of them are somewhat out of the way.

Abbey Pub 3420 W Grace St at N Elston Ave ☎773/478-4408; Blue Line to Addison. One of Chicago's unsung supporters of aspiring musicians and new music, with live music every night (Irish music on Sun). The only drawback is its location in Old Irving Park, northwest of Lakeview. Covers vary.

Baby Doll Polka Club 6102 S Central Ave ☎773/582-9706; Orange Line to Midway. Locals have been doing the polka, two-step and the tango here for forty years. The South Side location near Midway Airport means it's a considerable trek, so most Chicagoans don't bother, but if you're a Lawrence Welk fan or want a Polish experience in Chicago, then you'll find it worthwhile. There is no cover charge, and it closes at 2am.

Equator Club 4715 N Broadway St ☎773/728-2411; Red Line to Lawrence. Former speakeasy owned by Al Capone now has live African and Caribbean music, sometimes by internationally recognized recording artists.

Exodus II 3477 N Clark St ☎773/348-3998; Red Line to Addison. Across the street from the *Wild Hare* (see below), this smaller, lesser-known reggae venue in Wrigleyville is also a bit seedier, but if reggae's your thing, chances are you'll overlook the drawbacks. Rarely a cover and never the huge crowds you might find at the *Wild Hare*.

Fitzgerald's 6615 W Roosevelt Rd, Berwyn ☎708/788-2118; Blue Line to Harlem. Excellent venue for alternative country, Cajun and zydeco, but it's way out in the western suburb of Berwyn and hard to reach without a car. The club has live music every night, and despite the location, it's right alongside the *Abbey*, *Schubas* and the *Double Door* – the cream of Chicago's small-scale music venues.

Hideout 1354 W Wabansia Ave ☎773/227-4433; Red Line to North/Clybourn. This small, eclectic roots and country music bar is located two blocks north of North Avenue, in a no-man's-land east of Bucktown and

Wicker Park; best to call for directions. The music might as well be right in your lap and the crowd relishes the club's low profile. Fri till 2am, Sat till 3am.

HotHouse 31 E Balbo Drive, at S Wabash Ave ☎312/362-9707; Red Line to Harrison. Not your typical live music venue but a not-for-profit performing arts center in the South Loop that usually has a great lineup of world music and some jazz, blues and folk. Two-drink minimum; Fri till 2am, Sat till 3am.

Kitty O'Shea's 720 S Michigan Ave ☎312/294-6860; Brown Line to Harrison. Inside the *Hilton Chicago and Towers* in the South Loop, this great Irish pub offers Irish music most nights, starting at 9.30pm. The crowd is a mix of hotel guests and conventioneers, as well as a few discerning locals. Daily 11am–2am.

Martyr's 3855 N Lincoln Ave ☎773/404-9494; Brown Line to Irving Park. Restaurant and bar offering an eclectic roster of live entertainment by touring artists, with traditional Irish music on Monday and open-mic rockabilly on the first Thursday of each month.

Old Town School of Folk Music 4544 N Lincoln Ave ☎773/728-6000; Brown Line to Western. The fabulous new school and concert space in Lincoln Square for one of the city's enduring folk music traditions. It hosts a curious blend of concerts, usually some folk music, and attracts a literate, music-loving crowd. You might catch a blues band or something like a Woody Guthrie tribute – concerts start around 7pm, and tickets range from $5 to $25. Its curriculum of music classes (everything from fiddle to African drumming) is the best in the city.

Wild Hare and Singing Armadillo Frog Sanctuary 3530 N Clark St ☎773/327-4273; Red Line to Addison. Chicago's premier venue for reggae, located in Wrigleyville. There's no cover before 9pm, and the whole place feels like a Jamaican dancehall and gets packed and sweaty. Smoking not welcome.

Dance clubs

Chicago's **club life** is ever-changing, with new venues popping up all the time, especially in the old warehouses west of the Loop. In fact, the city owes its thriving club scene to its midwifing of house music during the early 1980s. Many of those warehouses have since evolved into extravagant dance clubs, with velvet couches, VIP rooms, mega-dancefloors, and expensive lighting and sound systems. These days, the "hot" club of the moment seems almost arbitrary – rather confusing given that they all offer, more or less, the same thing. In general, the larger and more ostentatious the club, the younger the crowd; the smaller, less known clubs tend to attract a late 20s and early 30s crowd with their more intimate settings.

Cover charges range from $5 to $25, and dress is typically upscale. Never wear jeans or sandals as you're likely to be turned away at the door. Also, be prepared for long waits to get in ($10–20 will usually persuade a bouncer to let you in immediately, though).

The clubs listed below have proven their staying power and are also among the best; if in doubt, or looking for the new hot thing, consult any number of the listings sections mentioned at the beginning of the chapter.

Betty's Blue Star Lounge 1600 W Grand Ave, at N Ashland Ave; ☎312/243-1699. Low-key West Side bar/club that transforms into a raging after-hours hotspot. Up-and-coming deejays spin nearly every night of the week and cheap drinks pull in both clubbers and some serious drinkers. Sun–Fri 7am–4am, Sat 11am–5am. You must be 23 or over to enter. Take a cab there and back.

Biology Bar 1520 N Fremont St ☎312/397-0580; Red Line to North/Clybourn. A club that tries to look like a science lab and mixes up the music with the occasional Latin beat, but overall an oddball place with a stiff cover ($15), pricey drinks and less room to dance than other nearby clubs west of Old Town, namely *Circus* (see below).

Circus 901 W Weed St ☎312/266-1200; Red Line to North/Clybourn. Celebrity hangout west of Old Town, featuring 20,000 square feet of cartoonish, technicolor decor and a trapeze act, stilt walkers and other flamboyant sideshows. It's a huge name in Chicago's club scene, but you might find it snooty and overpriced if you're not there strictly to dance and flirt.

Crobar 1543 N Kingsbury St ☎312/413-7000; Red Line to North/Clybourn. Hyper-trendy warehouse club, near the river west of Old Town, spinning the newest techno and house. More exclusive than the other big-name clubs – without ostentatious dress you may be turned away at the door. Sunday is gay night. Thurs, Fri & Sun 10pm–4am, Sat till 5am.

Excalibur 632 N Dearborn St ☎312/266-1944; Red Line to Grand. An institution in the city, and a bit touristy for it – not to mention for its Near North location – blasting rock, techno and R&B on several floors; Thursdays are dedicated to Latin music.

Funky Buddha Lounge 728 W Grand Ave ☎312/666-1695; Blue Line to Grand. Small and fashionably plush dance lounge on the West Side, open every night. A favorite of clubgoers for having a thoroughly mixed crowd and the city's top deejays.

Iggy's 700 N Milwaukee Ave ☎312/829-4449; Blue Line to Chicago. Not a club, per se, but a West Side restaurant that becomes fashionably loud and underground-like come 2am. The red-velvet interior gives it a bordello look, and there's a nice patio as well. Mon–Fri 7pm–4am, Sat till 5am.

Le Passage 1 Oak Place ☎312/255-0022; Red Line to Chicago. Hidden in an alley off Rush Street is the entrance to this chic French-Moroccan restaurant/lounge, a touch of South Beach and New York in Chicago's Gold Coast. It's popular with the after-work crowd, and, oddly, people do come here to eat, but the house music and dance scene is the reason to come here. The location's convenient if you're staying downtown, the crowd is upscale (as is the dress) and covers can be hefty ($20).

Red Dog 1958 W North Ave ☎773/278-1009; Blue Line to Damen. Small Bucktown club, or "funk parlor" as it likes to call itself, playing house, soul and, of course, funk. Mondays are great for house music and ladies get in free on Wednesdays (before midnight); the entrance is in the alley.

Rednofive 440 N Halsted St, near Grand Ave; ☏312/733-6699; Blue Line to Grand. Dark, underground space on the West Side that's quickly joined Chicago's A-list clubs with its cutting-edge deejay styles.

Smart Bar underneath *Metro*, 3730 N Clark St ☏773/549-0203; Red Line to Addison. Great techno and house on the weekend in post-industrial Wrigleyville surrounds. Weekdays see a mix of punk, Goth and Eighties nights. Open late – till 5am on Fri and Sat,

and especially crowded when shows at the *Metro* (see p.181) let out. Cover after 11pm (around $5).

Voyeur 151 W Ohio St ☏312/832-1717; Red Line to Grand. For clubgoers who take their people-watching seriously, this popular River North place offers two-way mirrors, fish-eye lenses, and closed-circuit TV cameras trained on the stainless-steel dance floor. Get beyond the gimmickry and you'll find that *Voyeur*'s hip-hop and house is among the best in town. No jeans. Open till 5am on Sat.

Performing arts and film

S econd only to New York in the States, **Chicago theater** is downright phenomenal, a unique blend of traditional "Broadway" plays and off-beat works by one of the soulful theater companies, the Steppenwolf or the Goodman.

With regard to **classical music**, the Chicago Symphony Orchestra is one of the best in the country, performing hundreds of shows a year, while a few smaller groups routinely put on free concerts around the city. Two **dance companies**, the classically inclined Joffrey Ballet, and the more avant-garde Hubbard Street Dance Chicago, are regarded as US emissaries to the world dance community, yet manage to remain quite visible throughout the city. Second City, with all its lore, has brought the spotlight to Chicago's **improv-isational comedy scene**, and should not be missed on even a short stay in town. And if none of this appeals, there is a strong film presence in Chicago, with ample opportunity to catch even the most obscure indie film or docu-mentary.

For **current information** about what's on, there is no better source than the free weekly paper, the *Chicago Reader*, available at cafés, bars and newsstands throughout the city. The *Chicago Tribune* and the *Chicago Sun-Times* also do a good job with current listings.

Theater

Typical of Chicago, its inhabitants have developed theater in their own style, daring and in-your-face, with two major theater companies leading the charge, the basement-born **Steppenwolf Theatre**, and the slightly more refined **Goodman Theatre**. In recent decades, Chicago actors and writers, following in the footsteps of John Malkovich, David Mamet and Gary Sinise, saw the local stage as a breeding ground and gateway to bigger and better, which is to say Broadway, but on the heels of much success and many a Tony award, the trend is changing, and Chicago has become a stage where actors strive to remain. Garage-theaters and local one-room theaters have grown in number and, as such, they've become a wonderful complement to the city's revived Theater District, in the Loop along Randolph Street. In the Theater District, gloriously restored old movie palaces like **The Oriental Theatre** and **The**

Chicago host touring productions of Broadway shows as well as pre-Broadway launches of productions. Outside the Loop, a number of mid-sized venues like **Victory Gardens** and **The Royal George** put on a mix of dramas, musicals and comedies, most of them locally produced, and smaller companies like **Black Ensemble Theatre** and **Red Orchid** ply their trade. The lists below represent only select venues and companies as the full list is far too long to include; consider them as a jumping-off point.

Information and tickets

For current **information** on plays and **tickets**, check with the League of Chicago Theaters (228 S Wabash Ave, Suite #300 ☎312/554-9800, ✆www.chicagoplays.com), a local alliance of most Chicago theaters formed to promote the scene, with all the current information on what's running where, and links to **Hot Tix**, the service for last-minute, half-priced tickets to shows. The Hot Tix booths (78 W Randolph St; the Chicago Water Works Visitor Center, 163 E Pearson St; and the Tower Records stores at 2301 N Clark St and 214 S Wabash Ave) and site (✆www.hottix.org) are an invaluable source for tickets. The *Chicago Reader* (✆www.chireader.com) is always a great source for listings and showtimes, as are the *Chicago Sun-Times* (✆www.suntimes .com) and the *Chicago Tribune* (✆www.chicagotribune.com), any of which you can buy (or simply get) at newsstands, cafés and bookstores. Alternatively, Broadway in Chicago (✆www.broadwayinchicago.com) is the website for three big-name, downtown theaters – the Cadillac Palace, Oriental Theatre, and the Shubert Theatre. Two radio stations, WBEZ 91.5 FM (✆www.wbez .org), and WFMT 98.7 FM (✆www.networkchicago. com/wfmt), are other sources of events happening around the city.

Theatre District auditoriums

Cadillac Palace Theatre 151 W Randolph St, at N LaSalle St ☎312/977-1700; **Brown, Blue, Green, Orange or Purple Line to Clark.** The facade has a boring high-rise look about it, but step inside and you'll see a space dripping with crystal chandeliers, huge mirrors, and gold add-ons, a bit like a French palace. This huge (2300 seats) theater was built in 1926, succeeded and suffered over the years, but thanks to a $20-million scrubbing it's now back on the national circuit for big-time plays and musicals.

Chicago Theatre 175 N State St, at E Lake St ☎312/902-1500; **Brown, Green, Orange, Purple or Red Line to State/Lake.** The Chicago was created with grand intentions, faced economic pressures and nearly succumbed to the wrecking ball. But in 1986, a city restoration team pumped $25 million into it, and the theater reopened, to welcome touring Broadway shows and large concerts.

Oriental Theatre, Ford Center for the Performing Arts 24 W Randolph St, at N Dearborn St ☎312/902-1400; **Brown, Green, Orange, Purple or Red Line to State/Lake.** Opened in 1927, the ornate and bizarre interior, with an impressive domed ceiling, swank chandeliers and an abundance of sculpted sea horses, goddesses and elephants, was built to resemble as Asian temple. It reopened in 1996 after a massive restoration project and puts on big-name shows.

Shubert Theatre 22 W Monroe St, at S State St ☎312/977-1700; **Blue or Red Line to Monroe.** Yet another impressively reclaimed theater house, the Shubert, one of Chicago's classier, elder Loop venues, puts on big-name, big-budget performances – unlike its days in the early twentieth century, when it was more or less a stage for vaudeville acts.

Mainstream companies

Chicago Shakespeare Theater 800 E Grand Ave, at Navy Pier ☎312/595-5600, ✆www .chicagoshakes.com. Spanking new Navy Pier stage that's the city's only all-Shakespeare company, in an intimate, courtyard-style theater (the actors perform on a catwalk-like stage that juts out into the audience). Constantly sold out, this company puts on consistently professional, if occasionally staid, productions of the Bard's plays.

Goodman Theatre 170 N Dearborn St, at E Randolph St ☏ 312/443-3800, ⓦ www.goodman-theatre.org; Brown, Green, Orange, Purple or Red Line to State/Lake. Even though they're the city's oldest and (arguably) most respected company, the Goodman puts on hip interpretations of classics, from Shakespeare to O'Neill, in this state-of-the-art theater complex which opened in 2000. The Goodman has two theaters: the 856-seat Albert Ivar Goodman Theatre, and the Owen Bruner Goodman Theatre, a moveable courtyard theater, with roughly 400 seats. Ask about "Tix-At-Six" for half-priced tickets on the day of performance. For further ticket information, call or stop by the box office.

Lookingglass Theater Company ☏ 773/477-9988, ⓦ www.lookingglasstheatre.org. Currently awaiting a permanent home in one of the Chicago Water Tower buildings, this relatively young itinerant company produces highly original work, mostly narrative-driven combinations of dance and music in what amounts to three main shows a year.

Organic Theater 1125 W Loyola Ave, at W George St ☏ 773/561-7702, ⓦ www .organictheater.com; Red Line to Loyola. A grungy counterpart to Steppenwolf, Organic is no less a Chicago theatrical landmark. Operating since the 1960s in several different locations, this group's alumni include Joe Mantegna, Dennis Franz and Dennis Farina. They've produced many Midwestern premieres, including Terrence McNally's "Love! Valor! Compassion!" and were the first company to stage a David Mamet play ("Sexual Perversity in Chicago").

Steppenwolf Theatre Company 1650 N Halsted St, at W Willow St ☏ 312/335-1650, ⓦ www.steppenwolf.org; Red Line to North/Clybourn. The cornerstone of the Chicago theater scene. See box below.

Off-Loop theaters

Apollo Theater 2540 N Lincoln Ave, at W Wrightwood Ave ☏ 773/935-6100, ⓦ www .apollochicago.com; Brown, Purple or Red Line to Fullerton. Smart, though relatively characterless space in Lincoln Park that hosts

children's productions on the weekends and has been home to Eve Ensler's wildly popular "Vagina Monologues" for a couple years now.

Athenaeum Theatre 2936 N Southport Ave, at W Oakdale Ave ☏ 773/935-6860; Brown Line to Wellington. This old performance complex (built in 1911) is one of the more widely used theater and performance spaces on the north side – there's always something happening on either the main stage or the smaller studios.

Bailiwick Arts Center 1229 W Belmont Ave, at N Racine Ave ☏ 773/883-1090, ⓦ www.bailiwick .org; Brown, Purple or Red Line to Belmont. Chicago's leading gay and lesbian theater center, which often offers concurrent performances.

Black Ensemble Theatre 4520 N Beacon St, at W Sunnyside Ave ☏ 773/769-4451; Brown Line to Montrose. A wonderful success story, this small and perennially popular company is basically a front for local impresario Jackie Taylor's musical homages to legends like Ella Fitzgerald and Jackie Wilson (the latter has been playing here and touring nationally for years).

Briar Street Theatre 3133 N Halsted St, at W Fletcher St ☏ 773/348-4000, ⓦ www.blueman.com; Brown, Purple or Red Line to Belmont. This no-frills Boystown theater is the current home of the long-running Blue Man Group show, a bizarre, multi-sensory production starring three famously bald, blue-headed men. Pop Dadaism for the masses.

Chicago Dramatists 1105 W Chicago Ave, at N Milwaukee Ave ☏ 312/633-0630, ⓦ www.chicagodramatists.org; bus #66. A small, bare-bones space that's home to some truly cutting-edge drama by up-and-coming local playwrights. Always good quality (and affordable).

Court Theatre 5535 S Ellis Ave, at E 55th St ☏ 773/753-4472, ⓦ www.courttheater.org. On the South Side's University of Chicago campus, the Court produces historically classic comedies and dramas, each deftly written. It will often host two shows simultaneously, and tickets range from $24 to $34, though half-price tickets are available two hours before the show.

ETA Creative Arts Foundation 7558 S Chicago Ave, at E 75th St ☏ 773/752-3955. The leading African American arts organization on the South Side that's been putting on

Steppenwolf Theatre

Steppenwolf is Chicago's most innovative and envelope-pushing company, a brand still seen today in the work of longtime members like **John Malkovich** and **Gary Sinise**. Three actors (including Sinise and "Oz" star Terry Kinney) founded the company in a church basement in the far north suburb of Highland Park in 1974. In the decades since, it has grown to three stages in a sleek, modern edifice in Old Town, and a 34-actor company which now includes familiar names like Joan Allen, Kevin Anderson, John Mahoney, Laurie Metcalf and Martha Plimpton. Their punishingly physical 1982 production of Sam Shepard's *True West*, directed by Sinise and starring Malkovich and Metcalf, was an unparalleled success, running for four months before transferring to New York (the first of many Steppenwolf productions to do so) and is regarded by many in the theater world. Subsequent high points include 1986's live stage extravaganza of Tom Waits' concept album, *Frank's Wild Years*, at the Briar Street Theatre, and the Tony Award-winning adaptation of *The Grapes of Wrath* in 1990. More recently, Sinise starred in their acclaimed 2001 adaptation of *One Flew Over the Cuckoo's Nest*, directed by Kinney, which transferred to London and then Broadway.

successful, often family-oriented, plays for some thirty years now.

Mercury Theatre 3745 N Southport Ave, at W Grace St ☎773/325-1700; Brown Line to Southport. Smallish live-theater venue (300 seats) two doors north of the Music Box Theater, along the Southport Corridor. Open only since 1996, it's quickly become one of the city's small-stage favorites, often hosting plays of the family-friendly variety for months at a time.

New Regal Theatre 1645 E 79th St, at S Cornell Ave ☎773/721-9301. A posh, opulent and restored old South Side vaudeville hall where the likes of Billie Holiday and Ella Fitzgerald once performed. Now a popular stop on the African American circuit of music revues and gospel plays.

Royal George Theatre 1641 N Halsted St, at W Willow St ☎312/988-9000; Red Line to North/Clybourn. Right across Halsted from Steppenwolf (see above), this is a modest, two-stage theater that hosts both long-running comedy shows and touring dramas.

Theater on the Lake 2400 N Lake Shore Drive, at W Fullerton Parkway ☎312/742-7994. Waterside venue where local theater groups like Steppenwolf and Second City put on sampler shows for a couple weeks at a time during the summer.

TimeLine Theatre 615 W Wellington Ave, at N Broadway St ☎312/409-8463, ⓦwww .timelinetheatre.com; bus #22. Spunky little group in a surprisingly nice theater tucked away on a quiet residential street in Lincoln Park.

Victory Gardens Theater 2257 N Lincoln Ave, at W Webster Ave ☎773/871-3000, ⓦwww .victorygardens.org; Brown, Purple or Red Line to Fullerton. This Tony-winning Lincoln Park company has produced a considerable number of premieres (more than any other in Chicago), and is known for helping nurture new and less experienced talent, especially of the local variety. Highly recommended.

Fringe theater and itinerant companies

Defiant Theatre ⓦwww.defianttheatre.org. Drama with a seriously punk rock attitude from a band of malcontents who've been around since the early 1990s, producing everything from Harold Pinter and John Guare to underground cult hits.

Famous Door Theatre ☎773/404-8283, ⓦwww.famousdoortheatre.org. A small, passionate group of actors that tends to put on lesser-known plays.

Redmoon Theater ☎773/388-9031, ⓦwww.redmoon.org. A Logan Square-based company that specializes in "theatrical spectacles" that fall somewhere between outré performance art, puppet shows and surrealist theater.

Wing & Groove 1935 1/2 W North Ave, at N Damen Ave ☎773/782-9416, ⓦwww .wingandgroove.com; Blue Line to Damen. A scrappy band inhabits this Wicker Park shoebox. Local comedy troupes often use this space, along with the company's own strange but worthwhile productions.

Comedy

Comedy on stage in Chicago is almost entirely made up. That is, there's an improvisational comedy troupe – based on a model invented by the legendary **Second City** theater back in the late 1950s – on seemingly every block and in every little theater space (most of them are itinerant) ready to take audience suggestions and spin them into a (possibly) funny routine; check the *Reader* for weekly listings. One of the few exceptions is the venerable **Zanies**, a straight-up standup-comic joint in Old Town.

ComedySportz Theatre 2851 N Halsted St, at W Wolfram St ☎773/549-8080, ⓦwww .comedysportz.com; Brown or Purple Line to Diversey. A wholly Chicago creation, this blend of sports and comedy – two comics battle against each other in song and scenes – is a fun, audience-driven experience, that you'll find outright weird or just plain funny. "Competitions" happen Thurs–Sat, beginning at 8pm; $17.

ImprovOlympic 3541 N Clark St, at W Addison St ☎773/880-0199, ⓦwww.improvolympic.com; Red Line to Addison. A couple of former Second City folks founded this Wrigleyville improv landmark back in the early 1980s. Their particular style of improv – called "The Harold" – takes one audience suggestion and spins it into a piece of instant comic theater lasting a half-hour or more. Alumni include Mike Myers, Andy Dick and Tina Fey. Rumor has it that their late founder Del Close (who died in 1999) willed his skull to the Goodman Theatre (see above), where it is kept, awaiting use in a future production of "Hamlet."

Neo-Futurarium 5153 N Ashland Ave, at W Foster Ave ☎773/878-4557, ⓦwww .neofuturists.org; bus #22. Up on the far north side resides this strange little place, wherein is performed the long-running "Too Much Light Makes the Baby Go Blind," a blitzkrieg of 30 mini-plays in 60 minutes. The (cheap) admission is determined at the door by a pair of dice.

The Noble Fool 16 W Randolph, at N State St ☎312/726-1156; Blue or Red Line to Washington. This troupe opened their new theater – with two performance spaces – next to the Oriental Theatre (see above) in spring 2002. They perform long-running and semi-improvised shows for a mostly tourist crowd.

The Playground 3341 N Lincoln Ave, at W Henderson Ave ☎773/250-3004, ⓦwww .the-playground.com; Brown Line to Addison. Solo, skit, team and improv comedy shows run every Thursday through Sunday night.

Second City 1616 N Wells St, at W North Ave ☎312/337-3992, ⓦwww.secondcity.com; bus #22. For over four decades, Second City has been a breeding ground for the nation's top comics, launching dozens of fledgling comics to stardom. The troupe performs a nightly series of sketches mixed with improvisation – never less than hilarious. There's also a smaller stage – Second City e.t.c. (1608 N Wells St) – producing similar material in the same building. Cover charge and two-drink minimum. See box on p.74 for more.

Zanies 1548 N Wells St, at W North Ave ☎312/337-4027, ⓦwww.zanies.com; bus #22. Pretty much the only place to see standup comedy in the city, Zanies packs them into their somewhat rough-at-the-edges club with two or three shows a night. Often the comics are less than stellar, but you can occasionally catch big names slumming. Cover charge and two-drink minimum.

Classical music and opera

Chicago's classical music scene is a straightforward affair – there's the internationally acclaimed **Chicago Symphony Orchestra** (CSO) and then all other groups a tier or two lower.

Chicago Symphony Orchestra

The CSO performs at Symphony Center, 220 S Michigan Ave (☎312/ 435-8122 or 435-8172; ⓦwww.cso .org), about ten times a month when they're not on tour domestically or internationally. With George Solti at the helm for many years, the one hundred-plus members of the CSO now follow the lead of Daniel Barenboim, a gifted award-winning composer who's trying to bring more contemporary music into the CSO repertoire, with frequent guest artists like Yo-Yo Ma, Wynton Marsalis, Itzhak Perlman, and others. Tickets can be pricey, between $25 and $200, the cheapest tickets for seats far away in the gallery.

Alternatively, CSO offers "RUSH" seating, general admission for any available seat just before the performance. Seats are not confirmed, so you may be asked to move to a free seat elsewhere if the original ticket holder should arrive late. Inquire about this last-resort option with the ticket agent in the lobby just before showtime.

Other classical groups

Beyond the CSO, there are a number of classical music groups in Chicago performing nearly every day of the week, at the Symphony Center when CSO is off, or smaller, **free concerts**

at the Chicago Cultural Center, 78 E Washington (☎312/346-3278 for details), Newberry Library, 60 E Walton, The 4th Presbyterian Church of Chicago (across from the John Hancock Center), Old St Pat's Church, 700 W Adams, Holy Name Cathedral, 735 N State St, The Museum of Contemporary Art, 220 E Chicago Ave, and a few other venues.

Classical music festivals

Grant Park Music Festival 78 E Washington St ☎312/742-4763, ⓦ www.grantparkmusicfestival .com. A summer-long series of outdoor classical music concerts put on by the city, held at the Petrillo Music Shell until the new Gehry-designed music amphitheater opens in 2004. The Grant Park Orchestra performs nights (Wed–Sat 6.30pm or 7.30pm), with various traveling musicians in the lineup.

Ravinia Festival Ravinia Park Rd, in Highland Park ☎847/266-5100, ⓦ www.ravinia.org. This is something different altogether: a wonderful outdoor music venue 25 miles north of the city in Highland Park. All types of music groups (from Tony Bennett to Los Lobos) pass through here in the summer

Smaller symphonies

The **Chicago Chamber Musicians** (333 S State St ☎312/692-9000, ⓦ www.chicagochambermusic.org) is a smaller cadre of devout musicians who put on some fifty concerts a year, many of which are held at DePaul University's Concert Hall, 800 W Belden Ave (☎773/325-7260), in Lincoln Park. They are best known (and loved) around town for their "First Monday" series, free lunchtime performances underneath the Cultural Center's Tiffany dome on the first Monday of every month. The **Chicago Chamber Orchestra** (☎312/922-5570) also perform at the Cultural Center though on Sunday afternoons. **Music of the Baroque**, the Midwest's largest group (60 musicians) playing 16th- to 17th-century music (☎312/551-1414, ⓦ www.baroque.org), perform in Old St Pat's Church, St Paul's Church, Holy Name Cathedral, as well as a bunch of suburban venues, weekdays throughout the year – single event tickets are available. The **Chicago Youth Symphony Orchestra** (☎312/939-2207) is what it sounds – a full (110 piece) orchestra comprising elite high-school musicians from the Chicagoland area; they perform a fall and a winter show each year, usually held at Symphony Center. **Chicago Sinfonietta** (☎312/236-3681, ⓦ www.chicagosinfonietta.org) of Evanston, under the leadership of Paul Freeman, has a multicultural feel to the music they produce, and tends to fuse classical with modern – everything from solos to orchestra-backed marimba performances. They hold a good number of their concerts at Symphony Center.

months, yet it is the definitive stage for summertime classical music – frequent shows by the CSO and immensely popular classical and world musicians. Metra trains from Ogilvie Transportation Center go directly to Ravinia's front gate.

Opera

Nearly as acclaimed at the CSO, the **Lyric Opera of Chicago** is tops for opera in Chicago, performing in the magnificent – and recently restored – Art Deco Civic Opera House, 20 N Wacker Drive (☎312/332-2244, ⓦwww.lyricopera.org). Its season is from mid-September to early February, and most performances are sold out. If you want even a chance at a (pricey, $50-150) ticket, you'll have to put yourself on the Lyric Opera mailing list and they'll send out a "Priority Individual Ticket brochure" in late July – this will have instructions about purchasing tickets and current availability.

The only real alternative is to call the **Chicago Opera Theater** (☎312/704 -8414, ⓦwww.chicagooperatheater .org), a company that puts on various lower-budget productions, often at the Athenaeum Theatre in Lakeview. Prices vary, but they're generally less than you'll pay at the Lyric for a show.

Cinema

Chicago is definitely on the shortlist of US cities with a big film culture, which means several things: there are growing lists of decent – and public – film festivals, a bunch of cool venues to see classics, indies, foreign flicks and documentaries, and a respectable number of mainstream theaters citywide, each pumping out the Hollywood hits. Venues range from mega-sized Omnimax theaters to music auditoriums that double as film houses to standard three- or four-theater first-run complexes.

For **information**, the free *Reader* (ⓦwww.chireader.com/movies/) always has up-to-date lists of showtimes, as does *New City* (ⓦwww.newcitychicago .com/chicago/film.html). Moviefone (☎312/444-3456) is a great way to find shows and showtimes at any theater in Chicago, though you'll need either the zip code or the theater's approximate area of town. Generally, the price of admission is about $9, though many of the smaller and second-run houses show films for half as much.

Film festivals

Chicago Outdoor Film Festival (mid-July to Aug) Free movie festival on Tuesday nights at Butler Field in Grant Park (Monroe St and Lake Shore Drive), where you can sit on a blanket with a picnic and watch flicks like *Vertigo* and *West Side Story*. ☎312/744-3315, ⓦwww.chicagooutdoorfilm.citysearch .com

Grant Park Film Festival (mid-July to end Aug) This is less a festival, really, than a popular (and free) series of outdoor screenings of classic movies like *Vertigo, Horse Feathers, Dr Strangelove*, etc. Put on by the City of Chicago and a few corporate sponsors, the festival happens every Tuesday night (beginning at sunset, usually around 8pm).

Black Harvest International Festival of Video and Film (Aug) A long-running and fascinating annual collection of new African and African American works which rarely (if ever) are screened anywhere else in the country. Held at the Gene Siskel Film Center (see below). ⓦwww.artic.edu/ webspaces/siskelfilmcenter

Chicago Underground Film Festival (late Aug) A little more unbuttoned than most, this fest was born out of frustration with the relative inaccessibility and mainstreaming tendencies of other fests. Two Columbia College students started it in 1993 and it's been a hit ever since, held for one week

each August at one or two theaters.
☎773/327-3456, 🌐www.cuff.org

Reeling: the Chicago International Gay and Lesbian Film Festival (late Aug to early Sept). See "Gay and lesbian Chicago," p.200.

Chicago International Film Festival (Oct) Held over a couple of weeks each October throughout the city's movie houses, this is now the oldest competitive film festival in North America (1964), and though it doesn't have the repute of say, the Sundance Film Festival, it is a highly respected event in the US motion picture world. Categories range from feature films, to first- and second-time directors, documentaries and short films, student and animated films. ☎312/425-9400, 🌐www.chicagofilmfestival.org

Chicago International Children's Film Fesrtival (Oct/Nov) The oldest and largest of its kind in the country, this showcases hundreds of feature and short films for (and often made by) children all over the world and also includes hands-on film workshops for kids. Held over two weeks in October and/or November at Facets cinémathêque (see below). ☎773/281-9075, 🌐www.cicff.org

First-run cinemas

600 North Michigan Avenue ☎312/255-9340; Red Line to Grand. Nothing special, but this nine-screener upstairs from Eddie Bauer and *Heaven on Seven* (see "Eating," p.152) shows a decent mix of mainstream and semi-arty films.

900 North Michigan Ave ☎312/787-1988; Red Line to Chicago. Two-screener underneath Bloomingdale's that's often deserted during the week (and so a great place to catch a flick while wandering about the Mag Mile).

Esquire 58 E Oak St, at N Rush St ☎312/280-0101; Red Line to Chicago. New releases and art/indie films at this tall, skinny theater slipped in between Oak Street boutiques.

Landmark Century Centre Cinema 2828 N Clark St, at W Diversey Parkway ☎773/248-7744; bus #22. The top couple floors of this vertical shopping mall, showing independent and foreign-language films – one of the city's better-run theaters.

McClurg Court 330 E Ohio St, at N McClurg Court ☎312/642-0723; Red Line to Grand. Streeterville theater with two unremarkable screens and one wonderfully massive,

practically IMAX-size one that's one of the biggest in the country.

Music Box 3733 N Southport Ave, at W Waveland Ave ☎773/871-6604, 🌐www.musicboxtheatre.com; Brown Line to Southport. The owners of this grand old neighborhood theater bill it as a "year-round film festival," and while it's not quite that, it is a good place to watch interesting flicks – cult, classic, indie, horror, whatever. Funky interior, and live organ music between films.

Pipers Alley 1608 N Wells St, at W North Ave ☎312/642-7500; bus #22. Three-theater complex in Old Town, always has a good pick of artsy movies that verge on mainstream.

Water Tower Theaters 157 E Chestnut St, at N Michigan Ave ☎312/274-1010; Red Line to Chicago. Formally a down-at-the-heels theater in the Water Tower shopping complex, this place was recently reincarnated as a new-release arthouse, pretty much the only one in the Mag Mile/River North area.

Second-run and indie flicks

Brew & View at The Vic Theatre 3145 N Sheffield Ave, at W Belmont Ave ☎773/929-6713, 🌐www.brewview.com; Brown, Purple or Red Line to Belmont. The name says it all: the place to come to watch flicks and drink beer (50¢ per cup, $2 per pitcher). Second-run movies, classics, and audiences that tend to sing and quote along. Admission is only $5; must be 18 to enter, 21 to drink.

Facets Cinémathèque 1517 W Fullerton Ave, at N Greenview Ave ☎773/281-4114, 🌐www.facets.org; Brown, Purple or Red Line to Fullerton. Daily screenings of cutting-edge films and, in their attached rental store, an enormous (and nationally renowned) cache of cult, experimental, and hard-to-find videos. Also hosts several annual film festivals.

Gene Siskel Film Center 164 N State St, at Randolph St ☎312/846-2600, 🌐www.artic.edu/webspaces/siskelfilmcenter/; Brown, Green, Orange, Purple or Red Line to State/Lake. Splashy, sleek new Loop two-screen complex (named for the beloved, late *Chicago Tribune* film critic), part of the School of the Art Institute of Chicago, with classics, revivals, indie premieres, festivals, etc.

Three Penny Theater 2424 N Lincoln Ave, at W Fullerton Ave ☎773/525-3449, 🌐www.3peny

cinema.com; Brown, Purple or Red Line to Fullerton. Aged but cheap little theater with two screens, showing second-run films, right across from the storied (and now only intermittently open) Biograph Theatre.
Univ. of Chicago DOC Films 1212 E 59th St, at S Woodlawn Ave ☎773/702-8575, ⓦwww .docfilms.uchicago.edu. On the University of Chicago campus and an appropriately brainy movie-house with daily screenings of just about any type. It's the longest continuously running student-film society in the nation, founded by students in the 1930s as an informal film society.
Village Theater 1548 N Clark St, at W North Ave ☎312/642-2403; bus #22. Always showing recently second-run films – with occasionally some stranger, cult fare and midnight flicks – at discounted prices.

Dance

Two companies, the **Joffrey Ballet** and **Hubbard Street Dance Chicago**, are Chicago's real gift to the world dance community, though there are a number of smaller dance companies that inevitably are a part of the local dance scene.

For current what's-on information, the **Chicago Dance and Music Alliance** (☎312/987-1123, ⓦwww.chicagoperformances.org) is a great source, the 2001 combination of the Chicago Music Alliance and the Chicago Dance Coalition. The Alliance website is loaded with numbers and venue information.

Companies

Ballet Chicago Studio Company ☎312/251-8838, ⓦwww.balletchicago.org. Roving like the Joffrey but not nearly as renowned a classical ballet troupe, Ballet Chicago does have a school, and has been performing – and training – since it opened doors in 1997. Geared toward the style of George Balanchine, famed 20th-century choreographer.

Chicago Moving Company ☎773/880-5402, ⓦwww.chicagomovingcompany.org. Modern dance under the guidance of Nana Shineflug, modern dance leader of great repute in Chicago. Concerts and classes since 1972.

Hubbard Street Dance Chicago 1147 W Jackson Blvd ☎312/850-9744, ⓦwww .hubbardstreetdance.com. More contemporary than Joffrey Ballet but equally talented, continually turning out some of the nation's best dance, with its characteristic blend of jazz, modern, ballet, and theatre-dance. For those interested in classes, Hubbard Street Dance Chicago has the comprehensive Lou Conte Dance Studio, with five state-of-the-art studio spaces and dozens of classes daily.

Joffrey Ballet 70 E Lake St ☎312/739-0120, ⓦwww.joffrey.com. The city's prime classically oriented dance company, one of the country's best. Transplanted from New York in 1995, the group uses Chicago as home base and performs in venues throughout the city, with tickets between $35 and $75 per seat.

Mordine and Company Dance Theatre ☎312/654-9540, ⓦwww.mordine.org. One of the nation's longer-running contemporary dance companies (1968), right behind the Joffrey Ballet and alongside the River North Dance Company. They were for many years headquartered at the Dance Center of Columbia College.

Muntu Dance Theatre ☎773/602-1135, ⓦwww.muntu.com. Dance troupe that performs all sorts of African tribal dances, with a contemporary take on everything. They usually perform only a few shows a year, sometimes at the Museum of Contemporary Art, or Hyde Park's DuSable Museum, among others.

River North Dance Company ☎312/944-2888, ⓦwww.rivernorthchicago.com. Created by four standout Chicago dancers in the late 1980s, River North (performing mostly at the Athenaeum Theatre, see p.187) comprises a mostly Midwestern cast, and devotes itself to jazz and contemporary dance.

△ Curtain call at the Steppenwolf Theatre

Venues

Athenaeum Theatre 2936 N Southport Ave, at W Oakdale Ave ☎773/935-6860 or 312/902-1500. See p.187 for details.

Auditorium Theatre 50 E Congress Parkway, at S State St ☎312/922-2110 or 902-1500, ⓦwww.auditoriumtheatre.org; Red Line to Harrison. Beautiful Sullivan-designed theater with exceptional acoustics, which often plays host to the Joffrey Ballet, as well as touring acts.

Chicago Cultural Center 78 E Washington Blvd, at N Michigan Ave ☎312/744-6630; Brown, Green, Orange or Purple Line to Randolph. Loft-like Sidney R. Yates Gallery on the fourth floor of the Cultural Center has frequent dance shows, usually free.

Dance Center of Columbia College 1306 S Michigan Ave, at E 13th St ☎312/344-8300, ⓦwww.dancecenter.org; Red Line to Roosevelt. Theater in a Columbia College building a few blocks from the main campus, with contemporary dance concerts, and classes in the other six studios, begun in 1969.

Harold Washington Library 400 S State St, at E Congress Parkway ☎312/747-4300; Red Line to Roosevelt. The Library often hosts dance performances in its lower-level auditorium.

Museum of Contemporary Art Theatre 220 E Chicago Ave, at N DeWitt Place ☎312/397-4010, ⓦwww.mcachicago.org; Red Line to Chicago. The MCA's street-level theatre often hosts dance performances.

Ruth Page Center for Arts 1016 N Dearborn St, at W Oak St ☎312/337-6543, ⓦwww.ruthpage.org; Red Line to Clark/Division. Designed to accommodate dance and theatre groups in search of a permanent residence, it hosts the performances of the various groups in residence there at any one time.

Gay and lesbian Chicago

A s the metropolis of the Midwest, Chicago has long been a magnet for small-town **gays and lesbians**, who make up a sizable minority here and are fairly visible, not just at the **Pride Festival** or **Northalsted Market Days**, two of the city's most popular summer events. Illinois' first openly lesbian mayor was recently elected in suburban Oak Park, and the Chicago city council in 2002 passed an ordinance outlawing discrimination against transgendered people.

Gay life in Chicago still revolves around the north side area known as **Boystown**, part of the Lakeview neighborhood that stretches east from Halsted Street to the lake and north from Belmont Avenue to Grace Street. Halsted in particular has been the long-standing center of gay life, and most of the action in Boystown focuses on the street's gay bars and gay-friendly restaurants around Roscoe Street.

Increasingly, however, the more affordable and less congested Swedish enclave of **Andersonville** (see p.102) to the north has been steadily luring gays and lesbians away from Lakeview for several years with a host of restaurants, bars and shops catering to the community. And even further to the north still-developing **Edgewater** and **Rogers Park** seem destined to be the next pockets in Chicago's already robust gay, lesbian, bisexual and transgender scene.

Gay travelers will have no problem finding friendly hotels in Chicago, though many prefer to stay around Lakeview, where gay-friendly accommodation abounds.

You can get a feel for Chicago's gay scene by picking up a copy of the *Chicago Free Press* (Ⓦww.chicagofreepress.com) or *Windy City Times* (Ⓦwww. outlineschicaco.com), both weeklies with extensive news and local event listings. For nightlife info, try *Gay Chicago* or *Boi Chicago*, weekly rags that detail just where the boys (and, occasionally, girls) will be partying next. All are free and can be picked up at corner boxes or in bars. Lesbians should check out Ⓦwww.dykediva.com, a fun, helpful site that lists upcoming lesbian parties, readings, concerts and seminars. A list of other gay resources and organizations in Chicago appears on p. 201.

Accommodation

While few properties in the area cater exclusively to gay men and lesbians, you'll feel right at home in just about every hotel in and around Boystown. For an explanation of the price codes, see p.131.

The Ardmore House 1248 W Ardmore Ave ☎ and ℻773/728-5414 (call before faxing), ⓦwww.ardmorehousebb.com; Red Line to Thorndale. Cozy, exclusively gay B&B in a comfortably furnished, restored Victorian on a quiet residential street close to the lake and a gay beach (Hollywood Beach). Three rooms share two full baths, plus an outdoor hot tub with secluded sundeck. Other amenities include Internet access, satellite TV and a nightly social hour, as well as continental breakfast on weekdays and full hot breakfast on weekends. Reservations required; two-night minimum stay on weekends. ❸–❹

Best Western Hawthorne Terrace 3434 N Broadway St ☎773/244-3434 or 1-888/675-2378, ℻773/244-3435, ⓦwww.hawthorneterrace.com. Red line to Belmont. Pretty even mix of gay and straight guests. For more details, see p.139. ❹–❺

Hotel Burnham 1 W Washington St ☎312/782-1111 or 1-866/690-1986, ℻312/782-0899, ⓦwww.burnhamhotel.com; Red or Blue Line to Washington; Brown, Green, Orange or Purple Line to State/Lake. This gorgeous boutique hotel in the Loop is very gay-friendly – mention the "pride rate" for a significant discount. Reserve months ahead. For more details, see p.131. ❹–❺

City Suites Hotel 933 W Belmont Ave ☎773/404-3400 or 1-800/248-9108, ℻773/404-3405, ⓦwww.cityinns.com; Brown, Purple or Red Line to Belmont. Just minutes' from Boystown, though the noise from passing trains and traffic can be a drag. Eclectic mix of gay men, artists and performers. For more details, see p.139. ❹

Days Inn Lincoln Park-North 644 W Diversey Parkway ☎773/525-7010, ℻525-6998, ⓦwww.lpdaysinn.com; Brown or Purple Line to Diversey. Great-value gay-friendly hotel with a mostly straight clientele, just a ten-minute walk from Boystown. For more details see p.138. ❸

Flemish House of Chicago 68 E Cedar St ☎312/664-9981, ℻664-0387, ⓦwww.chicagobandb.com; Red Line to Clark/Division. Gay-owned and friendly, but mostly straight clientele at these B&B apartments in a beautifully renovated 1892 Gold Coast row house. Six guest rooms done in attractive English Arts & Crafts style, each with full kitchen, bath, TV and phone. Rates include self-serve continental breakfast. No smoking, no children; two-night minimum stay. ❹–❺

The Gold Coast Guest House 113 W Elm St ☎312/337-0361, ℻337-0362, ⓦwww.bbchicago.com; Red Line to Clark/Division. Gay-friendly B&B with easy access to Mag Mile shopping and dining. For more details, see p.136. ❹

Majestic 528 W Brompton Ave ☎773/404-3499 or 1-800/727-5108, ℻773/404-3495, ⓦwww.cityinns.com; Red Line to Addison. Quiet, elegant inn near the lake on a residential Boystown street. For more details, see p.139. ❹

Old Town Chicago B&B Inn 1442 N North Park Ave, ☎312/440-9268, ℻440-2378, ⓦwww.oldtownchicago.com; Brown or Purple Line to Sedgwick. For more details, see p.136. ❺

Villa Toscana 3447 N Halsted St ☎773/404-2643 or 1-800/404-2643, ℻773/404-2416, ⓦwww.thevillatoscana.com; Red Line to Belmont. Six clean, smallish rooms in a gay-owned Victorian B&B, with a mostly gay male clientele. The house, in the heart of Boystown, set back from the street with a private sundeck, has three rooms with private bath; others are shared. No smoking, no pets. Basic amenities include phone, cable TV ands self-serve continental breakfast. Reserve at least a month ahead. ❸–❹

Cafés and restaurants

While many Chicago **restaurants** attract a sizable gay following (*Dinotto Ristorante* in Old Town, Randolph Street's *Blackbird* and *Marche*, for instance), the places listed below have become fixtures on the city's gay and lesbian scene. For an explanation of prices ranges, see box on p.142.

Angelina 3561 N Broadway St ☎773/935-5933; **Red Line to Addison.** Romantic, low-lit atmosphere and reasonable prices make this cozy Italian date spot a neighborhood favorite. Good, basic menu includes items like fettucine with artichokes and parmesan cream sauce, and angel-hair pasta with sun-dried tomatoes and asparagus. Moderate.

Ann Sather 929 W Belmont Ave ☎773/348-2378; **Red Line to Belmont.** Local Swedish chain. See p.161.

Buddies' Restaurant & Bar 3301 N Clark St ☎773/477-4066; **Red Line to Belmont.** Laid-back, country & western–themed gay bar/dining room serving up country-fried steak, grilled pork chops and other stick-to-your-ribs fare. Popular Sunday brunch, too. Moderate.

Caribou Coffee Company 3300 N Broadway St ☎773/477-3695; **Red Line to Belmont.** Not your typical chain coffee shop. Affectionately nicknamed "Cariboy," this comfortable, cruisy Boystown café is packed most nights and weekend afternoons with gay men reading, lounging in easy chairs and watching the scenery go by. Inexpensive.

Firefly 3335 N Halsted St ☎773/525-2505; **Red Line to Belmont.** This recent arrival, just down the block from the boy bars, is a loungey, late-night space offering creative bistro fare at reasonable prices. Don't miss the creamy parmesan deviled eggs or the flaky, tender grilled salmon with crunchy veggies. Open till 1.30am (Sun till 12.30am); closed Mondays. Moderate to expensive.

Joy's Noodles 3257 N Broadway St ☎773/327-8330; **Red Line to Belmont.** Good, super-cheap pan-Asian plates bring the boys out in full force at this very casual neighborhood BYOB joint. Good *lard na* (fried rice noodles with chicken and broccoli), baby egg rolls and more. Inexpensive.

Kit Kat Lounge and Supper Club 3700 N Halsted St ☎773/525-1111; **Red Line to Addison.** Clubby, cool South Beach-inspired decor, killer apple martinis and a playful atmosphere make this stylish, mixed Boystown spot worth a visit. The upscale comfort food menu includes a juicy beef tenderloin and mouthwatering eggplant bread pudding. Female impersonators perform nightly, strutting through the narrow room. Half-price martinis on Sundays and Tuesdays. Closed Mondays. Expensive.

The Room 5900 N Broadway St ☎773/989-7666; **Red Line to Thorndale.** Filmy curtains contrast with exposed brick walls at this romantic Edgewater BYOB. The lesbian-owned restaurant has a heavily gay clientele, and the menu's upscale comfort food includes tomato bisque with smoked gouda sandwiches and ostrich *au poivre* with fingerling potatoes. Don't leave without dessert, namely the delicious chocolate-chip cookie dough egg roll. Moderate to expensive.

She She 4539 N Lincoln Ave (a couple of miles northwest of Lincoln Park) ☎773/293-3690; **Brown Line to Western.** This cozy lesbian-owned Lincoln Square nook serves fun, flavorful dishes like wonton purses (mushroom potstickers) and she-she rolls (maki with salmon and wasabi) alongside potent martinis with cheeky names like the "RuPaul." Closed Mondays. Expensive.

Tomboy 5402 N Clark St ☎773/907-0636; **Red Line to Berwyn.** Lesbian-owned BYOB standby in Andersonville, with a hip gay and lesbian crowd and chic exposed-brick decor. Menu favorites include coconut-crusted "porcupine" shrimp and delicious peppercorn- and sesame-encrusted tuna with wasabi mashers. (Note: The new owners applied for a liquor license in late 2002; call ahead before you BYO). Moderate to expensive.

Voltaire 3441-3443 N Halsted St ☎773/281-9320; **Red Line Belmont.** This restaurant/cabaret on the Halsted strip has weekend song-and-dance shows by the Voltaire troupe and Monday-night sets by adored local diva Amy Armstrong. The eclectic, pricey dining room menu is hit-or-miss; more reliable is the bar food, like the tender ribeye steak sandwich and tasty chicken strips with sun-dried cherry aioli. Moderate to expensive.

Yoshi's Café 3257 N Halsted St ☎773/248-6160; Red Line to Belmont. If you can get past the generic, upscale diner decor, you're in for a treat. Chef Yoshi Katsumura brings a Japanese touch to French cuisine, resulting in delicious concoctions like chicken and mushroom spring roll with cucumber salad or grilled sea scallops with green tea pasta in pesto sauce. Closed Mondays. Expensive.

Bars and clubs

Most gay and lesbian **bars** in Chicago do not charge a cover; those that do are noted below.

Near North

Baton Show Lounge 436 N Clark St ☎312/644-5269; Red Line to Grand. You won't believe your eyes when you see the female impersonators at this famed River North club, which draws even more straight men and bachelorette parties than gay men. Showtimes Wed–Sun 8.30pm, 10.30pm and 12.30am. $10–12 cover with two-drink minimum.

Gentry of Chicago 440 N State St ☎312/836-0933; Red Line to Grand. This intimate cabaret, popular with showtune lovers and piano barflies, features live entertainment every day of the week and draws a mostly male crowd of suits from the neighborhood. Sunday nights are open mic.

Bucktown/Wicker Park

Red Dog 1958 W North Ave ☎773/278-1009; Blue Line to Damen. A young crowd hits this dance club on Monday nights to groove at "Boom Boom Room," a gay night of lively, cutting-edge house music. Cover $5.

Lincoln Park

Crobar Nightclub 1543 N Kingsbury St ☎312/337-5001; Red Line to North/Clybourn. Put on your tightest, most glittery clubwear for Sunday G.L.E.E. Club (Gay, Lesbian and Everything Else), a hugely popular night of progressive dance music for muscle boys and glam girls in the enormous Crobar dance complex. Cover $10.

Andersonville

@mosphere 5355 N Clark St ☎773/784-1100; Red Line to Berwyn. This far north side neighborhood bar, with exposed brick walls and metal decor, draws a crowd of mostly men and some lesbians. There's a small dance floor if the DJ music moves you, and tall windows that make for good Clark Street people-watching.

Big Chicks 5024 N Sheridan Rd ☎773/728-5511; Red Line to Argyle. Laid-back far north favorite with a dance floor, pool table, which despite its name fills with an eclectic, mostly male crowd. Free Sunday afternoon cookouts pack the place, and there's free parking in the alley behind the bar.

Star Gaze 5419 N Clark St ☎773/561-7363; Red Line to Berwyn. Chicago's main lesbian hangout, this dance club and restaurant draws an all-ages crowd, including some men. There's an inviting outdoor beer garden, plus pool tables, darts and a limited menu of bar food, salads and pastas. Fridays feature salsa music, with $2 drinks on Thursdays and karaoke on Sundays. Closed Mondays.

T's 5025 N Clark St ☎773/784-6000; Red Line to Lawrence. This casual local spot hosts an easy mix of gay and straight, offering good bar food up front and couches and a pool table in the back, where there's the occasional open-mic show or performance. Wednesday nights are popular with the lesbian crowd.

Lakeview

Berlin 954 W Belmont Ave ☎773/348-4975; Red Line to Belmont. Legendary dance spot where a pumped, mixed crowd grooves to some of Chicago's hottest DJs. The boys come out for Testosterone Tuesdays, while ladies gather for Women Obsession Wednesdays every week except the last of the month. Small cover on weekends.

Charlie's 3726 N Broadway St ☎773/871-8887; Red Line to Addison. Midwestern cowboys strut their stuff on the dance floor at this popular late-night country bar. Free line dance lessons Mondays and Wednesdays at 7.30pm and Saturdays at 9pm. After 2am on Friday and Saturday nights, the DJ spins house music until the wee hours. Small cover on weekends. Open Mon & Tues till 2am, Wed–Fri till 4am, Sat till 5am.

Circuit Nightclub 3641 N Halsted St ☎773/325-2233; Red Line to Addison. This cavernous nightclub is the place to be for circuit boys and club kids on Saturday nights, when the glowsticks come out and the techno starts pumping. Theme nights include Disco Bingo and karaoke in the adjacent Rehab Lounge, plus a spicy Thursday Latin night. Saturday night cover $15; small cover Thurs & Fri. Open Sun–Wed till 2am, Thurs & Fri till 4am, Sat till 5am.

The Closet 3325 N Broadway St ☎773/477-8533; Red Line to Belmont. Aptly named late-night lesbian hangout with a small bar and an even smaller dance floor. It's also very popular with the boys, who flood the place on weekends when the 2am Halsted bars let out. Open Sun–Fri 2pm–4am, Sat noon–5am.

Manhole 3458 N Halsted St ☎773/975-9244; Red Line to Belmont. Dark, cruisey after-hours bar and pumping dance club for the testos-terone set. You'll have to take your shirt off to get into the back bar and dance area. Small cover – more ($10–15) for special events.

Roscoe's 3356 N Halsted St ☎773/281-3355; Red Line to Belmont. Boystown's best hangout for younger guys, this comfortable video bar and club has five rooms plus a large dance floor, pool table and fireplace, plus an outdoor patio with food service in summer. Theme nights include karaoke Mondays, and game show Wednesdays. Small cover on Saturdays.

Sidetrack 3349 N Halsted St ☎773/477-9189; Red Line to Belmont. This sleek, friendly video bar draws a thirtysomething male crowd and sprawls over four connected rooms, including the recently added airy "glass bar," with lofty ceilings and a wall of windows looking out onto Halsted. Great frozen drinks, including a potent, purple Ketel One Crush. Theme nights are huge, particularly Sunday showtunes and Thursday comedy clips.

Spin 800 W Belmont Ave ☎773/327-7711; Red Line to Belmont. A tattooed and pierced mixed crowd call this bar and dance club home. Dollar drinks draw a big crowd on Wednesdays ($5 cover), as does the Friday shower contest. Small cover on Saturdays.

Festivals and events

Fireball (early Feb) Three days of nonstop dancing at clubs around the city. Proceeds benefit the Hearts Foundation, which supports local HIV/AIDS service organizations. ☎773/244-6000, ⓦ www.thefireball.com

International Mr Leather (weekend before Memorial Day) Leather-loving men (and even some women) come from all over the world to mingle, buy leather goods and check out the hottest leather man of all. ⓦ www.imri.com

Chicago Pride Festival (late June) Month-long series of events celebrating Chicago's gay community, with theater, panel discussions, athletic events and religious services culminating in the Pride Parade along Halsted St and Broadway on the last Sunday in June. ⓦ www.chicagopridecalendar.org

Northalsted Market Days (early Aug) One of the largest street fairs in the Midwest and the best people-watching of the year. This two-day event, staged in Boystown, draws more than 250,000 people with live music, hundreds of vendors and food from dozens of local restaurants. ⓦ www.northalsted .com/html/daze.html

Windy City Rodeo (third weekend in Aug) Cowboys and cowgirls from across the US compete in roping, bull riding, racing and more at this fundraising event. ⓦ www.ilgra.com

Reeling: the Chicago International Gay and Lesbian Film Festival (late Aug to early Sept) Over two decades old, running for two weeks at venues around the city. Good mix of entertaining and groundbreaking work. ⓦ www.chicagofilmmakers.org

Gay organizations and resources

About Face Theatre ☎773/784-8565,
🖳www.aboutfacetheatre.com. Theater company that explores issues of gender and sexuality both on stage and in performances and workshops at area schools.

Chicago Area Gay & Lesbian Chamber of Commerce 1210 W Rosedale ☎773/303-0167, 🖳www.glchamber.org; Red Line to Thorndale. Helpful community organization offering info packets for visitors and listings of shopping resources, jobs and more.

Gerber/Hart Library 1127 W Granville Ave ☎773/381-8030, 🖳www.gerberhart.org; Red Line to Granville. Circulating library with books, periodicals, videos and artifacts relating to gay, lesbian, bisexual and transgender individuals.

Illinois Gender Advocates 47 W Division St Suite 391 ☎312/409-5489, 🖳www.itstimeil.org; Red Line to Clark/Division. A political advocacy group for the transgender community, organizing demonstrations and vigils, publishing newsletters and more.

Lesbian & Gay HELPLine ☎773/929-4357. Provides crisis counseling and information on a variety of gay-related issues. Sun–Wed & Fri 6–10pm.

Test Positive Aware Network 5537 N Broadway St ☎773/989-9400, 🖳www.tpan.org; Red Line to Bryn Mawr. Resource for HIV patients, providing support groups, a medical clinic, yoga classes, social hour and more.

Unabridged Books 3251 N Broadway St ☎773/883-9119; Red Line to Belmont. Friendly, independent Boystown bookstore with extensive gay and lesbian sections, from literature to erotica, as well as a treasure trove of sale shelves.

Women & Children First 5233 N Clark St ☎773/769-9299, 🖳www.womenandchildrenfirst.com; Red Line to Berwyn. One of the nation's largest feminist bookstores, this Andersonville favorite stocks over 30,000 women's interest books, children's books and gay and lesbian titles. Frequent readings and discussion groups, too.

16

GAY AND LESBIAN CHICAGO | Gay organizations and resources

17

Sports and outdoor activities

I n Chicago, professional sports affiliation seems to permeate all levels of society, and you'll find that just about everyone has a handle on current teams in the NFL NHL and NBA, and the local outfit's respective standings. Supporting the local pro teams is a huge part of the Chicago mindset; walk the streets and you won't go far without passing some Chicago sports paraphernalia plastered across store windows or inside a crowded sports bar.

Attending a **professional sports event**, be it a baseball, football, basketball or hockey game, should be a priority for any visitor. If you can steal away for a Cubs game at Wrigley Field, you'll experience Chicago at its most prideful, as well as one of the great standing shrines to old-school sports stadiums.

As far as **participatory sports** are concerned, the city has been blessed with miles upon miles of lakefront parkland, fantastic for jogging, cycling, in-line skating, swimming, volleyball, fishing or simply lazing on a beach. Most of the action happens throughout Lincoln Park, the wide swath of greenery that stretches six miles north of downtown, the largest urban park in the country.

Baseball

Chicago has one of America's beloved ballparks, Wrigley Field, and one of the country's perennially worst professional baseball teams, the **Chicago Cubs** (☎773/404-2827, ⓦwww.cubs.com). Although the Cubs haven't won a World Series since 1908 and were caught up in the most scandalous event in the game's history (the 1917 World Series; see box on p.114), the team has a famously loyal and raucous group of fans that sell out Wrigley Park each season. Seeing a game there is a must even for non-baseball devotees.

While the popular Cubs have remained consistent non-achievers, their South Side rivals, the less celebrated **Chicago White Sox** (☎312/674-1000, ⓦwww.chisox.com) have fared slightly better at the more modern but sterile Comiskey Park – the previous Comiskey Park was demolished not many years ago, and used to be right next to where the new one is.

The baseball season runs between April and September. Ticket prices for Cubs games are $6–45; $12–45 for Sox games. For details on Wrigley Park, see p.100; for Comiskey Park, see p.114.

Game tickets

Buy **tickets** to most professional sporting events in Chicago through Ticketmaster (☎312/559-1212 or 559-1950, ⓦwww.ticketmaster.com), either online or by phone; it's also possible to buy them at one of several Ticketmaster outlets throughout the city (inside Carson Pirie Scott, Tower Records and at Hot Tix booths). You can also buy directly from the individual team's box office, especially at the last minute. If all else fails, you can try ticket brokers, although they usually charge higher prices. Try either Gold Coast Tickets (☎1-800/889-9100, ⓦwww.goldcoasttickets.com) or ticketsnow.com (☎1-800/927-2770).

Stadiums and venues

Allstate Arena Mannheim Road and Lunt Avenue, Rosemont ☎847/635-6601. Chicago Wolves hockey.
Comiskey Park 35th Street and Dan Ryan Expressway; ☎312/674-1000. Chicago White Sox baseball.
Soldier Field 425 E McFetridge Drive ☎312/747-1285. Chicago Bears football.

United Center 1901 W Madison St ☎312/455-4000, ⓦwww.unitedcenter.com. Chicago Blackhawks hockey and Chicago Bulls basketball.
Wrigley Field 1060 W Addison St, at Clark St ☎773/404-2827. Chicago Cubs baseball.

Basketball

Neither the **Chicago Bulls** (☎312/455-4000, ⓦwww.nba.com/bulls), nor the city of Chicago, had any real idea what impact one acquisition – Michael Jordan in the 1984 draft – would have on their next fifteen years. Jordan went on to become arguably the best player in the history of basketball, almost single-handedly changing the fortunes of the Bulls and the game as a whole. He led the team to win six NBA titles in the 1990s, and his gravity-defying antics defined the next generation of basketball hopefuls. His second retirement from the Bulls in 1999 (though he again unretired for a two-year stint with the Washington Wizards in 2001–2003) left the team reeling, and it hasn't recovered; it's now one of the lowest-ranked teams in the NBA, though fans do still pack the United Center for games.

The basketball season begins in the fall, and playoff games stretch into the spring. Standing-room tickets for Bulls games fetch about $25, with courtside seats running upwards of $500. For details on the United Center, see p.106.

Football

Known as the "Monsters of the Midway," football's **Chicago Bears** (☎312/295-6600, ⓦwww.chicagobears.com) have been playing at Soldier Field since the 1930s, although they've been temporarily relocated to the University of Illinois at Champaign's stadium while Soldier Field undergoes a massive renovation.

Despite years of down seasons, the Bears still pack the stadiums come fall, and tickets are highly coveted. As with other Chicago professional sports teams, fans are extremely loyal (verging on the obsessive), and routinely fill the seats despite the sub-zero temperatures at the lakefront stadium. The 1985 Chicago

Bears, under the lead of coach "Iron Mike" Ditka and the late running back "Sweetness" Walter Payton, won the Super Bowl and rank as one of the great teams of all time.

The football season opens the first week of September and runs through December. Tickets for Bears games are $45–65. For details on Soldier Field, see p.81.

Hockey

In this notoriously rough-and-tumble city, professional hockey has a major following. In fact, Blackhawk games have earned a reputation as the loudest sporting event in the country, and when the October to April season rolls around, tickets to **Chicago Blackhawks** (T312/455-7000, Wwww.chiblackhawks.com) games can be fairly hard to get. If you want to catch a Hawks game while in town, you'll have to see them at the United Center because the team's owners refuse to broadcast home games on TV. Standing-room tickets for Hawks games sell for around $20, with rinkside seats going for as much as $300. (For details on the United Center, see p.106.)

Alternatively, you can catch a minor league game at Allstate Arena with the **Chicago Wolves** (T847/724-4625, Wwww.chicagowolves.com), and while the play won't be as spectacular as you'd see at a Blackhawks game, it's still quite good.

Horse racing

One of the country's best tracks for thoroughbred horse racing is located northwest of Chicago in Arlington Heights – a half-hour's ride on Metra commuter rail. **Arlington Park Race Course**, 2200 Euclid Ave (T847/385-7500), is open May through September (Wed–Sun), with gates opening at 11am and post time (first race) usually at 1pm.

Besides the usual races, the track hosts "Party in the Park" on Friday afternoons, pulling in the after-work crowds with cheap drinks and live music on the front lawn; the first race doesn't start till 3pm.

To get here, board the Union Pacific Northwest line at Ogilvie Transportation Center and get off at the Arlington Park stop (round-trip $6). The train drops you right at the park.

Bicycling

With hundreds of miles of **bike trails** and a fifteen-mile lakefront trail, Chicago is a bicyclist's dream. The trail alone spans almost the northern suburb of Evanston and the University of Chicago in Hyde Park – passing by the heart of downtown – and it makes for one of the best outdoor experiences in the city.

Bike rental

Bike Chicago Navy Pier T312/755-0488, North Avenue Beach T773/327-2706, Wwww.bike chicago.com. This outfit has more or less cornered the bike rental market in Chicago, and with two key (and relatively accessible) rental outlets, it should be your first call for bikes and in-line skates. Prices start around $10/hour or $35/day on weekends, and on weekdays they offer the same hourly rates, though day rates drop significantly if you rent for three or four days. All rentals include locks and maps.

On the Route Bicycles 3146 N Lincoln Ave ☎773/477-5066, ⊛wwwontheroute.com. Full-service bike shop that also rents road bikes, mountain bikes and city bikes; the latter rent for around $35/day (24 hours), $20/half day.

Riding resources

Chicago Cycling Club ☎773/509-8093, ⊛www.chicagocyclingclub.org. Social club

that organizes rides every Saturday and Sunday between April and October, most leaving at 8.30am from the clock tower in Lincoln Park (at Waveland Avenue and the lakefront path, just south of the golf course). Rides range from 15 to 100 miles and are open to riders of all experience levels.

City of Chicago Bicycle Page ⊛www .cityofchicago.org/Transportation/BikeInfo.index. html. Resource with links to current informa-tion and bike route maps, including a detailed one of the lakefront bike trail.

Bird-watching

Chicago's best place for bird-watching is the **Magic Hedge**, east of Lake Shore Drive at Montrose Point (look out for the sign on Montrose Harbor Drive). Jutting out into Lake Michigan, this grassy area is right in a major migration path and can be visited year-round. For more on the Magic Hedge, see p.96.

Boating

As the city sits right on an enormous lake, the popularity and accessibility of boating is no surprise (see "Fishing" p.207 as well). The **Chicago Sailing Club**, 2712 N Campbell Ave (☎773/871-7245, ⊛www.chicagosailing club.com), organizes sailing lessons, rentals and charters from dock B at the north end of Belmont Harbor. Rentals are available to the public, with J22 boats from $35 to $55/hour, and J30 boats from $70 to $90/hour. The club also offer windsurfing lessons and equipment rentals, often from Montrose Beach, just north of the harbor.

Between May and September, there's a paddleboat rental service on Lincoln Park's South Pond, outside *Café Brauer*, 2021 N Stockton Drive ($10/30min or $15/hr). Boat rental is open from 10am to dusk.

Canoeing and kayaking

The Chicago Area Sea Kayaking Association ☎312/777-1489, ⊛www.caska.org. Offers evening paddles on Lake Michigan and is a good source for current information on

kayaking around Chicago.

The Lincoln Park Boat Club ☎773-549-2628, ⊛www.lpbc.net/Paddling. The club offers pad-dling and rowing classes, just south of W Fullerton Avenue, at the Lincoln Park Lagoon.

Bowling and pool

All but one of the following places offer both bowling and pool facilities.

The Corner Pocket 2610 N Halsted St, just north of W Wrightwood Ave ☎773/281-0050. Closer to a neighborhood pool hall (with a bar, and a kitchen in front) than the larger,

more sterile places, with nine regulation-size pool tables ($10/hr, Fri & Sat $12/hr after 8pm). Mon–Fri 4pm–2am, Sat & Sun noon–3am.

Diversey River Bowl 2211 W Diversey Parkway ☎773/227-5800, ⊛www.drbowl.com. A cheesy yet fun place to bowl amid flashing strobe lights, smoke machines and loud Eighties music. Lane prices vary by the day: Mon–Thurs $19/hr; Fri & Sat $32/hr; and Sun $26/hr. Shoes $3. Open daily noon–2am, Sat till 3am.

The Lucky Strike 2747 N Lincoln Ave ☎773/549-2695. Lincoln Park's Art Deco alley, with eight lanes and six regulation-size pool tables, two bars as well as decent finger food. The lanes may not be the best in the city, but the ambience makes up for it. Lanes cost $15/hr and shoes $2, while pool tables are $10/hr Sun–Thurs, $12/hr Fri & Sat. Mon–Fri 4pm–2am, Sat noon–3am, Sun noon–1am.

Marigold Bowl 828 W Grace St, at Broadway ☎773/935-8183. Keep score with pen and paper at this old-fashioned Wrigleyville alley, which has 32 lanes and is open 24hr on Friday and Saturday (when it does reams of business at $22 per hour). During the week, the prices drop ($2 per game before 5pm, $3.50 after 5pm), and the lanes close at midnight on most nights. The bar serves cheap beer and there's an arcade as well.

Southport Lanes & Billiards 3325 N Southport Ave ☎773/472-6600. Really a bar with four bowling lanes and a few pool tables, but the vintage setting – complete with human pinsetters – makes this a fun place to bowl. You'll need to call ahead as it's extremely popular. Rates are a little cheaper than usual ($16/hr, $2 for shoes). During the week, lanes open at 6pm and close when demand falls off or when the bar closes, usually around 1am. On weekends lanes open in the early afternoon and stay open later (but are often occupied by private parties and groups). As for pool, there are six regulation-size tables ($10/hr during the week, going up to $12/hr on peak nights).

Waveland Bowl 3700 N Western Ave, one block north of W Addison St; ☎773/472-5902, ⊛www .wavelandbowl.com; Red Line to Addison. The rare bowling alley that's open 24hr, 7 days a week – it's often full with leagues until around 9.30pm. Open since 1959, the recently refurbished alley has three regulation-size pool tables, an arcade and a little theater showing Disney flicks for kids. Prices depend on when you play, but expect to pay between $1 and $6 per game, with games being more expensive after 5pm and on weekends. Prices for pool table rental also vary, though you'll generally pay between $8 and $12/hr.

Chicago's beaches

Most visitors to Chicago don't know until they see firsthand that Lake Michigan not only is massive and appears very much like an ocean, but also has plenty of sand for the city to enjoy. In summer, the **beaches** are swamped with locals desperately trying to escape the oppressive heat and humidity.

All of the beaches listed below are free and usually open 9am–9.30pm between May and September, and you'll find public restrooms in the vicinity.

The main beaches

Foster Avenue Beach Sedate, clean beach near the northern tip of Lincoln Park. The beach house has concessions and outdoor showers.

Fullerton Avenue Beach Just east of Lake Shore Drive, this concrete stretch is popular thanks to the adjacent Theater on the Lake, which occasionally hosts evening shows on weekends during the summer (see p.188).

Montrose Beach Wide, sandy beach with volleyball courts; less crowded than the North Avenue and Oak Street beaches. You'll find Lincoln Park's bait shop here, as well a fishing pier (see "Fishing", opposite).

North Avenue Beach Just east of Lake Shore Drive, the city's most popular beach has volleyball nets, a Bike Chicago outlet (see p.204) and a boat-shaped beach house with concessions, volleyball equipment rental, along with *Castaway's Bar & Grill* (for review, see p.172).

Oak Street Beach This busy, fashion-conscious patch of sand, just east of Michigan Avenue, has skyscrapers as a backdrop.

Fishing

Few people come to Chicago with **fishing** in mind, but the city has a few places where anyone can put a line in the water. Chicago is, after all, on a lake well endowed with fish (especially coho and king salmon), and though angling trips and charter service are by no means plentiful, they do exist.

Most charter boats launch from north or south of the city, though a few service downtown fishermen (see below). Check the **Chicago Sportfishing Association**'s website (🅦www.great-lakes.org/il/fish-chicago/csa-list.html) for a list of charter boat operators. Prices usually start from $400 per six people per four hours.

If fishing from a boat doesn't appeal, there are a number of places where you can fish from shore. Popular fishing spots include Lincoln Park's **South Lagoon**, the pier at **Montrose Harbor** and just about anywhere there's a cement embankment along the lake. Fly fishermen often head to the pier at the south end of the North Pond to practice their casting – it's surrounded by floating rings that serve as targets.

The Park Bait Shop, at Montrose Avenue and Harbor Drive (☎773/271-2838) can set you up with bait (minnows and worms).

Charter operators

Captain A's Charter Service ☎312/565-0104, 🅦www.captainalscharters.com

Captain Bob's Lake Michigan Charters ☎1-888/929-3474, 🅦www.confusioncharters.com

Captain Randy's Charter Service ☎312/718-1995, 🅔r-schmidt@uchicago.edu

Golf

There are dozens of excellent **golf courses** within the greater Chicago area, as well as a few courses close to downtown.

Diversey Driving Range & Mini-Golf 141 W Diversey Parkway ☎312/742-7929, 🅦www.diverseydrivingrange.com. A terrific alternative to Waveland (see below), this driving range is open daily 7am–10pm, year-round (they have 25 heated mats), and rents clubs; a bucket of sixty balls costs $7, with the last bucket sold around 9.30pm.

Harborside International Golf Center 111th Street and Bishop Ford Expressway ☎312/782-7837. One of the best courses in the area – a links-style eighteen-hole course far down on the South Side. The only drawback is that you'll need your own transport to reach the course. Tee-time must be booked in advance, and greens fees start around $75 for eighteen holes.

Jackson Park Golf Course 63rd Street and Lake Shore Drive ☎312/747-2763. A decent eighteen-hole course on the South Side that's open year-round, from dawn to dusk. Greens fees start around $20.

Sydney R. Marovitz Golf Course 3600 Recreation Drive ☎312/742-7930. Also known as "Waveland," this popular nine-hole course is right on the lakefront near downtown and best suited for casual players who want to squeeze a few holes into their day (you'll need to book in advance, though). Rounds start around $15.

Jogging

Jogging remains one of the city's favorite athletic pastimes, thanks in large part to the extensive park system and the lakefront trail; jog either on the paved bike path or the dirt path – scenic routes either way. You can join the trail at most avenues and gauge your run using the mile markers along the way.

17

SPORTS AND OUTDOOR ACTIVITIES | Fishing • Golf • Jogging

The **Chicago Area Runners Association** (CARA: ☎312/666-9836, Ⓦwww.cararuns.org) organizes runs that meet at the north end of Diversey Harbor (membership not necessary). They can also provide information on upcoming races and fun runs, as well as training for the Chicago Marathon, the city's biggest running event (☎312/904-9800, Ⓦwww.chicagomarathon.com).

Festivals and events

D uring the freezing winter, Chicagoans tend to hibernate, with just a handful of citywide events able to lure locals out into the cold. But after St Patrick's Day, the Windy City comes alive with a host of **festivals and events**, with just about every neighborhood hosting its own weekend party. For a complete list of festivals, contact the Chicago Convention and Tourism Bureau (✆1-877/CHICAGO) or check out their website at ⊛www.chicago.il.org. Dates tend to change from year to year; call the numbers listed and check the local press for exact dates and times.

For a list of national public holidays, see Basics, p.32. Select festivals are listed in "Gay and lesbian Chicago," pp.196–201 and "Performing arts and film," pp.185–195.

January

Chicago Winter Delights (Jan–March) Family-friendly weekends of gourmet tastings, free blues and jazz shows, and discounts at city museums, hotels, restaurants and shops. ✆1-877/244-2246, ⊛www.877chicago.com

Chicago Boat, RV & Outdoors Show (early Jan) Boat-lover's extravaganza at McCormick Place, where you can check out more than 600 boats, 300 RVs and hundreds of booths catering to outdoor enthusiasts from all over the Midwest. ✆312/946-6200.

Chicago Cubs Convention (mid-Jan) Cub fans pay upwards of $40 to attend this popular

Information lines

Chicago Convention and Tourism Bureau ✆1-877/CHICAGO (244-2246) or 1-866/710-0294 (TTY)
Chicago Cultural Center ✆312/346-3278
Mayor's Office of Special Events ✆312/744-3315

weekend at the *Hilton Chicago and Towers* and get their favorite players' autographs, only to have their hearts broken again come summer. Oh well, at least the money goes to charity. ✆773/404-CUBS (2827).

February

African American Heritage Month (all month) Exhibits, special events and programs celebrating black history and culture all over the city, with many held at the South Shore Cultural Center. ✆312/747-2536.

Chicago White Sox "Soxfest" (early Feb) Fans of the South Side sluggers get their fix at this weekend event at the *Hyatt Regency Chicago*. ✆312/565-0769.

Chinese New Year Parade (date varies) Painted horses, traditional lion dancers and a 100-foot-long dragon snake along Wentworth from Cermak to 24th St, along with Miss Chinatown and her court in a flurry of fireworks at the neighborhood's biggest celebration of the year. ✆312/225-6198 or 689-0338, ⊛www.chicagochinatown.org

Chicago Auto Show (mid-Feb) The nation's largest auto show, a 10-day event at McCormick Place where the world's top automakers show off nearly 1000 different vehicles, from tame trucks to futuristic concept cars. ☎630/495-2282, ⊛www .chicagoautoshow.com

March

St Patrick's Day Parade (Sat before St Patrick's Day) One of the Chicago's most raucous celebrations, with the Chicago River dyed an emerald green for the occasion. Parade starts at Balbo and goes north on Columbus past Buckingham Fountain. ☎312/942-9188, ⊛www.chicagostpatspa-rade.com

South Side Irish St Patrick's Day Parade (St Patrick's Day) Less touristy and more authentic than the city event, this is the nation's largest neighborhood parade, drawing up to 300,000 revelers as it meanders through Irish communities Beverly and Morgan Park on Western from 103rd to 115th streets. ☎773/445-6764.

Flower & Garden Show (second week) Lush gardens, hands-on demonstrations and hundreds of product and educational booths highlight this weeklong event for green thumbs at Navy Pier. ☎312/222-5086, ⊛www.chicagoflower.com

Smelt Fishing (varies) For a couple of weeks each spring between March and May, thousands of finger-sized smelt (salmon-like fish, tasty when pan-fried) swarm along the lakeshore to spawn around 2–3am. When the call goes up ("The smelt are running!"), grab a net and head to the water; just south of Navy Pier's a good spot. ⊛www.chicagolandfishing.com

April

Earth Day Festival (third Sat) Eco-conscious Chicagoans browse the booths at this laid-back Lincoln Park gathering, where you'll see everyone from the Green Party and the Sierra Club to local vegan restaurants and organic clothing shops. ☎773/665-4682, ⊛www.chicagoearthmonth.com

Kids & Kites Festival (last Sat) Kids make and fly their own kites and watch professional flyers strut their stuff at this family-friendly event celebrating National Kite Flying Month at Montrose Harbor. ☎312/744-3315.

May

Cinco de Mayo Festival (first week) Five-day party celebrating Mexico's 1861 victory over the French, with live music, food vendors, soccer tournament and a parade that winds through Pilsen along Marshall Blvd, between Cermak Rd and 26th St. ☎312/399-9644.

Art Chicago at Navy Pier (early May) Works by more than 3000 international artists are on display and for sale at this Navy Pier contemporary art show, which also features lectures, panel discussions and special exhibitions. ☎312/587-3300, ⊛www.artchicago.com

Bike Chicago (mid-May to mid-June) Month-long festival promoting Chicago's bike-friendly streets, with a full slate of neighborhood rides, bike safety clinics, the Bike to Work Rally and more. ☎312/744-3315.

Asian-American Festival (late May) From Thai food to Indian stand-up comedy, this five-day event at Daley Center Plaza celebrates Asian culture with food vendors, activities and live entertainment. ☎312/744-3315.

Memorial Day Parade (Sat before Memorial Day) One of the nation's largest Memorial Day parades, with more than 10,000 participants and close to 300 marching units, veterans' groups and bands making their way from Balbo to Monroe along Columbus Drive. ☎312/744-0565.

Chicago Blues Festival (late May/early June) Without a doubt the best blues festival in the world, it's also Chicago's largest music festival, with four days of free performances in Grant Park by more than 70 performers, usually a roster of all-time legends. ☎312/744-3315.

June

Printers Row Book Fair (first weekend) Booksellers from around the country peddle their wares – new, used and antiquarian – under five tented blocks in the historic district on Dearborn St between Congress Parkway and Polk St. ☎312/987-9896, ⓦwww.printersrowbookfair.org

57th Street Art Fair (first full weekend) Hyde Park fair with more than 300 artists displaying and selling their work in painting, photography, jewelry, sculpture and other media. ☎773/493-3247, ⓦwww.57th streetartfair.org

Chicago Gospel Music Festival (first full weekend) Free concerts on three stages in Grant Park draw enthusiastic crowds of gospel music fans, some of whom sing a few bars themselves at the open-mic sessions in the Youth Tent. ☎312/744-3315.

Ravinia Festival (early June-early Sept) Pack a picnic basket and head north to suburban Highland Park, where for $10 you can get lawn seats to concerts ranging from the Chicago Symphony Orchestra to Tony Bennett. ☎847/266-5100, ⓦwww.ravinia.org

Wells Street Art Festival (2nd weekend) Fine art fair/street party for north side yuppies, with 250 exhibitors competing for attention. There's a live music stage, food vendors and children's theater, all on Wells St between North Ave and Division St. ☎773/868-3010, ⓦwww.chicagoevents.com

Andersonville Midsommarfest (2nd weekend) Everybody's a little Swedish on this weekend, as the city's Scandinavian enclave puts on a fun two-day party with live music, street vendors and a pet parade, all along Clark St from Foster to Balmoral avenues. ☎773/665-4682, ⓦwww.andersonville.org

Old Town Art Fair (2nd weekend) Crowded but fun weekend in one of the city's prettiest neighborhoods, with hundreds of booths hawking art, plus food and drink, and several lovely residential gardens open to the public. ☎312/337-1938, ⓦwww.oldtowntriangle.com

Juneteenth Celebration (mid-month) Celebrating the end of slavery, with events at venues around the city, including live music, storytelling, song and dance, food and a spirited parade along 79th St from Stony Island Ave to South Shore Drive. ☎773/684-6070 or 247-6200.

Northcenter's Ribfest (mid-month) Weekend-long neighborhood street party on Lincoln Ave between Irving Park Rd and Warner Ave, with a car show, two live music stages, an amateur cook-off, and ribs aplenty. ☎773/525-3609, ⓦwww.north centerchamber.com

Chicago Country Music Festival (last weekend) Big names often turn out for this free, foot-stomping two-day festival in Grant Park, which coincides with the opening weekend of Taste of Chicago (see below). With line dancing, dance lessons and music on two stages. ☎312/744-3315.

Taste of Chicago (late June to early July) More than three million people, packed like sardines in Grant Park, enjoy free concerts and scarf down deep-dish pizza, cheesecake and hot dogs at this massive ten-day festival in the heat of summer. ☎312/744-3315, ⓦwww.cityofchicago.org/ specialevents

July

Rock Around the Block (first weekend)
Lakeview traffic comes to a standstill as this local music festival takes over the intersection of Lincoln, Belmont and Ashland avenues, with thirty local bands jamming continuously on three stages. ☎773/665-4682, ⊛www.starevents.com

Independence Eve Fireworks Spectacular
(3rd) Cool, free pyrotechnic display in Grant Park accompanied by the Grant Park Symphony Orchestra, which opens the evening with a concert of patriotic favorites like *God Bless America* and *Stars and Stripes Forever*. ☎312/744-3315.

Chicago Yacht Club Race to Mackinac (mid-July)
Prestigious, invitation-only race from Chicago's Monroe Harbor 333 miles to Mackinac Island, Michigan. Watch the boats parade past Navy Pier with their ceremonial flags raised before the race. ☎312/861-7777.

Old St Pat's World's Largest Block Party (3rd weekend)
Touted as one of the city's best places to meet your mate, this church fundraiser draws 20,000 randy singles to the West Loop and raises money for its namesake church. ⊛www.worldslargestblockparty.com

Sheffield Garden Walk (3rd weekend)
Lincoln Park neighbors open their posh private gardens to the public (more than 100 on view), while attendees stroll through the neighborhood, guzzle beer and check out the decent live music. ☎773/929-9255, ⊛www.sheffieldfestivals.org

Venetian Night (late July/early Aug)
Half a million onlookers lounge along the lake at dusk as more than 35 elaborately decorated and illuminated boats promenade from the Shedd Aquarium to the Chicago Yacht Club, with further entertainment provided by the Grant Park Symphony Orchestra and a post-parade fireworks display. ☎312/744-3315.

Tall Ships Chicago (late July/early Aug)
Majestic racing yachts, clipper ships and replica trading schooners drop anchor along the lakefront; you can actually climb aboard and explore the impressive vessels during their five-day stay. ☎312/744-3315.

August

Retro on Roscoe (first weekend)
Yet another neighborhood street party, this one in fun, funky Roscoe Village (Roscoe St and Damen Ave) and featuring an antique car and motorcycle show, food and craft vendors, and a full lineup of bands playing tunes from the 1970s, 1980s and 1990s. ☎773/665-4682, ⊛www.starevents.com

Chicago 16" Softball Championship (second weekend)
More than one hundred men's, women's and co-ed teams compete in six classes at this Grant Park softball tournament, played with a 16-inch ball and no mitts. ☎312/744-3315.

Bud Billiken Parade (second Sat)
The largest African American parade in the US, named for a mythical guardian of children. Drill teams, dancers and local school kids march along King Drive from 39th to 51st streets, then live it up at a music festival and barbecue in Washington Park. ☎312/225-2400.

Chicago Air & Water Show (mid-month)
Sleek military aircraft zoom over the lake performing aerobatic stunts for onlookers; prime views can be had along the lakefront between Oak St and Fullerton Ave. Skip the water show, unless you don't mind fighting the crowds for a glimpse of the lackluster "Ski Show Team." ☎312/744-3315.

¡VIVA! Chicago Latin Music Festival (late Aug)
Tropical, merengue, salsa and mariachi bands jam in Grant Park at this two-day event, alongside local merchants selling traditional food, clothing and jewelry. ☎312/744-3315.

Mrs T's Chicago Triathlon (weekend before Labor Day)
Iron men and women swim, bike and run for glory along Lake Michigan in one of the world's largest triathlons. ☎773/404-2281, ⊛www.caprievents.com

Chicago Jazz Festival (Labor Day weekend)
A mellow holiday weekend crowd enjoys free jazz on three stages in Grant Park; there's an arts and crafts fair and wine garden, too. ☎312/744-3315.

September

German-American Festival (early Sept) The old German neighborhood of Lincoln Square throws a party with live oompah music and dancing, and more beer and schnitzel than you can shake a stick at. ☎773/728-3890, ⊛www.lincolnsquare.org

Mexican Independence Day (early Sept) The official holiday is Sept 16, but most of the festivities – including three separate parades at 26th St, 47th St and on Columbus Drive – happen in the two weeks before. ☎312/654-5314 or 773/579-1200.

Berghoff Oktoberfest (mid-Sept) This beer bash on Adams St in front of the legendary German restaurant packs the streets with after-work revelers enjoying the live music and gorging on knackwurst and potato salad. ☎312/427-3170, ⊛www.berghoff.com

Around the Coyote Arts Festival (mid-Sept) No beer tent and no bad live music, just local artists displaying and selling their works for a weekend in studios, galleries, and even bars and restaurants, in the Wicker Park neighborhood. ☎773/342-6777, ⊛www.aroundthecoyote.org

Chicago Celtic Festival (mid-Sept) Free art fair and music festival in Grant Park, with several stages of live music, dance, and storytelling, plus vendors hawking handmade clothing and jewelry, and plenty of Guinness. ☎312/744-3315.

World Music Festival (late Sept) Musicians from Niger, Turkey, Brazil and other faraway places take the stage at venues all over the city. ☎312/744-3315.

Italian Market Days (late Sept to early Oct) Lively lunchtime event at Block 37 (corner of State and Washington streets), where Italian singers and dancers entertain and vendors sell pastas, breads and cheese along with handmade dolls and masks. ☎312/744-3315.

October

Chicaglo (Oct–Dec) Three months of city-sponsored holiday events, from special markets and ethnic celebrations to ice-skating and parades. ☎1/877-244-2246, ⊛www.877chicago.com

Chicagoween (all month) Family-friendly Halloween events, from pumpkin-carving and spooky storytelling to haunted houses and even the Haunted "L" – a spooky tour of the Loop with costumed storytellers. ☎312/744-3315.

LaSalle Bank Chicago Marathon (second Sun) The fastest marathon in the world (thanks to the flat terrain), this event's also a hoot to watch – especially around mile seven at Broadway and Belmont Ave, where a cheering station of drag queens will make even the most tired runner smile. ☎312/904-9800 or 1-888/243-3344, ⊛www.chicagomarathon.com

Northalsted Halloween Parade (31st) The ghouls come out in full force for this parade and costume contest on Halsted St from Belmont Ave to Roscoe St. ☎773/868-3010, ⊛www.chicagoevents.com

November

Day of the Dead (1st) Traditional Mexican celebration of life and death; the Mexican Fine Arts Center Museum on 19th St (see p.110) boasts the nation's largest Day of the Dead exhibit, with colorful paintings, photography and sculpture from Mexico and the US. ☎312/738-1503, ⊛www.mfacmchicago.org

Dance Chicago (all month) Dance festival showcasing the Joffrey Ballet, Hubbard Street Dance and more than 200 other local jazz, ballet, tap and modern dance troupes. ☎773/935-6860, ⊛www.dancechicago.com

Lincoln Park ZooLights (late Nov to early Jan) Light displays, ice carving, train rides and a nightly laser show at the sea lion pool keep things hopping at this free zoo – though you will pay admission for this event (adults $8, kids 4–12 $6, free to kids 3 and under). ☎312/742-2165, ⊛www.lpzoo.com

Magnificent Mile Lights Festival (Sat before Thanksgiving) Mag Mile shops kick off the holiday season with an all-day celebration leading up to the lighting of more than one million lights strung from Oak St to Wacker Drive, followed by a fireworks show at the river. ☎312/409-5560, ⊛www.themagnificentmile.com

Thanksgiving Parade (last Thurs) More than a million spectators brave the cold to watch Kermit the Frog and the other balloons go by with marching bands on State St from Congress Parkway to Randolph St. ☎312/781-5678, ⊛www.chicagofestivals.org

Holiday Tree Lighting Ceremony (day after Thanksgiving) At Daley Plaza at 4pm, the mayor flips a switch and voila – the city's holiday tree (actually made of many smaller fir trees) lights up.

Christkindlmarket (late Nov to mid-Dec) Dozens of festively decorated timber booths at Block 37 (State and Washington streets) sell handcrafted ornaments, nutcrackers and other holiday trinkets, along with German fare like bratwurst, sauerkraut and hot spiced red wine. ☎312/644-2662, ⊛www.christkindlmarket.com

December

Carol to the Animals (first Sun) Carolers sing traditional holiday songs to the animals in the Lincoln Park Zoo; whether the animals like it or not is anyone's guess. ☎312/742-2000, ⊛www.lpzoo.com

Winter WonderFest (mid-Dec to early Jan) Family festival at Navy Pier with hundreds of decorated trees and plenty of entertainment, including puppet shows, storytellers, a skating rink, and Santa himself. ☎312/595-7437, ⊛www.navypier.com

Kwanzaa (Dec 26 to Jan 1) The DuSable Museum of African American History (see p.118) celebrates Kwanzaa (an African American holiday based on various African harvest festivals), with an exhibit of colorful textiles, paintings and artifacts that explores the holiday's history and meaning. ☎773/947-0600, ⊛www.dusablemuseum.org

Ethnic Market Chicago (late Dec) Last-minute Christmas shoppers escape the cold and sift through arts and crafts items from around the world inside a timber house set up at Daley Plaza (Clark and Washington streets). ☎312/744-3315.

Holiday Sports Festival (last weekend) All-ages event at McCormick Place where casual players try their hand at golf, martial arts, bowling, badminton and boxing, and more hard-core types compete in volleyball, soccer, table tennis and basketball tournaments. ☎312/744-3315.

New Year's Eve Fireworks (31st) Countdown to the new year with Buckingham Fountain's own fireworks display, followed by main pyrotechnic event above the lakefront at Montrose Harbor. ☎312/744-3315.

Shopping

S
hopping is one of Chicago's strong suits, right up there with blues music and modern architecture. Long on classy department stores nestled in historic buildings, especially within the confines of the Loop and Near North, Chicago ranks right up there near New York among US cities in terms of variety and experience; in addition, the spacious stores and down-to-earth service make shopping here relatively hassle-free. You'll be able to shop even in the dead of winter, thanks to the abundance of huge indoor malls, though eventually you'll come in contact with the freezing temperatures outdoors, not the most delightful proposition.

As for shopping **categories**, the city is especially strong in **malls** you'd actually be interested in visiting, esoteric **music** shops and **vintage and thrift stores**. This doesn't mean that trendy **boutiques** and the most modern fashions aren't accounted for as well; in truth, whatever you're looking for should be relatively easy to find.

Shopping by neighborhood

Shopping is concentrated in a few key areas of the city, all of them reachable by the El – we've indicated stops with each neighborhood overview below.

The Loop

As you might expect in the business district, some major department stores, like Marshall Field's and Carson Pirie Scott, line **State Street**, while **Wabash Avenue** has the pick of most everything else – camera shops, T-shirt shops, and other smaller service shops that are in no way specific to Chicago. You'll have no trouble getting here as all El trains stop in the Loop.

N Michigan Avenue (The Magnificent Mile) and Near North

The **Magnificent Mile**, Chicago's most famous shopping destination, is lined with malls and stores of all breeds, from big-name designers (Gucci, Armani) to commercial shopping (Niketown, The Gap, Bloomingdale's, Saks Fifth Avenue) to small Chicago-only establishments (Garrett Popcorn, Joy of Ireland). Pick an end, or one of the malls, and work your way in the opposite direction.

To reach N Michigan Avenue on the El, take the Red Line to Grand.

Gold Coast and Old Town

Boutique shopping at its priciest happens along **Oak Street**, adjacent to the north end of Mag Mile. It's never very crowded, and for those with some extra coin to throw around, it's the best place to do so – home to lots of ultra-fashionable designers. As for Old Town, the little strip of **Wells Street** between Division and North Avenue has a fair number of lesser-known boutiques.

The Gold Coast is reachable on the Red Line (get off at Clark/Division), while the Brown Line stops at Sedgwick in Old Town.

Bucktown and Wicker Park

The shopping in these parts happens on two main strips, **Milwaukee and Damen avenues**. South of North Avenue and the six corners intersection, Milwaukee more or less defines Wicker Park retro chic, with all sorts of oddball stores. Prices jump up as you head over to Damen Avenue, and then north of North Avenue: boutiques are geared more toward the yuppie than the starving artist, as the area grows a bit more in tune with its Lincoln Park neighbor.

To get to Bucktown and Wicker Park on the El, take the Blue Line to Damen. You can also hop to Lincoln Park from here on the efficient crosstown #73 bus, which runs along Armitage Avenue.

Lincoln Park

The center of the Lincoln Park shopping scene is the intersection of **Armitage Avenue and Halsted Street**, and for most Chicagoans, it's the best place to shop: away from the throngs on Michigan Avenue, reachable by the El or by car (with easy parking on the side streets), and plenty of restaurants, cafés, and bars to take a break from it all. The shops on Armitage tend to be of the local variety, many of which have been here for ages. Halsted Street receives plenty of spillover.

You can reach Lincoln Park on the El by taking the Brown Line to Armitage. The #73 Armitage bus runs to Bucktown and Wicker Park from here.

Lakeview

One thing to remember with Lakeview shopping: take the El, or hop a cab; if you're driving, most shops do not have their own parking and you're likely to search and search for a spot on the street for quite some time. **Belmont**, loaded with alternative and retro shops, is your best bet. **Clark Street**, which crosses through many neighborhoods, in fact hits its most interesting stride at its intersection with Belmont, though that's not to say that the rest of its length isn't worth exploring.

Take the Red Line to Addison to reach Lakeview.

Arts, crafts and antiques

Alaska Shop 104 E Oak St, Gold Coast ☎312/943-3393. This small gallery, hidden behind a jewelry store (Silver on Oak), has a fine selection of Inuit carvings, sculpture and scrimshaw.

Atom Antiques 1219 N Wells St, Old Town ☎312/867-2866. Set back from the street, this quirky antiques store is crammed with slot machines, stuffed animals, beer signs and vintage clothing. A fun place to browse; look for the life-size statues out front of subjects like Mike Tyson and Elvis.

Cielo Vivo 1528 N Milwaukee Ave, Bucktown ☎773/276-8012. You'll find everything from figurines made by the Lobi people of Burkina Faso to Japanese ceramics in this spacious shop, many from the owner's travels.

Eclectic Junction 1630 N Damen Ave, Bucktown ☎773/342-7865. A funky collection of handcrafted fixtures and trinkets for the house – arty-looking switchplates, painted knobs, funky wine racks and more.

Faded Rose 1017 W Armitage Ave, Lincoln Park ☎773/281-8161. Cozy store with an inviting selection of delicate linens and small housewares (bath products, picture frames, candlesticks), as well as custom-made living room furniture. Adjoins Tabula Tua (see below).

Findables 907 W Armitage Ave, Lincoln Park ⊤773/348-0674. This aptly named all-in-one gift boutique stocks a wide array of jewelry, china, candles, ornaments, picture frames and the like.

Gallery 37 Store 66 E Randolph St (inside Gallery 37 Center for the Arts), the Loop ⊤312/744-7274. Works by emerging and apprentice artists on view at the Loop's Gallery 37 – part of the School of the Art Institute of Chicago (see p.43) – can be bought in the gallery's store, be it lawn ornaments, mosaics, jewelry or furniture. Closed Sundays.

Idao Gallery 1616 N Damen Ave, Suite #3W, Bucktown ⊤773/235-4724. This gallery, which has been showcasing local and emerging artists for years, also has a wide selection of custom frames.

Lincoln Antique Mall 3141 N Lincoln Ave, Lakeview ⊤773/244-1440. Over sixty dealer booths hawk furniture, jewels, paintings, lamps and other antiques (from Victorian to mid-twentieth century) seven days a week, with dealers setting their own prices.

Pagoda Red 1714 N Damen Ave, Bucktown ⊤773/235-1188. Huge showrooms on two floors carrying high-quality eighteenth- and nineteenth-century Chinese art (pottery, rugs, furniture etc) – a nice change from the funky secondhand stores in the neighborhood.

Poster Plus 200 S Michigan Ave, the Loop ⊤312/461-9277. Three stories of fine art and vintage posters, as well as art-themed trinkets and custom framing.

Primitive Art Works 706 N Wells St, River North ⊤312/943-3770. Intriguing River North gallery featuring four floors of ethnic artifacts – jewelry, furniture, textiles etc – that makes for a fascinating hour's worth of browsing. The staff's enthusiasm for the place is infectious.

Tabula Tua 1015 W Armitage Ave, Lincoln Park ⊤773/525-3500. Linked to Faded Rose (see above), this small kitchenware store has unusual platters and place settings, engraved cheese spreaders and other gift-worthy items.

Books

Abraham Lincoln Book Shop 357 W Chicago Ave, River North ⊤312/944-3085. You'll find more than eight thousand new, used and antiquarian books on the shelves, covering the Civil War and other US military history, plus a host of collectibles and, of course, tomes on Lincoln himself.

Afrocentric Bookstore 333 S State St, the Loop (inside Chicago Music Mart at DePaul Center) ⊤312/939-1956. The city's best selection of African American-related books, along with plenty of magazines, calendars and greeting cards. The store also hosts occasional readings.

Barbara's Bookstore 1350 N Wells St, Old Town; ⊤312/642-5044. Independent Chicago bookstore chain without the corporate feel of a Borders or a Barnes & Noble. Well respected for its stock of literary titles.

Barnes & Noble 1441 W Webster Ave, Lincoln Park ⊤773/871-3610; 659 W Diversey Parkway, Lakeview ⊤773/871-9004. Either of these huge outlets will have any recent title you'd ever want, except perhaps for academic textbooks or highly specialized works.

Borders 150 N State St, the Loop ⊤312/606-0750; 830 N Michigan Ave, Near North ⊤312/573-0564; 2817 N Clark St, Lakeview

⊤773/935-3909. Massive, well-stocked book and music store. The N Michigan Avenue branch is the biggest and best of the city's chain bookstores, centrally located right on Mag Mile, with a café, frequent readings and signings, and loads of room to sit and browse.

Europa Books 832 N State St, Near North ⊤312/335-9677; 3229 N Clark St, Lakeview ⊤773/404-7313. This quaint neighborhood bookstore packs a lot into little space, including an excellent selection of foreign-language books, newspapers and magazines.

Myopic Books 1468 N Milwaukee Ave, Wicker Park ⊤773/862-4882. Artsy and academic Wicker Park book haven selling both new and used titles.

O'Gara & Wilson 1448 E 57th St, Hyde Park ⊤773/363-0993. Great little bookstore that has sold new and used books (both popular and obscure) since the late 1930s.

Prairie Avenue Book Shop 418 S Wabash Ave, the Loop ⊤312/922-8311. Serene and spacious place where you can browse the phenomenal architecture selection (12,000+ titles) to your heart's content. The store also hosts frequent readings and signings.

Rain Dog Books and Café 404 S Michigan Ave, the Loop ☎312/922-1200. Smallish bookstore carrying new and used books, known for its antiquarian collection (upstairs). Usually a sedate place to sit, read, have a coffee and listen to the ambient jazz.
Rand McNally Map & Travel Store 444 N Michigan Ave, Near North ☎312/321-1751. The map publisher's own store, with, no surprise, an array of maps, guides, travel gadgets and more.

Savvy Traveller 310 S Michigan Ave, between W Jackson Blvd and W Van Buren St, the Loop ☎312/913-9800. Travel guides, electronic translators, maps and anything else you might need on your trip.
Seminary Co-op Books 5757 S University Plaza, Hyde Park ☎773/752-1959. Cavernous basement bookstore with a devout following, where row upon row of shelves is crammed with academic titles.

Clothes and fashion

Chain stores

Anthropologie1120 N State St, Gold Coast ☎312/255-1848. Major fashion chain that blends in well with the neighborhood. Expensive women's clothing and home furnishings with a romantic/bohemian slant.
Banana Republic 744 N Michigan Ave, Near North ☎312/642-0020; 2104 N Halsted St, Lincoln Park ☎773/832-1172. The ubiquitous chain's flagship store is on Michigan Avenue, whose low-key men's and women's clothes are snapped up by huge swaths of the country's 20–40 age group.
Burberry 633 N Michigan Ave, Near North ☎312/787-2500. Michigan Avenue branch of the British stalwart clothier, known for its distinctive plaid and recently revamped to appeal to younger consumers.
The Gap 555 N Michigan Ave, Near North ☎312/494-8580. Affordable men's and women's basics (jeans, T-shirts) that coordinate with just about anything.

Designer stores

agnes b. 46 E Walton St, Gold Coast ☎312/642-7483. Beautifully cut, simple styles with a French twist – mainly in solid blues, blacks and whites. Neither cheap nor distinctive to Chicago, but very popular.
Cynthia Rowley 808 W Armitage Ave, Lincoln Park ☎773/528-6160. The native Chicagoan's designs cater to pretty young things, with a good selection of flirty dresses and dainty separates.
Giorgio Armani 800 N Michigan Ave, Near North ☎312/751-2244. The last word in classically styled luxury Italian fashion.

Gucci 900 N Michigan Ave, Near North ☎312/664-5504. Designer Tom Ford's empire of style; it doesn't get more expensive than this.
Ralph Lauren 750 N Michigan Ave, Near North ☎312/280-1655. All-American high-end fashion label.

Boutiques

apartment number 9 1804 N Damen Ave, Bucktown ☎773/395-2999. Slightly expensive men's boutique – the only one of its kind in the city – run by two down-to-earth sisters with an eye for intelligent fashion.
Betsey Johnson 72 E Oak St, Gold Coast ☎312/664-5901. Very distinctive, brightly colored and funky clothing from this New York designer; somewhat over the top for conservative Chicago.
Celeste Turner 859 W Armitage Ave, Lincoln Park ☎773/549-3390. Armitage Avenue staple, with cool dresses and funky tops, but a bit pricey – T-shirts might set you back $80, a sweater $180.
Jane Hamill 1115 W Armitage Ave, Lincoln Park ☎773/665-1102. Stylish dresses, shoes and jewelry from local designer Hamill. A good shop to find a sun dress.
Out of the West 1000 W Armitage Ave, Lincoln Park ☎773/404-9378. Cowboy-themed clothing and accessories, including boots, Lucky Jeans, Aztec-inspired turquoise jewelry, buckles, picture frames, lamps and much more.
p.45 1643 N Damen Ave, Bucktown ☎773/862-4523. Hip boutique that doubles as an art gallery for designers. Spacious, with plenty of attentive staff and a chic selection of casual and dressy styles. Recommended.

Sass 1456 N Milwaukee Ave, Wicker Park
☎773/342-7950. Super-trendy boutique where you'll find pieces from emerging talents on both coasts, as well as the UK, all at reasonable prices.

Shopgirl 1206 W Webster Ave, Lincoln Park
☎773/935-SHOP. Tiny boutique away from the Armitage strip that does well nonetheless by carrying some trendy labels including Three Dots, Trina Turk and Shoshanna. Expensive.

Sofie 1343 N Wells St, Old Town ☎312/255-1343. You'll find fashion with a slight edge, from New York and LA, at this friendly boutique.

Sugar Magnolia 34 E Oak St, Gold Coast
☎312/944-0885. Distinctive upscale Chicago boutique that's managed to hold its own against Oak Street's ultra high-end competition. Stocks new and established designers; not too funky but not cheap either.

Trousseau 711 W Armitage Ave, Lincoln Park
☎312/751-1450. Tops in women's lingerie, from brightly colored pajamas to lacey French bras.

Vagabonds 1357 N Wells St, Old Town
☎312/787-8520. Small, hip boutique with tasteful separates, pretty dresses, bags and accessories, all at affordable prices.

Vive la femme 2115 N Damen Ave, Bucktown
☎773/772-7429. One of the city's only boutiques for stylish, full-figured women (size 12–28).

Vintage, secondhand and thrift

Brown Elephant Resale Store 3651 N Halsted St, Lakeview ☎773/549-5943. Clothes – and actually much more, including records, books and furniture – with proceeds going to the Howard Brown Memorial Clinic.

Daisy Shop 67 E Oak St, Gold Coast ☎312/943-8880. Those willing to settle for gently worn couture will find a good selection from top designers at reduced – but still steep – prices.

Flashy Trash 3524 N Halsted St, Lakeview
☎773/327-6900. Men's and women's vintage clothing, jewelry and accessories on the playful side, in beautiful condition.

Hollywood Mirror 812 W Belmont Ave, Lakeview ☎773/404-4510. Sells more junky trinkets than you'd ever wish upon anyone, but it's a stimulating place nonetheless. While they do sell an assortment of vintage clothing, the main attraction here is the kitschy ambience, helped along by the

disco ball and lights, and loud punk music.

Lenny & Me 1545 N Damen Ave, Bucktown
☎773/489-5576. Friendly consignment store that has a great assortment of women's clothing, though mostly for petite frames.

McShane's Exchange 1141 W Webster Ave, Lincoln Park ☎773/525-0211. Basic, casual used clothing at bargain prices.

Phoenix Retro Resale 1932 N Damen Ave, Bucktown ☎773/862-6628.Fairly reasonably priced 1970s-era clothing for both men and women.

Recycle 1474 N Milwaukee Ave, Wicker Park
☎773/645-1900. Designer-conscious consignment store, with men's and women's jeans, shirts and more.

Una Mae's Freak Boutique 1422 N Milwaukee Ave, Wicker Park ☎773/276-7002. Affordable vintage clothes, perfumed candles and an odd array of knick-knacks make this a quintessential Wicker Park locale.

Discount clothing

Filene's Basement 1 N State St, the Loop
☎312/553-1055. One of those stores where you can find everything, from soap trays to brand-name clothes, all at discounted prices. Competitor TJ Maxx, in the same building, has a decent selection of housewares.

Marshall's 600 N Michigan Ave, Near North
☎312/280-7506. Though you'll have to plow through racks and racks of clothing – from discount to designer labels – you'll usually find a bargain or two.

Shoes

City Soles/Niche 2001 W North Ave, Bucktown
☎773/489-2001. Shoes with attitude – imports from Spain, Italy and beyond. Also carries bags and other wearables.

Hanig's Footwear 660 N Michigan Ave, Near North ☎312/642-5330; also Hanig's Birkenstock Shop, 847 W Armitage Ave, Lincoln Park
☎773/929-5568. Carries major brands of walking shoes like Ecco, Mephisto and Dansko. The Lincoln Park branch has one of the largest selections of sandals in the city.

John Fluevog Shoes 1539 N Milwaukee Ave, Wicker Park ☎773/772-1983. Flamboyantly trendy shoes from this Canadian label.

Johnston & Murphy 625 N Michigan Ave, Near North ☎312/751-1630. Staple for good-quality, conservative dress shoes.

Lori's Designer Shoes 824 W Armitage Ave, Lincoln Park ☎773/281-5655. The quintessential women's shoe store and one of the best in Chicago; styles run the gamut and there's also a good selection of one-of-a-kind bags and purses. Highly recommended.

New Balance Chicago 2369 N Clark St, Lincoln Park ☎773/348-1787. Low-key store selling one of the best brands in running shoes.

Niketown 669 N Michigan Ave, Near North ☎312/642-6363. This giant Nike retail outlet is a tourist attraction in itself, thanks in part to the video theater and miniature basketball court.

Shoe Soul 11 E Oak St, Gold Coast ☎312/475-9100; **2223 N Clybourn Ave, Lincoln Park** ☎773/528-1100; **3243 N Broadway St, Lakeview** ☎773/388-1100. High-quality, if funky, European styles that are on the pricey side.

Cosmetics and fragrances

Aroma Workshop 2050 N Halsted St, Lincoln Park ☎773/871-1985. A great place for candles, though you'll find scented oils, incense and the like here as well; there's also a mixing bar where you can create your own scents.

Fresh 2040 N Halsted St, Lincoln Park ☎773/404-9776. One of the hottest stores in Chicago, with knowledgeable staff and an extensive – though slightly expensive – selection of candles, soaps, lotions and other beauty products. Recommended.

MAC 40 E Oak St, Gold Coast ☎312/951-7310. Trendy make-up brand that caters to a youngish crowd, known for its glamour-heavy look.

Merz Apothecary 4716 N Lincoln Ave (at the intersection of Lincoln, Western and Lawrence), Lincoln Square ☎773/989-0900. Opened in 1875, this pharmacy is loaded with bath, body and natural-health products, including some rare European items.

Department stores and malls

Department stores

Barney's New York 25 E Oak St, Gold Coast ☎312/587-1700. Boutique department store carrying a highly edited selection of all the major designers. A more congenial and less crowded version of its New York counterpart.

Bloomingdale's 900 N Michigan Ave, Near North ☎312/440-4460. Flagship Midwest store of the famous New York retailer. You could easily spend half a day in here and skip the rest of the Mile; part of the 900 N Michigan Avenue mall, it's near a movie theater, restaurant and plenty of other shops.

Carson Pirie Scott & Co 1 S State St, the Loop ☎312/641-7000. Long-time competitor of Marshall Field's and always a step below, though it's still a great place to shop. The building itself is a tourist destination, considered a Louis Sullivan masterpiece (see p.42). Like Field's, they put on beautiful holiday-themed window decorations in December.

Lord & Taylor 835 N Michigan Ave, Near North ☎312/787-7400. Whether this conservative department store succeeds in revamping its slightly dated image remains to be seen, though its sales are usually worth a look. Located in the same mall as the larger Marshall Field's.

Marshall Field's 111 N State St, the Loop ☎312/781-1000; **835 N Michigan Ave, Near North** ☎312/335-7700. The original State Street location is Chicago's most famous store – a must if you intend to see what's behind the city's shopping appeal, especially around Christmas when the windows are decked in elaborate displays. Be sure and check out the blue Tiffany dome and the *Walnut Room* restaurant, a Field's institution. The smaller N Michigan branch still carries most designers.

Neiman Marcus 737 N Michigan Ave, Near North ☎312/642-5900. This high-end, designer-oriented store comes with more attitude than the others, but at least there's usually plenty of room to shop.

Nordstrom 55 E Grand Ave ☎312/464-1515.
Huge Seattle-based retail chain, with an
excellent shoe department and known for
top customer service.
Saks Fifth Avenue 700 N Michigan Ave, Near
North ☎312/944-6500. Similar to Neiman
Marcus in its clothing lines, but known for its
customer service and sales, and tends to
be among the most crowded of the city's
department stores. The first-floor make-up
department, especially, is especially popular.
Sears 2 N State St, the Loop ☎312/373-6000.
After several years' absence, the department store giant has returned to downtown
with its affordable, but rather staid, merchandise.

Malls

900 North Michigan 900 N Michigan Ave, Near
North ☎312/915-3916 or 915-3900.

Northernmost of the Michigan Avenue
malls. The six levels are home to
Bloomingdale's, Gucci, J. Crew and some
seventy stores, including a movie theater
and a few decent cafés.
Chicago Place 700 N Michigan Ave, Near North
☎312/642-4811. Eight-story space that
includes Saks Fifth Avenue, Joy of Ireland
and fifty other stores, plus the largest food
court on the Mag Mile.
The Shops at North Bridge 520 N Michigan
Ave ☎312/327-2300. Airy four-story complex
dominated by Nordstrom's, with a clutch of
children's stores, shoe stores and an
upscale food court.
Water Tower Place 835 N Michigan Ave, Near
North ☎312/440-3166. Chicago's most
famous mall – seven stories and over one
hundred big-name stores, including
Marshall Field's and Lord & Taylor.

Food and drink

Breadsmith (Wells Street Bread Co) 1710 N
Wells St, Old Town ☎312/642-5858. This small,
fabulous bread shop is a better alternative
to the numerous chain coffee and breakfast
joints in the area.
Fox & Obel Food Market 401 E Illinois St, Near
North ☎312/410-7301. You don't need to be
a gourmand to appreciate the superb
selection of cheeses, fresh fish, meats, deli
items and baked goods on offer at this
gourmet food emporium; there's a café
here, too.
Garrett Popcorn Shop 670 N Michigan Ave,
Near North ☎312/280-0162. A Chicago institution whose caramel and cheese flavored
popcorns are out of this world.
House of Glunz 1206 N Wells St, Old Town
☎312/642-3000. Small family-run wine shop,
purported to be the oldest wine shop in the

nation. Great place to pick up some unique,
inexpensive wines.
Lutz Continental Café & Pastry Shop 2458 W
Montrose Ave, Lincoln Square ☎773/478-7785.
Half-century-old German-style bakery
where you can soak up the Old World
ambience in the café at the back or take
home delectable strudels, cakes, pastries
and marzipan from the glass cases up
front.
Schmeissing's Bakery 2679 N Lincoln Ave,
Lakeview ☎773/525-3753. German bakery
that's been in Chicago for over seventy
years.
Wikstrom's Gourmet 5247 N Clark St,
Andersonville ☎773/275-6100. Assorted food
from all over Scandinavia: Gothenburg
sausage, Kavli flatbread, Danish pumpernickel
bread, Swedish lingonberries and the like.

Museum and gallery stores

ArchiCenter Shop 225 S Michigan Ave
☎312/922-3432; 875 N Michigan Ave (ground
floor of the John Hancock Center), Near North
☎312/751-1380. The Chicago Architecture
Foundation's retail arm, with a good selection of architecture-related books and
knick-knacks.

The Art Institute of Chicago Museum Shop
111 S Michigan Ave, at W Adams St, the Loop
☎312/443-3534; branch at 900 N Michigan Ave,
Near North ☎312/482-8275. Art books, repro-
ductions and a host of museum-related gift
items.

Bariff Shop for Judaica Spertus Museum, 618 S Michigan Ave, South Loop ☎312/322-1740. A small shop devoted entirely to Judaica, with art, ceremonial pieces, books and more.

The Library Store 400 S State St (in the Harold Washington Memorial Library), The Loop ☎312/747-4130. Good selection of books and even some art from local and emerging talent.

Music stores

Crow's Nest 333 S State St ☎312/341-9196. Huge store that looks like a national chain but isn't, carrying music in just about every genre (with imports as well), plus videos and DVDs.

Dave's Records 2604 N Clark St, Lincoln Park ☎773/929-6325. Vinyl only-store with largish selection: some 50,000 new and used LPs, 45s and 12-inch dance music and hip-hop.

Dr Wax 2523 N Clark St ☎773/549-3377; 5225 S Harper Ave ☎773/493-8696; 1203 N State Parkway ☎312/255-0123. This multi-branch outfit carries new and used CDs, LPs and tapes, but its strongest suit is its extensive secondhand CD bins.

Gramaphone 2663 N Clark St, Lincoln Park ☎773/472-3683. Packed to the gills with an outstanding selection of house, dance and techno discs, from mainstream to underground, from Chicago and anywhere else. DJs spin in the back, and you can listen to any CD before you buy.

Hi-Fi Records 2570 N Clark St, Lincoln Park ☎773/880-1002. One of Chicago's better outlets for used vinyl, not so much for the usual rock and pop stuff as for the 12-inch dance music. You'll also find overflowing bins of super-cheap used LPs, and a used music book section that turns up some good deals.

Jazz Record Mart 444 N Wabash Ave, The Loop ☎312/222-1467. Billing itself as "The World's Largest Jazz and Blues Shop," with the floor space and stock to back up the claim. In addition to aisles of new jazz and blues CDs, they also carry plenty of used vinyl, plus books and videos, and the occasional in-store performance. A must-stop for blues and jazz lovers.

Reckless Records 1532 N Milwaukee Ave, Wicker Park ☎773/235-3727; 3157 N Broadway St, Lakeview ☎773/404-5080. Chicago branch of the London-based used-music chain, with an extensive selection of CDs, DVDs and vinyl (especially indie, punk and imported electronica vinyl) at fair prices.

Sound Booth 1151 W Webster Ave, Lincoln Park ☎773/528-5156. Great selection of Grateful Dead, reggae and bootlegs, with some rock.

Symphony Store 220 S Michigan Ave, the Loop ☎312/294-3345. Maybe the place to go if you're looking for a classical music title, with a wide array in stock.

Tower Records 2301 N Clark St ☎773/477-5994; 214 S Wabash Ave, the Loop ☎312/663-0660. A couple of entries in the massive chain, with wide selections and in-store appearances.

Virgin Records 540 N Michigan Ave, Near North ☎312/645-9300. The biggest mainstream music store in the city, right in the heart of Mag Mile.

Sporting goods stores

Active Endeavors 935 W Armitage Ave, Lincoln Park ☎773/281-8100. A Lincoln Park mainstay and part of the Armitage Avenue shopping route, this small, popular retailer sells outdoor gear and clothes.

Eastern Mountain Sports 1000 W North Ave, Old Town ☎312/337-7750. Part of a large chain, but still a top outdoors store that can set you up with clothes and gear.

Erehwon Mountain Outfitter 1800 N Clybourn Ave, Old Town ☎312/337-6400. Probably Chicago's best selection of outdoor adventure clothes and gear.

The North Face 875 N Michigan Ave, Near North ☎312/337-7200. Function *and* stylish outdoor clothing and equipment, geared toward affluent adventure enthusiasts.

Orvis 142 E Ontario St, at N Michigan Ave, Near

North ☎312/440-0662. Mag Mile version of this dependable New England retailer, with fly-fishing gear and ruggedly fashionable outdoor wear.

Running Away 1753 N Damen Ave, Bucktown ☎773/395-AWAY. Very cool boutique runner's shop, with a yoga studio downstairs.

Specialty shops

All She Wrote 825 W Armitage Ave, Lincoln Park ☎773/529-0100. Warm, family-run stationery store with unique and cool gifts and decorations.

The Alley 854 W Belmont Ave ☎773/348-5000. A temple to all things Goth, this landmark of alternative and fetish Chicago is worth a look if you're in the area. Entrance is in the alley.

Blue Chicago Store 534 N Clark St, Near North ☎312/661-1003. The blues club's own store, packed with CDs, shirts, posters and assorted paraphernalia, including the club's signature art by John Carroll Doyle. For club review, see p.179.

Central Camera 232 S Wabash Ave, the Loop ☎312/427-5580. Good camera shop with touch of expert attitude, that's been in Chicago for over a century.

Chicago Tribune Gift Store 435 N Michigan Ave, Near North ☎312/222-3080. Hats, shirts and other souvenirs plastered with the *Tribune* logo.

City of Chicago Store 163 E Pearson St (across from the Water Tower), Near North ☎312/742-8811. As the name might suggest, Chicago souvenirs of all kinds.

F.A.O. Schwarz 840 N Michigan Ave, Near North ☎312/587-5000. Major toy store, with a huge selection of merchandise.

Iwan Ries & Co 19 S Wabash Ave ☎312/372-1306. This second-floor cigar shop has been a Chicago family business for nearly 150 years. Over one hundred different cigar brands, and at least 13,000 pipes on hand.

Joy of Ireland 700 N Michigan Ave, Near North ☎312/664-7290. Sift through Aran fisherman sweaters and other classic Irish wares (Waterford crystal, Guinness paraphernalia), then stop for a cup of tea and Irish pastries in the airy tea room.

Spacetime Tanks 2526 N Lincoln Ave, Lincoln Park ☎773/472-2700. If your idea of relaxation means floating in vats of water in complete darkness, this "float center" is for you. Four isolation tanks, each renting at $40/hr. Closes at 9pm every night except Sundays. Recommended.

Uncle Fun 1338 W Belmont Ave, Lakeview ☎773/477-8223. Wall-to-wall jokes and novelty toys – whoopee cushions, fake body parts and more.

Directory

Airlines Aero Mexico ☎1-800/237-6639; Air Canada ☎1-888/247-2262; Alaska Airlines ☎1-800/252-7522; America West Airlines ☎1-800/235-9292; American Airlines ☎1-800/433-7300; American Trans Air ☎1-800/435-9282; Continental Airlines ☎1-800/523-3273; Delta Air Lines ☎1-800/221-1212; Frontier Airlines ☎1-800/432-1359; Mexicana ☎1-800/531-7921; National ☎1-800/447-4747; Northwest ☎1-800/225-2525; Southwest Airlines ☎1-800/435-9792; Spirit ☎1-800/772-7117; United Airlines ☎1-800/241-6522; US Airways ☎1-800/428-4322.

Area code Chicago has two main area codes – ☎312 and 773 – but you may come across the following too: ☎630, 708, 815 and 847.

Banks Citibank ☎1-800/926-1067, ✆www .citibank.com; branches at 100 S Michigan Ave ☎312/419-9002; 233 N Michigan Ave ☎312/977-5881; 11 S La Salle St ☎312/853-5780; 69 W Washington Blvd ☎312/977-5131; 1 S Dearborn St ☎312/263-6660.
Northern Trust Bank; branches at 50 S LaSalle St ☎312/630-6000; 120 E Oak St ☎312/630-6666; 201 E Huron St ☎312/557-6200; 125 S Wacker Drive ☎312/444-7887.

Bus departures Call Greyhound (☎1-800/231-2222, in Chicago ☎312/408-5800), Lakefront Lines (☎1-800/638-6338) or Indian Trails (☎1-800/292-3831). Departures to Cleveland, Indianapolis, Milwaukee, Minneapolis, New York and beyond are from the terminal at 630 W Harrison St, at S Desplaines Street.

Currency exchange American Express: ☎1-800/528-4800, ☎www.americanexpress .com; offices at 605 N Michigan Ave, Suite 105 ☎312/435-2570; 55 W Monroe St

☎312/541-5440; 2338 N Clark St ☎773/477-4000; 122 S Michigan Ave ☎312/435-2595; Foreign Currency Exchange at terminals three and five, O'Hare International Airport. Northern Trust Co, 50 S LaSalle St ☎312/630-6000. World's Money Exchange, Mezzanine Level, Suite M1, 203 N LaSalle St ☎312/641-2151.

Doctors The Chicago Medical Society (☎312/670-2550) has a physician referral service that can point you to a doctor should you need one.

Electricity 110 volts AC. Plugs are standard two-pins – foreign visitors will need an adapter for any electrical appliances they bring.

Embassies and consulates Australia: 123 N Wacker Drive, Suite 1330, 60606 ☎312/419-1480; Canada: Two Prudential Plaza,180 N Stetson Ave, Suite 2400, 60601 ☎312/616-1860; Ireland: Wrigley Building, 400 N Michigan Ave, Suite 911, 60611 ☎312/337-1868; New Zealand: 8600 W Bryn Mawr Ave, Suite 500N, 60631 ☎773/714-9461; UK: Wrigley Building, 400 N Michigan Ave, Suite 1300, 60611 ☎312/970-3800.

Film times/tickets For current movie listings or to buy tickets in advance, call moviefone (☎312/444-FILM).

Hospitals Each of the following has a 24-hour emergency center: Cook County Hospital, 1835 W Harrison St ☎312/633-6000; Northwestern Memorial Hospital 251 E Huron St ☎ 312/926-2000; Rush-Presbyterian 1650 W Harrison St ☎312/942-5000; University of Chicago Hospital, 901 E 58th St, Hyde Park ☎773/702-6250.

Internet cafés Available at BEAN.net (inside Merchandise Mart), 350 N Orleans St ☎312/601-4430; Broadband Café, 58 E

Randolph St; Off the Wall Wireless Café, 1904 W North Ave, Wicker Park ☎773/782-0000; *Hostelling International–Chicago*, 24 E Congress Parkway, the Loop ☎312/360-0300; and the Harold Washington Library, 400 S State St ☎312/747-4999.

Libraries The main public library is Harold Washington Memorial Library, 400 S State St, in the Loop ☎312/747-4999. Alternatively, there's a Near North branch at 310 W Division St ☎312/744-0991 or 744-0992.

Tax Chicago sales tax is 8.75 percent; hotel tax 14.9 percent; restaurant tax 9.75 percent.

Taxis American-United ☎773/248-7600; Checker Taxi ☎312/243-2537; Wolley Cab ☎312/888-8294; Yellow Cab ☎312/TAX-ICAB.

Time Chicago is in the central time zone, which starts at Chicago (on the east end) and continues as far as the west border of Texas. This is six hours behind Greenwich Mean Time (-6 GMT). If flying from Australia or New Zealand, bear in mind that you will cross the international date line, and will, in effect, arrive in Chicago before you have left home.

Train departures Amtrak (☎1-800/872-7245 or 312/655-2101) operates out of Union Station, offering service to both coasts and beyond. You can buy (or reserve) your tickets on the phone, or on the Web (◉www.Amtrak.com), but in either case you'll need to pick them up at Union Station before you board. Trains serving the greater metropolitan Chicago area and suburbs are run by Metra (☎312/322-6777) and run out of Ogilvie Transportation Center; you can buy tickets at the station ticket office before boarding or pay slightly more on the train.

Travel agencies American Express: 605 N Michigan Ave, Suite 105 ☎312/435-2570; 55 W Monroe St ☎312/541-5440. STA Travel:1160 N State St ☎312/951-0585; 429 S Dearborn St ☎312/786-9050.

Weather In Chicago, both the *Chicago Tribune* and the *Chicago Sun-Times* print five-day weather forecasts. You can also visit weather.com and type in "Chicago."

Contexts

Contexts

A history of Chicago

The following account is intended to give an overall view of the city's development from a fur-trapping backwater through its industrialized apogee to the skyscraper-packed skyline of today. For more on the city's contribution to American architecture, see p.241.

1673–1833:
Chicago's early years

The first Europeans to officially sight Chicago were explorers from New France (now Quebec). **Louis Joliet**, a cartographer, and **Jacques Marquette**, a missionary, had been sent on an Empire-building expedition by Louis XIV, the so-called Sun King; Louis' plan was to shore up his country's holdings in the New World by connecting New France and New Orleans with fresh territory. Marquette and Joliet, guided by friendly local Powatomi Indians, arrived in what's now Chicago in the fall of 1673.

Native Americans had settled the area almost seven hundred years before, and it's also likely that other European settlers had passed through earlier as well. By this time the shores of Lake Michigan were a fur-trapping hub, and indeed, a year after their arrival, the explorers spent time with a fellow French-Canadian, Pierre Moreau – nicknamed "The Mole" – a trapper who'd already also established a thriving, illicit trade in alcohol to the Indians. The word *checagou* derives from Joliet's attempts to phonetically transcribe the local Native American name: it's been variously glossed as "great and powerful," "skunk" and "wild onion" (after the plants that grew in abundance locally), although no one has ever confirmed its true meaning.

Staking claim for France, Joliet and his party soon moved on, leaving a small settlement of three hundred or so. With a dash of magic and plenty of money, France planned for this town to be a gleaming metropolis, its answer to the powerful and thriving British settlements of New York and Boston. Sadly, it was a case of bad luck and bad timing: the royal coffers were running on empty, and there was little money left to spend on a town few in France would ever see. Soon, the settlement was abandoned and *Checagou* slipped back into obscurity: for the next few years, the territory flip-flopped between colonial powers, eventually landing in American hands after the War of Independence.

Given Chicago's recent, troubled race relations, there's a wry irony in the fact that the next non-native settler – acknowledged as the city's founder by most historians – was black: **Jean-Baptiste Point du Sable**. He was a Haitian-born fur trapper, who after arriving in 1779 amassed a sizable fortune, married a Powatomi Indian girl and built an estate where the *Chicago Sun-Times* building now stands. Du Sable's settlement was strategically important, and by 1803 – recognizing the continuing colonial threat from a disgruntled Britain – the American government had established a garrison here, known as **Fort Dearborn**. Indeed, open war with Britain did break out nine years later, and Fort Dearborn was the site of a major atrocity: British-backed Indians torched the building, and ambushed the evacuees from the fort, slaughtering two-thirds of them.

But America won the war, and Fort Dearborn was soon rebuilt. By the time of Chicago's incorporation as a town in 1833, there were 350 residents living in the area now bounded by Kinzie, Desplaines, Madison and State streets; that year, the town's first newspaper, *The Chicago Democrat*, went to press. The stop-and-start of Chicago's settlement was over: for the next seventy years it would grow at breakneck speed to become one of the largest, most prosperous cities in America and a symbol of nineteenth-century economic success.

1837–70:
The age of infrastructure

In fact, the first sign of Chicago's healthy future had come when the **Erie Canal** opened in 1825: by linking New York City's Hudson River with the hamlet of Buffalo, which sat on the eastern reaches of Lake Erie, the canal opened up the entire state of Illinois to commerce. Some savvy Chicagoans spotted how Buffalo exploded, virtually overnight, into a thriving transport hub – and were soon snapping up swaths of local land for next to nothing.

In the industrialized nineteenth century, Chicago had an advantage that no man could manufacture: its location. Those Buffalo-watchers recognized this, and so invested heavily in infrastructure like waterways and railroads; unusually, they also spent money on better sewers and drains. Indeed, Chicago city planners have always thought big and by treating their nascent town like a city, locals were well prepared to seize economic opportunities when they appeared.

The first of those was the construction of the **Illinois and Michigan Canal**, begun in 1836. This waterway would connect the Illinois River to the Mississippi, and so to the thriving shipping hub of New Orleans; a year later, swelled by the influx of thousands of construction workers, Chicago was large enough to incorporate as a city. Then it hit a snag: a nationwide depression that lasted for three years and was precipitated by President Andrew Jackson's ham-fisted meddling in the rickety national banking system.

After this, construction of the canal slowly resumed, while simultaneously local leaders turned their attention to Chicago's own water system. Since the city was built on marshy, swampy land, no cellars or drains had been possible at first, so now the streets were clogged with effluent. In 1849, an ingenious engineer, who'd recently arrived from New York State, devised a strange but simple solution: **raise the buildings**. Each structure was ratcheted off the ground to a height of four to seven feet, and drainage systems were then installed in the newly created first floor.

The engineer responsible was **George Pullman**, who'd later make his name as a railroad magnate; like Pullman, it's to the railroads that Chicago owes almost everything.

The railways arrive

As the railroads laid down tracks to and from the city, Chicago became the **terminus for cross-country travel**: few rail companies operated networks both east and west of the Mississippi River, and so all cargo, both freight and human, had to be unloaded there. This was the first key impact of the railroad: travelers would often stay (and spend) for several days before continuing their journey, while cargo hauling created hundreds of new jobs. In fact, during this time, the population of Chicago more than tripled – from 30,000 in 1850 to 110,000 ten years later.

If this first effect funneled America through Chicago, the second scattered Chicago across America. The rest of the US became a **market for goods** from merchants based in the city: soon, Chicago was the hub of America's grain and lumber trades. Businessmen here were best placed to reach any corner of the country and many became phenomenally wealthy: they then pumped money back into the city, building fabulous mansions and endowing institutions.

Third came the definitive **defeat of St Louis**, Chicago's snazzy southern rival three hundred miles away in Missouri. St Louis was already a thriving city in the early 1830s when Chicago was little more than a hamlet, linked by the Mississippi River to New Orleans and warm enough that its waterways wouldn't ice up in winter. But St Louis relied on the steamboat, which was easily eclipsed by Chicago's cheaper, more efficient railroad network. St Louis struggled on until the Civil War, which was the final, lethal blow: its Confederate economy depended on trade with the South, while Union Chicago was quick to provide the massive northern army with provisions, especially meat.

Chicago's **meatpacking plants** were perhaps the most visible by-product of its pole position in the railroad race – at one point it was even nicknamed Porkopolis. Since meat could be quickly transported cross-country from Chicago, it was a natural base during the Civil War, and by 1862, had become the largest meatpacking city in the world. The legendary Union Stockyards opened on the South Side in 1865: indeed, the stockyards were so large – ten miles of feed trough on one hundred acres of land – that they became a tourist attraction. Chicago's pragmatic leaders turned butchery into business. There was a disassembly line, where hog slaughter was so efficient that, unlike individual butchers who threw away almost half a carcass (like cartilage and bones), almost nothing was wasted: aside from meat, the plants turned out bouillon, brushes and even instrument strings. One local bigwig butcher used to boast that he made use of every part of a pig bar the squeal.

The railroads didn't just move food and goods, they also moved people: the train made travel speedy and convenient as never before. In essence they created a **commuter class**. Soon, the city's middle class was moving out of downtown and into larger houses and bigger yards further afield – in fact, Naperville, to the west of the city, was the world's first "railroad suburb."

Finally, the spaghetti of railroad lines meeting in Chicago spurred reform in one offbeat area: **time**. As late as 1883, there was no standard time in America – it could be 2.30pm in New York City, while a few hundred miles away it was 2.46pm in Washington, DC. Until the industrial age, variable timekeeping like this had caused few problems, but with the railroads came timetables, and so confusion. Often, companies synchronized the clocks along their own lines but this might bear little resemblance to local time; it also meant that many stations had several clocks, featuring the time according to each railroad company *plus* the local time. It's not surprising that Chicago, where fifteen railroad lines met, was one of the key drivers behind New York-based Charles Dowd's reforms of 1869, where he suggested four times zones, much like those we use today, be created.

Destruction and rebirth: 1871–1895

Chicago's transformation into a modern city was spurred on by a terrible city-wide fire, which would turn Chicago from a city of wood to a city of steel, and give the world the skyscraper. Subsequent progress was speedy, culminating with a high point of the World Fair in 1893.

The Great Fire of 1871

As Chicago's economic prosperity reached its peak, the most defining event in city history occurred – one which, at first, would seem to have doomed its progress but instead brought about its salvation: **the Great Fire of 1871**.

City fires weren't unusual in those days – most major American metropolises, Chicago included, had suffered at least one. In fact, there was a blaze there on October 7, 1871 (the day before the Great Fire) that had destroyed twenty acres west of downtown.

The subsequent fire started at around 9pm on October 8, in a barn owned by Patrick and Catherine O'Leary; it was situated at what's now the intersection of Jefferson and Taylor streets. The classic story tells how a kicking cow knocked over a nightlight and so started the blaze but the truth is probably more prosaic. Local cow-championing researchers have uncovered the existence of Daniel "Pegleg" Sullivan, whose mother's cow was also billeted in the same barn. Most historians now agree it's more likely that Sullivan, having stopped by to feed the animal, accidentally started the blaze and blamed the cow to save his skin.

Two factors hindered firefighters' immediate response: firstly, they were all exhausted after spending the previous night dousing the massive West Side blaze; secondly, an inept watchman misjudged the fire's location and sent the alert to the wrong crew. By the time they arrived, the flames were too strong to put out. For two days, until rain came in the early hours of October 10, Chicago burned at the rate of 65 acres each hour. Losses were staggering: exact statistics vary, but around 18,000 buildings were destroyed, damage was estimated at $200 million and 90,000 people were left homeless. Only 250 people died, thanks in part to the lake, into which many waded for safety away from the flames.

Only the Water Tower and the Pumping Station, gaudy Neo-Gothic hulks of stone lurking at the upper end of Pine Street (now N Michigan Avenue) didn't burn (see p.62). An architectural shame, perhaps, but at least the city's drinking water supply wasn't affected.

The city at its apogee

But Chicago's survival, despite the devastation across downtown, was due to more than clean(ish) drinking water. The only reason the city could bounce back as quickly as it did was that the fire had left Chicago's three major industries – the lumberyards, the stockyards and the railroads – untouched. Since Chicago was then at the heart of the country's economy, as well as its geography, businessmen across America turned their attention to rebuilding the city.

Hence, only two years later, downtown had been completely rebuilt. The creative opportunities afforded by Chicago's blank canvas also attracted men like

Louis Sullivan and Frank Lloyd Wright, whose architectural impact lingers even today – for more on them, see "Architecture" p.247. In the years following the fire, Chicago's buildings grew larger and more impressive until, in 1885, the **world's first skyscraper** was constructed downtown. Chicago seemed unstoppable, but the city was starting to show symptoms of urban blight.

The most famous – and telling - incident was the **Haymarket Riots** of 1886. Union leaders, always powerful in Chicago's massive factories and yards, had begun a movement for shorter working hours; a citywide strike was announced for May 1. Three days later, at a protest meeting over worker treatment, a bomb was detonated as police tried to clear the demonstrators. Officer Mathias J. Degan died instantly, while seven other policemen lingered for several days before also expiring. The citywide witch-hunt resulted in the trial of eight so-called "Haymarket Martyrs": seven were condemned to death and the eighth sentenced to fifteen years in prison. In the end, though, only four were executed; one committed suicide while two more saw their sentence commuted to life in prison. Although seven years later in 1893, Governor Altgeld would pardon and release the three remaining men, the Haymarket riots highlighted for the first time worker–owner friction that would reach paralyzing levels in the twentieth century.

If 1893 was the year when Chicago made a headline-grabbing debut on the world's stage (see below), it was also a difficult time for local industry: the country was in a depression and job losses in Chicago were significant. It was the year the paternalistic millionaire **George Pullman** – who'd masterminded the elevation of the city forty years earlier – also went from hero to villain in the eyes of the local working class. Pullman was a railroad millionaire, although he didn't own an inch of track: instead, inspired by the grueling trip he'd made from New York to Chicago, he turned his ingenuity to sleeping cars. Pullman's prototypes were well enough received but it was his flair for publicity, rather than his engineering know-how, that saw him through: after Lincoln's assassination, he offered his namesake car to bring Lincoln's body home to Illinois, and travel through towns across America on its way. Soon, Pullman cars were a common sight in every station and Pullman himself was a multi-millionaire, employing thousands of people at his factory in Chicago. The railroads weren't immune to industrial unrest like the Haymarket Riots; in fact, an 1877 national strike had driven home to Pullman the problems of keeping his workforce happy, or rather, docile. His answer was to build a town for them to live in, and so control every aspect of his employees' lives: buying up chunks of land far on the South Side, he started construction in 1879 and had quickly built a model community (albeit one where rents were 20 percent higher than elsewhere). The town prospered until 1893 when Pullman, his profits slashed by the depression, fired thousands of workers, cut wages by 25 percent but wouldn't lower rents. In response, union leaders called for a boycott of the sleeping cars across the network; although Pullman's strong-arming saw him eventually emerge victorious, it was at a high price - from then until his death four years later, he was vilified by his employees.

1893: The World's Columbian Exposition

Despite such economic unrest, 1890s Chicago considered itself a grand city, with a righteous claim to be a thriving rival to New York itself. But while New York had the prestigious Columbia University, the original **University of Chicago** had gone bust several years earlier. William Rainey Harper then masterminded the creation of a new university, located in the newly annexed

By 1910, almost one in two people in the United States lived in a city with more than 2500 inhabitants – and with such mass urbanization, problems like crime and disease became rife. Chicago, being a prime example of overnight urban growth, was no exception, a situation that led local architect **Daniel Burnham** to began investigating ways of imposing the moral order of a village onto growing cities. The far-reaching ideology he helped develop became known as the **City Beautiful Movement**.

Inspired by the harmony of Europe's new Beaux Arts style, as well as domestic successes like Frederick Law Olmsted's Central Park in Manhattan, reformers like Burnham pitched utopian cities, vaguely classical in style, whose beauty would inspire civic loyalty and upstanding morals in even the most impoverished resident. (Cynics might argue that food and better sanitation would have been more effective remedies.) Key features of the City Beautiful Movement included wide, tree-lined avenues, monumental buildings, ample greenspace and frequent plazas or fountains. There were even proscriptions on lampposts, which had to be attractive as well as functional, and straight roads, which had to be broken up by winding streets whenever possible.

Burnham outlined his blueprint for the perfect city at the **World's Columbian Exposition** in 1893, whose construction he oversaw: the fair's structures were uniform, and its parks enormous; a city built on these principles, he argued, would be crimeless due to a combination of civic duty and plenty of police. Burnham's evangelical plans weren't popular with everyone – Louis Sullivan, for example, moaned that his colleague's adoption of Old World Beaux Arts ideals enslaved turn-of-the-century commercial architecture in America and ended experimentation. (In hindsight, the moribund state of commercial design in the early twentieth century hints that Sullivan was right.)

But Burnham was unswayed and began hawking his ideas around the country, to cities including Washington DC (1901) and San Francisco (1906), which was at that time reeling from a fire similar to Chicago's devastating blaze in 1871. He enjoyed small successes in each place, but was itching to overhaul a city wholesale. Returning to his hometown of Chicago, he self-published plans for the town in 1909 – the first regional urban plans ever published in America, stretching out sixty miles from the lakefront past Chicago's current suburbs. The mayor responded to Burnham's prodding by creating a taskforce, the Chicago Plan Commission, to investigate the proposals, but as usual, the architect's ideals were battered by local bureaucracy and left in limbo: he died in 1912 having seen little progress. Ultimately, the commission only approved two of his ideas: the straightening of the river and, more importantly, the concept of a **public lakefront park**, which, more than any of his buildings, is perhaps Burnham's greatest legacy to the city.

area of Hyde Park on the South Side. The university would symbolize Chicago's egalitarian, pragmatic attitude: admitting both women and men from the outset, working on a quarters system to allow flexibility for its staff and overseeing an active university press to disseminate its ideals. Harper turned to John D. Rockefeller, nineteenth-century America's answer to Midas and a staunch Baptist to boot (the university was initially conceived as a Baptist bastion), for funds; Rockefeller pledged $600,000, contingent on the city raising $400,000. Since local Baptists couldn't cough up enough cash, the religious mission of the university was revised, and Marshall Field – who until then had never been known as a philanthropist – stepped in with additional funding. The university, designed in a Neo-Gothic style, opened in 1892. Sadly, the genial Harper would only live to see his dream realized for another fourteen years before dying at a young age in 1906.

The birth of the department store

Chicago may be lauded for launching the skyscraper, but it's rarely credited for its other contribution to modern life: the **department store**. Admittedly, the first such shop, Bon Marché, was actually in Paris (it's still there) but even if the French conceived the department store, it was immediately adopted and raised to adulthood by Chicago's shopkeepers along the "Ladies' Half Mile" of State Street.

The first retail genius was Potter Palmer, who invented the idea of the refund – in fact, for several years, the jaw-dropping practice of accepting returns, no questions asked, was known as the **"Palmer System."** He focused on female customers, greeting them at the door by name and escorting them round his store, and his refund system encouraged women to make impulse purchases for the first time. But it was Palmer's protégé Marshall Field who turned shopping into an art form. Field and his partner, Levi Leiter, bought a controlling stake in Palmer's store in 1865; sixteen years later, he renamed it and ran it solo. Trim, elegant and highly private, Field held fast to his rigid maxims: "The customer is always right" and "Give the lady what she wants." At its peak in 1900, **Marshall Field's** was serving 250,000 customers a day and employed 8000 people. Among the store's various innovations were bringing goods down from high shelves and putting them on counters so customers could touch and feel them; placing a perfume hall by the doors so that passers-by would be drawn in by the heady smells; opening a bargain basement; offering annual sales and gift certificates, and on down the line.

At the same time as Field was wowing downtown, local entrepreneur Aaron Montgomery Ward was servicing rural shoppers. Having worked at Field's store for two years before becoming a traveling salesman, Ward took what he learned from both jobs and produced a revolutionary new product in 1872: **the mail order catalog**. Mail-order shopping made merchandise, from basic to luxe, accessible to everyone; Ward opened up an entirely new market for consumer goods, much of it in rural, hard-to-reach places. Ward's business was a nineteenth-century hybrid of Wal-Mart and Amazon.com, buying goods in such vast quantities that he was able to undercut rural merchants by up to 75 percent. Soon, he had a rival in Richard Sears and Alvah Roebuck, who modeled their business after his - and eventually bested him thanks to Sears' instinct for snappy advertising. Both eventually opened brick-and-mortar stores and though Sears is now a household name, sadly Montgomery Ward's went into Chapter 11 bankruptcy in 2000 and closed its final few doors.

These shopping pashas have left their mark across the city: Marshall Field has his namesake museum (see p.78), the Merchandise Mart (see p.66) and even the University of Chicago (see p.116). Palmer's wife Bertha donated her extraordinary Impressionist collection to the Art Institute (see p.43); while Palmer has the greatest memorial of all – an entire neighborhood. By putting up his first magnificent mansion in what's now the Gold Coast, he encouraged his cronies to follow suit and almost single-handedly created the wealthy enclave (For more on the Gold Coast, see p.69).

But establishing the university was only a national coup; city bigwigs wanted to hog the world spotlight and turned to the idea of a Great Exhibition. The last fair had been in Paris in 1889, the centenary of the French Revolution; it was decided to hold a fair in America to acknowledge the four-hundredth year anniversary of Columbus' arrival. The catfight between New York and Chicago was fierce – in fact, it's where the nickname "Windy City" came from, when a Manhattan journalist derided the braggadocio of Chicago's committee. But the wind blew Chicago's way, and Congress finally voted in its favor: the city would host the **World's Columbian Exposition**, albeit a year late in 1893.

Daniel Burnham and Louis Sullivan, both beloved local architects, were appointed to oversee the fair, alongside legendary planner Frederick Law Olmstead (responsible for New York's Central Park). The site they chose, Jackson Park, was a swampy marshland close to the new university in the Hyde Park district. What's more, the 1892–93 winter was severe, even by Chicago standards, and hampered progress; so it wasn't until the fair actually opened on May 1, 1893, that anyone knew whether all construction would be completed in time.

The fair was an unqualified triumph and capped Chicago's century: known as the "White City" thanks to its burnished, floodlit white buildings, the fair covered six hundred acres, attracted more than 27.5 million visitors (almost half of the number of people then living in America), and featured 250,000 exhibits from 46 nations. Some of the most popular included the Electricity Building, which showcased the various uses of the new electricity including Elisha Gray's telautograph, a prototype fax machine that was designed to send writing or drawings by telegraph. The Streets of Cairo display was also popular, featuring raunchy belly dancers – although the legendary minx known as Little Egypt didn't, as is popularly supposed, make her debut at the fair: she surfaced for the first time two years later in Coney Island, New York. But it was **George Ferris' wheel** that grabbed the most headlines.

Burnham had challenged engineers across America to come up with a worthy retort to the Eiffel Tower of 1889: he received submissions including a replica of Dante's Hell (probably not a crowd-pleaser) and manmade mountains. But it was Ferris' idea to take the observatory from the Eiffel Tower and pivot it that won Burnham over. Ferris put up his 250-foot wheel in less than five months, using his own money: it was smart investment as 1.4 million riders paid 50¢ apiece to ride for two revolutions in one of its 36 cabins.

The fair's only surviving building is now the Museum of Science and Industry (see p.114): Burnham's Palace of Fine Arts, constructed in temporary materials, was painstakingly disassembled to its stone skeleton and then rebuilt in stone. The Midway Plaisance greenspace that Burnham & Co planned as a Venetian canal but had to abandon after flooding problems also emerged out of the fair.

1895–1920: Race and reforms

The years up to World War I would transform Chicago yet again, but it would never reach the level of fame and prosperity it enjoyed during the World Fair. Chicago's always depended on **immigration,** like the laborers who came to work on the first canal and turned it from a town into a city. But the new arrivals from Europe and the Deep South both enriched and complicated city life in new ways.

Some 2.5 million Europeans arrived in Chicago in the forty years from 1880. The largest communities were **Polish**, **Italian and Russian Jewish**, and each contributed in a different way to the new cosmopolitan make-up of Chicago. The Poles – stirred by Polish-language newspapers exhorting them *Swój do Swego* (Support Your Own) – created a self-sufficient, self-contained community that floated on the surface of existing society rather than integrating. The Italians also resisted integration, partly because many men had come alone and planned to return to Italy having earned extra money for their families: many of the Italians were from rural areas and so avoided working in factories, instead preferring lower-paid, outdoor jobs like construction and railroad maintenance.

The Russians established Maxwell Street Market (see p.108) and many worked as peddlers or shopkeepers, so coming into contact with many other immigrant and established groups, and therefore integrating most quickly of all.

African American immigration to Chicago was also significant – and unsurprising: Chicago was one of the main stops on the Underground Railroad, and had always had a liberal attitude to race relations (for example, D.W. Griffith's hit film *Birth of a Nation*, which glorified the KKK, was banned from the city's cinemas). More than such social concerns, though, there were pressing economic reasons: during World War I, European immigration all but ceased, and local white laborers saw their chance to agitate for higher wages; in response, business leaders turned to cheaper, black labor. Again, the railroad was also part responsible: many Pullman porters on the trains were African American, and they would take copies of *The Chicago Defender*, the city's black newspaper, along with them to distribute during their travels. The net result was that Chicago's African American population more than doubled from 44,000 in 1910 to 109,000 ten years later.

There was little integration, though: most blacks were confined to a small strip along S State Street, part of which was an entertainment district known as **The Stroll**. Despite the segregation, racial violence wasn't commonplace: the one major exception was the 1919 Race Riots, sparked by the death of a black teenager, Eugene Williams. On July 27, Williams had been out swimming with friends in the lake when they drifted past a "whites only" beach: struck on the forehead by a rock thrown by a white sunbather, he fell unconscious and drowned. When his friends called in the local police and pointed out the man responsible, the officer refused to arrest him. Six days of riots ensued, only calmed when the state governor sent 5000 troops to the city. It's worth noting that the Williams' story is shot through with unreliable, contradictory facts and that perhaps the severe nationwide depression of 1919 (and ensuing unemployment) was as much the reason for the violence as his death.

Around this time of massive immigration, the **Progressive Movement** was sweeping the country: this new political sense focused on social justice and the harms of industrialization. Predictably, gritty Chicago was a prime focus - see Upton Sinclair's groundbreaking fictionalized account of the stockyards, *The Jungle*, for an example. Groundbreaking social worker Jane Addams established Hull-House (see p.108) after a trip to London's Toynbee Hall, which was designed to provide social services to the working-class poor. From its founding in 1889, Hull-House mushroomed into a massive complex that even included a library and a gym (for her efforts, Addams was awarded the Nobel Peace Prize in 1931). It was also in the early part of the century that Daniel Burnham conceived of and began to implement his City Beautiful plan, which was as much about civic pride as it was architecture (see box on p.234 for more on this).

Gangsters and glamor: Chicago's Roaring Twenties

Despite the city's best efforts to paper over its associations with organized crime, Chicago will always be known as the home of **Al Capone**. It's ironic that the era of molls, mobsters and murderous ambushes was brought about by zealous reformism like the Progressive Movement. National temperance advocates had jostled for a ban on alcohol for several years and many prominent women's groups focused on its harmful effects on the modern family (in other words, the number of abusive alcoholic husbands it produced). Although Chicago's voters came out 6:1 against **Prohibition**, it was introduced nation-wide in January 1920.

Predictably, banning alcohol only glamorized it further, especially among the upper classes for whom serving a cocktail before dinner became a subversive sign of power and wealth. Chicago's illicit alcohol industry was controlled by individual gangs, each of whom supplied different districts of the city: the so-called Beer War, much like many gang murders today, broke out when one man decided to take over the whole city.

That man, born Alphonse Caponi in New York, but better known as Al Capone arrived in Chicago in 1919: he ran speakeasies for a while, before widening his ambitions and soon taking control of the booze supply on the city's South Side. He was never averse to offing troublesome competitors and ten years after his arrival, Capone made his final, decisive move. On the morning of February 14, his henchmen (dressed as local cops of course) gathered seven members of the rival Bugs Moran gang, lined the men up against a wall in a garage and shot them at point blank range. The so-called **St Valentine's Day Massacre** cemented Capone's legend, as well as scaring off Bugs (who'd overslept and therefore escaped execution); Moran ceded his north side territory to Capone, who finally controlled the whole city. He wouldn't enjoy his spoils for long: in 1931, Capone was sent to Alcatraz by his nemesis, Eliot Ness, whose determined investigators earned the nickname "The Untouchables" since they were so bribe-resistant. The gangster was actually convicted of tax evasion, and served a short sentence before retreating to his mansion in Miami where he expired in 1947 of an advanced case of syphilis.

1930–55: The World's Fair, the war and waning fortunes

By 1933, when it was clear that Prohibition was all but useless, the laws were repealed. Chicago, now known more for robberies than railroads, decided to up its image by launching a new **World's Fair**, this time in celebration of the city's own centenary and called "A Century of Progress." But despite the massive attending numbers (39 million visitors over two years) and the fact that it even operated at a slight profit, the 1933 fair had none of the cultural impact its predecessor had enjoyed. Tellingly, there's little evidence left that it ever took place and its architectural impact was minimal.

There is plenty of evidence of the other major event in Chicago from this era – although the only local reminder is a small plaque on the campus of the University of Chicago. Underneath the squash courts there, on a cold December afternoon in 1942, visiting Italian professor **Enrico Fermi** and his team achieved the first controlled release of nuclear energy. Fermi had been brought to Chicago to undertake such secret experiments only ten months before; at 3.25pm on December 2, he achieved his goal of a controlled nuclear chain reaction. His work paved the way both for fossil fuel-free power stations and the wrenching devastation of the atom bomb, which when dropped on Japan three years later finally ended World War II.

The years after the war were difficult for Chicago, as race relations grew contentious as elsewhere in America: many white locals fled to the new suburbs, leaving downtown an underinvested ghetto. Less than sixty years since its first, world-busting fair, Chicago was on a downward slide until the arrival of one in 1955, legendary man: Richard M. Daley.

The Boss

Richard M. Daley (aka The Boss) served five consecutive terms as mayor of Chicago, establishing a political dynasty and ruling the city as *de facto* king in a way that few other mayors anywhere in America have ever managed. He secured such governmental *carte blanche* through Chicago's unique local political cal structure: as a staunchly Democratic city, the local party (Cook County Democratic Party, or CCDP) effectively selects then elects the mayor uncontested. Daley had worked to fill the CCDP (nicknamed, somewhat ominously, The Machine) with his supporters over several years and by rewarding them handsomely – as was expected – after his election, his path to power remained clear.

Born in 1902, Daley was an unremarkable, hardworking young man; his eventual ascension was never prefigured in his early years. Pragmatic and no-nonsense, Daley's politics were a comfortable fit for this blue-collar, industralized town: he was socially conservative, but financially liberal. He's most infamous for his gross mishandling of the protests around the **1968 Democratic Convention**. When a group of antiwar demonstrators, who'd turned up as part of a so-called "Festival of Life" organized by counter-culturalists the Yippies, started to protest outside the convention, local police steamed into the crowd and brutalized them in an incident that came to be known as the **Battle of Chicago**. When eight demonstrators were arraigned in federal court the following year, the circus-like trial mesmerized the media and demonized Daley; eventually, all eight were found not guilty of inducing a riot.

Despite this debacle, Daley made many valuable contributions to the city: he was a great builder, if not a sensitive handler of his staff or opponents. He poured money into the Loop, and managed to keep Chicago solvent in the 1970s when cities like New York, Detroit, Cleveland and Philadelphia were hobbled by their financial troubles. Daley's most visionary act was the attention he lavished on hitherto forgotten Douglas Aircraft field; the city had purchased it in 1946, but left it languishing until Daley realized that a great city like Chicago needed a world-class airport. He thus became the driving force behind the development of **O'Hare airport**, as the field had been renamed, the largest airport in the United States when it opened and decades later still one of the busiest in the world. Incidentally, its call letters – ORD – derive from its original name, Orchard Airport, when it was under ownership by Douglas.

Chicago today

Both supporters and opponents of Daley were shocked when he died in office in 1976: this political hiccup was compounded when his spunky protégée **Jane**

Byrne ran for mayor against the incompetent incumbent in 1979. She was desperately ill-suited to the job. A great headline grabber (Byrne moved into the deprived Cabrini Green projects for a short but highly publicized period), who'd pledged to fight the grinding wheels of the Machine, she was instead crushed by it and booted out of office by another Democrat, **Harold Washington** in 1983.

The city's first black mayor was an unwilling victor: he'd never wanted to run and had already incurred the wrath of the CCDP during his campaign. He won simply because the two other candidates – Byrne and **Richard J. Daley**, Daley senior's son – split the white vote. Nearly three-quarters of African Americans in Chicago voted during his election, and one precinct on the South Side even called the Board of Elections in mid-afternoon and asked if they should close, since everyone registered in that ward had already voted. Sadly, Washington was a lame-duck mayor during his first term (the CCDP opposed everything he supported and vice versa); when he won for a second time, Washington was slowly achieving a constructive political consensus when, like Daley, he unexpectedly dropped dead in office.

Since then, it's been Daley Jr all the way: unlike his father, he's a CEO-style mayor, delegating duties and running the city like a corporation. It's a smart move in a place that has always been driven by commerce and, as a city, has always been run by big business. There was shock locally when, in the 1990 census, Los Angeles' population finally eclipsed Chicago's and seized second place to New York; in fact, with its second-city moniker stolen, in some ways the city's still searching for a new identity. Ironically, the one factor that proved such a boon to the burgeoning Chicago – its location in the center of the North American continent – is an albatross for any city that has international ambitions. **Boeing's** recent decision to switch its headquarters from Seattle thus has to be considered a coup, as the city tries to chart its course in twenty-first century America.

Architecture

I n a prize fight of great buildings between America's biggest cities, there's no question that Chicago would win by a knockout, thanks both to sheer volume and variety. The devastation of the Great Fire proved to be every megalomaniac architect's dream, and grand-thinking men flocked here from around the country for the unlimited opportunities in innovation it afforded. The story of Chicago's buildings since the Great Fire – and of its leading role in world architecture – centers mainly around four men: William Le Baron Jenney, Louis Sullivan, Frank Lloyd Wright and Mies van der Rohe (although numerous others were on hand to contribute; see the box below for short bios on all, along with their career highlights).

The Chicago Style

The revolutionary style that appeared in Chicago in the wake of the fire, which came to be known as the **Chicago School of architecture**, was inspired by the city's status in the 1870s: it was the capital of America's heartland, isolated from the influence of the East Coast and Europe. Locals needed to rebuild, of course, but rather than replicate what had come before, they sought a signature architectural style that would embody the city's spirit of industry and efficiency. Being a wealthy city with no polite proscription against flashy uses of such wealth, as there was in cities like Boston and New York, Chicago was willing and able to try out fresh designs in its new downtown.

Local architectural innovations didn't work immediately, however – several early buildings like City Hall had such badly built foundations that they sank into the soft soil. Enter architect **William Le Baron Jenney** – already in town before the Great Fire to oversee urban planning projects, he gleefully turned his attention to downtown office space. It was Jenney who perfected the Chicago School's central innovation: the steel skeleton for high-rise buildings. Before then, in order to build a multistoried structure, architects incorporated monumentally thick walls at ground level, whose very thickness effectively limited the building's height. When Jenney produced the Home Insurance Building, at LaSalle and Adams streets (1883; now demolished), he designed what's acknowledged to have been the first modern skyscraper, using a metal structural skeleton to support its exterior walls on metal shelves, instead of thickening its lower walls.

Aside from making slimmer, taller buildings possible, Jenney's remarkable invention had several significant effects. Since the walls no longer bore the brunt of the massive structural strain, the masonry was opened up for windows, creating lighter, more livable office space. As well, the Chicago Style produced two new window treatments that fused form with function: oriel windows, bay windows that ran the height of a structure to emphasize its giddy verticalness (terrific examples can still be seen at the Fisher Building (see p.50); and the better-known Chicago windows, which had three sections – a huge fixed central pane and two smaller sash panes on either side to make cooling and heating more controllable (see the Marquette Building – p.51).

The man who was single-handedly responsible for the Chicago School's preoccupation with the idea that form should follow function (and whose

The men who built Chicago

Remarkably, many of the breathtaking buildings in the Loop were the work of just a handful of gifted architects. For easy reference, we've provided below brief biographies of the boldfaced names who built Chicago, noting their key works in and around the Loop.

DANIEL H. BURNHAM (1846–1912) was a forward-thinking architectural giant with an evangelical zeal for city planning, and one of the driving forces behind the City Beautiful Movement. He designed and oversaw the 1893 World's Columbian Exposition on Chicago's South Side and later exported his vision to other places, including Washington DC, and San Francisco. With his partner, John Wellborn Root, he designed the show-stopping **Rookery**, 209 S LaSalle St (p.54), known for its gorgeous light court. Burnham was also the mastermind behind the **Reliance Building**, at 32 N LaSalle (p.42), the world's first steel-framed building and a forerunner of today's giddying skyscrapers.

Although **BERTRAND GOLDBERG** (1913–97) was trained at the Bauhaus in Germany and thus influenced by Mies van der Rohe (see below), he soon found his own highly individual style. Technically eccentric, Goldberg saw rectilinear shapes as unnatural and so designed overwhelmingly circular buildings to encourage community and interaction. He also believed round structures had better wind resistance and provided more usable interior space. **Marina City** at 300 N State St is Goldberg's best-known work (p.67) – a controversial, mixed-use complex aptly nicknamed the Corncobs.

WILLIAM HOLABIRD (1854–1923) **AND MARTIN ROCHE** (1855-1927) met while working together in the offices of William Le Baron Jenney (see below). Together, they were pioneers of architecture's "Chicago School" and credited with popularizing the "Chicago window" – a fixed central pane flanked by moveable sash windows. The pair are remembered for the **Marquette Building**, 140 S Dearborn St (p.51); with its open facade and steel frame, it was the prototype for many modern office buildings. After the architects' deaths, the firm was taken over by Holabird's son **JOHN** (1886–1945); together with **JOHN WELLBORN ROOT JR** (1887–1963), son of Burnham's partner, the younger Holabird designed the one major Art Deco masterpiece downtown, the **Board of Trade**, at 141 W Jackson Blvd (p.54).

Though both **HELMUT JAHN** (1940–) and Mies van der Rohe (see below) were German expatriates drawn to Chicago by the Illinois Institute of Technology (the former to study there, the latter to help found it), their work could not be more different. Jahn's buildings are a playful counterpoint to Mies' minimalism, combining color, humor and reflective glass to convey energy and fun. His local masterpiece is

precepts still ricochet through design today) was **Louis Sullivan**. The moody but inspired architect was one of many major names to be employed by Jenney, soon after he arrived in town in 1873, but Sullivan transformed his mentor's ideas with a rule-breaking flair. He rejected the cookie-cutter concept that modern buildings should ape historic structures: instead of copying past work (whether his own or others), Sullivan worked on one-off designs for each client alongside his level-headed engineering partner Dankmar Adler. Sullivan & Adler's aesthetic was heavily influenced by the British Arts and Crafts school, which is why the firm's buildings often feature nature motifs and scrolling ironwork, as well as plentiful terra-cotta ornamentation. In fact, terra-cotta was a key material for all modern skyscrapers: steel skeletons risked melting in a the **James R. Thompson Center**, 100 W Randolph St (p.53), with its brightly colored atrium and curving facade.

WILLIAM LE BARON JENNEY (1832–1907) is known as the "father of the skyscraper." Originally from Massachusetts, Jenney came to Chicago in the 1860s to work on urban planning projects, including the railroad suburb of Riverside; after the Great Fire, though, he became heavily involved in the rebuilding of downtown. Yet despite his many technical achievements, his greatest impact was as mentor to many great architects of the late 1800s and early 1900s – Burnham, Holabird, Roche and Sullivan were all at one time employed by his firm. Don't miss the **Manhattan Building**, 431 S Dearborn St (p.50) – one of his earliest works that prefigures many later advances in structural engineering. Sadly, his 1883 Home Insurance Building at LaSalle and Adams streets – widely regarded as the "first skyscraper" because it used a metal skeleton to help support the exterior wall – no longer stands.

LUDWIG MIES VAN DER ROHE (1886–1969) was so influential that he's even spawned an adjective, "Miesian," to describe the work of the many architects who hero-worshipped him. German by birth, van der Rohe was the founder of the "International Style," a consummate modernist who fused classical proportions with sleek minimalism. Lured to Chicago to run a design school (and in the process escape the Nazis) in 1937, Mies went on to produce some of his best work there. The **Federal Center Complex**, 200 S Dearborn St (p.50), with its calm and ordered simplicity, is one of his masterpieces; for an account of another of his attention-grabbing designs, the jet-black **IBM building** (see p.67).

The rule-breaking genius of **LOUIS SULLIVAN** (1856–1924) spawned the revolutionary tenets that were the foundation of the "Chicago School" of architecture. Born in Boston, and trained at MIT and in Paris, Sullivan came to Chicago after the Great Fire to put into practice his maxim, "Form Follows Function" – which soon had many adherents among architects. Often working with brilliant engineer **DANKMAR ADLER** (1844–1900), he built masterpieces like the **Carson Pirie Scott** department store at 1 S State St (p.42). Note its practical, modular design and nature-inspired cast-iron decorations, among them a touch of the architect's ego – Sullivan's own initials (LHS), woven into the design.

Tiny, ornery **FRANK LLOYD WRIGHT** (1867–1959) is probably America's best-known architect, the man who single-handedly created the "Prairie style," with its open common spaces and flowing horizontal lines. Much of his work is in Chicago, notably Oak Park (see p.120) and Hyde Park (see p.114). His one notable project downtown was the remodeling of the **Rookery** in 1907 – the wonderfully airy atrium he oversaw during the renovations is well worth a detour.

fire, so early architects learned to fireproof them by covering the frame in flame-resistant, terra-cotta tiles.

Sullivan stood out from among his peers in the Chicago School, his love of decoration being unusual (and expensive) among his more commercially minded colleagues. Contemporary firms like Burham & Root or Holabird & Roche were known for their simple and similar designs, often co-operating on single buildings, which had the effect of giving the Chicago School a pleasing and powerful uniformity. Only one other person – one of Sullivan's former employees – would prove to have an even greater impact on modern buildings, developing a new residential style that swept America in the early twentieth century: Frank Lloyd Wright.

The Prairie style

Frank Lloyd Wright was an ambitious young architect from Wisconsin who moved with his mother to Oak Park in the Chicago suburbs in 1887. He started as a draftsman in the architectural office of Joseph Lyman Silsbee, quitting that job when he discovered that his colleague George Maher (who designed the Pleasant Home, another early Prairie-style building – see p.124) made more money than he did. He then snagged a position in Louis Sullivan's firm, though he was soon fired for moonlighting on his own projects (the clash of both men's moody artistic temperaments can't have helped either). But Sullivan's fascination with nature - and his dedication to functional buildings – would make a lasting impression on his youthful ex-employee. Wright set up on his own, in a small studio in Oak Park – a savvy move, as he was taking commissions from his neighbors in what was one of the wealthiest suburbs of the city. From there, he never looked back and rapidly became arguably America's most famous architect.

Wright's style echoes Sullivan's version of the Chicago School. Many of Wright's designs feature heavily ornamented stained-glass windows, whose abstract patterns owe much to Sullivan's swirling terra-cotta and ironwork. Wright also believed in blurring the line between man-made structures and nature – hence the large porches or open entranceways he often designed, which blend indoors and out, and even the tree that grows through his home

△ Detail of cast-iron grill, Carson Pirie Scott building

and studio. Wright was similarly passionate in his belief that form should follow function, and he designed houses where the flow from room to room would create a cozy but open atmosphere. These flowing designs prefigured modern multiuse spaces, as Wright installed wide archways instead of the doors that connected the honeycomb of box-like rooms in most Victorian houses. (This was also a reaction to a general shift toward an informal living style, plus innovations in central heating that reduced the costs of heating whole houses.)

Like the Chicago School, Wright was inspired by his Midwest surroundings, but while predecessors like Jenney had looked skyward to create precipitous buildings that would embody the city's efficiency and wealth, Wright turned to the wide, flat prairies of farmland for ideas, in the process creating the first all-American residential style.

Wright's status as a national icon has eclipsed how stubborn a man he was; indeed, his unbending nature was one of the reasons many of his designs have aged poorly. Wright's aversion to including downspouts meant that water gushing from the roof has frequently damaged ground level concrete. Similarly, the forced-air heating system he designed for the Unity Temple in Oak Park broke down as soon as it was activated and makeshift radiators were installed that have clunked and gurgled their way through services ever since.

But it's undeniable that the Prairie style changed the face of American residential architecture; occasionally, Wright even worked on commercial buildings, like the gracefully columned S.C. Johnson & Sons' headquarters in Wisconsin or his last, most famous commission, the whirly white Guggenheim Museum in New York. As well, his legacy has reached far beyond America: Wright's former employee Walter Burley Griffin entered (and won) a contest to design a new capital for Australia and moved there to oversee the city – known as Canberra – in 1914, taking the Prairie style's precepts with him.

The International Style and today

While Wright was transforming American homes, there was no guiding hand to architecturally oversee Chicago's commercial structures. The early twentieth century was a directionless period, when a hodge-podge of styles invaded downtown, from the Neo-Gothic Tribune Tower to the Art Deco Board of Trade (designed by the firm of Holabird & Root, both sons of key members in the Chicago School). This all changed with the arrival in the city of an architecturally gifted German refugee, **Mies van der Rohe**, in 1938.

Summed up by his motto "Less is more" and "God is in the details," Mies van der Rohe honed his minimalist style while director of the Bauhaus design school in Germany. Faced with few prospects under the Nazis, he left Germany in the late 1930s to run the architectural program of the Armour Institute of Technology on Chicago's Near South Side. It was a fateful assignment: practical, no-nonsense Chicago was an ideal match for the pragmatic architect, who soon established a private practice; his first project was redesigning the school itself, which had changed its name to the Illinois Institute of Technology. Soon, he was working on skyscrapers in America's post-war economic boom, and for almost thirty years, his modernist International Style helped define America's urban landscape.

This influential style derived much from the simplicity and functionality of the Chicago School: both are known for their lack of ornamentation, flat walls and user-friendliness. But Mies and his followers also mixed in a healthy helping of Frank Lloyd Wright: thanks to technological advances, they were able to open up the floor plans in skyscrapers as Wright had in homes, wrap windows round corners (a project Wright struggled with throughout his life) and emphasize horizontal lines even in tall buildings. The signature flourish of the International Style was to paint a building white, further underscoring its lack of ornamentation. Another skill Mies shared with Wright was furniture design, but while the latter's chairs feature primarily in museums (since few people would choose to sit on them voluntarily), Mies' designs – most famously the Barcelona armchair – continue to be reproduced for sale today.

Mies still looms large over Chicago, even after his death in 1969, whether in the firm of Skidmore, Owings & Merrill, whose Miesian designs include the Sears Tower, or in the work of Helmut Jahn, who aggressively rejects Mies principles in favor of whimsical, oddball buildings like the James R. Thompson Center.

Two modern structures exemplify Chicago's continued openness to architectural experimentation, one gloriously successful, the other an embarrassingly costly mistake. The Smurfit-Stone building (1983) is the former, its diamond-shaped, sloping roof makes it a stylish, idiosyncratic addition to the skyline and, like New York City's Empire State Building, the colors in which it's illuminated at night change according to season. The latter is the eighty-story Amoco Building (1973), now officially known as the Aon Center: less than ten years after its completion, the imported Italian marble – brought from the same quarry as Michelangelo's *David*, no less – started warping and falling off; no one, apparently, had thought about the effect of Chicago's bitter winters on the stone. It cost the shortsighted owners a staggering $60 million in the early 1990s to replace the marble with tougher pale granite.

Chicago blues

Chicago has been nearly as central to the evolution of modern **blues** as New York was to the evolution of modern jazz. While far from the only area where country blues musicians started to plug in, it was where more decided to do so than anywhere else. Throughout the first half of the 1900s, blacks poured into Chicago from the South, bringing with them the music of their birthplaces, yet also needing to adapt to the ways of the big city. It took a while before loud, stinging electric guitar leads, harmonicas and a hard-hitting rhythm section became the law of the land. Once this format had established supremacy in the 1950s, though, it pretty much stuck, characterizing not just Chicago blues but most electric blues worldwide.

Early Chicago blues

Between 1900 and 1960, the black population of Chicago increased from about 30,000 to over 800,000. Many of them came from the South, especially Mississippi; by 1930, Chicago had more Mississippi-born residents than any other town outside of Mississippi. Displaced southerners wanted to hear the kind of blues music they had grown up with, and gravitated toward performers from the lands they had left. At the same time, relocated southern musicians were adapting their styles to the northern way of life, playing louder and at a more energetic pace. Chicago blues became more urban throughout the 1930s and early 1940s via fuller ensembles, a more pronounced beat and some early ventures into amplification.

The most important figure of early Chicago blues was not a performer, but producer/A&R director **Lester Melrose**. Melrose built a stable of Chicago's leading talent under one umbrella, arranging for two major labels, Columbia and Victor, to record **Big Bill Broonzy**, **Memphis Minnie**, **Tampa Red**, **Washboard Sam**, **Big Joe Williams**, **Arthur "Big Boy" Crudup**, **John Lee "Sonny Boy" Williamson** and **Bukka White** (much of the music was released on the Bluebird label, a subsidiary of Victor, and thus referred to as "the Bluebird beat"). By using this pool of musicians to back up each other in the studio, Melrose created a "house sound" of sorts, a concept that in the decades to come would be widely applied both within and outside of the blues field. He aimed for a band sound, using not just guitar but also piano, and often a bass and washboard or drums for a rhythm section.

Modern listeners may find the Melrose/Bluebird beat stuff tame even in comparison with the early Chess sides of a few years later, yet they were directly influential upon the performers that would up the wattage. Big Bill Broonzy, who linked folk and blues styles, was a key inspiration on Muddy Waters, who would record a tribute album to Broonzy in the 1960s. John Lee "Sonny Boy" Williamson was crucial in making the harmonica a viable lead instrument in blues. A southern musician, Rice Miller, would call himself Sonny Boy Williamson after John Lee was murdered in 1948; causing never-ending confusion among record-buyers, Miller recorded his own influential body of work for Chess in the 1950s and 1960s as "Sonny Boy Williamson," and blues reference books have to resort to calling John Lee Williamson "Sonny Boy Williamson I" and Rice Miller "Sonny Boy Williamson II." **Big**

Maceo was the king of the early Chicago blues piano players with his forcefully direct style, often accompanied by guitarist Tampa Red; his trademark tune was "Worried Life Blues," a core nugget of the fatalistic blues repertoire.

Muddy Waters and Chess Records

Lester Melrose seemed to have locked up the Chicago blues market, but after World War II changes in the music business and society made the Bluebird beat sound passé. Independent companies were spurting up to challenge the Columbia/Victor dominance, and a more amplified, rhythm-and-blues-oriented sound was ascendant. One of these labels was **Chess Records**, and after some false starts it would become a power in the R&B market with the electric Chicago sound, particularly with transplanted Mississippian **Muddy Waters**.

Waters was well known as a young blues player in Mississippi, where he was recorded for the Library of Congress by folklorist Alan Lomax in the early 1940s. His decision to move to Chicago in 1943 was typical of the circumstances that led many to pack up their bags: a dispute with the boss over his sharecropping wages led him to try his luck up north, where discrimination was not so rife and economic opportunity better. Muddy at first found work as a truck driver, but his heart was in playing the blues, as he moonlighted at rent parties and clubs. Like musicians all over the country, he was finding that amplification and a band were needed to make himself heard in urban crowds. Waters didn't dilute his Mississippi Delta blues slide and moaning vocals; he just fleshed them out and made them louder. In a way this was a throwback to a sound that predated the Lester Melrose stable, but it had a clear bite and power that was modern and more forceful.

Waters made his first recordings (unissued at the time) for Melrose, but found a more sympathetic outlet when he began recording for Aristocrat, a label run by brothers **Phil and Leonard Chess**, which was making some tentative forays into the blues market. His 1948 single "I Can't Be Satisfied"/"I Feel Like Going Home" wasn't much different from what he had sung in the Delta; in fact he had cut both songs under different titles for his Library of Congress sessions. Now he had the urban market, however, and the single became an R&B hit, to be followed by other classics like "Long Distance Call" and "Rollin' Stone." Despite his success, his studio sound lagged behind the advances he had made as a live performer, heading a full band; still, reluctant to tinker with the winning format of "I Can't Be Satisfied," the Chess brothers – who had changed the name of their label to Chess by 1950 – recorded Muddy almost as a solo artist, with only a string bass to accompany him. Waters was on the verge of leaving Chess when Leonard Chess relented and starting using a full band, with guitars, harmonica, piano, bass and drums in the early 1950s.

If for nothing more than his records, Muddy Waters would be a blues giant – "Hoochie Coochie Man," "I Just Want to Make Love to You," "Mannish Boy," "Got My Mojo Working," and "Trouble No More" are classic staples of rock and blues setlists, and his B-sides and outtakes were scarcely less accomplished. In addition to being an excellent guitarist, he was more importantly a singer whose confidence suffered no fools, putting over both boasting and sorrowful lyrics with a last-word bearing, absent of any meekness or resignation. Waters also had an eye for assembling the best Chicago blues talent, and several of his sidemen would become star or respected solo artists, including guitarist Jimmy Rogers, pianist Otis Spann, and a slew of harmonica players: Little Walter, Junior Wells, James Cotton and Walter Horton.

More classic Chess blues

Chess is most associated with the sound of what in-the-know blues hounds call the four big Ws: Muddy Waters, Little Walter, Howlin' Wolf and Sonny Boy Williamson. It had a harsh (in the good sense of the word) sheen with upfront electric guitar leads and searing harmonica, propelled by a granite-hard, propulsive rhythm section. Like Sam Phillips at Sun Records, Chess added an otherworldly echo (with primitive tape delay) that, along with their skill at recording the instruments at slightly overamplified levels, added to the room-filling depth of the recordings.

Little Walter made his initial impression as harmonica player in Muddy Waters' band in the early 1950s, and started a solo career after his instrumental, "Juke," tore up the R&B charts in 1952. What Jimi Hendrix was to rock guitar, Little Walter was to blues harmonica, redefining the parameters of the instrument in a way that permanently changed how it was played, and has not been matched to this day. Walter used his harp like a horn, swooping and improvising jazzy phrases, amplifying it so that it could compete on equal terms with electric guitars, and boldly using the more complex chromatic harp to get tones and shadings that were impossible to coax out of standard models. On top of this he was a good singer with an arsenal of great material: the instantly memorable "My Babe" was his biggest hit, while "Mean Old World," "Mellow Down Easy," and "Off the Wall" weren't far behind. Although he was still a young man, he went into a dreadful artistic and health tailspin in the 1960s, culminating in death resulting from a street fight in 1968, aged only 37.

Howlin' Wolf was engaged in an ongoing battle with Muddy Waters for supremacy in the Windy City blues scene, and while he never dislodged Waters' unofficial crown, his raspy, haunted voice projected more charisma than any other classic Chicago blues stars did. Wolf was already well on his way to prominence with his recordings at Sun Studios in Memphis in the early 1950s, but after his move north his music grew in frightening intensity and hard-rocking drama. "Smokestack Lightning," "The Red Rooster" (aka "Little Red Rooster"), "Spoonful," "Wang Dang Doodle," and "I Ain't Superstitious" are delightfully bone-rattling performances removed from the reckless thrust of rock 'n' roll by only a thin margin, accounting for the entry of many of his songs into the sets of famous 1960s rock groups like the Rolling Stones and Cream.

Sonny Boy Williamson, aka Rice Miller, had already recorded and performed in Arkansas and Mississippi for a while before hooking up with Chess. In a brazen act of nerve he appropriated the name of the first, late John Lee "Sonny Boy" Williamson; unlike just about everybody else who tried similar tricks throughout the music biz, he got away with it, not least because his talent was equal to or greater than that of the original Sonny Boy. Less experimental and more country in his harmonica playing than Little Walter, Williamson was still a wizard at making wordless witty comments with his riffs. Already in his middle age when he began his stint at Chess, he was also a humorous yet wizened songwriter and vocalist, contributing his own stack of blues standards with tunes like "One Way Out," "Don't Start Me to Talkin'," "Eyesight to the Blind," and "Nine Below Zero."

The four Ws only represented a fraction of the company's blues output. Chess had some less adventurous piano-based blues hits with **Eddie Boyd** and **Willie Mabon**, and odd records with **J.B. Lenoir**, whose voice was so high-pitched that many mistook him for a woman, and who exhibited unusual sociopolitical consciousness on numbers like "Eisenhower Blues" and "Korea Blues." Part of the company's success was based on the presence of session musicians and songwriters that never became widely known to the public as recording artists. Even when signed to Chess as solo artists, some musicians would back up other performers; Little Walter, for instance, was appearing on Muddy Waters songs throughout the 1950s, long after he had made it on his own and stopped performing with Waters live. Drummer **Fred Below**, who appeared on many Chess sessions, was an unsung architect of rock 'n' roll, his jazzy, swinging backbeat laying part of the foundation for the steady, insistent rhythm that would take over popular music. No one was more important to Chicago blues' classic era than **Willie Dixon**, the songwriter who devised stone-cold greats for many of the Chess artists and other performers in the Chicago area: "Hoochie Coochie Man," "I Just Want to Make Love to You," "Back Door Man," "Wang Dang Doodle," "My Babe," "Spoonful," "Little Red Rooster," and "Pretty Thing" were all from his pen – and Dixon also found time to play bass on many sessions.

1950s blues

Chess was at the vanguard of a mini-explosion of Chicago independent labels that recorded blues in the 1950s. J.O.B., Chance, United/States, Parrot – none achieved anything like the success of Chess, and reissues of their material are far more sporadic, but they recorded fine blues records by solid Chicago bluesmen who weren't quite on the front line of the city's best, such as J.B. Lenoir, Johnny Shines, Sunnyland Slim, Walter Horton, Snooky Pryor and J.B. Hutto.

Aside from Chess, the most significant of the local labels recording blues was **Vee-Jay** (often abbreviated as VJ). Like Chess it wasn't limited to blues, also doing R&B and rock 'n' roll, but it did land two of the most prolific and popular blues singers of the era, **John Lee Hooker** (more appropriately part of the Detroit blues scene) and **Jimmy Reed**. Reed's success was based on his simplicity – he sang with an easygoing, unruffled charm over a steady, rockish beat decorated by simple but effective guitar figures and harmonica riffs. Another fine VJ performer was harmonica player and vocalist **Billy Boy Arnold**, a Bo Diddley sideman whose frugal but stellar VJ output had thumping beats and charged guitar–harp interplay that could stray close to rock.

Most of the early Chicago blues was played in the city's **South Side**, but black neighborhoods were also spreading to the West Side neighborhood. In the 1950s a style of blues began to be identified with the West Side that was funkier and more modern in nature, in the mold of B.B. King, than the entrenched South Side approach, sometimes using saxophones. **Cobra** was a notable short-lived West Side blues label, employing Willie Dixon as its musical director when the great songwriter and arranger left Chess for a while in the late 1950s. Cobra's jewel was guitarist **Otis Rush**, the most skilled blues artist bar none when it came to working in minor keys, whose anguished vocals were complemented by devilish twisting riffs that both thrill the ears and give you the hives. "Double Trouble," "I Can't Quit You, Baby," and "All Your Love" were instant standards, yet Rush, only in his early twenties when he made his Cobra singles, has never been able to fully capitalize upon his genius. Throughout the 1960s and the first half of the 1970s, he was dogged by lousy record deals that curtailed his studio opportunities. Still active today, he never seems to marshal resources for recording sessions that represent him to the best of his abilities.

Elmore James flitted from label to label often, and did not confine his base of operations to Chicago, also recording in Mississippi, New York and New Orleans over the course of his nomadic discography. He nevertheless rates as an all-time Chicago blues great, as he was the most influential electric slide blues guitarist of all time. "Dust My Broom," with its classic opening descending riff, had been around in the blues repertoire since Robert Johnson had cut it back in the 1930s. James was the guy who made it an instantly recognizable standard, though, giving the slide riff a gripping super-amped chill. Though he was to rely on this riff often, he did vary his slide style in interesting ways, creating a crying effect on slow burners like "The Sun Is Shining" and its close cousin "The Sky Is Crying." He died in 1963, too soon to see his immense impact upon 1960s rock: Brian Jones of the Rolling Stones was so besotted with James that he called himself "Elmo Lewis" in the pre-Stones days, and Jeremy Spencer of the original Fleetwood Mac based almost his entire style around James's licks.

Chuck Berry and Bo Diddley

In 1955, two Chess guitarists recorded a new brand of blues-rooted music that had the ironic effect of mostly driving hardcore blues off the charts for good. **Chuck Berry**, although from St Louis, recorded at Chess in Chicago, often with stalwart Chess musicians such as Willie Dixon and Fred Below. Berry was not as grounded in country-blues as most of the city's leading players; he was born in St Louis, not a plantation, and had absorbed the innovations of jump-blues stars like Louis Jordan and country and western singers. Slow down the tempo of his first single, "Maybellene," and you can imagine a hillbilly singer having a hit with it. In fact, it had started out as a demo called "Ida May" that bore some resemblance to a country tune called "Ida Red", recorded by Bob Wills. But "Maybellene" was rock 'n' roll pure and simple, with that sped-up backbeat and furiously riffing guitar.

Berry has defined much of the basic vocabulary of rock 'n' roll, not only in guitar riffs but in lyrical content, venturing into almost journalistic observations on the nuances and frustrations of teenage and young adult life, and celebrating the joys of rock 'n' roll itself. For the rest of the 1950s, he knocked off one classic after another: "Roll Over Beethoven," "Sweet Little Sixteen," "Rock & Roll Music," "School Day," "Johnny B. Goode," "Brown Eyed Handsome Man," "Too Much Monkey Business" and "Carol" were some of the best. They were also inspirations for the best rockers of the 1960s – not just the Beatles and the Stones, but also Bob Dylan (whose "Subterranean Homesick Blues" is much like "Too Much Monkey Business") – to write and sing their own material.

Lagging far behind Berry in sales, **Bo Diddley** over time proved to be almost as influential. A wild and wacky guitar innovator, he produced oceanic layers of reverb from his ax that sounded like outer-space shock waves by 1950s standards. Like Berry he was a witty songwriter with acute powers of observation, but while Berry kept a detached ironic eye on things Diddley yukked it up like life was just one big put-on. Diddley too was a great performer: Elvis Presley was said to have studied Bo's act closely, and Diddley featured oddly shaped guitars (most famously a square model) and acrobatic antics that anticipated Jimi Hendrix's even bolder moves along those lines in the late 1960s.

Yet above and beyond his deeper skills, Bo Diddley's trademark is his beat. Described sometimes as a "hambone" or "shave-and-a-haircut," its bomp, ba-bomp-bomp, bomp-bomp pattern is one of the most irresistible rhythms known to humankind, and although Diddley used it over and over it didn't get tiresome. Others adapted it for their own ends: Buddy Holly used it for "Not Fade Away," which when covered by the Rolling Stones gave them their first big British hit. It was that beat, and that wild guitar playing, that made it impossible to call Diddley a bluesman, even though his music was soaked right through with R&B feeling. He built a catalog of wonderful songs – "I'm A Man," "Bo Diddley," "You Can't Judge A Book By Its Cover," "Road Runner" and "Who Do You Love?" – that were ready-to-order for cover by bands all over the US and Britain.

Blues in transition: the 1960s

In the early 1960s blues had became a less significant part of the R&B singles market; rock 'n' roll had eaten into its audience since the mid-1950s, and soul music was beginning to gather steam. Both Chess and Vee-Jay were directing their resources toward their soul stars, and while there was still work for blues musicians in local clubs, there was less opportunity to record and innovate in the studio. However, a blues and folk revival was generating an interest among young, white Americans in blues music that had hitherto been confined to an almost exclusively black listenership; British rock bands were covering blues and R&B tunes, and bringing the original artists to the attention of young white listeners in the US and UK who had never heard the sources. The Rolling Stones were the biggest of such acts; to their credit they didn't limit themselves to covering tunes in their effort to bring their heroes into the spotlight, recording in Chess Studio on their first visit to the US in 1964 (and naming an instrumental, "2120 South Michigan Avenue," after the address of the Chess building), and having Howlin' Wolf guest on one of their television spots.

Other progress came in the form of how the music was recorded and packaged. **Junior Wells'** *Hoodoo Man Blues* (1965) was a departure in that it was hardcore modern Chicago blues recorded for the local Delmark label as an *album*, not a more or less random array of sessions. It was doubly significant for being the greatest Chicago blues recording of its time. Harmonica player Wells had been on the scene since the early 1950s, doing time in the Muddy Waters band and recording some fine sides as a leader on several labels. Like several of the younger veterans of the 1950s scene, he was not averse to adding some irreverent rock and soul flourishes to his sound. The result took the Chicago blues in new, exciting directions, Wells sometimes coming on like a blues James Brown on cuts like "Snatch It Back And Hold It," bluesing up rock tunes like "Hound Dog," even putting in a Latin influence on "Chitlin Con Carne." The band on the album was tops, too, especially guitarist **Buddy Guy**, who was eventually to have an amazing rebirth in the 1990s, chalking up a bunch of

Grammies with new recordings and establishing one of the city's best blues clubs, *Buddy Guy's Legends*.

Harmonica player **James Cotton**, yet another alumnus of the Waters band, made some fine assertive soul-rock-blues in the late 1960s and was one of the most dependable fixtures of the live blues circuit through the 1990s, although he was always more impressive as an instrumentalist than as a singer. **Magic Sam** was the most mature exponent of the West Side sound, his finger-picked tremolo guitar and R&B-ish material marking him as one of the more versatile performers in the city. He had short hitches with several labels before finding a home on Delmark, where he made a couple of assured albums that found a satisfying midpoint between the soul-flavored direction the blues was being pulled towards, and the loose-limbed spontaneity more characteristic of the 1950s. Unfortunately, he died unexpectedly of heart trouble in 1969, only 32 years of age.

At the same time as young whites were beginning to listen to the blues, young whites were beginning to play the blues, not just in Britain but also in Chicago. The local white blues acts tended to be well-meaning but stiff interpreters of the form, the exception being the **Paul Butterfield Blues Band** (which was actually integrated, though its front line was white). Butterfield was only an adequate singer, but a fine harmonica player; his group was more noteworthy for two exceptional guitarists, **Mike Bloomfield** and **Elvin Bishop**. The Butterfield band played lean and mean, and were more open to rock and soul influences than most African-American bluesmen, as was especially evident in Bloomfield and Bishop's fiery solos; a black rhythm section that had played with Howlin' Wolf refuted accusations of inauthenticity.

Although Chess's glory days as a blues powerhouse had passed, the label did record some quality blues in the 1960s. Howlin' Wolf and Muddy Waters made some good sides through 1965 or so, Buddy Guy spent his early career there, and Chicago's best woman blues singer, **Koko Taylor**, got her start at Chess. A tough and swaggering belter in the mold of the most aggressive blueswomen, such as Big Mama Thornton, Taylor's anthem was Willie Dixon's "Wang Dang Doodle." Originally recorded by Howlin' Wolf in 1960, Taylor made the hard-partying song her own and even got to #4 in the R&B charts with it in 1966, when top-selling blues singles had become a rarity. That didn't guarantee an easy ride for Taylor, who in the early 1970s was working as a maid to make ends meet. A long-running association with Alligator Records from the mid-1970s onwards, though, solidified her reign as the queen of the Chicago blues.

Modern Chicago blues

In the last generation, Chicago blues has adopted a brassier polish than its previous incarnations, both figuratively (in its good-time strutting) and literally (in the frequent deployment of horns in addition to guitars and a rhythm section). Soul, rock and funk shadings have become more prominent than they were in the 1960s; the tempo has generally become slower and funkier, and the vocals more cocksure. The good-natured, sometimes carefree and boasting tone of much current Chicago blues could perhaps be said to mirror the improved lot of blacks in America in general; sure there's a long way to go before justice is achieved for all, but the social and economic oppression of today's African Americans is not as severe as it was earlier in the 1900s.

The label mostly responsible for giving both old-timers and newbloods a chance to record is **Alligator**, founded in the early 1970s. In addition to giving steady exposure to artists like Son Seals that had somehow missed out on studio opportunities, it also revitalized the careers of veterans like Koko Taylor, James Cotton and Billy Boy Arnold. Over the years it expanded its roster to include blues artists from all over the country, but Chicago performers remain central to its release schedule. Alligator's best records (aside from those by Koko Taylor) have been by guitarists. Its first release, by **Hound Dog Taylor**, was a throwback to the spontaneous, just-short-of-sloppy club and juke-joint blues of the 1950s, albeit with fuzzier tones, in a no-nonsense trio featuring Taylor's slide guitar. **Son Seals** was more a man for the times, speaking both through lengthy, feverish solos and gruff, unruffled vocals, using a funky bottom and beefy horn section. **Fenton Robinson**, whose "Somebody Loan Me A Dime" had already been exposed to rock listeners through Boz Scaggs' cover version, was a notable example of Alligator giving a proper chance to an artist who had only been able to record here and there. Other notable Chicago guitarists who took time-honored yet updated styles to a fairly wide audience were slide guitarist **Lil' Ed Williams** (of **Lil' Ed & the Blues Imperials**); **Jimmy Johnson** and **Eddy Clearwater**, who could uncannily approximate vintage Chuck Berry.

Since the 1970s, Chicago blues has been in the best of times and the worst of times. On the positive side, general public awareness of the blues is higher than ever, particularly among whites, with clubs featuring blues mostly or occasionally springing up in Chicago and all over the US. On the negative side, the form has grown stale as fewer and fewer young African Americans dedicate themselves to the style, as either listeners or musicians. Its original audience has changed too: blues is still played in some South Side joints, but the real popular clubs are on the affluent north side, drawing white patrons almost exclusively. Rock, soul and then rap music siphoned off a lot of talent as trends changed, and musicians in the blues field are now well aware that, with rare exceptions, they will be playing and selling to a specialist market that's a small slice of the industry pie. Chicago blues, like New Orleans jazz and R&B, is in something of a preservationist mode. There's lots of competent, energetic electric blues in classic styles for locals and tourists to enjoy, on stage and on record, but the time of greatest artistic innovation seems gone. Changing public tastes are only part of the reason: the blues is a more rigidly defined style than most American popular styles, and it's difficult to make an original statement when its boundaries and signature riffs have been so firmly laid down.

Discography

The following is a select list of essential blues recordings, which should all be available on CD.

Billy Boy Arnold *I Wish You Would* (Charly). Both sides of Arnold's six Vee-Jay singles from the mid-1950s, plus a couple of rare bonus items. An underrated source point for blues-rock with its propulsive beat and riffs, especially on "I Wish You Would" and "I Ain't Got You."
Chuck Berry *His Best Vol. 1 & 2* (Chess). Almost every song on this pair of twenty-track anthologies is

immediately familiar; if you haven't heard the original version, you've heard it covered by someone. Besides the big hits like "Sweet Little Sixteen," "Maybellene," "Johnny B. Goode" et al, there are relatively undiscovered secondary goodies like "Little Queenie," "Oh Baby Doll," and "I Want To Be Your Driver."
Big Maceo *The King of the Chicago Blues Piano* (Arhoolie). Twenty-five

sides from 1941 to 1945, sometimes with bass and drums, and even some electric guitar.

Bo Diddley *The Chess Box* (Chess). Two CDs that don't even get to all of his first-rate waxings, but it does have most of 'em: "Bo Diddley," "I'm A Man," "Pretty Thing," "Diddy Wah Diddy," "Who Do You Love?," "Road Runner," "You Can't Judge A Book By Its Cover," "Mona," and hidden treasures like "Down Home Special" and "You Don't Love Me." For less dough there's the single-disc *His Best*, which sticks to the most celebrated tunes.

Buddy Guy *The Very Best of* (Rhino). Serviceable eighteen-song best-of doesn't reach into his 1990s comeback phase, but covers highlights from the late 1950s to the early 1980s, including some Chess sides and supersession-ish tracks with guest spots by Junior Wells, Dr John, Bill Wyman and Eric Clapton.

Howlin' Wolf *His Best* (Chess). Twenty tracks from the 1950s and 1960s, with a lineup including "Spoonful," "Smokestack Lightning'," "Wang Dang Doodle," "Back Door Man," "The Red Rooster," "Killing Floor" and "'I Ain't Superstitious." Great stuff that's simultaneously scarifying and exhilarating, and even if you're familiar with the above tunes you'll also be blown away by more obscure items like "Shake For Me," which has some of the snakiest blues guitar playing ever.

Elmore James *The Sky Is Crying: The History of Elmore James* (Rhino). Collecting James can be frustrating, as he recorded for numerous labels and did multiple versions of some of his best tunes. This smart 21-song compilation of 1951–61 material has the essentials, including the first "Dust My Broom," "The Sun Is Shining," "The Sky Is Crying," "Shake Your Moneymaker" and "It Hurts Me Too."

J.B. Lenoir *Vietnam Blues: The Complete L&R Recordings* (Evidence). Lenoir was a solid journeyman Chicago bluesman in the 1950s, and grew remarkably as a songwriter in the 1960s, exploring Vietnam and racial discrimination with a directness rare in the blues; he also went to an acoustic format with minimal, almost African percussion. These mid-1960s recordings, still largely unknown even in blues circles (they were only available in Europe for a long time), are an intriguing glimpse into a road seldom taken.

Little Walter *The Essential Little Walter* (Chess). Two CDs of Little Walter is not too much, even if you're not a blues specialist. Besides ace standards like "Boom, Boom Out Goes The Light," "My Babe" and "Mellow Down Easy," there's a bounty of hidden gems like the virtuosic bop-jazzy instrumental "Fast Large One," the classic minor-key downer blues "Blue And Lonesome" and just plain-hot party blues like "Too Late" and "It Ain't Right."

Jimmy Reed *Speak The Lyrics To Me, Mama Reed* (Vee-Jay). There have been, and will always be, a bunch of Jimmy Reed best-of compilations on the market that largely duplicate each other in track selection. This 25-song one is about the best, with the familiar hits and some less overexposed songs.

Otis Rush *His Cobra Recordings, 1956–1958* (Paula). All sixteen of the tracks Rush officially released on Cobra, plus four alternate takes. Most of this is also on the two-CD box *The Cobra Records Story* (Capricorn), which adds some interesting material from the same vintage by Magic Sam, Buddy Guy, Walter Horton, Sunnyland Slim and others.

Hound Dog Taylor *Hound Dog Taylor & The Houserockers* (Alligator). From the first dirty-amped run of notes, this is Chicago blues at its rawest, in a boogieing trio style that never gets too fussy or shambling. It's much more together and enjoyable, by the way, than the somewhat similar minimal Mississippi juke-joint blues that has gotten so much attention in the 1990s.

Koko Taylor *What It Takes: The Chess Years* (Chess). Eighteen cuts from 1964 to 1971, including "Wang Dang Doodle" and other cuts reinforcing her persona as a woman not be messed with.

Muddy Waters *His Best, 1947 to 1955* (Chess). Great twenty-song compilation is mostly killer – "I Can't Be Satisfied, "I Feel Like Going Home," "Rollin' Stone," "Hoochie Coochie Man," "I'm Ready," "Trouble No More" – and also charts his progress from the spare near-Delta blues of his first recordings to the full-bore electric sound of the mid-1950s. Also worthwhile is the next installment, *His Best, 1956 to 1964* (Chess), which has material not quite as well known, including "You Need Love" (the riff of which was nicked by Led Zeppelin for "Whole Lotta Love").

Junior Wells *Hoodoo Man Blues* (Delmark). From the opening crash of "Snatch It Back And Hold It," this varied set grabs your gut and doesn't let go, Wells blowing his harp feverishly and working the vocals like a soul showman while Guy drives things along with sharp and snazzy blues licks. Blues albums don't come any better than this.

Sonny Boy [John Lee] Williamson *Sugar Mama* (Indigo). Twenty-four songs from 1937 to 1942, including one, "Good Morning School Girl," that became one of the all-time blues standards, covered by everyone from Junior Wells to the Grateful Dead.

Sonny Boy Williamson [aka Rice Miller] *His Best* (Chess). To-the-point twenty-song anthology

that zeroes in on his most essential output: "Born Blind," "Your Funeral And My Trial," "Down Child," "Help Me," "One Way Out" and "Bye Bye Bird" just for starters.

Various Artists *The Alligator Records 20th Anniversary Collection* & *The Alligator Records 25th Anniversary Collection* (Alligator). Two double-CD retrospectives of Alligator's output. This doesn't stick solely to Chicago artists, but a lot are on these compilations, including Son Seals, Koko Taylor, James Cotton, Fenton Robinson, Hound Dog Taylor, Billy Boy Arnold, Carey Bell, Big Walter Horton, and Jimmy Johnson.

Various Artists *Blues Masters, Vol. 2: Postwar Chicago* (Rhino). Decent introductory sampler of tracks from 1950 to 1961 within and without Chess, by legends like Howlin' Wolf, Muddy Waters, Little Walter, Jimmy Reed, Buddy Guy and Junior Wells, as well as significant artists such as J.B. Lenoir, Robert Jr Lockwood, Earl Hooker and Jody Williams.

Various Artists *The Chess Blues-Rock Songbook* (Chess). This is what you want to have handy if you're dead set on putting someone straight about all the Chess artists who cut original versions of songs that sold a lot more units after getting covered by white guys. Classics like "Spoonful," "I Just Want To Make Love To You," "Johnny B. Goode," and less obvious choices like John Brim's "Ice Cream Man" and Willie Mabon's "The Seventh Son," let the music do the talking.

Various Artists *Chicago: The Blues Today!, Vols. 1–3* (Vanguard). Important series of compilations that documented the mid-1960s Chi-town blues scene with cuts by enjoyable second-line artists such as J.B. Hutto, Otis Spann, Homesick James, Big Walter Horton and Johnny Young, as well as tracks by Junior Wells and Otis Rush.

Adapted from *The Rough Guide to Music USA* (1999), by Richie Unterberger.

Books

W here the books we recommend below are in print, the publisher's name is given in parentheses after the title: the US publisher's first, separated, where applicable, from the UK publisher by an oblique slash. Where books are published in only one of these countries, we have specified which one; when the same company publishes the book in both, it appears just once. Books available in only one country are usually easily ordered online at Amazon or similar sites. Books tagged with the ✳ symbol are particularly recommended.

History and society

Jane Addams, *Twenty Years at Hull-House* (US Signet). Reformer Addams tells the story of her upbringing and remarkable life working at the innovative settlement house she helped start in Chicago's industrial and impoverished West Side. A perceptive, extremely detailed account of the settlement's day-to-day struggles to improve the social conditions in the city's slums in the late nineteenth century.

✳ **Nelson Algren**, *Chicago: City on the Make* (US U of Chicago Press). Grittily lyrical time capsule highlighting the state of mid-twentieth century Chicago. Algren has deep affection for the city, but he also has an unsentimental determination to point out its social carbuncles. A must-read for anyone keen to understand the history of blue-collar Chicago.

Eliot Asinof, *Eight Men Out: The Black Sox and the 1919 World Series* (Henry Holt). Though little known now, this 1919 scandal – when the heavily favored White Sox threw the final game in the World Series in return for high bribes – rocked America after World War I. This brilliant book astutely examines the cause and effect of what the White Sox did, and frames the story with lashings of anecdotes. A terrific, revealing read, even for non-sports fans.

Adam Cohen and Elizabeth Taylor, *American Pharaoh: Mayor Richard J Daley, His Battle for Chicago & the Nation* (US Little, Brown & Co). Cohen and Taylor take Daley as touchstone for the city, cannily fusing his life story with the story of Chicago itself through the twentieth century. Readable enough, and strong on Daley's poor handling of race relations in the city, but Royko's book (see p.260) is better known and better.

Nadine Cohodas, *Spinning Blues into Gold* (US St Martins Press). A lively look at Chess Records, the blues label that began on the South Side of Chicago. Cohodas is strongest when examining the savvy marketing and business flair of the Chess brothers, but much weaker when analyzing the music they packaged in its cultural or musical context.

Robert Cromie, *The Great Chicago Fire* (US Rutledge Hill). Picture-packed recap of the Great Fire that's evocative with its imagery, but skimpy on substance – stick with Donald Miller's (see below) detailed, more serious approach if you're looking for hard facts about the fire.

David Farber, *Chicago '68* (US U of Chicago Press). Riproaring examination of the seminal event in Daley

Sr's tenure as mayor – the (mis)handling of hippie protests at the Democratic Convention of 1968. Farber evokes the energy and excitement of the time, though he trips slightly when trying to draw wider conclusions from the highly localized events.

Peter Golenbock, *Wrigleyville: A Magical History Tour of the Chicago Cubs* (US St Martin's Press). Riveting account of the lame-duck team in sports-mad Chicago: the Cubs have hobbled from season to season for almost fifty years while headline-grabbers like the Bears and the Bulls have basked in glory. This affectionate, anecdote-packed account of the team provides terrific insight into why and how it kept stumbling.

★ **Libby Hill**, *The Chicago River: A Natural and Unnatural History* (US Lake Claremont Press). This eclectic, unusual study follows the Chicago River from its origins through the interference in its flow by man to the present day. It's offbeat and highly readable, taking a refreshingly quirky approach to historical events.

★ **Blair Kamin**, *Tribune Tower* (US Tribune Co). The *Chicago Tribune*'s Pulitzer Prize-winning architecture critic has written a lovingly detailed, piercingly astute account of his owner's HQ. It's packed with sprightly stories and offers not only a glimpse at the story behind one of Chicago's best-loved buildings, but also an understanding of what happened to the city in the years between World Wars I and II.

Richard Lindberg, *To Serve & Collect* (US Southern Illinois U Press). White Sox historian Lindberg has produced a heavily researched, controversial account of the corrupt cops who populated Chicago's police system for more than a hundred years. His prose can tangle at times, and the text would have been shaped better by a sharper editor, but it's a worthwhile, if depressing, read.

Harold Mayer and Richard Wade, *Chicago: Growth of a Metropolis* (US U of Chicago Press). Coffee-table classic, filled with glossy pictures and a correspondingly airbrushed account of the city's evolution. Not the pithiest of histories perhaps, but fun to flick through.

Donald Miller, *City of the Century: The Epic of Chicago and the Making of America* (Simon & Schuster). Chicago's apogee was the nineteenth century, and this account of the city from its founding through 1899 takes in every major historical figure from Marquette to Marshall Field. Miller's obsession with detail is admirable, but it also rather clogs his rollicking story; he's on surest footing when writing about later events, notably the World's Columbian Exposition of 1893 and the Great Fire.

Dick W. Simpson, *Rogues, Rebels and Rubberstamps: The Story of Chicago City Council from the Civil War to the Third Millennium* (US Westview). Himself a former local alderman, Simpson brings an insider's relish to the story of America's most battle-scarred, corruption-blighted local government. Simpson's use of Chicago's infamous city council as a touchstone for larger political themes is sometimes questionable, and his prose can be clunky, but it's a fascinating story nonetheless.

Biography

John Kobler, *Capone: The Life and World of Al Capone* (US DaCapo Press). Punchy, ambivalent account of the world's greatest gangster, pepped up by a vivid eye for period detail and a refusal to make simple judgements. Capone's the part of its past that Chicago is most determined to forget, but Kobler's juicy biography fills in many of the blanks that the city leaves undiscussed.

Mike Royko, *Boss: Richard J. Daley of Chicago* (US New American Library). Local journalist Royko turns his take-no-prisoners sights on Chicago's mythical mayor. Given Royko's well-known antipathy towards his subject, he turns in a readable, surprisingly balanced account that documents the inner workings of the local Democratic party's Machine.

Robert Schoenberg, *Mr Capone* (Quill/Robson Books). A more scholarly, sober-minded take of Capone's myth than Kobler's thrill-ride, this biography adds much on Capone's pre- and post-Chicago lives – from his birth in Brooklyn to his syphilis-riddled final years in Miami. Schoenberg's prose is sprightly enough to keep his story pacey despite wads of detail. Arguably the definitive account of Capone and his times.

★ **Robert Spinney,** *City of Big Shoulders* (US Northern Illinois UP). A brisk survey of city history from its founding to today and one of the best introductions to the city. It's an easier read than Miller's much lauded tome (see p.259), and makes quicker, punchier points about the city's urban evolution. Highly recommended.

Travel, journalism and impressions

Mike Royko, *One More Time: The Best of Mike Royko* (US U of Chicago Press). The Pulitzer Prize-winning columnist chronicled the foibles and follies of the powerful for more than thirty years; this book brings together some of his pithiest, most enjoyable rants and shows anyone unfamiliar with his work why his name is legend in Chicago. There is another collection of his columns called *For the Love of Mike: More of the Best of Mike Royko*.

★ **Studs Terkel,** *Division Street: America* (US New Press). Terkel's the undisputed chronicler of the voice of working-class Chicago – and his reputation was founded on this absorbing, extraordinary book. His first-person interviews with men and women, black and white, as they tell the story of their lives in the city are unputdownable. For a similarly absorbing collection of personal testimonies from working Chicagoans, read Terkel's *Working: People Talk About What They Do All Day and How They Feel About What They Do* (Random House).

Architecture, music and photography

Willie Dixon with Don Snowden, *I Am the Blues* (Da Capo). The autobiography of the greatest behind-the-scenes architect of modern blues doesn't have as many absorbing stories as hoped. Still, producer, arranger, bassist and songwriter Dixon offers some fascinating insights into the gestation of numerous classic recordings.

David Lowe, *Lost Chicago* (US Watson-Gupthill). Splendid pictorial record – with more than 250 illustrations – of the city's vanished architecture. Spanning the early nineteenth century through the twentieth century, historian Lowe engagingly, and in great detail, dwells on the grand mansions, stockyards, skyscrapers, movie houses and magnificent train stations that helped shape Chicago's architectural legacy.

Mike Rowe, *Chicago Blues* (Da Capo). Originally titled *Chicago Breakdown*, this can get too detailed for the uncommitted blues fanatic, but has a wealth of information on Chicago blues from the 1930s to the 1960s. It includes background on all the big and small Chicago blues labels and all of the city's major classic blues artists, as well as lots of minor ones. Cool vintage photos, too.

★ **Pauline A. Saliga** (ed), *The Sky's the Limit – A Century of Chicago Skyscrapers* (US Rizzoli). Lushly illustrated, exhaustive survey of Chicago's significant buildings, emphasizing those that still stand over demolished masterpieces. Useful, detailed background for sightseeing, especially on modernist structures from the 1970s and 1980s.

Franz Schulze and Kevin Harrington (eds), *Chicago's Famous Buildings: A Photography Guide to the City's Architectural Landmarks and* *Other Notable Buildings* (US U of Chicago Press). Regularly updated pocket guide to Chicago. Though the descriptions are a bit brief, each entry is accompanied by a black and white photo. Buildings have been organized by geographical location, including a number in the suburbs.

★ **Alice Sinkevitch** (ed), *AIA Guide to Chicago* (Harvest/Harcourt). Pocket-sized encyclopedia on local buildings, useful mostly for its detailed maps and brief but detailed essays on the city's most important structures. It's let down somewhat by the fact that every entry isn't accompanied by a corresponding photograph.

Susan Sirefman, *Chicago: A Guide to Recent Architecture* (Artemis/Ellipsis). This palm-size guide manages to squeeze in a diverse crop of notable buildings (one hundred in all), built in Chicago within the last decade – from major office towers to houses and restaurants, and even *McDonald's* hamburger university. Crisp black and white photographs accompany architect Sirefman's concise text.

Sandra B. Tooze, *Muddy Waters: The Mojo Man* (ECW Press). Competent and lengthy bio of the pre-eminent Chicago blues musician, covering his life thoroughly from his Delta days to his ascendancy to stardom on Chess Records and his final years as a revered elder statesman, but it doesn't catch fire as often as you'd expect.

Fiction and poetry

Nelson Algren, *The Neon Wilderness* (Seven Stories Press). Think of Algren's short stories as what Hemingway might have written about Chicago had he not fled the city as soon as he was able. Not the most uplifting collection, but the muscular, no-nonsense style and punchy stories are still a knockout.

Of Algren's other titles, the best is probably *The Man with a Golden Arm.*

★ **Saul Bellow**, *The Adventures of Augie March* (Knopf/Penguin). Given what a grumpy curmudgeon Bellow himself has become, it's refreshing to read this early novel with its relentless optimistic hero.

Dickensian in scope, it echoes Dickens in its sometimes knobbly style – persevere, and once you find the rhythm of Bellow's writing, it's a hugely satisfying read.

★ **Theodore Dreiser**, *Sister Carrie* (Penguin). Convention-busting turn-of-the-nineteenth-century novel, with a resourceful, resolutely amoral heroine who sins but still succeeds in this ambiguous fable. Her story also spotlights the power department stores (and their seductive goods) had on working-class women – it's a quiet determination to acquire such finery that drives Carrie's every action.

James T. Farrell, *Studs Lonigan* trilogy (Penguin). Farrell's legendary novel follows an idealistic Irish American boy as he's gradually ground down by the drudgery of life. Famed for its realism and unblinking depiction of early twentieth-century urban life, the novel's not aged well: to a modern reader, its awkward prose can be wearing, especially given how little actually happens to Studs during this doorstopper of a book.

Andrew Greeley, The Blackie Ryan mysteries. University of Chicago lecturer Greeley moonlights as a writer of intriguing thrillers, whose hero, Bishop Blackie Ryan, is a Catholic priest on Chicago's north side. Try *Happy Are the Peacemakers* (o/p), where Blackie's just about the only man able to resist sexy widow Nora MacDonaugh's charms (and so investigate why her husbands keep dying) or *The Bishop and the Missing L Train* (Forge) which centers on a logic-defying kidnapping.

Eugene Izzi, *The Criminalist* (US Avon). Izzi's last novel (he hanged himself soon after the book was completed) is one of his best, filled with believably imperfect characters trawling through the grubbiest corners of the city. This time, homicide detective Dominick di Grazia investigates the brutal murder of a young,

pregnant prostitute with the help of a feisty, fiftysomething female colleague.

Frank Norris, *The Pit: A Story of Chicago* (Penguin). A strong companion novel to *Sister Carrie* (see above), Norris' story revolves around a greedy speculator and his complicit, compliant wife. Though less brutally amoral than Dreiser's take, it offers similar lessons about the lure of Chicago's wealth and power, and is a good snapshot of the caffeinated early days of the Chicago Stock Exchange.

Sara Paretsky, The V.I. Warshawski mysteries. Paretsky's ballsy, bittersweet female private eye V.I. Warshawski prowls the streets of Chicago solving crime. Try *Bitter Medicine* (Dell/Penguin) where Warshawki's investigating malpractice in an Emergency Room, or the first book *Indemnity Only* (Dell/Penguin), centering on the serpentine search for a missing co-ed.

Carl Sandburg, *Chicago Poems* (US Dover). The celebrated poet and Illinois native made his literary breakthrough with this earthy, evocative collection of free-verse poetry, a tribute to the beauty and violence of industrial Chicago. Highlights include such well-known poems as "Chicago" and "Fog."

Upton Sinclair, *The Jungle* (Bantam/Penguin). A hundred years before Eric Schlosser's recent megaseller, *Fast Food Nation*, came Sinclair's disturbing portrait of the squalid meatpacking industry in Chicago. The brawny prose tells the story of stockyard worker Jurgis Rudkus, who eventually finds salvation in socialism. The book's derailed when Sinclair's ideological rants take over toward the end, but it's still a vivid story.

Richard Wright, *Native Son* (Harper Perennial/Vintage). Bleak but powerful, Wright's potent novel tells the story of Bigger Thomas, an African American in 1930s Chicago who kills a white woman by accident and tries to cover it up with awful results. An indictment of ghet- to life whose message about racial inequality still resonates seventy years on.

Index

and small print

Index

Map entries are in color

Twenty years of Rough Guides

In the summer of 1981, Mark Ellingham, Rough Guides' founder, knocked out the first guide on a typewriter, with a group of friends. Mark had been traveling in Greece after university, and couldn't find a guidebook that really answered his needs.There were heavyweight cultural guides on the one hand – good on museums and classical sites but not on beaches and tavernas – and on the other hand student manuals that were so caught up with how to save money that they lost sight of the country's significance beyond its role as a place for a cool vacation. None of the guides began to address Greece as a country, with its natural and human environment, its politics and its contemporary life.

Having no urgent reason to return home, Mark decided to write his own guide. It was a guide to Greece that tried to combine some erudition and insight with a thoroughly practical approach to travelers' needs. Scrupulously researched listings of places to stay, eat and drink were matched by careful attention to detail on everything from Homer to Greek music, from classical sites to national parks and from nude beaches to monasteries. Back in London, Mark and his friends got their Rough Guide accepted by a farsighted commissioning editor at the publisher Routledge and it came out in 1982.

The Rough Guide to Greece was a student scheme that became a publishing phenomenon. The immediate success of the book – shortlisted for the Thomas Cook award – spawned a series that rapidly covered dozens of countries. The Rough Guides found a ready market among backpackers and budget travelers, but soon acquired a much broader readership that included older and less impecunious visitors. Readers relished the guides' wit and inquisitiveness as much as the enthusiastic, critical approach that acknowledges everyone wants value for money – but not at any price.

Rough Guides soon began supplementing the "rougher" information – the hostel and low-budget listings – with the kind of detail that independent-minded travelers on any budget might expect. These days, the guides – distributed worldwide by the Penguin group – include recommendations spanning the range from shoestring to luxury, and cover more than 200 destinations around the globe. Our growing team of authors, many of whom come to Rough Guides initially as outstandingly good letter-writers telling us about their travels, are spread all over the world, particularly in Europe, the USA and Australia. As well as the travel guides, Rough Guides publishes a series of dictionary phrasebooks covering two dozen major languages, an acclaimed series of music guides running the gamut from Classical to World Music, a series of music CDs in association with World Music Network, and a range of reference books on topics as diverse as the Internet, Pregnancy and Unexplained Phenomena. Visit **www.roughguides.com** to see what's cooking.

SMALL PRINT

Rough Guide credits

Text editor: Yuki Takagaki
Series editor: Mark Ellingham
Editorial: Martin Dunford, Jonathan Buckley, Kate Berens, Ann-Marie Shaw, Helena Smith, Olivia Swift, Ruth Blackmore, Geoff Howard, Claire Saunders, Gavin Thomas, Alexander Mark Rogers, Polly Thomas, Joe Staines, Richard Lim, Duncan Clark, Peter Buckley, Lucy Ratcliffe, Clifton Wilkinson, Alison Murchie, Matthew Teller, Andrew Dickson, Fran Sandham, Sally Schafer, Matthew Milton (UK); Andrew Rosenberg, Richard Koss, Hunter Slaton (US)
Production: Link Hall, Helen Prior, Julia Bovis, Katie Pringle, Rachel Holmes, Andy Turner, Dan May, Tanya Hall, John McKay, Sophie Hewat

Cartography: Maxine Repath, Melissa Baker, Ed Wright, Katie Lloyd-Jones
Cover art direction: Louise Boulton
Picture research: Sharon Martins, Mark Thomas
Online: Kelly Martinez, Anja Mutic-Blessing, Jennifer Gold, Audra Epstein, Suzanne Welles, Cree Lawson (US)
Finance: Gary Singh, Edward Downey, Mark Hall, Tim Bill
Marketing & Publicity: Richard Trillo, Niki Smith, David Wearn, Chloë Roberts, Demelza Dallow, Claire Southern (UK); Simon Carloss, David Wechsler, Megan Kennedy (US)
Administration: Julie Sanderson, Karoline Densley

Publishing information

This first edition published March 2003 by
Rough Guides Ltd,
80 Strand, London WC2R 0RL.
345 Hudson St, 4th Floor,
New York, NY 10014, USA.
Distributed by the Penguin Group
Penguin Books Ltd,
80 Strand, London WC2R 0RL
Penguin Putnam, Inc.
375 Hudson St, NY 10014, USA
Penguin Books Australia Ltd,
487 Maroondah Highway, PO Box 257,
Ringwood, Victoria 3134, Australia
Penguin Books Canada Ltd,
10 Alcorn Avenue, Toronto, Ontario,
Canada M4V 1E4
Penguin Books (NZ) Ltd,
182–190 Wairau Road, Auckland 10,
New Zealand
Typeset in Bembo and Helvetica to an
original design by Henry Iles.

Printed in Italy by LegoPrint S.p.A

312pp includes index
A catalogue record for this book is available from the British Library

ISBN 1-85828-755-3

The publishers and authors have done their best to ensure the accuracy and currency of all the information in **The Rough Guide to Chicago**, however, they can accept no responsibility for any loss, injury, or inconvenience sustained by any traveler as a result of information or advice contained in the guide.

SMALL PRINT

Help us update

We've gone to a lot of effort to ensure that the first edition of **The Rough Guide to Chicago** is accurate and up to date. However, things change – places get "discovered", opening hours are notoriously fickle, restaurants and rooms raise prices or lower standards. If you feel we've got it wrong or left something out, we'd like to know, and if you can remember the address, the price, the time, the phone number, so much the better.

We'll credit all contributions, and send a copy of the next edition (or any other Rough Guide if you prefer) for the best letters. Everyone who writes to us and isn't already a subscriber will receive a copy of our full-colour thrice-yearly newsletter. Please mark letters: **"Rough Guide Chicago Update"** and send to: Rough Guides, 80 Strand, London WC2R 0RL, or Rough Guides, 4th Floor, 345 Hudson St, New York, NY 10014. Or send an email to **mail@roughguides.com**

Have your questions answered and tell others about your trip at
www.roughguides.atinfopop.com

Acknowledgements

Rich McHugh I want to thank my friends, confidants, dinner companions and late-night compadres. Despite the fact that I had a legitimate excuse to keep chatting you up and dragging you out, you didn't have to say yes, and more often than not you did. Thanks to Trip Baby, Michael and Kim Burke, Michael Callahan, Shannon Collins, Sean Cunningham, Amanda Donovan, Michael Dressel, Daniel Dunn, Jeff Fioresi, Molly and Tobin Flavin, Steven Glunz, Elizabeth Goldberg, Peter Hickey, Chad Jashelski, Brian Kelly, John Kleiderer, Mark Marinacci, Molly McDonnell, Tom and Sinead McHugh, Maureen Phenner, Katie and Greg Ranke, Brittan Reilly, Tony Scelzo, James Taylor, David Wells, Gretchen Wochner, Michele Benedetto, Jamie Frank, Heather Morgan, Leslie Sharpe, Anne Tschanz, Megan Warren, Colette Misutka and James Walsh, Blaine Bell, Greg Christopher.

And a huge, huge thanks to Danie Donovan, whose love, patience and support kept me afloat throughout, to Daniel and Pippa McHugh, for their overall advice, and to my parents, Tom and Joan McHugh, who never say no and always give more than they should.

Thanks also Mark Ellwood, J.P. Anderson, Chris Barsanti and Richie Unterberger, and especially Monique Duwell, for her help with the South Side chapter – as well as Niki Smith, Richard Trillo, Hunter Slaton, Amy Copley, Martin Dunford, Andrew Rosenberg and Yuki Takagaki at Rough Guides.

I was fortunate to cross paths with countless hospitable, interesting and downright fun Chicagoans while researching and writing this, so to all of you, thank you.

J.P. Anderson I'd like to thank Barry Flynn from the Chicago Area Gay and Lesbian Chamber of Commerce, and Cindy Gatziolis from the Mayor's Office of Special Events.

Mark Ellwood Thanks to Letizia Treves for eleventh hour art input; Derrek Hull; the Ladies of PR 21 (Bridget, Rebecca, Casey, Susanna, Jam and Tricia – and Grant, too); Nancy Norton at Pleasant Home; but most of all to Pat & Jack Ricard, who first welcomed me to Chicago and made it feel like home.

The editor would like to thank Helen Prior, Katie Pringle and Julia Bovis for impeccable production work, Melissa Baker and Ed Wright for fine mapmaking, Amy Copley for dogged picture research, Russell Walton for his eagle eye and Andrew Rosenberg for lighting the way. Special thanks to J.P. Anderson, Chris Barsanti and Mark Ellwood for pitching in when we needed it most.

Photo credits

Cover credits

Front top small picture – Art Institute ©Neil Setchfield
Front lower small picture – Ferris wheel ©Alamy
back cover top picture – ©Neil Setchfield
back cover lower picture – Buckingham Fountain ©Pictor

Color introduction

University of Chicago ©Churchill and Klehr Photography
Chicago Theatre ©Rich McHugh
El train ©Churchill and Klehr Photography
Calder sculpture ©Rich McHugh
Deep-dish pizza ©Courtesy of Lou Malnati's Pizzeria
Pizzeria Uno ©Churchill and Klehr Photography
Grant Park ©Churchill and Klehr Photography

Window shoppers ©Rich McHugh
Boats by the lakefront ©Churchill and Klehr Photography
Berghoff ©Churchill and Klehr Photography

Things not to miss

1. Aerial view of Chicago ©Courtesy of the John Hancock Tower Observatory
2. Chagall's *American Windows*, the Art Institute of Chicago ©Courtesy of the Art Institute of Chicago
3. El train above street ©Royalty-Free/CORBIS
4. Sunbathers, Oak St Beach ©Churchill and Klehr Photography
5. Tiffany Dome, Chicago Cultural Center ©Courtesy of the Chicago Department of Cultural Affairs, photo by Hedrich-Blessing
6. Chicago Mercantile Exchange ©Churchill and Klehr Photography
7. Wrigley Field sign ©Rich McHugh

8. Billy Goat Tavern ©Rich McHugh
9. 2146 Caton St, Wicker Park ©Rich McHugh
10. Navy Pier ©Churchill and Klehr Photography
11. *Palm Court Lounge, The Drake Hotel* ©Courtesy of *The Drake Hotel*
12. Mr. Beef sign ©Churchill and Klehr Photography
13. Museum of Science and Industry ©Churchill and Klehr Photography
14. Chicago Symphony Orchestra, Symphony Center ©Courtesy of the Chicago Symphony Orchestra
15. Frank Lloyd Wright Studio (left) ©Courtesy of the Frank Lloyd Wright Preservation Trust, photo by Jon Miller, Hedrich-Blessing; Frederick C. Robie House (right) ©Courtesy of the Frank Lloyd Wright Preservation Trust, photo by Hedrich-Blessing
16. Chicago Architecture Foundation boat tour ©Courtesy of the Chicago Architecture Foundation
17. Michigan Avenue during the holiday season ©Churchill and Klehr Photography
18. Lakefront path ©Churchill and Klehr Photography
19. "Sue," Field Museum of Natural History ©Rich McHugh

20. Eddie Shaw performing at B.L.U.E.S. ©William A. Allard, National Geographic Image Collection
21. Marina Park tower ©Churchill and Klehr Photography
22. Glessner House ©Courtesy of the Chicago Architecture Foundation
23. Second City sign ©Rich McHugh
24. Marshall Field's department store ©Courtesy of Marshall Field's
25. Ravinia Festival pavilion ©Courtesy of the Ravinia Festival

Black and white photos
Rookery staircase ©Churchill and Klehr Photography (p.46)
Buckingham Fountain ©Churchill and Klehr Photography (p.82)
Lincoln Park ©Churchill and Klehr Photography (p.95)
Rockefeller Memorial Chapel ©Churchill and Klehr Photography (p.113)
Celtic Crossing bar ©Churchill and Klehr Photography (p.170)
Steppenwolf Theatre Company ©Courtesy of the Steppenwolf Theatre Company (p.194)
Carson Pirie Scott ironwork detail ©Courtesy of the Chicago Architecture Foundation (p.245)

Rough Guides travel

Rough Guides publishes new books every month

TRAVEL • MUSIC • REFERENCE • PHRASEBOOKS

Music

Acoustic Guitar
Blues: 100 Essential CDs
Cello
Clarinet
Classical Music
Classical Music: 100 Essential CDs
Country Music
Country: 100 Essential CDs
Cuban Music
Drum'n'bass
Drums
Electric Guitar & Bass Guitar
Flute
Hip-Hop
House
Irish Music
Jazz
Jazz: 100 Essential CDs
Keyboards & Digital Piano
Latin: 100 Essential CDs
Music USA: a Coast-To-Coast Tour
Opera
Opera: 100 Essential CDs
Piano
Reading Music
Reggae
Reggae: 100 Essential CDs
Rock
Rock: 100 Essential CDs
Saxophone
Soul: 100 Essential CDs
Techno
Trumpet & Trombone
Violin & Viola
World Music: 100 Essential CDs
World Music Vol1
World Music Vol2

Reference

Children's Books, 0–5
Children's Books, 5–11
China Chronicle
Cult Movies
Cult TV
Elvis
England Chronicle
France Chronicle
India Chronicle
The Internet
Internet Radio
James Bond
Liverpool FC
Man Utd
Money Online
Personal Computers
Pregnancy & Birth
Shopping Online
Travel Health
Travel Online
Unexplained Phenomena
Videogaming
Weather
Website Directory
Women Travel

Music CDs

Africa
Afrocuba
Afro-Peru
Ali Hussan Kuban
The Alps
Americana
The Andes
The Appalachians
Arabesque
Asian Underground
Australian Aboriginal Music
Bellydance
Bhangra
Bluegrass
Bollywood
Boogaloo
Brazil
Cajun
Cajun and Zydeco
Calypso and Soca
Cape Verde
Central America
Classic Jazz
Congolese Soukous
Cuba
Cuban Music Story
Cuban Son
Cumbia
Delta Blues
Eastern Europe
English Roots Music
Flamenco
Franco
Gospel
Global Dance
Greece
The Gypsies
Haiti
Hawaii
The Himalayas
Hip Hop
Hungary
India
India and Pakistan
Indian Ocean
Indonesia
Irish Folk
Irish Music
Italy
Jamaica
Japan
Kenya and Tanzania
Klezmer
Louisiana
Lucky Dube
Mali and Guinea
Marrabenta Mozambique
Merengue & Bachata
Mexico
Native American Music
Nigeria and Ghana
North Africa
Nusrat Fateh Ali Khan
Okinawa
Paris Café Music
Portugal
Rai
Reggae
Salsa
Salsa Dance
Samba
Scandinavia
Scottish Folk
Scottish Music
Senegal & The Gambia
Ska
Soul Brothers
South Africa
South African Gospel
South African Jazz
Spain
Sufi Music
Tango
Thailand
Tex-Mex
Wales
West African Music
World Music Vol 1: Africa, Europe and the Middle East
World Music Vol 2: Latin & North America, Caribbean, India, Asia and Pacific
World Roots
Youssou N'Dour & Etoile de Dakar
Zimbabwe

Rough Guides music, reference & CDs

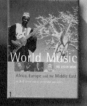   

NOTES

NOTES

The ideas expressed in this code were developed by and for independent travellers.

Learn About The Country You're Visiting

Start enjoying your travels before you leave by tapping into as many sources of information as you can.

The Cost Of Your Holiday

Think about where your money goes - be fair and realistic about how cheaply you travel. Try and put money into local peoples' hands; drink local beer or fruit juice rather than imported brands and stay in locally owned accommodation. Haggle with humour and not aggressively. Pay what something is worth to you and remember how wealthy you are compared to local people.

Embrace The Local Culture

Open your mind to new cultures and traditions - it will transform your experience. Think carefully about what's appropriate in terms of your clothes and the way you behave. You'll earn respect and be more readily welcomed by local people. Respect local laws and attitudes towards drugs and alcohol that vary in different countries and communities. Think about the impact you could have on them.

Exploring The World – The Travellers' Code

Being sensitive to these ideas means getting more out of your travels - and giving more back to the people you meet and the places you visit.

Minimise Your Environmental Impact

Think about what happens to your rubbish - take biodegradable products and a water filter bottle. Be sensitive to limited resources like water, fuel and electricity. Help preserve local wildlife and habitats by respecting local rules and regulations, such as sticking to footpaths and not standing on coral.

Don't Rely On Guidebooks

Use your guidebook as a starting point, not the only source of information. Talk to local people, then discover your own adventure!

Be Discreet With Photography

Don't treat people as part of the landscape, they may not want their picture taken. Ask first and respect their wishes.

We work with people the world over to promote tourism that benefits their communities, but we can only carry on our work with the support of people like you. For membership details or to find out how to make your travels work for local people and the environment, visit our website.

www.tourismconcern.org.uk

TourismConcern
Campaigning for Ethical and Fairly Traded Tourism

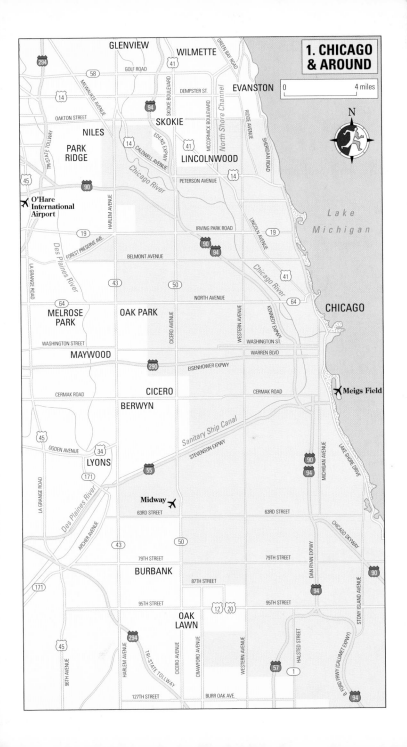

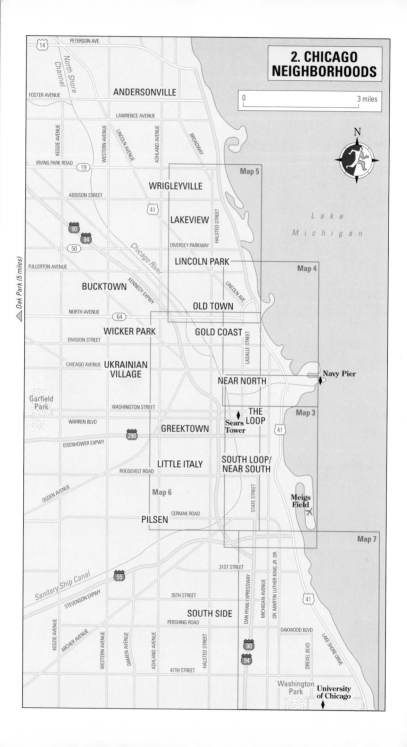

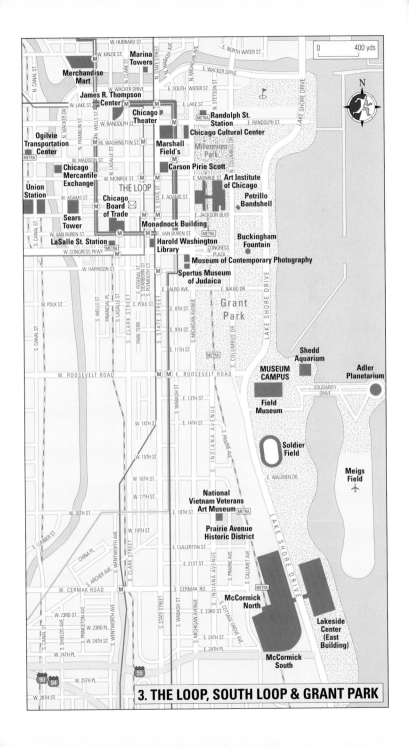

3. THE LOOP, SOUTH LOOP & GRANT PARK

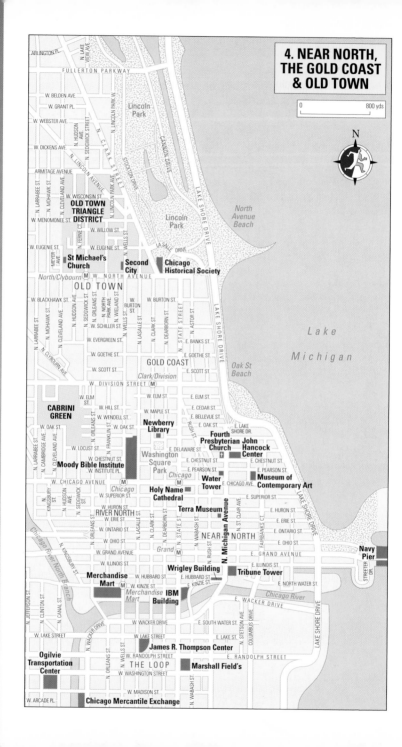

4. NEAR NORTH, THE GOLD COAST & OLD TOWN

0   800 yds

N

ARLINGTON PL.

N. LAKE VIEW AVE.

FULLERTON PARKWAY

W. BELDEN AVE.

Lincoln Park

W. GRANT PL.

N. LINCOLN PARK W.

W. WEBSTER AVE.

N. HUDSON AVE.

N. SEDGWICK STREET

W. DICKENS AVE.

CANNON DRIVE

ARMITAGE AVENUE

N. LARRABEE ST.

N. MOHAWK ST.

N. CLEVELAND AVE.

N. LINCOLN AVENUE

N. LINCOLN PARK AVE.

W. WISCONSIN ST.

OLD TOWN TRIANGLE DISTRICT

W. MENOMONEE ST.

STOCKTON DRIVE

W. WILLOW ST.

Lincoln Park

North Avenue Beach

N. FERNE CT.

N. WELLS ST.

W. EUGENIE ST.

W. EUGENIE ST.

LA SALLE DRIVE

MEYER AVE.

St Michael's Church

Second City

Chicago Historical Society

North/Clybourn Ⓜ W. NORTH AVENUE

OLD TOWN

LAKE SHORE DRIVE

W. BLACKHAWK ST.

N. SEDGWICK ST.

N. ORLEANS ST.

N. NORTH PARK AVE.

N. WIELAND ST.

W. BURTON ST.

W. BURTON ST.

Lake Michigan

N. LARRABEE ST.

N. MOHAWK ST.

N. CLEVELAND AVE.

N. HUDSON AVE.

N. CLYBOURN AVE.

W. SCHILLER ST.

W. LASALLE ST.

N. CLARK ST.

N. DEARBORN ST.

N. STATE STREET

E. BANKS ST.

W. EVERGREEN ST.

W. GOETHE ST.

E. GOETHE ST.

N. ASTOR ST.

GOLD COAST

Oak St Beach

W. SCOTT ST.

E. SCOTT ST.

Clark/Division Ⓜ

W. DIVISION STREET Ⓜ

W. ELM ST.

E. ELM ST.

CABRINI GREEN

W. HILL ST.

W. MAPLE ST.

E. CEDAR ST.

W. WENDELL ST.

E. BELLEVUE ST.

N. FRANKLIN ST.

E. LAKE SHORE DR.

W. OAK ST.

W. OAK ST.

Newberry Library

E. OAK ST.

RUSH ST.

W. LOCUST ST.

Fourth Presbyterian Church

John Hancock Center

N. LARRABEE ST.

N. CAMBRIDGE AVE.

N. CLEVELAND AVE.

N. ORLEANS ST.

W. CHESTNUT ST.

E. DELAWARE PL.

E. CHESTNUT ST.

E. CHESTNUT ST.

Moody Bible Institute

W. INSTITUTE PL.

Washington Square Park

E. PEARSON ST.

E. PEARSON ST.

W. CHICAGO AVENUE Ⓜ

Chicago

Water Tower

Museum of Contemporary Art

N. KINGSBURY ST.

N. HUDSON AVE.

N. SEDGWICK ST.

W. SUPERIOR ST.

Chicago Ⓜ

Holy Name Cathedral

E. CHICAGO AVE.

E. SUPERIOR ST.

W. HURON ST.

RIVER NORTH

W. ERIE ST.

Terra Museum

E. HURON ST.

N. LASALLE ST.

N. CLARK ST.

N. DEARBORN ST.

N. STATE ST.

N. WABASH ST.

N. RUSH ST.

N. ST. CLAIR ST.

FAIRBANKS CT.

E. ERIE ST.

W. ONTARIO ST.

E. ONTARIO ST.

LAKE SHORE DRIVE

W. OHIO ST.

N. MICHIGAN AVENUE

NEAR NORTH

E. OHIO ST.

W. GRAND AVENUE

Grand Ⓜ

E. GRAND AVENUE

Navy Pier

W. ILLINOIS ST.

E. ILLINOIS ST.

Wrigley Building

STREETER DR.

N. JEFFERSON ST.

N. CLINTON ST.

N. CANAL ST.

N. KINGSBURY ST. NORTH BRANCH

Chicago River

Merchandise Mart

W. HUBBARD ST.

E. HUBBARD ST.

Tribune Tower

E. NORTH WATER ST.

Merchandise Mart Ⓜ

W. KINZIE ST.

E. KINZIE ST.

IBM Building

Chicago River

E. WACKER DRIVE

W. WACKER DRIVE

E. SOUTH WATER ST.

N. WELLS ST.

N. ORLEANS ST.

STETSON AVE.

COLUMBUS DRIVE

LAKE SHORE DRIVE

W. LAKE STREET

W. LAKE STREET

E. LAKE ST.

James R. Thompson Center

W. RANDOLPH STREET

E. RANDOLPH STREET

Ogilvie Transportation Center

THE LOOP

Marshall Field's

N. WABASH ST.

W. WASHINGTON STREET

W. MADISON ST.

W. ARCADE PL.

Chicago Mercantile Exchange

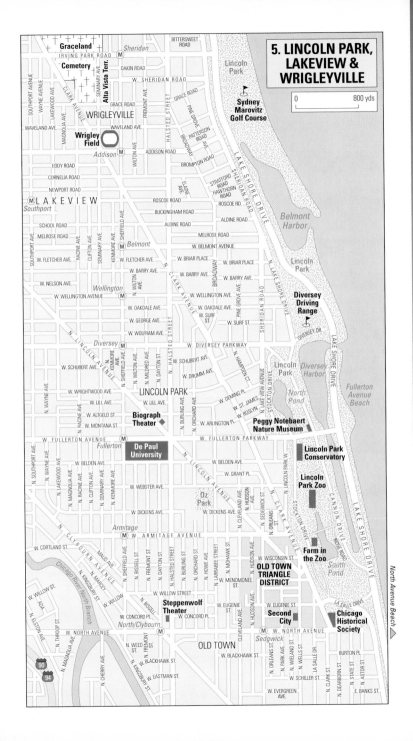

5. LINCOLN PARK, LAKEVIEW & WRIGLEYVILLE

0   800 yds

Graceland Cemetery

Sheridan

Lincoln Park

IRVING PARK ROAD
DAKIN ROAD
W. SHERIDAN ROAD
GRACE ROAD
GRACE ROAD
Alta Vista Terr.
BITTERSWEET ROAD

Sydney Marovitz Golf Course

SOUTHPORT AVENUE
WAYNE AVENUE
LAKEWOOD AVE.
CLARK AVENUE
SEMINARY AVE.
FREMONT AVE.
PINE GROVE
HALSTED STREET

WRIGLEYVILLE

WAVELAND AVE.
MAGNOLIA AVE.
WAVELAND AVE.

Wrigley Field
Addison

WILTON AVE.
BROADWAY
PATTERSON ROAD

ADDISON ROAD
BROMPTON ROAD

EDDY ROAD
CORNELIA ROAD
NEWPORT ROAD

ELAINE AVE.
STRATFORD ROAD
HAWTHORN ROAD

LAKEVIEW

Southport

ROSCOE ROAD
BUCKINGHAM ROAD
ALDINE ROAD
MELROSE ROAD

ROSCOE RD.
ALDINE ROAD

SCHOOL ROAD
MELROSE ROAD
SOUTHPORT AVE.
RACINE AVE.
CLIFTON AVE.
SEMINARY AVE.
KENMORE AVE.
SHEFFIELD AVE.

W. FLETCHER AVE.
Belmont
W. FLETCHER AVE.

W. BELMONT AVENUE
W. BRIAR PLACE
W. BRIAR PLACE

W. BARRY AVE.
W. BARRY AVE.
W. BARRY AVE.

Belmont Harbor

Lincoln Park

W. NELSON AVE.
Wellington
W. WELLINGTON AVENUE
W. WELLINGTON AVE.

N. WILTON AVE.
CLARK AVENUE
BROADWAY
PINE GROVE AVE.
SHERIDAN ROAD
N. LAKE SHORE DRIVE

W. OAKDALE AVE.
W. OAKDALE AVE.
W. GEORGE AVE.
W. SURF ST.
W. WOLFRAM AVE.
W. SURF ST.

Diversey Driving Range

Diversey
W. DIVERSEY PARKWAY
DIVERSEY DR.

N. LINCOLN AVENUE
W. SCHUBERT AVE.
N. WAYNE AVE.
N. RACINE AVE.
N. KENMORE AVE.
N. SHEFFIELD AVE.
N. WILTON AVE.
N. MILDRED AVE.
N. DAYTON ST.
N. HALSTED STREET
W. DRUMM AVE.
HAMPDEN CT.

Lincoln Park *Diversey Harbor*

W. SCHUBERT AVE.

W. WRIGHTWOOD AVE.
LINCOLN PARK
W. LILL AVE.
W. LILL AVE.

W. DEMING AVE.
W. ST. JAMES PL.
N. LAKE VIEW AVENUE
STOCKTON DRIVE
North Pond

Fullerton Avenue Beach

W. ALTGELD ST.
W. MONTANA ST.

Biograph Theater

N. BURLING AVE.
N. ORCHARD ST.
W. ARLINGTON PL.
W. ROSLYN

Peggy Notebaert Nature Museum

W. FULLERTON AVENUE
Fullerton
W. FULLERTON PARKWAY

De Paul University

W. BELDEN AVE.
W. BELDEN AVE.
W. GRANT PL.

N. SOUTHPORT AVE.
N. WAYNE AVE.
N. LAKEWOOD AVE.
N. MAGNOLIA AVE.
N. RACINE AVE.
N. CLIFTON AVE.
N. KENMORE AVE.

W. WEBSTER AVE.

N. LINCOLN AVENUE
N. CLEVELAND AVE.
N. HUDSON AVE.
N. SEDGWICK ST.
N. ORLEANS ST.
N. CLARK AVENUE
STOCKTON DRIVE
N. LINCOLN PARK W.
CANNON DRIVE
LAKE SHORE DRIVE

Lincoln Park Conservatory

Lincoln Park Zoo

Oz Park
W. DICKENS AVE.
W. DICKENS AVE.

Farm in the Zoo

Armitage
W. ARMITAGE AVENUE
South Pond

N. CLYBOURN AVENUE
W. CORTLAND ST.
MAUD AVE.
N. BISSELL ST.
N. FREMONT ST.
N. DAYTON ST.
N. HALSTED STREET
N. BURLING ST.
N. ORCHARD ST.
N. HOWE AVE.
N. MOHAWK ST.
N. LARRABEE STREET

W. WISCONSIN ST.

OLD TOWN TRIANGLE DISTRICT

W. WILLOW ST.
W. MENOMONEE ST.

Chicago River North Branch
W. WILLOW ST.

W. WILLOW STREET
Steppenwolf Theater

W. CONCORD PL.
W. CONCORD PL.
North/Clybourn

W. EUGENIE ST.
N. HUDSON AVE.
W. EUGENIE ST.
CLEVELAND AVE.

Second City

LA SALLE DRIVE
Chicago Historical Society

W. WILLOW ST.
N. ELSTON AVE.
W. ADA ST.
N. THROOP ST.
N. MAGNOLIA AVE.
N. CHERRY AVE.
N. KINGSBURY ST.

W. NORTH AVENUE
Sedgwick
OLD TOWN
W. NORTH AVENUE

N. WEED ST.
N. FREMONT ST.
N. BLACKHAWK ST.
W. BLACKHAWK ST.

N. ORLEANS AVE.
N. PARK AVE.
N. WIELAND ST.
N. WELLS ST.
N. LA SALLE DR.
BURTON PL.

90
94

W. WILLOW ST.
W. CONCORD PL.
W. EASTMAN ST.
N. KINGSBURY ST.

N. CLARK ST.
N. DEARBORN ST.
N. STATE ST.
N. ASTOR ST.

W. SCHILLER ST.

W. EVERGREEN AVE.
E. BANKS ST.

North Avenue Beach

6. WEST SIDE

Bucktown & Wicker Park

Oak Park

W. WABANSIA AVE.
W. CONCORD PL.

W. NORTH AVENUE
W. PIERCE AVE.
N. WICKER PARK AVE.
N. WILMAUKEE AVENUE
JULIAN ST.
W. BEACH AVE.
W. BLACKHAWK ST.
N. BOSWORTH AVE.
N. GREENVIEW AVE.
N. CLEAVER ST.
W. SCHILLER ST.
W. LE MOYNE ST.
W. ELLEN ST.

N. ELSTON AVE.
N. NORTH BRANCH AVE.
N. CHERRY AVE.

N. SHEFFIELD AVE.
N. WILLOW ST.

FREMONT ST.
N. DAYTON AVE.
N. CLYBOURN AVE.
W. BLACKHAWK ST.

N. WILLOW ST.
N. BURLING ST.
N. ORCHARD ST.
N. HOWE ST.
N. LARRABEE ST.
N. MOHAWK ST.
N. EUGENIE ST.
N. CLARK ST.
LA SALLE DR.

M Sedgwick

North/Clybourn

N. CLEVELAND AVE.
W. NORTH AVENUE M
N. SEDGWICK ST.
N. ORLEANS ST.
N. PARK AVE.
N. WIELAND ST.
W. SCHILLER ST.

CABRINI GREEN

W. EVERGREEN AVE.
W. GOETHE ST.
W. SCOTT ST.
Clark/Division M
W. DIVISION STREET M

Division M W. DIVISION STREET
90 94

W. HADDON AVE.
W. THOMAS ST.
W. CORTEZ ST.
W. AUGUSTA BLVD.
W. WALTON ST.
W. CHESTNUT ST.
W. FRY ST.

N. DAMEN AVE.
N. WINCHESTER AVE.
N. HONORE ST.
N. HERMITAGE AVE.
N. MARSHFIELD AVE.
W. IOWA ST.
W. PEARSON ST.

UKRAINIAN VILLAGE

W. CHICAGO AVENUE
W. SUPERIOR ST.
W. HURON ST.
W. ERIE ST.
W. OHIO ST.

N. WOLCOTT AVE.
N. WOOD ST.
N. ARMOUR ST.
N. BISHOP ST.
N. ADA ST.
N. NOBLE ST.
N. THROOP ST.
N. ELIZABETH ST.

M Chicago
W. SUPERIOR ST.
W. HURON ST.
W. ANCONA ST.
W. ERIE ST.

N. ELM ST.
W. HILL ST.
W. WENDELL ST.
W. OAK ST.
W. MAPLE ST.
W. OAK ST.

STATE STREET

W. OAK ST.
N. LARRABEE ST.
N. CAMBRIDGE AVE.
N. CLEVELAND AVE.
N. ORLEANS ST.
N. FRANKLIN ST.
N. WELLS ST.
Chicago M
N. HUDSON AVE.
N. SEDGWICK ST.
W. SUPERIOR ST.
W. HURON ST.
W. ERIE ST.
W. ONTARIO ST.
W. OHIO ST.
Chicago M
N. LASALLE ST.
N. CLARK ST.
N. DEARBORN ST.
Chicago M

N. KINGSBURY ST.

Chicago River North Branch

W. GRAND AVE.
W. FERDINAND ST.
W. HUBBARD ST.
W. KINZIE ST.
W. CARROLL AVE.
W. FULTON ST.
W. WALNUT ST.
W. LAKE STREET

N. PAULINA ST.
N. ASHLAND AVE.
N. JUSTINE ST.

N. OGDEN AVENUE

N. CARPENTER AVE.
W. HUBBARD ST.
W. KINZIE ST.
W. CARROLL AVE.
W. FULTON ST.

N. MORGAN ST.
N. PEORIA ST.
N. GREEN ST.

Grand M

N. DES PLAINES ST.
N. JEFFERSON ST.
N. CLINTON ST.
N. CANAL ST.

W. GRAND AVENUE M
W. ILLINOIS ST.

Merchandise Mart M
W. HUBBARD ST.
W. KINZIE ST.

N. STATE ST.
Grand M

W. WACKER DR.
W. LAKE ST.

N. WACKER DR.

M Ashland

Harpo Studios ■
W. RANDOLPH STREET

Clinton M
Ogilvie Transportation Center

THE LOOP

WARREN BLVD.

W. WASHINGTON STREET

W. MADISON STREET
W. MONROE ST.
W. ADAMS ST.
W. QUINCY ST.

N. LOOMIS ST.
N. ADA AVE.
N. THROOP ST.
N. ELIZABETH ST.
S. LAFLIN ST.
S. ABERDEEN ST.
S. HALSTED ST.

United Center ■

GREEKTOWN

S. GREEN ST.

W. ARCADE PL.

Union Station ■

DAN RYAN EXPWY

W. WACKER DR.
N. FRANKLIN ST.
N. WELLS ST.
N. LA SALLE ST.
N. CLARK ST.
N. DEARBORN ST.
S. STATE STREET

W. ADAMS ST.
W. JACKSON BLVD.
W. VAN BUREN ST.

Sears Tower ■

W. JACKSON BLVD.
W. VAN BUREN ST.

DWIGHT D. EISENHOWER EXPWY

W. CONGRESS ST.
Racine M
290
UIC-Halsted M

DWIGHT D. EISENHOWER EXPWY

Medical Center M
W. FLOURNOY ST.
Polk M
W. FLOURNOY ST.
W. LEXINGTON ST.
W. POLK ST.
W. CABRINI ST.
W. ARTHINGTON

W. HARRISON ST.

Clinton M
W. HARRISON ST.

University of Illinois ✚

S. WOLCOTT AVE.
S. MARSHFIELD AVE.

S. MAY ST.
S. ABERDEEN ST.
S. CARPENTER ST.
S. MILLER ST.

UIC ■
Jane Addams Hull-House Museum ■

N. SHERMAN ST.

Cook County ✚

W. FILMORE ST.
W. GRENSHAW ST.

LITTLE ITALY

W. POLK ST.
W. TAYLOR ST.

COLT AVE.

W. POLK ST.

S. CANAL AVE.

South Branch

W. TAYLOR ST.

W. ROOSEVELT ROAD

W. WASHBURN AVE.
W. 13TH ST.
W. HASTINGS ST.
W. 14TH ST.
W. 15TH ST.

S. DAMEN AVE.
S. WOOD ST.
S. PAULINA ST.
S. ASHLAND AVENUE
S. LAFLIN ST.

UIC ■

W. WASHBURN AVE.
W. 13TH ST.
W. HASTINGS ST.
W. 14TH
W. 14TH PL.
W. 15TH ST.

S. LOOMIS ST.
S. RACINE AVE.
S. BLUE ISLAND AVENUE

W. MAXWELL ST.

S. MORGAN ST.
S. PEORIA ST.
S. NEWBERRY AVE.
S. SANGAMON ST.
S. UNION AVE.

90 94

W. MAXWELL ST.
W. 14TH ST.
W. 14TH PL.
W. 15TH ST.
W. 16TH ST.

S. CLINTON ST.

Chicago River

W. 14TH ST.
W. 15TH ST.
W. 16TH ST.

Mexican Fine Arts Center ■

18th M

PILSEN

W. 16TH ST.
W. 17TH ST.
W. 18TH ST.
W. 18TH PL.
W. 19TH ST.

S. THROOP ST.
S. ALLPORT ST.

W. 18TH ST.
W. 18TH PL.

S. CARPENTER ST.
S. MILLER ST.
S. PEORIA ST.
S. SANGAMON ST.

S. UNION AVE.
S. HALSTED ST.
S. DESPLAINES ST.
S. JEFFERSON ST.

DAN RYAN EXPRESSWAY

S. CLARK ST.
S. FEDERAL ST.
S. DEARBORN ST.

W. CULLERTON ST.
W. 21ST ST.
W. 21ST PL.

W. 21ST ST.

W. CULLERTON ST.

W. 21ST PL.

S. CANAL PORT AVE.

W. CERMAK RD.
Cermak/Chinatown M

S. LUMBER ST.

W. CERMAK RD.
S. ARCHER AVE.
S. 23RD ST.
S. 23RD PL.
S. 24TH ST.
S. 24TH PL.

CHINA PL.

S. CLARK ST.
S. FEDERAL ST.
S. STATE STREET

S. PRINCETON AVE.
S. WENTWORTH AVE.

N

0   800 yds

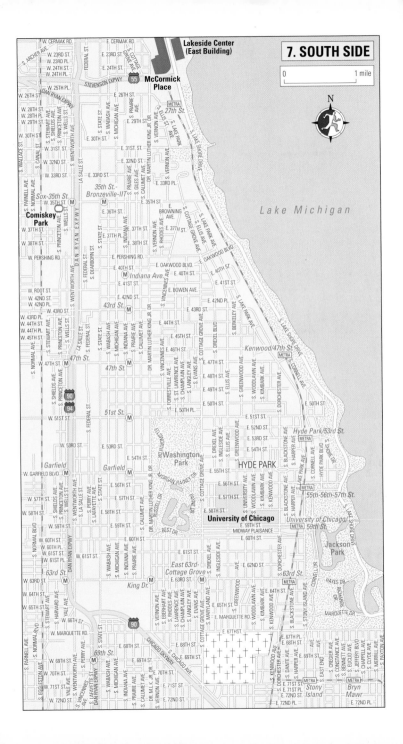

7. SOUTH SIDE

Lakeside Center
(East Building)

McCormick
Place

Lake Michigan

Comiskey
Park

Kenwood/47th St.

Washington
Park

Garfield

HYDE PARK

University of Chicago

Jackson
Park

55th-56th-57th St.

University of Chicago/59th St.

Midway Plaisance

King Dr.

East 63rd-
Cottage Grove

Bryn
Mawr

Stony
Island

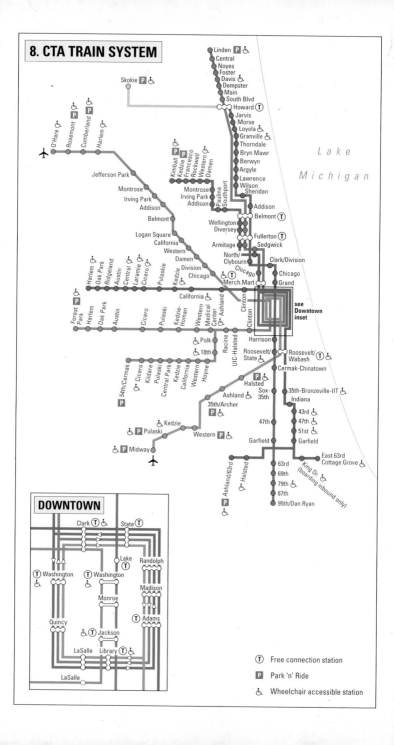

8. CTA TRAIN SYSTEM

Linden P &
Central
Noyes
Foster
Davis &
Dempster
Main
South Blvd
Howard (T)
Jarvis
Morse
Loyola &
Granville &
Thorndale
Bryn Mawr
Berwyn
Argyle
Lawrence
Wilson
Sheridan

Skokie P &

O'Hare
Rosemont
Cumberland
Harlem

Kimball P
Kedzie
Francisco
Rockwell
Western
Damen

Jefferson Park

Montrose
Irving Park
Addison
Belmont

Logan Square
California
Western
Damen
Division
Chicago

Montrose
Irving Park
Addison

Paulina
Southport

Addison
Belmont (T)

Wellington
Diversey

Fullerton (T)
Sedgwick

Armitage

North/
Clybourn

Clark/Division

Chicago

Chicago

Merch.Mart

Grand

Lake   Michigan

Harlem &
Oak Park
Ridgeland
Austin
Central &
Laramie &
Cicero &
Pulaski
Kedzie

California &

see
Downtown
inset

Forest
Park P
Harlem
Oak Park
Austin
Cicero
Pulaski
Kedzie-
Homan
Western
Medical
Center
Clinton
Clinton

Polk &
18th &

Racine

UIC-Halsted

Harrison

Roosevelt/
State &

Roosevelt/
Wabash (T) &

Cermak-Chinatown

54th/Cermak
Cicero
Kildare
Pulaski
Central Park
Kedzie
California
Western
Hoyne

Halsted P &

Sox-
35th &

35th-Bronzeville-IIT &

Indiana

35th/Archer P &

43rd &
47th &
51st &

Kedzie &
Pulaski P &

Western P &

47th

Garfield

Garfield

Midway P &

East 63rd
Cottage Grove &

63rd
69th
79th
87th
95th/Dan Ryan

King Dr.
(boarding inbound only)

Ashland/63rd

Halsted

DOWNTOWN

Clark (T) &

State (T)

Lake
(T)

Randolph

(T) Washington
&

(T) Washington
&

Madison

Monroe

Quincy

(T) Jackson

Adams

LaSalle

Library (T) &

LaSalle

(T) Free connection station

P Park 'n' Ride

& Wheelchair accessible station